STEEPED IN BLOOD

Steeped in Blood

Adoption, Identity, and the Meaning of Family

FRANCES J. LATCHFORD

McGill-Queen's University Press
Montreal & Kingston · London · Chicago

© McGill-Queen's University Press 2019

ISBN 978-0-7735-5680-5 (cloth)
ISBN 978-0-7735-5681-2 (paper)
ISBN 978-0-7735-5799-4 (ePDF)
ISBN 978-0-7735-5800-7 (ePUB)

Legal deposit third quarter 2019
Bibliothèque nationale du Québec

Printed in Canada on acid-free paper that is 100% ancient forest free
(100% post-consumer recycled), processed chlorine free.

This book has been published with the help of a grant from the
Canadian Federation for the Humanities and Social Sciences, through
the Awards to Scholarly Publications Program, using funds provided
by the Social Sciences and Humanities Research Council of Canada.

Funded by the   Financé par le
Government   gouvernement
of Canada   du Canada

Canada Council   Conseil des arts
for the Arts   du Canada

We acknowledge the support of the Canada Council for the Arts.
Nous remercions le Conseil des arts du Canada de son soutien.

Library and Archives Canada Cataloguing in Publication

Title: Steeped in blood : adoption, identity, and the meaning of family /
    Frances J. Latchford.
Names: Latchford, Frances J. (Frances Joan), author.
Description: Includes bibliographical references and index.
Identifiers: Canadiana (print) 20190103973 | Canadiana (ebook) 2019010399X
    | ISBN 9780773556812 (paper) | ISBN 9780773556805 (cloth) |
    ISBN 9780773557994 (ePDF) | ISBN 9780773558007 (ePUB)
Subjects: LCSH: Adoption. | LCSH: Adoptees. | LCSH: Families.
    | LCSH: Identity (Psychology)
Classification: LCC HV875 .L38 2019 | DDC 362.734—dc23

This book was typeset by True to Type in 10.5/13 Sabon

To my family, Frank and Joan,

Vancel, Carol, Ira, Michael, Benjamin, Alphonse, and Jay,

who made these thoughts possible

Contents

Acknowledgments

Thank you to my parents, Frank and Joan Latchford, and to my siblings, Vancel, Carol, Ira Cromwell, Michael, Benjamin, Alphonse, and Jay Latchford, for all of your love, laughter, and support, as well as for the intimacies and experiences of family that continue to inspire my critical interest in meanings of family and its formations. Suzy Richter and Jackie O'Keefe, my oldest friends, what would I have done without your never-ending warmth, encouragement, and love? Patti Phillips, your willingness to talk adoption and theory, and your friendship, have meant so much to me and my work. Dear John Grundy and Paul Halferty, thank you for listening to me read aloud every paper I have ever written on adoption, your campy wit and intelligence, and your enduring friendship throughout this process. To the rhyming couplet Marlene Warnick and Sharelene Wallace, the cake, your company, and your encouragement have mattered so much. Dr Andrea O'Reilly, my generous colleague, thank you for your ongoing support of my adoption research and the trail you have blazed academically and professionally for me and so many women like me who study the family, mothering, and issues related to them. Thank you to the Alliance for the Study of Adoption and Culture, which has been the most important forum for the presentation of my work. I also extend a personal thank you to Emily Hipchen and Kimberley Leighton, long-time alliance members, for all our post-conference debates in bars across the United States and over the years. Great thanks to Jonathan Crago, executive editor of McGill-Queen's University Press, for your ear and insight, and thanks to the press itself for supporting this project for the duration, as well as to managing editor Kathleen Fraser, associate managing editor Lisa Aitken, copy editor Robert Lewis, and indexer Alexandra Peace for their expertise and fine work. The author and publisher would like to thank the Faculty of Liberal Arts and Professional Studies at York University, Toronto, for its support of this work. Thank you also, Susan Dimock, for your belief in the philosophical significance of this project at the very start. Julia Gotz, your clarity of mind and the inestimable pieces of practical advice have kept me going. To my "outlaws," Thelma Bird, Ken Jones, Jan Bird, and Mary Ruth Wright, thank you too for your love and encouragement and for holding a spot open on the coffee table for this book. To my partner, Dr Kym Bird, the fun and laughter you stimulate, your love and playfulness, your infinite patience with me and excitement about my work, and your persistence in telling me to "get going" and "gird my loins" have always sustained me and moved me forward on this journey. Thank you, Birdie. I would not have done this without you!

STEEPED IN BLOOD

Introduction

What is the nature of the relationship between your identity or self-experience and knowing your biological genealogy? Does your identity, your sense of self, turn on this knowledge or its absence in a real and necessary way? Let me illustrate with a story. Not so long ago, my mother presented me with an old manuscript, which she claimed was a copy of a journal and letters written by my great-great-great-great-grandfather Timothy Rogers (1756–1827). Inside the journal was a genealogy dating back to the thirteenth century that apparently links me not only to John Rogers the martyr (1505) but also to Edward I, king of England (1272). With the genealogy in hand, I was, of course, utterly seduced by these apparent bio-facts. They impressed me with myself. My immediate response to my mother's revelation was a deeply *felt* sense that this bio-genealogical knowledge – preserved magically, simply, materially, incontestably in the mere fact of a biological tie – reflected on me and said something unique about myself. In the course of this momentary seduction, I felt a rightful claim to identify with martyrs and kings. Feeling the powerful and immediate pull to identify with this bio-genealogy, however, does not erase for me the question of whether or not this kind of knowledge really does or should be understood to genuinely reflect *who I am*. This idea is operative in me at the same time that I am strongly suspicious of it. Surely, King Edward's relations to his contemporaries, including his serfs, had a much more profound impact on their identities and self-experience than any biological relation to me, revealed midlife, can or will ever have on my sense of self, assuming this bio-genealogy that is said to be mine is even true.

One significant aspect of this seduction story is that if each of us had equal access to our bio-genealogies and were related to kings, it would be completely unremarkable. But, of course, people's bio-genealogies are not equally valued. Neither are *people* equally valued when they do not know or cannot access their bio-genealogies. It is for these reasons that this story ultimately has philosophical, psychological, social, political, and historical significance with regard to the relationship between human experience and bio-genealogical knowledge. This royal revelation story illustrates how bio-genealogical knowledge shapes our experiences of self and identity. It also elicits important questions about how bio-genealogical knowledge produces differentiated "family" subjects in the modern Western context. It has implications for how the possibilities of "family" experience are limited and determined in a social-political-historical context that insists on giving distinct meanings to the absence and presence of biological ties, or a knowledge of the latter, between "family" members. In effect, the question this story raises about whether or not my lately learned bio-genealogy now circumscribes *who I am* in any profound sense points to how different kinds of "family" subjects in the modern Western context, particularly "adoptees" and "biological children," are produced. It bears on how adoptees come to be differentiated from biological children insofar as they do not know (or do not know as fully as the biological child) their bio-genealogy in an environment that conflates a firm identity and the reality of family ties with the self's possession of this kind of knowledge.

The idea that biological ties (even to someone who lived impossibly long ago) are self-defining forces is pervasive in our culture and its institutions. For instance, the proliferation of contemporary websites like ancestry.com and dnaancestryproject.com, television series such as NBC's *Who Do You Think You Are?* and PBS's *Faces of America*, and DNA ancestry research services akin to 23andMe is evidence that this idea contours popular culture and engages us as selves. It functions for and within us as a *bio-genealogical imperative*. It demands that the self *know* its bio-genealogy at the same time that it produces the self as a kind of being that *needs* to know its bio-genealogy. As we will see, therefore, *to be* an "individual" and a real member of a "family" in the Western context today has been made, by various modern institutions and discourses, to depend on the self's ability to meet the demands of this imperative.[1] It is an imperative that limits and determines the self's identity and "family" experience relative to the self's access or lack of access to bio-genealogical knowledge. And it underpins the production of different kinds of family subjects. It differentiates the kinds of "family" experiences that are available to "adoptees," as opposed to "biological children," or even available to "half-siblings" or "stepchildren" for that matter.

How is a bio-genealogical imperative implemented and maintained within our culture and in such a way that it effectively differentiates the subjectivity of "biological children" and "adoptees"? To put it another way, how does bio-genealogical knowledge come to be socially, politically, and historically constituted as the self's most authentic and complete truth? This is the fundamental question addressed by this book. And to answer it, this work critically examines the idea that bio-genealogical knowledge is something that can and does ensure both the *reality* of "family" ties and the self's sense of itself as "complete" or "whole." It considers how this idea is reiterated through the modern Western discourses of individualism, naturalism, psychoanalysis, and incest, all of which shape contemporary constructs of self-knowledge. It also examines how, through the human sciences (i.e., biological medicine, psychiatry, psychology, and sociology), these discourses converge upon the institution of adoption and give rise to the adopted subject. At the same time that it demonstrates how the bio-genealogical imperative is entrenched in our culture, social institutions, and experience, this book responds to the largely uncritical idea in adoption discourse that, due to a lack of bio-genealogical knowledge, the adoptee is necessarily prone to suffer identity problems, pathology, and weak family connections compared to the self who does not lack such knowledge. The aim of this work, therefore, is to resist the effects of a mode of being that denigrates adoptees and adoptive family ties through the reiterative demand that the self seek *and* know its bio-genealogy. It is a response to a mode of being that underpins a dominant concept of self wherein *to be* the ideal "individual," one that is healthy and normal, is also *to be* a real or "biological" child and family member.

Where individualism, naturalism, psychoanalysis, and incest meet within the human sciences, the bio-genealogical imperative operates broadly in a modern Western context that is increasingly fashioned by these sciences. It is through the influence of the human sciences that these discourses are able to play a central role in the proliferation and maintenance of the adopted subject. Individualism and Darwinian naturalism ask new questions: "*Who am I?*" and "*What am I?*" respectively. Taken up as they are by the human sciences, they act as portals to new truths that are sought, then and now, about the self's nature and identity. Under the influence of individualism and naturalism, the human sciences arrive at an answer to these questions: "*I am* my bio-genealogy." Psychoanalysis reinforces this answer because it invents the psychic necessity of the child's proximity to its biological parents in "normal" identity formation at the same time that it maps bio-narcissistic identifications in "normal" child development onto human being. Where incest is set up as a biological, psychic, and/or cultural taboo that is universal, it further prompts the human sciences to reiterate the idea that bio-genealogy is the self's best answer to questions about its nature and identity. The determination that the incest taboo is universal heightens the self's obligation and need to know biological kin so that it may avoid overstepping that prohibition. Together, these discourses regulate the self's identity and family experience through the human sciences, even today, as they bear on law, medicine, psychology, and the institutions of family and adoption. Their part in implementing the self's *need* to know its bio-genealogy plays a formidable role in the production and maintenance of what counts as self-knowledge and "normal" identity formation.

The self's need for bio-genealogical knowledge further culminates in the early and ongoing development of modern Western adoption discourse, the guiding principle of which is the "best interests of the child." As a branch of the human sciences, the institution of adoption generally capitulates to the demands of the bio-genealogical imperative. It accepts and popularizes the idea that bio-genealogical knowledge is a fundamental human need and, therefore, that access to this knowledge serves a child's best interests. It reinforces the bio-genealogical imperative because it explicitly and implicitly defers to the human sciences, which engage a biological family bias because they treat the biological tie both as an inherently superior conduit for bio-genealogical knowledge and as the superior basis for the experience of "family." The institution of adoption's deference to this bias occurs primarily in and through its application of human biology, psychiatry, psychology, and sociology to the "problem" of adoption. Through the use of these sciences, it draws the differentiated boundaries of adoptee identity and degrades (as *lack*) the nature of the adoptive tie. It does so through the normalization of "adoptee" experience as something that is either pathological or inescapably different. As a result, the institution of adoption is an apparatus that mediates the (inferior) meaning, value, and experience of ties between selves who claim each other as "family" in spite of having no common bio-genealogy. Indeed, it responds to the absence of bio-genealogical knowledge or biological ties between adoptive parents and children with the bio-genealogical imperative because it reiterates the idea that the self in general and the adoptee in particular need access to bio-genealogical knowledge.

The current ontological status of the adoptive tie is the effect of the bio-genealogical imperative; the adoptive tie is inferior to the biological tie because this tie is thought to exist in ways that the adoptive tie does not. It is treated as an immaterial bond because it is a social and legal bond, whereas the biological tie is understood to be material. One way that this difference in status is evidenced clearly is in the extent to which people who share adoptive ties are treated as social curiosities. They are curiosities because people with adoptive ties are subject to the imperative in unique ways. Their ties, specifically the knowledge and experience of them, are scrutinized in ways that do not directly affect people with biological ties. Once identified as an "adoptee" or "adoptive parent," a person is frequently asked to testify that her ties are a real basis for "familial" love and affection: "do you love your child as much as you would if you had given birth to her?"; "can you really bond with your adopted child the way you do with a biological child?"; "if you could have chosen, would you have had your *own* or still adopted?"; "do you ever wonder who your *real* parents are and what life would have been like with them?"; "do you really feel your adopted parents are your *real* parents?" The adoptee's bio-genealogical knowledge is also scrutinized: "do you know your birth parents?"; "what do you know about your biological parents?"; "would you like to know your birth parents?"; "do you know anything about any of your ancestors?"; "how do you deal with not having this information?" Questions like these are familiar to adoptive family members everywhere, and they are signs that the imperative is at work. Essentially, these kinds of questions are aimed at making people with adoptive ties prove (or disprove) that their bonds and ontological status as "family" members are real. This kind of social exercise in tie substantiation is not imposed upon people who share biological ties with their family. Still, families with biological ties are subject to the same imperative, although its effects manifest differently. They are asked to parade their bio-genealogical knowledge from time to time, and since they are able to do so, their status as "family" members is reinforced rather than undermined. Ultimately, these social exercises serve a deep purpose: they effectively differentiate the ontological status of adoptive ties from biological ties and maintain a biological family order.

These effects of identification also concern me as the author of this book: I do not identify my social location or relationship to adoption in this text, even though the reader might expressly desire to know it. This choice is strategic. It is aimed at undermining the epistemological impact of the bio-genealogical imperative on the reader. Many theorists who enlist feminist epistemology, sometimes in conjunction with poststructuralism, do locate their identity and/or relation to their object of study for two reasons: the "personal is political" and the theorist's self-reflexive consciousness of social location manifested in the articulation of her identity helps to expose and combat critical blind spots rooted in her epistemological standpoint and privilege. As Patricia Hill Collins observes in a discussion of black feminist epistemologies, this self-disclosure resists, among other things, the bias of "an idealist analysis whereby the background, worldview, and interests of the thinker are deemed irrelevant in assessing his or her ideas."[2] Relative to adoption studies, Sally Haslanger and Charlotte Witt suggest that the utility of standpoint theory, in part, is that "those in the adoption triad typically have available to them a different perspective on family, love, race, and knowledge than those who are not," wherein the adoption triad includes birth parents, adoptees, and adoptive parents.[3] They also characterize a feminist "self-disclosive style" as an approach to "philosophical argumentation that makes explicit its sources and its basis in experience, so that its strengths and limitations, bias and insight, can be better evaluated."[4] One obvious effect of self-disclosure, therefore, is that it provides the reader with a basis from which to judge the theorist's work against a knowledge that is thought to be granted or denied typically by her identity. The question that standpoint theories do not address is whether feminists can be self-reflexive about the impact of personal bias, experience, and worldview on their theories without a *public* "confession" that can effectively lead to their theories being judged *by the reader* against the constraints of a given theorist's identity or subject position, the implications of which are socially constructed or enframed as well. For instance, as I argue in this book, the institution of adoption overdetermines and limits the main meanings currently associated with the subject positions of the triad. To identify as a member of the triad or as excluded from it would be to immediately overlay the text with a number of possible bio-genealogical narratives that it wants to resist; a central thesis of this book is that the imperative it critiques already informs the contemporary construction of the subject positions of the triad.

Like many unqualified poststructuralists and queer theorists, therefore, I do not assert an identity precisely because self-disclosure *can* create epistemological blind spots on the part of the reader. Michel Foucault, for instance, sometimes wrote anonymously or under a pseudonym to resist the reader's epistemological inclination to receive or reject a work not in and of itself but in light of an author's fame, biography, identity, and/or social location, which is why he also refused to identify as "Gay."[5] For Foucault, "Visibility ... is a trap."[6] He thought identity should not be allowed to operate as a differentiated limit on how a critical work must be read; this knowledge effectively constrains how the author is heard, as well as what the author may be permitted to say and/or critically investigate.[7] As this book addresses a reader and engages Foucault's work and queer theories, I find myself aligned with them on this point, even as feminism is central also to this work. Where the choice not to identify my relationship to adoption troubles the reader, therefore, I urge you to consider as you read this book how having this knowledge might serve the institution of adoption and/or the dominant bio-family epistemologies and narratives that this book intends to resist.

The idea that adoption experts and discourse normalize the differentiation of adoptive ties, and do so in such a way that they are experienced as ontologically inferior to biological ties, is fundamental to this book. It shows how the inferiority of adoptive ties is the effect of a social and cultural Western logic that insists on differentiating family ties in support of a biological family order. To demonstrate its central claim, the book already assumes a well-established idea in continental, poststructural, feminist, queer, and postcolonial theories of difference and otherness: the meaning of difference, notably the need or desire to mark, map, and interrogate it, is never neutral in the social and cultural contexts of thought, language, power/knowledge, and/or institutionalized discourses that structure our realities, whether as sexed, gendered, racialized, pathologized, and/or adopted subjects. This book does not, therefore, focus so much on proving *whether* the differentiation of adoptive ties leads to their being treated and experienced as inferior. It primarily takes this idea for granted to properly address a more pressing question: *how* does the differentiation of adoptive ties give rise to a bio-genealogical imperative, one that produces and maintains the social and political inferiority of these ties? A brief comment on the question of *why* differentiation breeds ontological hierarchies, even as this effect is well known in the context of continental, poststructural, feminist, queer, and postcolonial theories of difference, will nevertheless clarify for the reader what is at issue with respect to the basic assumption with which this book begins.

The idea that differentiation is an aspect or apparatus of normalization and subject formation is discussed by Foucault in *Discipline and Punish*. He elucidates the relationship between difference and social hierarchies in a discussion of disciplinary power, which, he explains,

> refers individual actions to a whole that is at once a field of comparison, a space of differentiation and the principle of a rule to be followed. It differentiates individuals from one another, in terms of the following overall rule: that the rule be made to function as a minimal threshold, as an average to be respected or as an optimum towards which one must move. It measures in quantitative terms and hierarchizes in terms of value the abilities, the level, the "nature" of individuals. It introduces, through this "value-giving" measure, the constraint of a conformity that must be achieved. Lastly, it traces the limit that will define difference in relation to all other differences, the external frontier of the abnormal ... The perpetual penality that traverses all points and supervises every instant in disciplinary institutions compares, differentiates, hierarchizes, homogenizes, excludes. In short, it *normalizes*.[8]

Although Foucault is concerned with penal institutions, he would agree that the measurement or (de)valuation of difference is a disciplinary tactic at work within all social institutions (i.e., science, law, medicine, psychology, and social work), including the institution of adoption. What I take this insight to mean with respect to adoption, therefore, is that its discourse, which both differentiates and pathologizes adopted subjects and families, sustains a hierarchy that normalizes the biological tie *as* a kind of family tie that is ontologically "real" or more real than the adoptive tie.

Sandra Lee Bartky's work encapsulates a variation on the theme of difference and its inherently devaluating effects. She explains how, from a feminist, poststructuralist, and Derridian perspective, difference functions within signifying systems, or language, to produce binary oppositions:[9]

> [T]he founding concepts of metaphysics are implicated in binary oppositions (God/world; mind/matter) in which the superior term depends covertly for its intelligibility on the inferior term, which it typically denies or tries to ignore. The binary oppositions that ground racism, imperialism, and sexism function in just the same way and are typically linked to more familiar philosophical binaries: Masculinity, for example, in a philosophical tradition that values rationality, is associated with a superior ability to reason, femininity with a denigrated intuition or emotion.[10]

Bartky's observation with respect to the signification of gender difference is not unlike this book's view of adoption discourse as something that similarly opposes, as it differentiates, adoptive and biological ties: the differentiation of family ties in adoption discourse fundamentally sustains the superiority of biological ties over adoptive ties.

Another look at relational hierarchies to which processes of differentiation give rise is offered by Diana Fuss in her now classic feminist, queer, and postcolonial text *Identification Papers*. Here, she draws connections between Edward Said's and Frantz Fanon's ideas on the matter as it pertains to questions of subjectivity and race: "Edward Said's enormously influential theory of orientalism, which posits the Muslim 'Orient' as a phobic projection of a distinctly Western imaginary, echoes elements of Fanon's own theory of colonial psychopathology in which the black man is subjugated to the white man through a process of racial othering: 'for not only must the black man be black; he must be black in relation to the white man.'"[11] The idea that the discursive differentiation of adopted and biological family subjects undergirds what could be called a *monoracial bio-family imaginary* is not unlike Fuss's observation insofar as she shows how a relational "Western imaginary" is used to other the East and racialized subjects in support of Western superiority and whiteness. Likewise, this book shows how our contemporary Western social and cultural context idealizes biological subjects and ties at the expense of adoptees and adoptive ties. If Fuss's imaginary is taken seriously, therefore, the idea that there is a bio-genealogical imperative, or a bio-family imaginary, which is explored herein, is not merely plausible; it is also persuasive! That is because a frequent and real similitude between concepts of race and biology can be understood to produce similar, and sometimes identical, effects.

In a discussion of difference, postcolonial subjectivity, the body, and race, Bill Ashcroft, Gareth Griffiths, and Helen Tiffin also provide perspective on the idea that differentiation impacts ontological status, self-experience, and/or subjecthood: "The 'difference' of the post-colonial subject by which s/he can be 'othered' is felt most directly and immediately in the way in which the superficial differences of the body and voice (skin colour, eye shape, hair, texture, body shape, language, dialect or accent) are read as indelible signs of the 'natural' inferiority of their possessors."[12] Analogously, the material lack of a biological tie others adoptee experience or subjectivity in direct and visceral ways too. Just as the body is (mis)used to manifest a socially constructed reality of race, which nonetheless is treated normatively as a bio-material reality, the adoptee's body, voice, skin colour, hair, and eyes are scrutinized also for proofs of difference in relation to adoptive parents' and siblings' bodies, voices, skin, hair, eyes, and so on. The ontological impact of this use of the adoptee body is that it diminishes the status of adoptive ties, an outcome that is compounded when adoption is transracial.

In all of these instances, the historical, social, and political project or will to know and demarcate difference *as such* within the human and social sciences as well as within culture and language is exposed as a strategy of relational power that renders inferior an "other" subject, body, group, or continent to sustain the "natural" superiority of those that are dominant. These social and political analyses of difference and the hierarchal relations of power to which they give rise are not, however, particularly new; they are well established in feminist, poststructuralist, postcolonial, and queer theories. What is novel about this book, therefore, is its exposure of how the explicit and implicit operations of differentiation limit our possibilities for "family" experience given that the institution of adoption consistently conflates the meaning of adoption with difference.

This book interrogates the question of adoption *as* difference because adoption experts and discourse insist that adoptees and adoptive family ties are "different" relative to biological family subjects and their ties. It critically examines the notion of adoptee difference not to show that biological and adoptive ties are the same but to demonstrate how the reiteration of adoptee difference within adoption discourse makes only particular meanings and experiences of family (im)possible for adoptees and adoptive families. It exposes how contemporary meanings and discourses of adoption set the ontological status of biological and adoptive ties at odds in such a way that the latter is made inferior to the former. It shows how the discourse of adoption produces this effect, regardless of whether adoption experts intend to elicit the effect or not.

To further establish how a biological family order is realized, this book examines discourses that are local and perimetric to the institution of adoption, ones moreover that work in concert with individualism, naturalism, psychoanalysis, and incest. These discourses concern adoptee identity, the twin bond, and the adoptee reunion phenomenon known as "genetic sexual attraction" (GSA). Adoptee identity discourse, both within adoption psychology and search and reunion literature, interrogates the relationship between the adoptive tie and an adoptee's proneness to identity problems and pathology. Conversely, discourse about the psychology of the twin bond focuses on the nature of the relationship between twins' genetic similarity and the similarity of twins' identities and personalities. Adoptee identity and twin bond discourses intersect because the best subjects for "twin studies" are twins who have been separated at birth by means of adoption. Additionally, the adoptee is regarded as the best "control" for nurture, as opposed to nature, in twin studies. Genetic sexual attraction refers to the sexual (and potentially incestuous) feelings adoptees and birth parents or birth siblings may feel for each other following a successful search and reunion. It is a relatively new discourse in the context of adoption and search and reunion. It maps out a psychology of how and why sexual feelings can occur in spite of the prohibition against incest, and it warns reunitees against acting upon these feelings.

Adoptee identity, twin, and GSA discourses are alike in that they treat the biological tie's presence or absence as a problem or object of concern, and they do so uncritically because they never seriously question the fundamental assumption that it *is* the tie's presence or absence that (de)stabilizes the self's identity. The effect, as I show, is that these discourses are tactical outports of the bio-genealogical imperative. In part, that is because the range of theories they encompass, those that surround adoptee identity formation, the twin bond, and genetic sexual attraction, *appear* to take opposing positions on the nature-nurture debate. The theories out of which these broader discourses are formed make fundamental claims that explicitly locate them on one side or the other of this familiar debate, but as I demonstrate, even within the theories that appear to side with nurture, there is an implicit nature bias. The essence of this bias is a pervasive and uncritical acceptance of the idea that the biological tie's presence, in and of itself, is a necessary condition for the self's ability to obtain a complete and normal sense of identity as both an "individual" and a "family" member, as well as the idea that the biological tie's presence is a sufficient condition for *being* either a "biological child" or a "biological family."[13] This bias has obvious implications for what it means *to be* "adopted" simply because adoption entails a lack of biological ties. As a result, the nature bias that informs these discourses is coextensive with the bio-genealogical imperative because the theories that comprise them, like the institutions that are founded upon them, overdetermine the knowledge and experience of "biological" and "adoptive" families.

A key goal of this book is to philosophically investigate conditions of knowledge – specifically individualism and naturalism, psychoanalysis, and universalized incest – that contour the human sciences and, thereby, adoption in order to show how bio-genealogy is set up as the etiology of both the "adoptee's" and the "biological child's" subjectivity. It considers how this etiology of identity occurs out of a convergence of the human sciences with the institution of adoption and the adoption rights movement (ARM); it examines how this convergence engineers and overdetermines the possibilities of adoptive and biological "family" experience. By way of a collage of philosophical ideas that I draw from the likes of Michel Foucault, Judith Butler, and Adam Phillips, to name only a few of the theorists with whose work I engage, this book initiates a genealogy of the modern bio-genealogical imperative. It does so both to propose a critical ontology and epistemology and to subvert the ritualized uses of bio-genealogy as the etiology of normal identity and family experience, an etiology that both affects and is affected by the problematization and pathologization of adoptee identity and adoptive ties.

There are three main movements or parts in this book, and three chapters are dedicated to each one. The first, fourth, and seventh chapters present discourse analyses that uncover the operation of the bio-genealogical imperative in adoption, twin, and GSA discourses respectively; the second, fifth, and eighth chapters provide theoretical and genealogical investigations of each discourse and its implications for "family" experience, as well as its production in light of the broader modern Western discourses of individualism, naturalism, psychoanalysis, and incest; finally, the third, sixth, and ninth chapters offer critical analyses that intervene in the knowledge and effects of each discourse.

One purpose behind this tripartite arrangement is to expose, account for, and then resist the reiteration of the bio-genealogical imperative as it occurs in (seemingly) different or independent discourses that are shown nonetheless to intersect within the institution of adoption in myriad ways. The book exposes varied and complicated reiterations of the imperative through close textual analyses of adoption and family discourses that either propose or (appear to) resist bio-essentialist attitudes and bias; it demonstrates that the imperative's constant reiteration is an inherent function of contemporary adoption and family discourse, regardless of whether the discourse takes the perspective of nature or nurture or pertains to transnational, domestic, transracial, monoracial, and/or infant or late-adoption theories and practices. The idea that the institution of adoption is contoured fundamentally by the bio-genealogical imperative and the persistent demonstration of this fact via discourse analyses potentially leave this book open to the critique that it oversimplifies an otherwise diverse range of adoption literature and theory or, worse, that the book, not the discourse, is repetitive. However, when we scrutinize adoption and family discourse, as I do in the book, we see that the efficiency of the imperative lies simply and precisely in its repetitions throughout variegated literature that theorizes various kinds of adoption and family psychologies and relations. In other words, where the book attunes the reader to the multiform machinations of the imperative in adoption and family discourse, the reader cannot help but begin to see it everywhere because the traces of the imperative really are pervasive. Albeit to different degrees, the imperative occurs in all adoption theories, regardless of whether these theories are nature or nurture perspectives on adoptee identity. This argument is not an oversimplification but points to a formerly unobserved over-presence of the bio-genealogical imperative in the literature, which this book exposes. The book's main concern, therefore, is not to show that the imperative's operations vary in form and/or by degree, although it does discuss this too, but to demonstrate that there always is a form and/or degree of the imperative at work in both historical and contemporary adoption discourse, regardless of whether the discourse addresses transnational, domestic, transracial, monoracial, infant, and/or late adoptions. It shows precisely that the imperative has a very wide reach. In transracial adoption discourse, for instance, racial difference, or racial identity per se, appears to be the central issue. But there is an undeniable degree to which race operates *as* the biological tie's presence or absence within a family given that to be intelligible as a biological family is also to be seen as a monoracial family. That is why the experiences of mixed-race families with biological ties are not entirely unlike those of mixed-race adoptive families; in both instances, race functions as the degree to which a family has "failed" to observe the bio-genealogical imperative. And these degrees, in tandem with others that may or may not concern race in adoption discourse, are what manifest the imperative's almost totalizing force in the (re)production of the ontological inferiority of the adoptive tie and the problematization of adoptee identity.

In addition, the organization of the book's chapters embeds within the text a series of strategic repetitions or counter-reiterations that provoke readers to think more critically and anew about adoption and family discourse. It pushes readers to reconsider their own "biopowered" (re)inscription in the bio-genealogical imperative.[14] It enlists strategic repetitions against the dominant reiteration of the bio-genealogical imperative to (over)familiarize readers with the explicit and implicit ploys of a bio-logic that is highly nuanced and pervasive throughout adoption theory and practice; the process of (re)familiarization via strategic repetition is one that feminist and queer poststructuralists, such as Judith Butler, enlist for the purposes of resistance, as it can serve a counter-reiterative function that interrupts dominant discourse and knowledge, which in this instance are bio-genealogical.

Chapter 1 of this book examines how the dominant answer to a central modern Western question about the self – "*Who am I?*" – is bound to the bio-genealogical imperative by the institution of adoption as both a mode of family discourse and an arm of the human sciences. It examines the theories and psychologies that adoption experts typically use to explain adoptees' "identity problems" and/or the need to search for biological parents and siblings. It uncovers a paradox within adoption discourse. Adoption psychologies assume, implicitly and explicitly, that adoptees search because of an *essential* and *natural* need to know their bio-genealogical history and relations in order to establish a normal identity. In effect, adoption experts treat the need for bio-genealogical knowledge as essential and natural because this knowledge enables the self to experience the *presence* of the biological tie materially and as the foundation of a normal identity.[15] In this way, among others, adoption discourse confers an inferior, because immaterial, ontological status upon the experience of adoptive ties.[16]

The discussion of adoption discourse in chapter 1 details the main theories and psychologies of nature and nurture that adoption experts typically use to explain the patterns and pathologies of adoptee identity. It not only describes the dominant contemporary accounts of adoptee identity and experience but also demonstrates how apparently conflicting perspectives about nature and nurture in adoption discourse ultimately share a common commitment to bio-essentialist assumptions about the centrality of bio-genealogical knowledge to normal identity formation. In effect, the dichotomy between nature and nurture theories about adoptee identity is shown to collapse on the side of nature: I argue that adoptee identity theories that claim to be nurture perspectives subscribe, often inadvertently, to important nature assumptions, and I do so to bring the uncritical treatment of these theories, and their effects, as nurture perspectives into question. In this chapter, nurture perspectives founded on implicit nature assumptions are shown to function covertly as, and in tandem with, nature theories on adoptee identity; they reinforce the effects of nature theories and naturalize the relationship between normal identity and the presence of biological ties. Chapter 1 concludes with the idea that for these reasons adoption experts are a univocal group in that they subscribe to some semblance of bio-essentialist notions of family and identity.

Both the relationship between adoption revelation and self-knowledge and its implications for family subjectivities are explored in chapter 2. In the middle of the twentieth century, adoption experts in North America began to emphasize the necessity of telling children they were adopted as early as possible and reiterating this truth throughout childhood. The aim of this process, then and today, is to protect the adoptee from identity crises, or the self-altering trauma of late revelation.[17] Early revelation allows children to incorporate the knowledge of adoption into their sense of identity during the earliest stages of development. The idea is that telling minimizes or prevents the risk of terrible identity crises. These crises occur if the adopted child is allowed to develop the identity of a "biological child," or a false self-knowledge, only to find out in adulthood that she was adopted. These crises inevitably arise when adoption is kept secret.

Although adoption experts generally understand the adoptee's knowledge of adoption to elicit identity conflicts because of their bio-
genealogical alienation, a hidden adoption is an even greater concern
because it gives rise to a genuinely false, and thus more fragile, identity that is likely to be shattered not *if* but *when* the truth of adoption
is discovered.

In chapter 2, therefore, the depiction of late revelation as a universal threat to normal identity formation is shown to mean that, in
adoption discourse, *being* a "biological child" turns absolutely on the
factual presence of a biological tie between parent and child. The purpose of this demonstration is to question whether the conflation of
biological fact with the truth of being is, or should be treated as, the
superior basis for identity, self-definition, and experience. In effect,
this chapter examines the phenomenon of late revelation and considers philosophical questions about whether there is a natural and essential ontological difference that distinguishes the "adoptee's" being
from that of the "biological" child. It shows how this idea functions as
the bedrock of contemporary adoption discourse and that it does so
because adoption experts treat the effects of late revelation uncritically as a sign that the ontological difference of adoptee identity is natural and essential. The chapter further contends that this assumption
is flawed because adoption experts never really ask *whether* the experience of being a "biological" child turns on the factual, material presence of the biological tie or on the belief that the tie is materially present. It also explores the idea that a person who *knows* herself solely *to
be* a "biological" child, even though she may have been adopted, is no
less a "biological child" than the child who was not adopted. It considers that experiences based on the self's beliefs about its ties, which
are factually false beliefs, are no less real than the same sorts of experiences based on factually true beliefs. It argues that adoption experts
are mistaken to locate the origins of adoptive and biological families'
ontological differences in the material presence or absence of biological ties, as opposed to the knowledge itself that such a tie is present
or absent.

Foucault suggests that a generalized moral obligation to know oneself is imposed upon the modern Western subject; the genealogy of
this imperative is examined in chapter 3 as a central force in the production of "adoptee" subjectivity today. This chapter shows how the
"individual," who at the same time is a "family" subject, is ensnared in
this demand through the intersection of central tenets of individual-

ism and naturalism, which together conflate the meaning of knowing oneself with the self's bio-genealogy. It demonstrates how the meaning of self-knowledge *as* bio-genealogical knowledge subjects the adoptee and would-be "individual" to a demand that cannot be met within the confines of the adoptive family. It shows how the subjectivity of the "adoptee" is constituted as the obvious effect of the self's inability to fulfil this obligation, how this obligation is imposed generally on the family through the rise of individualism and naturalism, and how this obligation is inflicted specifically on the adoptive family with the emergence of the institution of adoption. It also contends that the institution of adoption maintains a biological family order because it reiterates the idea of the self's inherent psycho-structural need to address the bio-genealogical imperative with bio-genealogical knowledge, which experts deem essential in normal development and identity formation. This chapter's main argument is that, in contrast to the "individual" who *is* a biological family subject, the modern "adoptee" emerges precisely *as* the experience of incomplete self-knowledge that is due to the *meaning* of lack, as opposed to the lack itself, that occurs when the self cannot access bio-genealogical knowledge. It maintains that the self's need to meet a bio-genealogical imperative is inculcated through events in modern Western knowledge, wherein the bio-essentialist effects of individualism and naturalism are compounded for the family in and through the human sciences and the institution of adoption.

Since the late nineteenth century, human scientists have used twin and adoption studies to debate questions about whether biology or genes drive personality, identity, experience, and ultimately the quality of familial ties.[18] By examining the use that behavioural geneticists, psychologists, and psychoanalysts make of twins and adoptees in this debate, chapter 4 investigates the effects of the bio-essentialist discourse to which this use gives rise. Twin discourse, which treats the adoptee as the twin study's ideal control, is on a continuum with adoption discourse in that it too (re)produces the bio-genealogical imperative of the family that informs adoptee subjectivity. What chapter 4 suggests is that twin and adoption studies are not impartial apparatus that discover and unearth objective truths about nature and nurture in human experience; instead, the human sciences' invention and application of these studies is a social-political-historical event that participates in the overdetermination of family knowledge and experience as biological in essence and nature. For some time, twins and their bonds have served as a relatively uncomplicated and definitive standard against which other *kinds* of family ties are and can be measured. This chapter suggests that the main reason twin studies function this way, and so readily, is due as much to the questions human scientists do not think to ask as it is to the questions they do think to ask about genetic similarity and its possible meanings.

Much like "adoptees," therefore, "twins" are examined in chapter 4 as a modern touchstone against which family subjectivities are evaluated, constituted, and determined. Moreover, the discourse to which the event of the twin and adoption study gives rise is explored as an instrument of the bio-genealogical imperative. It is shown to render human biology or genetics a necessary, indubitable, and ontological basis for family experience. Thus, as germane as adoption discourse is to formations of adoptee subjectivity, so too is twin discourse given that the modern fascination with "twins" produces a qualitative distinction between our experiences of ties that are *more* or *less* biological. Where a concern with the "twin bond" emerges as a key focal point of the twin study, it further establishes biology *as* the essential basis for familial *kinds* of bonds; this situation is reflected in the behavioural geneticist's and psychologist's belief that the experience of a bond is an inherited genetic predisposition *and* in the psychoanalyst's belief that these bonds are a psychic response to an environment of genetic similarity. As a final goal, this chapter examines the nature-nurture debate that surrounds twins and the twin bond to expose how this dichotomy, in and of itself, (re)produces the modern Western bio-genealogical imperative and the superiority of the biological tie.

In chapter 5, what I call "bio-narcissism" is explored as a dominant mode of being in modern Western culture. In fact, I argue that it is a central and common aspect of modern Western experience. Bio-narcissism and the bio-genealogical imperative are shown to be integral to one another. That is because contemporary family and adoption psychologies are imbued with the idea that familial love is predicated upon bio-narcissism, an assumption that affirms the self's need to know the individuals it is most and least like. A key question that informs this chapter is how the modern Western self comes to identify with experiences that are overdetermined by the logic of bio-narcissism. To answer this question, I explore the experience of bio-narcissism as an effect of psychoanalysis and its influence: the intelligibility of psychoanalytic discourse, which elicits a bio-logic of the self-same – by which I mean a bio-logic that privileges the self's love of what appears to be like the self in an *other* – is realized through its emergence in a social, political, and historical context that is permeated already by individualist and naturalist discourses. As psychoanalysis gains influence, bio-narcissism becomes a key component of the human psyche and family relations. In particular, psychoanalysis produces the self's love of the self-same as it "discovers" the psychic universality of narcissism in the myth of Narcissus; the antiquity of this Greek myth operates in psychoanalysis as the evidence that narcissism is a timeless attribute of the human psyche. Once the myth's uncritical use as a universal and its impact on family subjectivity are established, this chapter resists this truth of psychoanalysis with the idea that bio-narcissism is no more than a proof that the influence of psychoanalysis is pervasive; it is a sign that psychoanalysis has successfully imposed the knowledge of bio-narcissism upon modern Western human experience.

The psychoanalytic concept of narcissism is introduced in chapter 5 to address the question of how it is that psychoanalysis "discovers" and, thereby, determines the human psyche's inherent propensity for narcissism. Although it appears to uncover narcissism as an inherent psychic phenomenon and, on this basis, maps it out, I argue that psychoanalysis's greatest success is really that it maps the conventional meaning of the Narcissus myth *as* a love of the self-same *onto* human experience and attachment. Contrary to psychoanalytic theory, therefore, I do not assume that psychoanalysis "discovers" a genuinely universal truth about the human psyche when it concludes that human beings are prone to narcissism. Instead, I show how the influence of psychoanalytic discourse, which is accomplished further by its share in the logic of individualism and naturalism, institutes bio-narcissism as a now too pervasive mode of "family" experience. I also examine how psychoanalysis garners the status of objective truth for its claim that the human psyche and, by implication, family relations are essentially bio-narcissistic. And with respect to adoptee subjectivity, I contend that the critical accomplishment of psychoanalysis is that its production of the modern Western self *as* a narcissistic subject elicits "family" experience as a mode of being that must now conflate love and intimacy with the presence or experience of (biological) sameness. In other words, I argue that the influence of psychoanalysis as either a family or adoption psychology plays a very important role in the maintenance of the bio-genealogical imperative.

Sigmund Freud modelled the psychology of human attachment and love on Narcissus, along with Oedipus, because he understood myth to reflect a truth about the nature of our psyches. He regarded Ovid's myth, in particular, to be a universal narrative that mirrors the original state of desire of all human beings; the infant is like Narcissus in its initial and unconscious state of self-absorption because it is incapable of realizing or addressing the other's needs and desires. Freud also believed that narcissism plays a key role in all stages of human development; it is the psychic foundation of all forms of love and identification. Freud drew a *psychology*, not a morality, from the tragedy of Narcissus, a psychology that, because of psychoanalysis's continued influence, informs twin, family, and adoption discourses today. As a result, my project in chapter 6 is to show how psychoanalysis marks our knowledge and experiences of identity and family with narcissism. I investigate how that is accomplished through the institution of narcissism, particularly bio-narcissism, as the first principle of both a normal identity and "family" relations. I examine how the biological double operates as the medium through which the self is driven to understand itself and its family bonds. I explore how the use of *the same* by psychoanalysis, when coupled with the bio-genealogical imperative, constitutes narcissism as the foundation of family psychology. But I do so to resist narcissism as the truth of our psychology. In effect, this chapter questions the discursive location of a narcissistic desire for the "double" in the self and, on this basis, critically interrogates this idea's role in the maintenance of self-knowledge as something that is treated as complete and authentic only to the extent that the self knows and experiences its bio-genealogy. The chapter critically rethinks this desire and how it limits our possibilities of experience within both biological and adoptive families. It does so by considering four psychoanalytic concepts that inform our "family" experiences and psychologies today; it examines the role of childhood history, the unconscious, narcissism, and identification as key constructs that are operative in contemporary family and adoption psychologies. In response to the limits of intelligibility that narcissism imposes on family experience, this chapter re-examines the Narcissus myth not as a psychology but as a critical epistemology. It recounts a version of the myth, as told by Pausanias, to facilitate an understanding of how and why the idea of difference, which is and can be a basis for family bonds, remains largely unintelligible to us today.

Adoption discourse surrounding genetic sexual attraction is the main focus in chapter 7. What is considered here is how adoption experts' appeals to incest discourse in order to explain GSA enlist them in the differentiation and degradation of the adoptive tie that they strive to minimize. It explores the function of adoption discourse *as* incest discourse in the case of GSA theory and psychology. Moreover, it demonstrates how this discourse (re)inscribes the bio-genealogical imperative because the adoptee's ability to avoid GSA necessarily demands that she know her bio-genealogy. It observes that questions of GSA are taken up in much the same way as questions that concern adoptee and twin identity; they are tackled primarily within a matrix of behavioural genetics (or sociobiology), psychoanalysis (including theories on object relations and on loss and attachment), and socialization discourse. Chapter 7 suggests that GSA theories, like adoptee identity and twin bond theories, also bestride the nature-nurture debate. Thus theories normally thought to be opposed are shown to be mixed and matched, largely uncritically, by adoption experts. Indeed, adoption experts seem to appeal too easily to both nature and nurture simultaneously in order to give a comprehensive view of the origins of GSA. In this chapter, however, I argue that the blending of nature and nurture perspectives to explain GSA is easy not because it is comprehensive but because it is an effect of the bio-genealogical imperative that already informs adoption discourse. I also tender the idea that this blending is due to the function of the meaning of incest *as* the biological tie. Inevitably, the current meaning and experience of family maps onto that of incest in that both pivot on the presence of the biological tie. So despite the legal fact that the adoptive tie severs all rights and responsibilities normally founded upon the biological tie, there is an important sense in which the ontological status of "family" as biology remains utterly intact via the meaning of incest and, ultimately, GSA. This situation is made evident by a number of facts: adoption experts warn reunited birth families against the trauma of acting on GSA; reunited birth parents and birth children or birth siblings are subject to incest law following life-long separations through legal adoption; and adoptive parents or siblings who commit sexual abuse against an adoptee are not legally understood to commit incest. The final aim of chapter 7, therefore, is to expose how the meaning of incest, as it intersects both with GSA (or adoption) discourse and with the bio-genealogical imperative, (re)produces and opposes "biological" and "adoptive" family subjects.

The meanings and laws used to regulate incest are polyvalent, varying in different times and locations; it has been condemned, ignored, and even accepted in different historical moments. Following a brief historical discussion of incest's mutability, which is evident in the diverse social-political-economic uses that have been made of incest, chapter 8 primarily investigates its meaning within the human sciences. The chapter examines the modern meaning of incest and its role in the differentiation of biological and adoptive ties. It considers the idea, proposed by Foucault, that the human sciences' problematization of incest as a *universal* leads to the "affective intensification" of what I assume is the biological family's experience and adds to this idea the argument that it diminishes the intensity of the adoptive family's experience.[19] As biology, psychology, sociology, and feminism all play a role in the universalization of incest, the chapter examines the impact of these modern disciplines on a new knowledge of incest that further bolsters the bio-genealogical imperative. I argue that where incest intensifies biological ties, it attenuates the experience of adoptive ties. In the end, chapter 8 returns to the relationship between adoption and incest discourse and the emerging knowledge of GSA in order to illustrate the often unwitting role that the institution of adoption plays in rendering the adoptive family's experience inferior to that of the biological family.

Chapter 9 takes on the quintessential incest narrative: the myth of Oedipus. It is the narrative to which human scientists turn as the testimony that incest and its prohibitions are universal. Here, the dominant reading of the myth as a *tragedy* is shown to undergird the truth of incest as it is told by the human sciences. The Oedipal tale's contemporary operation as a mode of universalized incest in family and adoption discourse is also established. The tragic fate of Oedipus – his blinding, dethroning, and exile – is a metaphor for the dissolution of culture, family, and self that awaits all those who fail to comply with the modern Western imperative that to know oneself is to know one's bio-genealogy – an imperative that is ultimately commensurate with the imperative of incest. Just as the modern Western experience of biological family is a problem of Oedipal knowledge or incest, so too is the experience of the adoptive family such a problem because it is equally subject to the same bio-genealogical imperative. The myth bears a special resonance within the institution of adoption because it is the inimitable reunion story and because the Oedipal tragedy is manifested through Oedipus's lack of bio-genealogical self-knowledge, or his ignorance about the true identity of his biological parents. As we see, adoption experts often read the truth of adoptee experience through the Oedipal narrative as interpreted by the human sciences, and they do so especially in response to phenomena such as GSA, search, and reunion. To act on GSA, they claim, is to risk great biological, psychological, and social perils, a warning that is mirrored in the tragic fate of Oedipus, a reunitee who sleeps with his biological mother.

Working with the idea that the meaning of incest and GSA is informed by a modern Western meaning of *tragedy* that is attached to the Oedipus myth, I arrive at the final question addressed by this work: what new possibilities for the meaning of family reside in the story of Oedipus if and when the myth's meaning as tragedy is rejected? Some reunitees, as we shall see, embody this question simply because they refuse current Oedipal interpretations of their sexual desire, a refusal that rejects the idea that they are "family" simply because they share biological ties. To read Oedipus outside a meaning of tragedy is to get at the heart of what the experience of adoption can be: in a social-political-historical moment that does not attach arbitrary and hierarchical values to either adoptive or biological ties, adoption is an experience of family that is essentially no better and no worse than that of biological family. To put it another way, an alternate tragedy emerging out of the Oedipus myth is its use in bolstering the modern Western imperatives of bio-genealogy and incest (prohibition) that effectively constitute the ontological reality of family *as* the biological tie.

This book responds to the impact of adoption as a system of knowledge that impacts real lives. It is a rejoinder to a pathology that defines adoptees and adoptive families' experiences as inauthentic. It reacts to harms that are experienced today by families and selves that dare to love across difference. It challenges notions of family and identity that are rooted in bio-essentialism. It counters the demand of bio-narcissism, which is treated uncritically as the matchless foundation of familial love. It is a genealogy of the bio-genealogical imperative to which biological and adoptive family subjects all subscribe far too readily. It troubles family practices and pleasures that emerge through our regulated desires to obey such an imperative. This book is one way that we might begin to decentre the biological family, rethink the possibilities of our bonds, and multiply our abilities *to be* family. So let's begin.

I

"Who Am I?":
Adoption as Identity Loss

I said, "Who am I?"
Looking into the mirror my eyes searched for clues.
There were none.
Nor were there likely to be.
For I am adopted.

Betty Jean Lifton, *Twice Born*

We now know that although it can end the legal ties, adoption can never end the genetic and psychological connections between children and their birth families.

Kenneth W. Watson, "Family-Centered Adoption Practice"

The viability of the adoptive family has come under review as more and more adopted individuals have seemingly failed to achieve a sense of personal identity within the adoptive family which is satisfying or complete.

Charlene E. Miall, "The Stigma of Adoptive Parent Status"

Why do many adoptees feel a need to search out their biological parents and siblings? The reasons given are various. Adoptees may search for medical reasons because medical history is important and useful for addressing concerns related to mental and physical health. Adoptees may feel they do not "belong" to their adopted parents or family, so they may search to abrogate this feeling.[1] They may wish to know the reasons "why" they were given up for adoption: were they "wanted" and were they "loved"?[2] But as Robert S. Anderson puts it, a "fairly consistent reason adoptees give for searching ... is that they hope for a change in the way they experience themselves as people."[3] What is it, then, that is sought out in order to bring about this change? Paradoxically, adoption discourse that addresses issues of adoptee identity and the search tends implicitly or explicitly to assume that the reason so many adoptees search is that they are motivated by an *essential* need that is also a *natural* need to address their self-experience or identity in light of *knowing* their bio-genealogical history and relations. Adoption discourse treats the need for bio-genealogical knowledge as essential and natural, especially when it conflates this kind of knowing – which is said to underpin normal identity formation – with the self's ability to experience the *presence* of the biological tie. It is in this way, I argue, that adoption discourse confers an inferior ontological status upon the experience of adoptive ties.

This way of describing adoption discourse may seem to treat adoption experts as a homogeneous group. For reasons that will become clear, adoption experts are a univocal group in a number of important respects. Below the surface of what initially appear to be conflicting perspectives on adoption held by experts who are ostensibly opposed lies a common set of fundamental assumptions about the importance of bio-genealogical knowledge. For example, there is a growing debate about whether the need for bio-genealogical knowledge is essential to normal identity formation or whether it is socially produced by a cultural climate that stigmatizes adoptive ties to such an extent that adoptees feel compelled to seek their origins. Upon closer examination, however, the apparent dichotomy between the nature as opposed to the nurture of adoptee identity problems can be shown to collapse on the side of nature; that is, adoption identity theories that fundamentally claim to be nurture perspectives can be shown to subscribe inadvertently to important nature assumptions. Uncovering the nature assumptions of these theories brings into question their categorization as nurture perspectives: nurture perspectives that entail implicit nature assumptions (covertly) function as and reinforce nature theories on adoptee identity; they reinforce the implications of nature theories that claim an essential relationship exists between normal identity formation and the presence of the biological tie. One of the main reasons these nurture arguments collapse into nature arguments is that they can be shown, implicitly, to subscribe to what is explicitly assumed by the nature side of the debate. Both nurture and nature arguments about adoptee identity give an essential significance to the presence of the biological tie as the best source of bio-genealogical knowledge, which is said to prevent the identity problems commonly associated with being adopted.

Another reason the dichotomy appears to collapse in the context of adoptee identity theories is that many contemporary adoption experts summon up, as cause and consistent, a variety of psychological theories that pertain to both nature and nurture. Some experts do so inadvertently, and others do so expressly insofar as they argue that adoptee identity problems cannot be attributed solely to nature or nurture, which appears to explain the contradiction. All the same, I argue that the real reason adoption experts *can* blend nature and nurture perspectives, implicitly or explicitly, is that most, if not all, adoptee identity theories *do* subscribe to a biological bias, albeit to greater or lesser degrees. In my discussion of how adoption's impact on identity is characterized by the experts, it is worth noting, therefore, that adoptee identity theories can be confusing where they appear, due to their assumptions, to be aligned concurrently with inconsistent schools of thought. Nevertheless, I examine the broadest range of these theories to isolate the main kinds of causes that adoption experts, historically and currently, attribute to the problem of adoptee identity.

The image of the adoptee's search for her birth family as a quest for self-identity is widely developed within the institution of adoption.[4] This quest, however, is associated largely with pathology by adoption experts (i.e., geneticists, psychiatrists, psychoanalysts, psychologists, sociologists, social workers, and search activists). In the discourse that surrounds adoptee identity and adjustment, the idea that adoption "can present lifelong developmental and psychological challenges to adopted persons" is a powerful theme that shows no sign of waning soon.[5] The relationship between adoption and identity formation became a focal point among adoption experts in the 1940s.[6] The adoption rights movement (ARM) also began to emerge at this time. Jean Paton, an American adoptee and the earliest known search activist, first proposed the idea of a "national, mutual-consent, voluntary adoption registry" in 1949.[7] A radical idea for the time, the import of a registry is that it allows adoptees and birth parents to record "identifying information" or the explicit particulars of their adoptions and relinquishments in hopes of being matched with each other in order to facilitate reunion. Although the ARM is critical of the institution of adoption and its historical role both in the legal sealing of birth records and in the mediation of identifying information, its main justification for

demanding adoptee access to birth records is the identity pathology
that other adoption experts say adoptees face due to their lack of
bio-genealogical knowledge. In fact, important support for the ARM
also comes from a number of influential geneticists, psychiatrists,
psychoanalysts, psychologists, and social workers within the traditional institution of adoption.[8]

For instance, E. Wayne Carp claims that the prolific work of child
psychiatrist Arthur Sorosky and social workers Annette Baran and
Reuben Pannor currently serves as the ARM's single most important
and effectual justification for the disclosure of adoption records.[9]
Sorosky, Baran, and Pannor argue that "the problem of identity is
that it must establish a continuity between society's past and the
future," adding that "very few adoptees are provided with enough
background information to be incorporated into their developing
ego and sense of identity."[10] They also suggest that adopted children
suffer unnecessary and sometimes disabling identity and emotional
problems that disclosure of bio-genealogical knowledge can ease. To
address these problems Sorosky, Baran, and Pannor further support
the idea of "open adoption," where the birth parent relinquishes all
legal rights to a child but retains a right to ongoing contact and
knowledge of the child's well-being and whereabouts if desired.[11]
For Sorosky, Baran, and Pannor, open adoption averts identity problems in adoptees because it provides them with the knowledge and
experience of their birth parents that are deemed essential to normal identity formation. In fact, Baran and Pannor are so convinced
of the import of such knowledge and experience, as Barbara Melosh
observes, that they completely reject adoption as a viable family
form, "advocat[ing] an increased emphasis on family preservation –
providing all possible support to enable single mothers to raise
their children."[12]

Search activists continue to use the work of adoption experts like
Sorosky, Baron, and Pannor to give credibility to the case for adoption
record disclosure and the right to consensual reunions that adoption
record secrecy prevents. As a result, search activists have popularized
the dominant psychology surrounding adoptee identity and prolifer-
ated adoption discourse through public debate.[13] For these reasons,
search activists are like adoption experts to the extent that they play a
crucial role in reinforcing the idea that there is an essential relation
between bio-genealogical knowledge and normal identity formation.
In the context of this discussion, therefore, search activists are consid-

ered to be among adoption experts, and the ARM is assumed to be an important part of the institution of adoption where issues of adoption and identity converge.

A cursory glance at the theory on adoption and identity since the 1940s tells the story that, compared to nonadopted people, adoptees are historically understood to be highly susceptible to identity and mental health problems.[14] Since then, a main pivot upon which the adoptee's identity problems have continued to turn is her alienation from bio-genealogical knowledge, which nonadopted children normally glean through their proximity to the biological family. Search narratives also reinforce this idea because they assume that the adoptee's need for bio-genealogical knowledge is a "natural and intrinsic" aspect of normal identity formation and that it "is a natural – even universal – response to adoption."[15] Yet, insofar as adoption experts think the need to search is normal and natural, "implicitly or explicitly, the absence of blood relations has generally been thought to render adoption pathogenic *per se*."[16] In fact, it can safely be said that beliefs about the pathology of adoption are so deeply embedded in historical and contemporary adoption identity discourse that the motivating question behind most research is not *whether* but *how* growing up in the absence of biological ties makes adoptees different from nonadopted people.

For instance, the implications of claims that adopted adolescents are "more prone than nonadopted adolescents to aggressive, sexual, identity, dependency-independency, and social conflicts" are and have been used to support some pretty extreme ideas that link adoption to serious anti-social behaviour and psychopathology.[17] Concepts such as Sorosky, Baran, and Pannor's "adoption syndrome" and David Kirshener's "adopted child syndrome" locate a propensity for violence in *some* adoptees because they are particularly incapable of dealing with the effects of their adoptions.[18] In fact, by the late 1980s, these notions had garnered enough currency to be used in a number of court cases and to explain why some notorious criminal adoptees, such as Joel Rifkin and Patrick DeGelleke, had engaged in serial killings or murder.[19] Of course, the idea that adoption is inherently pathogenic is not uncontested. For example, Lorne Loxterkamp appears to challenge this view when he considers whether biological ties, or access to them, can be the cause of, rather than the cure for, identity problems. Specifically, he argues that in cases where the biological family has abused the adoptee, a sense of identity is going to be better secured through a sense of belonging that she may experience only in the adoptive family. In effect, in some instances, "contact" with the biological family via open adoption can, through retraumatizaton, cause identity problems that the contact is meant to prevent. Unfortunately, his objection does not target the patho-ontological question surrounding the heightened valuation of biological ties as the best foundation for identity formation, which concerns us here. Instead, Loxterkamp essentially weighs one harm (adoption) against "another kind of harm" (abuse or retraumatization) and comes out in favour of the former. He does not dispel the idea that adoption, on its own, is a threat to identity but merely implies that it is or can be a lesser of two evils.[20] There are important works, however, that do explicitly critique the pathology surrounding adoption and identity: Elizabeth Bartholet's *Family Bonds* and Katarina Wegar's *Adoption, Identity, and Kinship*. And they contest this idea in provocative and powerful ways that do question the superior ontological status of biological ties that is taken for granted by adoption experts. Yet, as we will see, even these theorists, among others, do not deny that the *need* for bio-genealogical knowledge, a need that is normally treated as the source of adoption-related pathology, is *real*.[21]

To indicate just how prevalent the idea that adoptees are prone to identity problems continues to be, we need only consider any clinical or popular reunion manual or adoption handbook.[22] Compiling the most influential research on adoption, search, and reunion, the recent *Handbook of Adoption: Implications for Researchers, Practitioners, and Families* is a case in point. The idea that adoptee identity goes hand in hand with the threat of pathology is a central theme in this anthology that targets both adoption experts and families touched by adoption. For example, in the foreword to the book, David Brodzinsky asserts that the psychodynamics of adoption are "unique" and that "[i]ssues related to separation and loss, trauma, attachment disruption, and conflicted identity ... are viewed as core components of the adoption experience."[23] In *Birthright: The Guide to Search and Reunion for Adoptees, Birthparents, and Adoptive Parents*, Jean A.S. Strauss also exemplifies this idea when she states, "My natural heritage was an important piece of my identity. That it was withheld, I felt, denied me the opportunity for complete self-knowledge."[24] Adoption handbooks for lay audiences interested in adoption are even more illustrative in this regard. Given that the audience is the (potential) adoptive parent, these handbooks generally aim to present adoption as a normal and positive (as opposed to pathological) family experience. For instance, in *Raising Adopted Children*, Lois Ruskai Melina acknowledges dissenting views concerning the idea that adoptees are "at risk" for identity and emotional problems, but she does so at the same time that she arguably over-acknowledges the theory that supports this idea.[25] She provides (potential) adoptive parents a blend and balance of information that she deems will enable them to make fair and informed decisions about adoption and all that it entails as a family form. But she qualifies this discussion, saying that although "[i]t is too simple ... to explain away any behavioral or emotional problems an adoptee has as being related to her adoption ... it is also unwise to ignore the fact that the adoptee has had experiences in her life that children who have been raised by their biological parents do not have."[26] Regardless of the dissenting views she discusses, Melina's balanced discussion still leaves the (potential) adoptive parent with a distinct impression that, because of the absence of the biological tie or parents, the *possibility* that adoptees are prone to identity problems *must* be considered seriously both in the choice to adopt and throughout adoptive parenting. This impression is compounded by the book's more general claims because, even though Melina is a proponent of various nurture perspectives, such as that of H. David Kirk, these perspectives contain an implicit bio-bias, which is examined later in this chapter.[27] Early in her book, for instance, she asserts that "[w]e have come to realize that family is as much about relationships as it is about biology," a claim that perhaps more covertly, but no less powerfully, implies that the biological tie's absence will necessarily impact the adoptee simply because it excludes the idea that family and the things it impacts, like identity formation, can or indeed might be *only* about relationships.[28] So although one goal of her book is to minimize the (potential) adoptive parent's concern about the development risks facing adopted children, the discussion nonetheless strongly conveys the idea that the association between being adopted and pathology is real. What the *balance* of Melina's discussion illustrates, therefore, is that despite being called into question, the association between adoption and identity problems remains prevalent and forceful within the institution of adoption, which affects any constituency it addresses.

What, then, are the ways that adoption experts have answered the question of the origin of the adoptee identity conflict? A number of theories originally proposed in the 1940s through to the 1960s continue to influence contemporary perspectives on adoptee identity. These early theories emphasize the import of biological family continuity and frame adoptee identity problems in relation to concepts such as "genealogical bewilderment," "genetic ego," and Sigmund Freud's "family romance." All of these theories assume that a lack of bio-genealogical knowledge due to the absence of the biological tie undermines the normal process of identification, which is what underpins identity conflicts in adoptees.

In 1943 Florence Clothier argued that blood ties bind the child to the past and future and that by definition the adopted child has therefore "lost the thread of family continuity."[29] On the basis of psychoanalysis and allowing for the idea that genetics plays a role in identity formation, she claims that "the severing of the individual from his racial antecedents" and from the biological mother is what underpins the psychology of the adopted child.[30] Identification, particularly with forebears, she suggests, is experienced precisely through the mother-child bond, which is also fundamental to the formation of a child's sense of security. As a result of separation, the adopted child is also traumatized and deprived of a necessary "primitive relationship" with the mother, one that underpins normal development.[31] What separates the adopted child from the nonadopted child, therefore, is that her ego "in addition to all the normal demands made upon it, is called upon to compensate for the wound left by the loss of the biological mother."[32] For Clothier, normal identity formation depends on the "the physiological and the psychological" relationship between biological mother and child, a relationship that, she claims, is doubtfully "replaced by even the best of substitute mothers."[33]

Although coined by E. Wellisch in 1952, the notion of "genealogical bewilderment" was fully developed by H.J. Sants only in 1964. Like Clothier, Sants takes a psychoanalytic perspective and works with the idea that there are "genetic aspects of identification."[34] Generally, genealogical bewilderment occurs in the child "who either has no knowledge of his natural parents or only uncertain knowledge of them," leading to a "state of confusion and uncertainty ... [that] fundamentally undermines his security and thus affects his mental health."[35] More specifically, Sants suggests that it occurs because differences in the nonbiological parents' "genetic structure" and "appearance can severely hamper a child's capacity to identify with his parents in order to reinforce any feelings he may have of belonging as the result of loving care."[36] Unable to identify biological aspects of himself in his adoptive parents – such as appearance or character traits granted through heredity – the adopted child experiences a sense of alienation that can lead to mental health or identity problems in adolescence and to an obsessive need to know his origins.[37] In effect, Sants assumes that the normal process of identification and the experience of belonging entails that a child experiences and knows himself *as* biologically like his parents and family.

Max Frisk introduced the concept of a "genetic ego" in 1964. On the basis of Erik Erikson's psychoanalytic views, Frisk suggests that, especially during adolescence, the adoptee is prone to "identity crisis" or an inability to achieve a "firm sense of self."[38] On the basis of his psycho-therapeutic experience with adoptees, he adds his ideas about the role and nature of the genetic ego in identity formation: "They were not born, they had no 'genetic' ego but in its place was a hereditary ghost, they also lacked the egotistical family rights acquired by birth. In the formation of identity this 'genetic' factor seems essential ... They now asked themselves 'What am I and where do I come from?' ... A new identity has to be found and formed. To be able to integrate the aspects connected with heredity and 'genetics' they must get to know their own biological parents."[39] Frisk further explains that adoptees struggle with their inability both to discern "common features between the [adoptive] parents and themselves" and to gauge their "prospects ... on the basis of their biological inheritance."[40] Treated as a fundamental aspect of normal identity formation, the concept of genetic ego, which is lacking in the adoptee, depicts bio-genealogical knowledge as an essential component of identity that is best acquired within the context of the biological family.

Frequently, the Freudian concept of the "family romance," first presented in 1909, is used to explain adoptee experience. Freud suggests that in the course of normal development, a child must free himself from an original state wherein "his parents are at first the only authority and the source of all belief."[41] The family romance is a stage at which the child, by comparing his parents to other children's parents, initially experiences his parents' love as inadequate. Resenting any inadequacy as a withdrawal of love, the child makes sense of this loss by fantasizing that he was adopted simply because he does not believe his (real) parents could deny him complete love.[42] The biological child ultimately resolves this conflict when he accepts that his parents *are* his own, and this facilitates his identification with them. In the adoptive family, however, resolution is problematic because the child's adoptive parents are *not* his own (i.e., not his biologically real parents). The knowledge of being adopted, therefore, causes a "prolongation and reinforcement of the family romance fantasy" and "impedes the adolescent's identification with the adoptive parent" and, as a result, his identity formation.[43] In the context of the family romance, the idea that the child must identify with parents whom he knows and accepts as *real* is tantamount to the idea that normal identification relies on bio-genealogical knowledge *as* the presence of the biological tie.

Family continuity, genealogical bewilderment, genetic ego, and the family romance are concepts that adoption experts still take seriously and incorporate into contemporary perspectives on adoptee identity.[44] By the late 1980s, however, the scope of ideas surrounding adoptee identity theory had greatly expanded. This progression is reflected in McRoy, Grotevant, and Zurcher Jr's book *Emotional Disturbance in Adopted Adolescents*, which attempts to address the fact that there is "no comprehensive theoretical framework that contributes to a full understanding of the development of children and adolescents within adoptive families."[45] In this light, and without neglecting the import of the earliest adoptee identity theories, they identify seven main approaches that they agree are most relevant and applicable to the question of adoptee development and adjustment: psychoanalytic theory, genetic theory, attachment theory, goodness-of-fit theory, cognitive developmental theory, Kirk's adoptive kinship theory, and attribution theory.[46]

Traditionally regarded as a nurture perspective, psychoanalytic theory proposes a number of possible causes that can give rise to adoptee identity problems.[47] The adoptive parents' (usually the mother's) unconscious aversion to parenting, which originates with unresolved feelings about infertility or with guilt and shame about raising someone else's child, may negatively affect the adoptee's identity development. Adoptee identity may also be undermined if the adoptee is overly concerned with the idea that she has been relinquished because she is "bad" or that her birth parents' character or nature is "bad." In adolescence, therefore, she may identify herself as bad or identify with the bad birth parent. Finally, identity problems may also be the result of the child's inability to successfully resolve the family romance, examined above.[48]

Genetic theory suggests that identity conflicts in adoptees are caused by "bad" genes for a number reasons. The birth mother's genetic makeup or her health during pregnancy may affect adoptee identity at the level of the gene. Thus adoptees may inherit psychological diseases that are genetically transmitted from parent to child. Or the mother's age, socio-economic status, and possible substance abuse during pregnancy may cause identity problems that are genetic in origin. McRoy, Grotevant, and Zurcher Jr note that some genetic theories suggest that a birth mother's genetic makeup may also be the cause of her early pregnancy and willingness to relinquish her child and that this genetic makeup, in turn, leads to the adoptee's identity problems. Fundamentally, genetic theory further suggests that genetic similarity within a family is adaptive or that an important aim of inheritance is to increase genetic similarity. The benefit of the presence of genetic similarity in a family is that it decreases conflict associated with (genetic) differences in personality and intellect that, in the adoptive family, are said to give rise to adoptee identity problems. This assumption, as we shall see, informs the goodness-of-fit theory, which is a preventative response to the identity problems that behavioural geneticists claim are due to the genetic differences between adoptee and adoptive parent.[49]

Introduced in the 1960s, John Bowlby's attachment theory is a psychoanalytic perspective that, in part, is influenced by evolutionary biology. This theory "suggests that a genetic anchoring of the tendency toward an attachment disorder exists."[50] It contends that interruptions in the infant's proximity or relationship to a caregiver undermine her ability to develop a consistent sense of security or trust in her attachment to others. This situation can lead to psychopathology in adoptees that manifests as an insecure sense of self and an inability to form lasting attachments to others. Although the frequency of interruptions and the child's age at which they occur are said to play a role in the likelihood that a child will develop identity problems, adoption itself is understood to be a cause of identity problems because it necessarily *is* an interruption, the impact of which is magnified if and when placements do not occur in early infancy.[51]

Linked to nature-based genetic theories, the goodness-of-fit theory underpins what are commonly known as "matching" practices in adoption.[52] Ultimately, the concept of matching is fundamental to modern and contemporary adoption practice and discourse and, in many respects, can be traced back historically to eugenic science and thought. The idea of "finding a 'match' between adoptive parents and adoptable children in which racial background, religious faith and the intellectual potential of the child were the most important factors" became "'sound adoption practice'" as early as the 1940s in Canada and the United States.[53] And although it is true that the individual criteria for a match have changed and been debated over time, it is also true that the idea that adoptive parents and adoptable children must be matched has never waned.[54] As proposed by Mc-Roy, Grotevant, and Zurcher Jr, this view suggests that adoptee adjustment is enhanced by the extent to which the adoptee's physical, intellectual, and personality traits are closely paired with those of her adoptive parents. Matching practices, it is argued, minimize experiences of difference, which are thought normally to be absent in the biological family and are thought to negatively impact adoptee identity formation.[55] These practices target differences that are said to heighten the likelihood of misunderstandings between adoptive parents and the adoptee, an outcome that increases conflict and, thereby, the chance that normal development in the adoptee will be hindered. Embedded in the arguments that support matching is the idea that adoptees, by nature, are more prone to developmental problems because genetic difference inevitably means that they are going to be less like their adoptive parents (i.e., physically, emotionally, and intellectually) compared to biological children and their biological parents.[56]

Arguments in favour of matching have long applied to questions of race and transracial adoption. Throughout the 1930s and 1940s in Canada and the United States, there was "strict adherence to racial matching in adoption placement," which, "combined with the dearth of agency-approved non-white adoptive homes, made it highly unlikely that non-white children surrendered to social agencies would find permanent adoptive homes, at least before the mid-1950s."[57] As definitions of a child's "'adoptability'" began to change in light of "Civil rights activism and increasing racial pluralism," so too did the stringency of attitudes about race as a necessary criterion for matching.[58] This shift opened the door to transracial adoption throughout the 1950s and 1960s, but a new controversy over matching peaked in the early 1970s when the National Association of Black Social Workers (NABSW) rejected transracial adoption, a

rejection rooted in the history and activism of the civil rights movement. In the United States, racial matching was reinstituted as a
social work practice to respond to "the 1972 NABSW statement
against transracial adoption." The NABSW "placed the highest value
on the development of Black cultural identity and survival skills for
African American children living in a racist society, and led to a shift
in policy in favor of 'racial matching' between children and parents."[59] As with many things, Canada followed suit, a fact for which
Karen A. Balcom provides ample evidence, although policies and
practices on this front varied provincially.[60] North American debates
over matching heated up again in the 1990s as "whites willing to
adopt children of other races" increasingly demanded that they be
able to do so.[61] Policy surrounding the practice was then reversed in
the United States in favour of "color-blind adoptions" under "the
Multiethnic Placement Act of 1994 (MEPA) and the Interethnic
Placement Act of 1996."[62] This move, however, has not put an end to
the debate – "[t]ransracial placements for African American and
other racialized children in both Canada and the United States have
... remained controversial" – especially because the interplay between colour-blind adoption and systemic racism (and classism) is
real.[63] As Dorothy Roberts observes, "[a]ll of the literature advocating the elimination of racial considerations in child placements
focuses on making it easier for white people to adopt Black children" in that "[t]ransracial adoption advocates don't mention the
possibility of Blacks adopting white children."[64] Of course, the fact
that colour-blind adoption *is* problematic does not mean that racial
matching is *not* (and vice versa), particularly because there is a further interplay between matching and the bio-genealogical imperative insofar as constructs of race and biology also intersect.

The upshot of what is an ongoing debate over racial matching,
therefore, is that it does continue to operate within the institution of
adoption, even though it is no longer centrally mandated by social
work policy. It continues to be advocated, more informally, as a best
practice by many contemporary social workers and social work
associations, such as the NABSW, as well as by child-focused organi-
zations like the Canadian Pediatrics Society.[65] Policy has shifted, but
the idea retains important influence. For instance, the Ontario government's Ministry of Children and Youth Services indicates that
"[w]e support efforts to match children with families of the same
race, culture and language if it is clearly in the best interests of the

child," even though it also contends that "these policies should be informed by current evidence" and that "placement should not be unduly delayed and no child should go without a stable, permanent home simply because an adoptive family who can meet a great majority of a child's needs is not of the same race, cultural or linguistic background as the child." The government also indicates that "there is great variability in the emphasis CASS [Children's Aid Societies] place on racial and cultural matching, and many different iterations of what factors matter when matching children with families (e.g., physical appearance, cultural practices)." It further notes that "policies about placing children in families with a similar cultural background are applied differently across the province."[66] Wegar also suggests that many adoption workers still view matching to be "an important mechanism in ensuring 'successful' adoptions."[67] Ultimately, therefore, current circumstances are such that even if the rigidity of past *policies* has changed, normative *preferences* and *practices* that amount to racial matching have not disappeared. On a final note, it could be proposed that matching need only be treated as a means of maintaining cultural, not biological, continuity – which implies that the idea of matching could logically map onto nurture perspectives. But this view of matching is dubious in one important respect: to pair race and culture is not necessarily to break the epistemic or discursive bond between race and biology in contemporary Western social contexts that have yet to transcend an enduring history of scientific racism. Arguably, it only sets culture up as race's stand-in or twin, which thereby (re)links culture or cultural identity to biology. For instance, few if any adoption experts challenge the idea that within the context of transnational and/or transracial adoption a child's birth culture or culture of origin is relevant to normal development and identity, even if the child, once born, never lives in that culture. The idea that the location of one's *birth* in and of itself matches a child to a culture, rather than only to a lived experience in that culture, *is* a bio-logic that roots culture in bio-materiality, wherein birth is the biology and birthplace (i.e., as in nation or land of origin) is the materiality that (re)grounds culture in biology. In other words, in contemporary family and adoption practice and experience, "conflations and slippages around questions of blood, race, and cultural origins of the child and family" remain commonplace, as Sara K. Dorow and Amy Swiffen's parent study of Chinese transnational and transracial adoptions suggests.[68] Where matching is advocated in adoption, therefore, even for the sake of cultural continuity, it has implications for the reiteration of the bio-genealogical imperative simply because biology, race, and culture are inextricably linked to identity and family experience in and by adoption and family discourse.

Cognitive developmental theory is a nature perspective that assumes the mind and learning are subject to a biologically rigid structure that predetermines the onset and stages of psychological development. David Brodzinsky, who is sympathetic to genetic theory, applies this perspective to the question of adoptee identity formation, arguing that it is a life-long process.[69] On this view, adoptee identity is profoundly impacted by how well adoptive parents address the meaning of adoption with the adoptee through "adoption revelation" (i.e., telling the child that she was adopted) and through ongoing discussion of the issue during childhood and adolescence. Generally, this view posits that the cause of identity problems is either that an adoptee is given too much information before she reaches the stage of development where she is able to properly assimilate and adapt to this knowledge or that she is given too little knowledge too late, which also undermines her comprehension and adjustment. Either way, identity development is hindered because the inappropriate allocation of knowledge occurs before or after the appropriate stages of biologically determined development, which is detrimental to the adoptee's ability to reach a mature understanding of what it means to be adopted.[70]

As McRoy, Grotevant, and Zurcher Jr explain, H. David Kirk's adoptive kinship theory is a "social-role theory," or nurture perspective.[71] According to Kirk, adoptive families are at a disadvantage because there are no clearly defined roles for adoptive parents and adopted children, as opposed to biological parents and children, in a social context that values the biological family more highly. In other words, as the Western "cultural script" solely addresses the biological family, adoptive families are rendered less "competent" than biological families in enacting their roles.[72] Therefore, the *adoptive* parent and *adopted* child experience a "role handicap."[73] They cannot perform the roles of *biological* parent and child simply because the presence of the biological tie is treated socially as categorically essential to that role. To respond to this handicap, Kirk argues that clearer social roles for adoptive parents and adopted children must be discerned. Once they are achieved, adoptee identity problems will decrease because clearer social roles will increase role competence and, therefore, adoptee adjustment.

To this end, Kirk further examines how adoptee adjustment is thwarted when, in order to cope with the stigma of adoption, adoptive parents reject, as opposed to acknowledge, their difference as "adoptive parents" in comparison to "biological parents." The key to adoptee adjustment, therefore, lies in an "acknowledgment-of-difference," whereas a "rejection-of-difference" undermines parent-child communication and thus adoptee development. Where an adopted child cannot communicate openly with her adoptive parents about her difference relative to biological children – a difference that Kirk believes is inherent to adoption – the child is forced to try to make sense of her self-experience *as* difference, even though it is at odds with her parents' denial of difference. The conflict caused by the rejection of difference causes identity confusion in the adoptee.[74]

Finally, attribution theory is a cognitive developmental perspective about interpersonal relationships that is used to address the question of adoptee identity.[75] In the context of adoption, it is used to examine the meanings that adoptive parents and adoptees may "attribute" to each other's behaviour, including their assumptions about the causes for that behaviour. The downside of attributions is that they can result in the wrong intentions or responsibilities being associated with the parents' or child's behaviour. Therefore, the success of attributions, and ultimately adoptee identity, is undermined by various biases that occur as attribution errors, such as the *"self-serving bias," "confirmation bias,"* and *"feature-positive bias."*[76] When exercising the self-serving bias, adoptive parents wrongly attribute a child's negative behaviours to facts pertaining to her adoption (e.g., her unknown genetic history) and thereby unfairly absolve themselves, for instance, of being dysfunctional parents. Furthermore, once parents make an initial set of judgments about adoptee behaviour, all subsequent behaviours are likely to be read through the preceding judgments, at which point parents are engaging in a confirmation-bias. Parents may enact a further bias that is termed feature-positive, wherein the frequency of attributions and thus errors increases relative to any and all of the adoptee's overt or positive behaviours, such as acting out, which makes a bad situation worse. The adoptee may also make attribution errors that can heighten conflict, thereby alienating her from her adoptive parents. Through attribution errors, therefore, adoptee adjustment and identity are said to be undermined by means of misjudged behaviours that are specifically interpreted in relation to the fact of adoption.[77]

Among the theories discussed by McRoy, Grotevant, and Zurcher Jr, psychoanalytic theory, attachment theory, and Kirk's adoptive kinship theory are typically characterized as nurture perspectives. Genetic theory, goodness-of-fit theory, cognitive developmental theory, and attribution theory are nature theories. Nevertheless, the nature-nurture dichotomy that normally characterizes these theories collapses in favour of nature when they are applied to the issue of adoptee identity. That is because each of these theories entails either explicit or implicit nature biases, which assume that normal identity, or the prevention of adoptee identity problems, turns on whether a child's inherent need for bio-genealogical knowledge and/or the presence of genetic similarity is met within the course of development.

Psychoanalytic theory invokes an implicit nature bias when it associates adoption with identity pathology in such a way that it logically construes bio-genealogical knowledge and the presence of biological ties as fundamental aspects of normal identity formation. The subtext of the idea that adoptee development is hindered by the guilty, infertile, adoptive mother is that a child's identity is inherently stronger if it emerges within the biological family. That is because the fertile mother, whose fertility is manifested by the *presence* of her biological child, does not experience the *kind* of guilt or shame (i.e., that associated with infertility) that gives rise to "adoptee" identity problems. So although a biological mother might experience some other kind of guilt and shame that causes identity problems in her biological child, those problems are not "adoptee" identity problems. Thus psychoanalysis treats adoptee identity problems as being essentially due to the absence of the biological tie. Furthermore, the family romance depicts bio-genealogical knowledge *as* the presence of the biological tie insofar as a foundation of normal identity is the child's realization and acceptance that her parents are *real*. Given the very structure of this fantasy, the litmus test of the parents being real is the child's concrete knowledge that a biological tie is present; it alone confirms that no other *real* parents exist.

Genetic theory posits that the presence of genetic similarity and bio-genealogical knowledge is essential to normal identity formation because it assumes that genes *are* identity in two important ways. Genes are identity in the biologically determined sense that psychological personality traits are due to genetic inheritance. They are also identity in the sense that having bio-genealogical knowledge, as the experience of genetic similarity or personality traits held in common between the (biological) parent and child, is thought to be adaptive. The experience of genetic similarity supports normal identity formation or prevents (adoptee) identity conflicts that can create divisiveness in the (adoptive) family because the more genes there are in common, the more personality traits there will be in common, and thus the more likely it is that the (biological) parent and child will get along or avoid conflict. In genetic theory, as it is applied to adoption, the experience of genetic difference *as* personality difference between adoptive parent and adoptee is the central cause of "adoptee" identity problems. Thus, even if the adoptee suffers a genetic mental illness that gives rise to some of her identity problems, that genetic illness, in and of itself, is also a kind of genetic difference. As a result, it merely compounds or heightens the more general effects on identity that genetic theory already attributes to the adoptee's basic experience of genetic difference, effects that occur in the absence of any other mental illness from which she may suffer. The nature bias of genetic theory, therefore, lies in the claim that the experience of *genetically determined difference* creates a particular kind of parent-child conflict, one that underpins the "adoptee" identity conflict and does not occur between a biological parent and child. Whatever the identity conflicts of biological children, they are not subject to "adoptee" identity conflicts because, on this view, the latter arise only due to the presence and experience of genetic difference. The nature assumption of genetic theory, therefore, is that normal identity formation is dependent on both the presence of genetic similarity and the possession of bio-genealogical knowledge *as* the experience of that similarity.

The nature bias of genetic theory is also illustrated in a number of other ways. For instance, the goodness-of-fit theory, which is a genetic theory, proposes that adoptee identity problems, or the effects of genetic difference that cause them, are minimized through matching practices. The practice of matching reinforces this bias simply because it is an attempt to *mimic* the presence of genetic similarity between an adoptive parent and child in order to avert identity conflict. In effect, the motivation behind this practice is the assumption that normal identity formation pivots on the presence of genetic similarity, which matching is aimed at forging. Genetic theory further emphasizes, *as* real, the need for bio-genealogical knowledge where having this knowledge is construed as adaptive with regard to genetic identity problems that are thought to be avertable through bio-genealogical knowledge that enables medical and therapeutic responses to those problems. Finally, by claiming that birth mothers who relinquish their offspring are more likely to produce children who are genetically prone to identity problems because of the mother's genes, health, socio-economic status, and/or substance abuse, genetic theory effectively concludes that being adopted is a *sign* of being subject to identity problems in a way that being a biological child is not.[78] Essentially, therefore, genetic theory draws an explicit causal link between normal identity formation as an outcome of bio-genealogical knowledge and the presence of genetic similarity.

The nature bias in attachment theory turns on its assumption that adoption *is* interruption, or a break in the stability of a primary attachment that otherwise is a lynchpin in normal identity formation. The idea that adoption, in and of itself, *is* interruption creates an epistemic bio-bias because it implies a converse idea: the presence of the biological tie *is* attachment because it is not an interruption in and of itself. The result is that attachment theory differentiates biological and adoptive ties categorically; it locates adoption among a class of things that threaten normal identity formation, and it sets the biological tie apart from all of these things and thus apart from the adoptive tie with respect to the promise that the biological tie holds over and above the adoptive tie in relation to development and identity. So even as attachment theory acknowledges there are many types of interruptions that can pose a threat to identity, the biological tie is not understood to be among them, even if an interruption is due to the actions of a biological parent. For instance, where an abusive biological parent is a threat to attachment, the threat is commonly understood to lie in the abuse, not the biological tie, but in adoption the tie alone, as interruption, is a threat, even when no other threat exists. Where attachment theory treats the meaning of adoption as interruption, it implies further that the biological tie, as attachment, can combat, mediate, or temper interruptions that the adoptive tie cannot, regardless of whether a child is placed at birth or three years old. Of course, Bowlby's idea that a child forms attachments to a primary "caregiver," as opposed to a biological parent specifically, does suggest that attachment theory allows for the idea that normal identity formation can occur within the adoptive family. Nonetheless, insofar as the meaning of adoption in attachment theory is always and only interruption, the concept of "caregiver" necessarily entails an implicit bio-bias or meaning that favours biological parents over adoptive parents as givers of care who can potentially and unequivocally prevent interruption.

The meaning of adoption in attachment theory affords the adoptee no possibility of escaping interruption, whereas the biological child, *as such*, is always afforded this possibility, even if it is not ultimately realized. So even though the biological child *might* experience prolonged interruptions that parallel aspects of adoption (e.g., the death of a parent or a long-term interruption due to divorce, temporary foster or kinship care, or an illness that results in prolonged hospitalization of a parent or child), attachment theory still entails a bio-logic that grants her a *possibility* for noninterruption that it simply cannot grant the adoptee. The theory positions interruption as merely possible and contingent for biological children but as necessary and inevitable for adoptees. As a result, it renders the adoptive tie ontologically inferior to the biological tie as a foundation for attachment that prevents identity problems; it is inferior because the conflation of the meaning of adoption with interruption produces the adoptive tie logically and epistemologically as a sufficient condition for identity problems and casts the biological tie as a necessary condition for normal identity formation, even though other conditions exist that must be met too (i.e., no, few, and/or short interruptions). The adoptive tie is posed as an obstacle, or disadvantage, to normal identity formation in *all* cases, whereas the biological tie is not posed in this way at all, and this difference discursively subverts the adoptive tie to the biological tie.

Cognitive developmental theory is biased in favour of the idea that the biological tie is essential to normal identity formation insofar as Brodzinksy characterizes being "adopted" *as* a unique process. There is an inverse conclusion to be drawn from the notion that *being* "adopted" is something to which the self must adapt itself in order to avert "adoptee" identity problems. That is, *being* a "biological" child is not something to which the self must adapt itself, insofar as being this *kind* of child is not linked to the kind of identity problems that are tied to being adopted. To put it another way, the presence of the biological tie averts the need for a *process* of assimilation and adaptation that must be addressed in its absence. This bias is also reflected in attribution theory as a branch of cognitive developmental theory. In the adoptive family, attribution biases are categorically different in nature compared to those occurring in a biological family simply because they pivot on the fact of adoption. Attribution biases linked to adoptee identity problems, therefore, become nonexistent in the presence of the biological tie. In effect, the biological tie functions as a conduit for bio-genealogical knowledge, which inherently prevents "adoptee" identity problems because its presence does not facilitate the kinds of attribution errors, or responsibility avoidances, that are germane only to the adoptive family. For instance, a biological child's behaviour cannot be blamed upon *unknown* genes in a biological family.

Although Kirk rejects adoptee identity theories with "'biologistic' or 'hereditarian' sentiments'" when he argues that the cause of adoptee identity problems is social, he also subscribes to an implicit nature assumption.[79] Largely, this assumption is the result of what is implied by his prescription that the remedy for adoptee identity problems is the "acknowledgment of difference." This remedy is pragmatic: it suggests that knowing the rules (or roles) helps one to play the "social-role" game "competently." Competence at being adopted entails knowing the social meaning of adoption and living in accordance with that meaning. To the extent that the social meaning of adoption *is* difference, therefore, competence pertains to how well the social role of adoption is lived *as* difference through its acknowledgment.[80] The social prescription that adoption must be lived as difference, however, is not necessarily at odds with nature-based theories that also depict adoptive families as different from biological families. In effect, Kirk's social prescription that adoption be lived *as* difference (inadvertently) reinforces some of the same nature assumptions embedded in nature theories.

Kirk assumes that adoption's difference *is* social and encourages the adoptee to live her adoption *as* difference in order to achieve the goal of role competence. The problem, however, is that the achievement of role competence is equivalent to the experience of the adoptive tie *as* inferior if and when that role is defined by a *social* context that knows and responds to the difference of adoption as both an *essential* and *natural* difference. Where the adoptive tie is *socially* considered *to be* essentially different from and inferior to the biological tie, competence at being "adopted," by definition, is going to entail a role that must be lived as though it were inherently different from the role of being a "biological" child. Furthermore, where the difference of adoption is *socially* known *as* a natural difference, competence is going to demand playing a role that reflects the social belief that the biological tie is genuinely a necessary basis for the development of normal identity and bonds between the parent and child. In accordance with the social meaning that the adoptive tie *is* a lack of nature (because it is the absence of the biological tie), the role associated with having adoptive ties is going to be one that is (or should be) lived as an experience of the adoptive tie as though it is unlike and inferior to the biological tie.

Given the predominance of these social beliefs, the risk of living adoption as difference is that it means living adoption in accordance with a predominant set of social beliefs and expectations that construe being "adopted" as being essentially and naturally different from, and inferior to, being a "biological" child – a point that Kirk completely fails to address. To put it another way, even if the knowledge of adoption as essential and natural difference *is* social, being adopted is only treated as difference *socially* if and when it is also known and treated as though it is *really* an essential and natural difference. If this difference were genuinely *known* socially to be inessential and irrelevant to questions of nature, no difference would need to be acknowledged or performed by the adoptee at all because socially *the difference* would be known *not* to exist at all.[81] For these reasons, the prescription of role competence, because it supports *living* rather than resisting the (social) meaning of adoption, reinforces nature-based theories that claim adoption *is* an essential and natural difference.

Kirk's notion of "shared fate," or the practice of empathy, also makes his view complicit in a more subtle nature assumption. Empathy, he proposes, is a means by which the adoptive family acknowledges its difference. Specifically, adoptive parents empathize with the child's loss of her biological parents, and with the birth parents' pain surrounding relinquishment, through the pain of their infertility, which further promotes mutual understanding within the adoptive family about the loss of real or potential biological ties. Empathy also increases the adoptive family's role competence in general and that of the adoptee in particular because it enables her to feel understood, to understand herself *as* "adopted," and to glean important knowledge about her relinquishment and her bio-genealogical origins.[82] The nature bias of the empathy strategy, however, is that precisely to enable the adoptive family to acknowledge its *difference* relative to the biological family, the strategy directs the adoptive family to act *like* the biological family. There is an important sense, therefore, in which this strategy, albeit empathic, is a kind of seeking and sharing of bio-genealogical knowledge for the sake of role competence or a firm sense of identity. In this light, Kirk clearly accepts the idea that the resolution of adoptee identity conflicts fundamentally turns on knowing bio-genealogy. Furthermore, the role Kirk gives to empathy contradicts the import he gives to the adoptee's need to acknowledge her difference. His emphasis on empathy actually magnifies the adoptee's need of bio-genealogical knowledge and fundamentally de-emphasizes or "rejects" her social difference from the biological child, who also has this need, even though the latter's need is met more readily as a result of her location within the biological family. By putting so much emphasis on the biological tie, or its loss, as *the* mutual basis for empathy within the adoptive family, Kirk's strategy effectively reinforces the nature assumption that there is an intrinsic need for bio-genealogical knowledge that must be met in order to prevent or cure adoptee identity problems.

Fundamentally, therefore, the distinctions that McRoy, Grotevant, and Zurcher Jr make between the nature and nurture theories they discuss are superficial because all of these theories do agree that adoptee identity problems are due to a lack of bio-genealogical knowledge and/or the presence of the biological tie, which is regarded as the best conduit for this kind of knowledge. Furthermore, none of these theories suggest that this need is not real, nor do they focus critically on the question of *whether* normal identity entails that this need be met out of any necessity. They already assume the need is real and simply explore *how* this need is best met by the adoptee given her alienation from the biological tie and the knowledge its presence conveys.

Perhaps the most obvious evidence that the nature-nurture dichotomy (as it is normally applied to adoption identity theories) is collapsible is that McRoy, Grotevant, and Zurcher Jr, along with many prominent adoption experts, do not engage in any real debate about whether or not nature, as opposed to nurture, plays the weightier role in the formation of adoptee identity. Following their discussion of the differences they identify between theories, McRoy, Grotevant, and Zurcher Jr plainly assert that *all* these theories should, and thus can, be integrated into a single framework because "behavior is multiply determined and no single causal factor leads directly to emotional disturbance."[83]

Indeed, many other adoption experts also acknowledge and incorporate theories from both sides of the nature-nurture dichotomy into their perspectives. For instance, McRoy, Grotevant, and Zurcher Jr present Brodzinsky's cognitive developmental approach as one of seven distinct perspectives, but in *Being Adopted: The Lifelong Search for Self*, Brodzinsky, Marshall D. Schechter, and Robin Marantz Henig present a view that brings a number of nature and nurture perspectives to bear on adoptee identity too. Framing adoption as a lifelong process, they fundamentally accept Kirk's "rejection of difference," the concept of "genealogical bewilderment" discussed prior to McRoy, Grotevant, and Zurcher Jr, Bowlby's attachment theory, the "family romance," and the idea "that genetic tendencies are more important than environment in determining who it is we become."[84] In *Journey of the Adopted Self: A Quest for Wholeness*, Betty Jean Lifton does much the same thing. She makes use of Kirk's "rejection of difference," "genealogical bewilderment," Bowlby's attachment theory, the "family romance," and genetic theory to explain why adoptee identity is adversely affected by legally sealed birth records, which she argues deny adoptees their right to bio-genealogical knowledge.[85] John Triseliotis also claims that the idea of adoptee identity formation on the basis of "internal experiences" should not be opposed with that of "social influences" because "the two types of experience are not separate but part of the same developmental continuum."[86] He explains that "[c]uriosity about our immediate and more distant ancestors is *natural*" and that, therefore, "the meaning and importance to all children and adults of the *truth* about their genealogy" must be recognized and taken seriously.[87] He accepts the import of the social and the notion of genealogical bewilderment.[88] Finally, he emphasizes the significance of personal narratives and historical continuity in identity formation and characterizes the need to know bio-genealogy as a "deep emotional and social need" in Western culture.[89]

Arguably, the fact that traditional nurture theories on adoptee identity entail implicit nature biases and the fact that adoption experts concurrently accept nature *and* nurture theories, when taken together, suggest that many adoption experts unknowingly commit a *reductive fallacy*.[90] That is, adoption experts appear to accept the idea that the social plays a *real* role in causing adoptee identity problems. But, given the implicit nature biases of the nurture theories in question, nature still functions unobserved as an *essential* cause, and it does so in such a way that it trumps nurture's ontological status *as* cause. To put it another way, adoption experts clearly suggest that adoptee identity is a complex whole that is attributable to a number of causes at once, but they also essentially reduce the origins of adoptee identity to only one of the different parts or causes that *they* have attributed to it; specifically, they reduce it to the lack of bio-genealogical knowledge and/or the absence of the biological tie.

McRoy, Grotevant, and Zurcher Jr, along with Brodzinsky, Lifton, and Triseliotis, typify the traditional tendency within the institution of adoption to collapse nurture into nature because they simply assume that bio-genealogical knowledge is essential to normal identity formation or a strong sense of self. Subsequently, however, a small but increasingly significant number of adoption experts, such as Elizabeth Bartholet and Katarina Wegar, have attempted to problematize the preceding adoptee identity theories in important ways. In fact, they do delve more deeply into the idea of *whether*, as opposed to *how*, the fundamental cause of identity problems is due to nature at all.[91] Still, as I argue, their work inadvertently reinforces some of the same nature biases it aims to challenge.

Elizabeth Bartholet's work offers one of the most direct critiques of "the biologic bias" that governs contemporary notions of family and its impact on the system of adoption.[92] She argues that the adoption system discriminates against (potential) adoptive parents as a result of social work matching practices that are based on "age, race, religion and disability" and that it does so at the expense of the "best interests" of children who need loving homes.[93] In her view, the adoption social work system violates the "the right to privacy and the 'civil rights'" of would-be adoptive parents because matching entails an invasive interview process wherein would-be adoptive parents must bare all – for instance, financially, racially, spiritually, psychically, physically, and even sexually, as well as via the "home visit" – to social workers who decide where to place children.[94] She challenges the social stigma that adoptee identity theories create around adoption and argues that adoptee identity is not undermined by the absence of the biological tie out of any inherent necessity. Bartholet's challenge to these theories targets the biologic reasoning behind matching practices because they assume that difference (e.g, biology, race, personality, and disability) between adoptive parents and children threatens normal identity formation in adoptees. To critique this assumption, she discusses numerous studies that show, by early adulthood, adoptees' emotional adjustment is equivalent to, or greater than, that of biological children, and she includes studies of interracial and transnational adoptions, as well as monoracial adoptions.[95] These studies, as Bartholet observes, contradict the conclusions of adoption experts who link pathology in adoptees to monoracial, transracial, and/or transnational adoption; they offer "striking findings, since the vast majority of international adoptees have had problematic preadoptive histories which could be expected to cause difficulties in adjustment" if you believe adoptee identity theories and clinical adoption research.[96] Bartholet compellingly argues that these studies undercut the monoracial, "biologic" family model that matching practices reinforce. In addition, her discussion of adoptee identity theories shows that the results of clinical adoption research are skewed for various reasons: clinical samples are not random insofar as they survey only adoptees who are already seeking help from mental health professionals; clinical studies tend to ignore that many adoptees belong to other subgroups that are prone to maladjustment (e.g., as a result of abuse, neglect, or physical or mental disabilities that occur prior to adoption), which is ultimately irrelevant to adoptee status; and nonclinical studies tend to show opposite results.[97] She adds that "[t]here is simply no basis for assuming that a multicultural identity is problematic from the perspective of the children involved."[98] And she affirms "that adoption has for the most part been extraordinarily successful in enabling even those children who have suffered extremely severe forms of deprivation and abuse in their early lives to recover and flourish."[99] For Bartholet, the problem lies not in adoption but in adoption research, which has not been "designed to assess potentially positive aspects of adoption" and thus "reflects as it reinforces the adoption stigma."[100]

Bartholet's critique of the biologic bias that is maintained within contemporary adoption theory and practice is provocative, especially because she rejects the idea that, whether racial, genetic, or otherwise, sameness is the only sound foundation for a family bond. Indeed, she lauds difference as an excellent basis for family bonds.[101] She also exposes the significant contradiction between adoption identity theories and the psychic realities of many adoptees, a contradiction that is commonly overlooked by adoption experts. She is radical in her intention to decentre the biological family and/or the biologic bias that is fundamental within adoptee identity theory and literature. For example, she writes, "What if they started with the assumption that the norm and the ideal was the adoptive family, and the question was whether biologic parents should be allowed to raise the children they produce? What might the studies 'find' if their starting assumption was that biologic parenting had inherent risks?"[102] In effect, she clearly articulates the idea that it is the social idealization of the modern biological family that causes the social differentiation and denigration of the experience of adoption because "[i]n a world in which adoptive status is degraded, it will not feel good to be adopted."[103]

Still, in spite of her critique of the *social* idealization of the biological tie and its effect on the adoptive family, Bartholet does manage, perhaps inadvertently, to reinforce important aspects of the biological biases she sets out to challenge. In particular, she adds a number of problematic qualifications to her position with regard to the difference, and thus the normative value, that attaches to adoptive versus biological family ties. Surprisingly, I think, Bartholet affirms that there is an *essential* difference between biological ties and adoptive ties, although this difference in and of itself is not precisely the source of, but contributes to, a self-contradiction in her view: she claims that adoptive and biological ties are different but equal, which in and of itself creates an epistemological contradiction in that difference, normatively speaking, in this social, historical, and political context, continues to invoke meanings of hierarchy and thus inequality, although this is not a point on which I wish to focus now.[104] This affirmation is merely implied in some moments, such as when she explains that her "attack on the adoption stigma should be understood as an argument for adoption but not against biology" and that "this does not necessarily mean that we should see biologic family bonds as shackles to be cast off as simply irrelevant."[105] And it is explicit in other moments, such as when she argues that although adoption is "not ... the same as biologic parenting ... it should be recognized as a positive form of family, not ranked as a poor imitation of the real thing on some parenting hierarchy."[106] Thus Bartholet's position appears to be that although these two kinds of ties are essentially different, they ought to be or could be treated as socially equal and positive in value. The biological tie's ontology does not determine the (im)possibility of whether adoptive ties can be valued equally as a positive family form; the culprit alone is the social idealization of the biological tie. Bartholet's position, therefore, reasonably favours both biological *and* adoptive parenting and rejects only biological reason or bias, or so it seems.

The real problem with Bartholet's position is that although she claims that biological and adoptive ties are different but equally positive family forms, she still decides to pander to people who are inclined or biased toward biological parenting; she wants her readers to know that she is not advocating "a universal baby swap at the moment of birth."[107] She also claims that "there are many good reasons for having some presumption in favor of biologically linked parenthood."[108] She discusses the value of biological ties and demonstrates her openness to the idea that "their absence may create a greater potential for problems. Genetic heritage is an important influence on intellect and personality, and it may be that for many parents some level of likeness is important and too much difference is problematic. Adoption may require parents who are more open to difference, more flexible, and more imaginative than the norm."[109] Even if her nod to behavioural genetics is put aside, Bartholet effectively acquiesces to the norm or biologic bias with this argument. She accepts the idea that if, in the majority of instances, biological likeness is socially important to would-be parents, this is a good and sufficient reason to favour biological parenting over adoptive parenting. Her point is that a preference for biologic parenting in these instances prevents the socially denigrating effect of these types of parents' attitudes on an adopted child's identity, simply because it encourages them *not* to adopt. The problem with this argument, however, is that by making it at all, Bartholet reproduces the biological bias she wants to thwart. On the one hand, she argues that biological and adoptive ties are different but equal family forms; on the other hand, she effectively claims that there are good reasons not to favour both kinds of ties equally in a social context that is not equally in favour of adoptive ties.

The biological bias of Bartholet's position is that if biological and adoptive ties really are different but *equal*, why argue that there are *any* good reasons for some presumption in favour of biological ties, especially if her main goal is to dispense with the social denigration of adoptive ties and the impact it has on adoptee identity? Why not argue – at least in theory, if not in practice – that logically speaking a universal baby swap at birth would have no inherently negative impact on family bonds or identity? Indeed, if biological ties are different but equal, such a practice, were it to become a social norm, would break down the social stigma that surrounds adoption. If there are equally good reasons to think adoptive and biological families are positive family forms, even if those reasons are essentially different, why favour one or the other at all? Even if a majority of parents currently do think, for instance, that genetic likeness is important or that too much difference is problematic, why should such judgments be respected or catered to in this theoretical context or even in reality? To support, rather than challenge, these parents' choices, which are biologically biased, is to support the biologic reasoning behind those choices. This is especially the case when we consider that the greatest source of stigma against the adoptive family is its location in a social context that assumes normal identity and family bonds depend on bio-genealogy *as* the presence of the biological tie. Therefore, biological family bonds, or the meaning attached to their absence, *are* shackles that should be cast off as wholly irrelevant; where the presence of the biological tie is *known* to support normal identity formation and the adoptive tie is not so known, the former will be experienced as doing so, and the latter will not.

Katarina Wegar characterizes the relation between adoptee identity and "genealogical knowledge" as inessential.[110] She argues that the "need to search" is socially constructed by means of "a genetic and universal biological imperative," which produces the inferior meaning of adoption.[111] In part, this situation is evidenced by the fact that there are many "adoptees who do not wish to search" or who have little or no desire for what I call bio-genealogical knowledge.[112] In this light, Wegar critiques the adoption rights movement's use of adoption pathology as a justification for opening sealed records, simply because such arguments do nothing to negate the adverse effects of adoption pathology on adoptees.[113] She explains that "[a] more powerful argument for opening adoption records would *emphasize* the cultural context of adoption: since American society places so much emphasis on blood ties, it is both inconsistent and unfair to deny this information to adoptees who want it."[114] In other words, the *need* for bio-genealogical knowledge can be *real*, even if it is not inherently necessary for normal identity formation, merely because it is rooted in a current social construction that says this need is universally true.[115] Having made this argument, Wegar, unlike Kirk and Bartholet, explicitly recognizes that her proposal is double-edged in relation to the reinscription of a nature bias. Supporting a socially constructed need for bio-genealogical knowledge that is *known* as essential does pose the profound likelihood that this need will be reinscribed *as* essential. Somewhat anti-climactically, therefore, Wegar concludes that, with regard to the social "truth" that bio-genealogical knowledge is essential to normal identity formation, "the possibility of escaping the trappings of rhetoric is slim ... but new insights can replace old ones."[116]

Within the conventions of analytic philosophy and practical ethics, Sally Haslanger takes a nurture position that, although informed by Kirk, is more optimistic about resistance.[117] Nevertheless, she succumbs to the bio-genealogical imperative to the extent that, somewhat like Bartholet, she subtly tips her hat to the bio-family. She also does so discursively. In a critique of David Velleman's bio-ethical discussion of gamete donation, she enlists adoptee identity theories to challenge his bio-ethics. Velleman argues that gamete donation *should* be rejected on the moral grounds of "well-being" and writes that "'[w]hat is most troubling about gamete donation is that it purposely severs a connection of the sort that normally informs a person's sense of identity, which is composed of elements that must bear emotional meaning, as only symbols and stories can.'"[118] Haslanger likens Velleman's position to adoptee identity theories that are "bionormative" and parses his main contention to show that he conflates the social with the biological in failing to acknowledge that his emphasis on "symbols and stories," or narrative, entails that social, not biological, relations are the progenitors of normal identity formation. Haslanger also rejects the biological family as a necessary promisor of normal identity formation, as well as the idea that an inherent or moral value should be granted to biological ties over and above ties that are adoptive in kind, including ones due to donated gametes. Like Kirk, she understands the greater value normally attributed to biological ties to be an outcome not of biology but of social forces, particularly a dominant "social schema," one that favours biological families over other families, although she does think that the dominance of the bio-family can be resisted. In fact, she believes that neither knowledge of nor contact with the biological family is necessary for proper identity formation, nor is it morally required; however, like Bartholet, she stops just short of forswearing the idea that knowledge and contact are "a good thing":

> I believe that knowing one's biological relatives can be a good thing, and that contact is valuable in the contemporary cultural

context largely because this context is dominated by the natural nuclear family schema. Even in this context, the formation of a full self and the formation of a healthy identity do not require contact with, or even specific knowledge of, biological relatives. Identities are formed in relation to cultural schemas, and fortunately our culture provides a wealth of schemas that sometimes fit with and sometimes run counter to the dominant ideology. Living under the shadow of the natural nuclear family schema, it is reasonable to provide children with information about or contact with their biological relations, if and when this becomes an issue in their forming a healthy identity. However, if we are to avoid harming our children, then rather than enshrining a schema that most families fail to exemplify and which is used to stigmatize and alienate families that are (yes!) as good as their biological counterparts, we should instead make every effort to disrupt the hegemony of the schema.[119]

Acontextually, Haslanger's position is that if there is a diversity of family schemas that are *equally good*, which she thinks there is, then the schema that serves a child's needs or adjustment best *is* best and reasonable for that child; in essence, there is no objective or inherent reason a normal identity cannot be had either way (i.e., in biological or adoptive families) or both ways (i.e., in adoptive families with adoptee access to bio-genealogical knowledge and contact) because adoptive families are "(yes!) as good."

Within a social context dominated by a bio-family schema, Haslanger can nevertheless be said to reinforce the bio-genealogical imperative because of her nod to the bio-family. That is, if the upshot of her position is that *a number of diverse family schemas are equally good*, why affirm *at all* within a bio-family context (i.e., our own) that she "believe[s] that knowing one's biological relatives can be a good thing" because, arguably, the refusal to do so more acutely undercuts the bio-family schema's dominance? Admittedly, she is conscious of this effect. It is evident in an analogy she draws to show why there is value in bio-family contact or knowledge *within* the bio-family schema, even though she thinks the dominance of this value is "pernicious" and problematic. Her analogy pertains to race and how she teaches her own children "to situate themselves as Black (and gendered) within that [i.e., the current racial] structure" or "hierarchy" because "their lives will be easier," even though in doing so "it plausi-

bly also reinforces the structure" of racism she wants to resist.[121] It is
in this light that she asks, "What do we owe our children here?" and
"How do we choose?" – questions she leaves with us because "[j]ustice
and happiness, knowledge and security do not always coincide," which
is to say the questions are rhetorical. The question aside of whether or
not racial situatedness and bio-familial situatedness are analogous,
Haslanger's rhetorical move reinforces the bio-genealogical imperative.[120] Her questions perpetuate doubt about when adoptive families
of any kind are or can be equivalent to biological ones, not because
these questions imply an answer but because they refuse one. To clarify, therefore, Haslanger's real position appears more to be that
although adoptive families and ties are "equal to" or are "as good" as
biological ones, it is wrong or dangerous to make an unequivocal
choice as a parent or a family, and perhaps as a self, against bio-family
contact or knowledge, at least *within* a context dominated by a bio-
family schema; thus, where children are concerned, parents should let
it play out and keep their options open without making a permanent
choice, hence her gesture toward the bio-family. But as much as I
respect Haslanger's work, and I do, if gesturing toward the bio-family
is a part of the strategy to resist, then I would suggest her strategy still
amounts to a *promise to repeat* not the ubiquity perhaps (i.e., some
families may resist or may do so at some times and not others) but certainly the dominance of bio-family schemas and thus the bio-
genealogical imperative.

To compound matters, Haslanger's assertion that adoptive families are "(yes!) *as* good" is a comparative claim that implicitly reiterates the adoptive tie's inferiority relative to the biological tie because
the latter already *is* something that *is* "valuable in the contemporary
cultural context."[122] Within a context that overvalues the biological
family, the comparative meaning of "*as* good" already renders suspect the adoptive family's *equivalence* as a good basis for identity.
Within the biological family hierarchy, "*as* good" is an epistemic
relation that perpetuates the hierarchy between the comparators
(i.e., adoptive and biological families). At best, to say that families
without biological ties are "*as* good" as ones with them signifies that
adoptive families are *equally good, but still different*; however, differentiation *within* the contemporary context is also the main instrument of the hierarchy in question. Think of it this way: "*as* good" is
a phrase that is commonly used when what is said to be "*as* good" is
still not yet believed to be as such. For instance, "*as* good" is what my

parents said when they tried to pawn powdered milk off for fresh. It is what you say to yourself when you settle for the new, but lower-priced, car on the lot. It is what pharmacists say when they swap out your Viagra for a no-name generic brand. In other words, no one makes these comparisons the other way round because epistemologically, in our cultural context, we already *know* that milk is better than powdered milk, that the more expensive model is better (i.e., because it has more and better features) than the cheaper, and that Viagara in hand breeds more confidence than the no-name brand when one is walking out of the pharmacy. Put simply, "*as good*" cannot signify equality in contexts that utilize comparative differentiation to realize and stabilize the inferiority of one category beneath another; this turn of phrase is always and already an acknowledgment that B is *known* to be less than A, which is why the case needs to be made for B in the first place.[123] In the face of "*as* good" comparatives, therefore, the best discursive strategy is to avoid them. Better to demonstrate what is *the same*, which, generally speaking, does appear to be the actual intention of Haslanger's critique of Velleman. For if, as Haslanger argues, identity formation in *all* families is a process of socialization that emerges out of "symbols and stories" or a "narrative project" in line with any family schema that may or may not be, and need not be, biological, the process of identity formation in all families really is *the same* even if individual identities are not. Ultimately, therefore, claiming that adoptive families are "*as* good" as biological families is detrimental to Haslanger's argument because, implicitly, it means the discourse of the argument has already acquiesced to the comparative difference that is the undoing of the value or status of the families, ties, and identities the argument intends to affirm.

Increasingly, there are adoption experts whose theories and methodologies are social constructionist at the same time that they wittingly affirm the bio-genealogical imperative. There is a relatively new inclination to argue that adoptee identity is not a matter of *either* nature *or* nurture but of *both* nature *and* nurture; this move from either/or to both/and is poststructuralist and often feminist in its aim to sidestep binary thinking and the hierarchies it produces. To circumvent the binary, adoptee identity is posed as a product of both nature and nurture on the basis of the idea that biology (or genetics) and culture (or the social), equally, are discursive forces that impact adoptee subjectivity: the difference between the two is "conceptual."

In *BirthMarks: Transracial Adoption in Contemporary America*, Sandra Patton offers a very good example of the both/and move in contemporary analyses of adoption studies:

> The tension between "nature" and "nurture," or "biology" and "culture" is usually present in the discourse about adoptees. I employ the concept of social construction to encompass both culture and biology. To argue that identity is socially constructed is to see individual selves developing through complex interactions between biologically, genetically embodied people, cultural meaning systems, material circumstances, social institutions, public policies, and socioeconomic politics. With regard to the specific tension, generally present for adoptees, between heredity and environment, I accept recent scientific research that emphasizes the interdependence of these two categories, and points out that the separation of the two is conceptual rather practical. Indeed, in my view, the existence and use of these categories as *separate* forces shaping individuals reflects Western dualistic frames of organizing the world. I am not arguing that these are not *real* forces, for in fact the widespread, unquestioning belief in and the use of these two ways of explaining identity makes them real in their effects. Genetics is one system of meaning to explain who we are, but let us be clear that none of us – adoptees and non-adopted people alike – knows our actual DNA structure. Rather, we infer these genetic maps by comparing our phenotypic characteristics with those of our family members. Thus, it is the *cultural discourse of genetics*, as opposed to our DNA, that gives meaning to our identities.[124]

Patton's foundational argument explicitly couples biological or genetic theories of adoptee identity with nurture theories in that she apparently treats both as modes of cultural discourse, a position to which I am partial in many respects. As it concerns the bio-genealogical imperative, however, Patton's affirmation of a both/and position is not precisely the problem. The problem is the use to which Patton puts it. She enlists it strategically not only to avoid a traditional nature-nurture debate but also to circumvent any detailed or meaningful critique of bio-genetic *discourse* and its effects; it merely becomes one discursive force among many that she accepts as obviously impacting adoptee identity, along with the unknowable, material force of DNA. At best, her critique of bio-genetic adoptee identity discourse is *en passant*. She affirms that "[t]he concept of an 'authentic self' linked to genealogical origins seems overly simplistic," and she articulates a "resistance to the idea that biology *fully* defines our identities," but she does not elaborate on what adopted and bio-family subjects might do, not simply, to sidestep the nature-nurture debate but also to resist a bio-genealog-ical family order that frequently produces painful and traumatic effects that are discursive and that an uncritical sidestep leaves intact.[125] Patton's assertion that "adoptee identities are intricately constructed and reconstructed by our biological histories, the vari-ous cultural meaning systems we encounter, and our interaction with public policies and social institutions" does not, in and of itself, *really* undercut the effects of bio-genealogical discourse.[126] Her view "encompasses" and, thereby, accepts *both* nature *and* nurture as dis-cursive forces in the production of adoptee identity, but her sidestep *really* reintegrates bio-essentialist thought or knowledge back into the foundation of adoptee identity, which is now accepted as a com-posite of the discursive effects of the categories of nature and nur-ture. As she observes, discourses are "*real* forces" that produce effects if and when they are accepted, reiterated, and practised dominantly as truths, which currently they are, not only by adoption experts, the institution of adoption, adoptive families, and adoptees, as well as biological families, family institutions and experts, and popular cul-ture at large, but also by Patton because she carries on a social, polit-ical, and historical tradition that does not meaningfully challenge either nature arguments or bio-genetic discourse.

Why does Patton fail or refuse to engage in such a critique? Obvi-ously, one reason is that a both/and position enables her to do so but it does not preclude her from doing so; we might accept the idea that biological and social meaning systems that are discursive inform bio-logical family and adoptee identities, which Patton does, and then meaningfully challenge those constructed systems, which she does not. Another reason, arguably, is that Patton's position cannot actu-ally withstand such a critique, a fact that the both/and sidestep also obfuscates. In particular, this is evident in the slippage or conceptual collapse of the discourse of genetics into genetic causality that is exposed when some of Patton's claims are re-examined in light of each other. Patton claims that identity is due to "complex interactions between biologically, genetically embodied people, cultural meaning systems, material circumstances, social institutions, public policies, and socioeconomic politics" and "that none of us – adoptees and non-adopted people alike – knows our actual DNA structure." These two claims work together to support her claim that genetics is a discursive force: in light of the first claim, the second, the idea that we do not or cannot *know* our *actual* DNA structure, implies that the *knowledge* of genetic science, which is a socio-cultural production, is always only discursive and thus not objective or objectively true. However, the meaning of these two claims is troubled by another claim Patton makes elsewhere. She asserts that adoptees "know we have 'alien' origins that guide our bodily development with biological, genetic maps sketched in indecipherable code."[127] This claim highlights the ambiguity within Patton's first two claims and exposes a weakness in the both/and position. Although her third claim reiterates the second, it contradicts the first, the idea that genetics is a *discursive* force, and it reinstitutes genetics as a bio-deterministic force in identity formation. Patton's assertion that there is a genetic "code" or "map," albeit indecipherable, is an affirmation of the nature, not the *discursive* nature, of bio-genetics in identity formation. The idea that adoptees' origins lie in *alien* genetic code because they are located in adoptive, not biological, family contexts – a code that guides bodily development and, thereby, identity because biologically related bodies are the "familial genetic touchstones by which to guide our construction of family and self" – (re)situates the *real* force of bio-origins outside bio-discourse and within the material domain of bio-genetics and nature.[128] It reinstitutes a covert logic of nature as cause within Patton's argument that otherwise claims that the force of nature in adoptee identity is discursive. Patton's both/and argument boils down to a nature argument but one that is let in uncritically through the backdoor.

Another facet of the nature problem at work in Patton's position, one that is compounded by a both/and position, is that she equivocates with respect to the meaning of "embodiment." Her concept of embodiment is confusing in that it is not expressly defined nor theoretically contextualized within the text, yet it is fundamental to her position. At times, Patton's claim that we are "biologically, genetically embodied people" appears to convey something like a feminist post-structuralist or Foucaultian notion of the body as discursive, just as it does above (i.e., "[g]enetics is one system of meaning to explain who we are"), whereas at other times it appears to refer to an objective "aspect of being" or identity that is independent of "the *cultural discourse of genetics.*" The latter is evident when Patton writes,

> A focus on cultural differences alone often translates into arguments by "social constructionists" and cultural studies scholars that deny the power of biology; focusing on culture to the exclusion of politics and policy often forces progressives, through the logic of the dualistic contrast, into an untenable opposition to biology that cannot hold its own in public debate. In my view, identity formation is shaped by the biological, embodied aspects of being, the cultural meaning systems available to individuals and the public policies, social institutions and political economy of the society in which a person lives.[129]

Patton's view of the body, here, appears altered into one that now understands biology as a causal and independent corporeal force that impacts identity, even as discursive forces, including discursive genetics, also influence identity. There is a certain ambivalence in Patton's text, therefore, over the hard question of whether nature, rather than discursive nature, should be clearly, not obliquely, said to impact adoptee identity. Coupled with the pitfalls of an uncritical both/and position, Patton's equivocation on the subject of embodiment reproduces the implicit nature bias that is largely unchallenged by adoption experts. Patton's equivocation over the meaning of embodiment aside, her both/and approach to adoptee identity, because it is also uncritical, does not challenge and resist the bio-genealogical imperative: with respect to the question of nature or nurture, her ambivalence works in the service of the nature bias.

Sara K. Dorow also enlists a both/and approach to adoptee identity in *Transnational Adoption: A Cultural Economy of Race, Gender, and Kinship*, one that is feminist and postcolonial and that adapts Jacques Derrida's notion of "hauntology" to characterize adoptee experience in relation to questions of identity and belonging; hauntology refers to that which is "neither living nor dead, present nor absent: it spectralizes. It does not belong to ontology, to the discourse on the Being of beings, or to the essence of life or death."[130] Dorow employs Derridian hauntology, as opposed to ontology, to characterize how transnational, transracial adoptees, and their families, are impacted by "architectures of race, family, and nation that more broadly haunt the cultural politics of identity in the contemporary United States."[131] She characterizes adoptees as visited by "the ghosts of unsettled pasts, foreclosed relationships, and excluded others that haunt the present and push for recognition and for the restoration of history to the present," and she argues that for these reasons adoptees face various "restrictions on their imagined belonging."[132] She also presents these architectures, or ghosts, of biology, race, gender, class, culture, and nation as a series of "'impossible contradictions'" to be faced by transracial and transnational adoptees and their families; transracial, transnational adoptee experience is contradictory because it is situated "in between" or at intersections of biology, race, gender, class, culture, nation, and family as meanings that when compounded often conflict in relation to identity and experience or subjectivity.[133] Dorow considers the contradictions that haunt adoptees to be "an invitation to think in new ways about the stuff of which identification is made, narrated, and imagined – that is, if we can live with the contradictions."[134] She argues that transnational, transracial adoption foregrounds the ambiguity of identity, belonging, and family overall because "[i]t pushes us to address the 'in between' of race as neither essence nor illusion but rather as historically relational and fluid; it pushes us to consider all forms of familial and national kinship as unstable concoctions of blood and culture; and it pushes us to recognize that social relatedness is made in exchanges both marketized and humanitarian."[135] Dorow's analysis is nuanced and convincing on many fronts. Her idea that transracial and transnational adoption exposes the contradictions of blood, race, class, and culture, which contour and constrain the possibilities of identity and family that are imaginable, is compelling and instructive. Her hauntological exploration of adoption also captures the *presence of absence*, if you will, or lack of identity and belonging that adoptees and adoption experts repeatedly describe throughout past and present adoption literature. Moreover, her analyses of adoption's powerful contradictions, or ghosts, are insightful and illustrative, perhaps especially in relation to nation, race, and class. She also shifts the ground of traditional debates within adoption, such as when she moves us deconstructively "from asking whether we are 'for or against' transnational or transracial adoption to asking what adoption, *as practiced*, is for and against."[136]

Yet there are important ways that Dorow's ideas also reinscribe the bio-genealogical imperative. They do so insofar as Dorow takes a both/and position at all. She urges adoptive families not only to consider and anticipate but also to accept the contradictions that haunt adoption because they "are pushed to live with it" anyway.[137] The problem Dorow creates with this move is that it fortifies the bio-genealogical imperative: the bio-essentialist meanings of family that the imperative entails are an inevitable part of the whole of the contradictions to be accepted, even as another part encompasses meanings of family that are social and akin to a "'poststructural' global kinship beyond borders of difference," a possibility Dorow proposes and then strangely undercuts because such a possibility always "should remain a question."[138] Dorow's idea that adoptees and their families must strive to accept the contradictions of adoption also reinscribes the bio-genealogical imperative in that she likens it to H. David Kirk's "acknowledgment-of-difference," which she argues is "easily expanded and applied to other forms of (potentially subversive) difference that mark the adoptive relationship, such as miscegenated class privilege, nonexclusive motherhood, and transnational kinship."[139] Thus, just as Kirk's position was shown earlier to reinforce the bio-genealogical imperative, Dorow's integration of Kirk implicates her acceptance-of-contradiction strategy in a similarly implicit bio-logic. Fundamentally, Dorow's both/and strategy reinforces the bio-genealogical imperative because she advises adoptees and their families to live *with* – not to subvert and resist *any* or *all* – the contradictions that haunt, interrupt, or undermine adoptee narratives of identity and belonging. So even if Dorow's premise that adoptees and their families are a unique opportunity to examine how architectures of biology, race, gender, class, and nation haunt us all is intriguing, and I think it is, why not go further and argue that resistance against the marginalizing and pathologizing effects of these forces on adoptee identity, experience, and belonging demands that we "give up the ghosts," exorcize them, with radical critiques of bio-genealogical discourse as a contemporary and dominant force that makes the very construction of adoptees *as* "haunted" possible in the first place? In effect, is it not precisely by virtue of historical and contemporary meanings of biology *as* family, *as* race, *as* gender, *as* nation, and even *as* class and culture, in certain respects, that adoptees are and can be represented and stigmatized, again and again, as "haunted?"

Dorow's idea that adoptees and their families should strive to live with the contradictions that haunt them is cause for concern for a number of other reasons too. It puts adoptees and their families in an untenable position. It (re)places – inadvertently but nonetheless unfairly – the burden of living with ghosts and contradictions squarely on the shoulders of adoptees and their families. In theory, Dorow's position is one that treats the burden as one to be shared among adoptive and biological family subjects alike. She argues that it has value outside of adoption contexts because "[h]aunting potentially pushes not just adoptive parents, adopted persons, and adoption practitioners but others of us to ask these questions of the racial and sexual and national spaces we occupy."[140] The problem with this idea in reality, however, is that biological family subjects do not and need not share this burden because they are not (*really*) haunted; they are not haunted because the taken-for-grantedness of their bio-family experience conforms with, rather than contradicts, bio-normativity and all that it implies for race, class, and culture. In effect, Dorow's view is too quick to assume that biological family subjects (i.e., people who enjoy bio-normative privilege) are *haunted* rather than comfortably *constructed* by the same architectures as adoptees. It assumes they are consciously able and willing to see the ghosts that appear as such to adoptees and their families; this is not to say that no biological family subject ever sees the same ghosts that adoptees face (e.g., many mixed-race children or children in racially blended families do too), but it is impractical and unrealistic to rely on these subjects to do so or to do so in a way that profoundly eases, shares, or removes the burden of the acceptance of contradiction that Dorow places inescapably on adoptees. To put it another way, the ghost metaphor, or the idea of adoption hauntology, reinforces the bio-genealogical imperative given that only adoptees, and to a different extent their families, are *necessarily* subject to visitation by what might more accurately be described as bio-ghosts, precisely because of the particularities of adoption as a discursive context that subscribes to the bio-genealogical imperative.

Additionally, Dorow's idea that the contradictions of adoption are *ghosts* at all too readily lends itself to the popular (mis)characterization of adoptee experience, or pathology, as an unresolved interior, psychic battle with remnants of an adoptee's past; the metaphor does not fully convey the degree to which adoptee subjectivity is an ongoing and contemporary effect of a blend of social, political, historical, and cultural forces that, being bio-normative, externally operative, and adaptive, are constantly (re)internalized and reiterated. Although it does effectively represent a common kind of adoptee affect, Dorow's ghost metaphor is too easily reterritorialized by adoption discourse in that it already construes adoptees as psychically troubled (e.g., in terms of identity) because they are haunted by "'ghost parents.'"[141] The unqualified ghost metaphor lends itself too easily to the idea of the haunting as a psychic matter and thereby to an espistemic failure that yet again shifts our focus away from the *nature* of the ghost that is assumed to call upon the adoptee as such given that the paranormal metaphor does not sufficiently distinguish or problematize what is accepted as bionormal about the ghost; Dorow's enlistment of Derrida to refer to the ghosts of adoption as "'others not present'" is too plain an invocation because it does not unfailingly expose that the adoptee's ghosts (i.e., those of gender, race, nation, and class) are also always and already operating discursively as *biological* others or bio-genealogies not present.[142]

The idea of adoption hauntology, as opposed to ontology, also obfuscates the extant bio-ontology of adoption: adoptees are not merely haunted by ethereal or intangible spectres; they are troubled by the bio-ontological facticity of parents not present, parents "who are both real and unreal in the experience of the child," and thus by a facticity that I argue in chapter 2 is materialized by means of bio-normativity.[143] In this light, Dorow's (re)presentation of adoptees *as* haunted does not convey the important degree to which bio-ontology, as opposed to adoption hauntology, plays a key a role in the formation of the adopted subject. Adoption hauntology, as merely the ghosts of "past events whose effects are still with us," or "'social hieroglyphics,'" diminishes our perception of adoptee subjectivity as an effect of a contemporary discursive context that reiterates family ties and experience as the presence of bio-genealogy.[144] It allows the bio-genealogical imperative's present, as opposed to past, formations to go unrecognized as such.

Where it summons up the "ghosts of unsettled pasts," pushes for a "restoration of history to the present," and maps the presence of absence, or yet again a lack, back onto adoptee experience, Dorow's adoption hauntology not only reiterates key tenets of adoption and adoptee identity discourse but also renders the bio-genealogical imperative invisible as a contemporary changeling that is ferociously adaptive. Although I do not deny that the production of bio-spectres is among the bio-genealogical imperative's operations, so is the ongoing (re)territorialization of contemporary, emergent, and new meanings of family in order to bring those meanings back in line with bio-normativity. Dorow's Derridian metaphor, insofar as it locates adoption's contradictions in shadow-meanings of the past, does not convey how the bio-genealogical imperative (re)produces adoptive subjects through the (re)innovation of present, as well as past, architectures. For this reason, adoption hauntology, as something past and absent, not present, inadvertently contributes to an illusion of progress (e.g., poststructural kinship) bio-normatively speaking and in the following ways: adoption remains a second to last choice or substitute for the biological child that today continues to be experienced as the balm that genuinely satiates the desire and quest for family bonds; adoption continues to be construed as the infertile's surrogate; fertility is increasingly framed as a human *right* that is prior to adoption rights because, for instance, would-be parents in Ontario and Quebec are now entitled to government-funded fertility treatments but not to government-funded adoption as opposed to fostering; and fertility clinics catalogue the genetic attributes of sperm and egg donors to facilitate "matching practices" that mimic a biological connection between the parents and child. In other words, even if the identities of parents are changing (e.g., single, straight, queer, or poly), the desire for biological ties over adoptive ties is not. Indeed, it is arguably intensifying – for instance, because fears surrounding the decline of the nuclear family are increasing and because there is a steady increase in demands for equal access to fertility services. In addition, the popular, political, and scientific preoccupation with genetics (e.g., as evidenced by the International Human Genome Project and the National Human Genome Research Institute) – including its meanings with respect to identity, personality, sex, race, gender, health, behaviour, and family, as well as all that it implies historically and presently for meanings of adoption, adoptee identity, and adoptive ties – is as powerful as ever. Indeed, even the idea that race is genetic, which has further implications for meanings of family *as* biological (or monoracial), continues to capture the popular and scientific imagination. For instance, Nicholas Wade's recent spin on what is an essentially eugenic stance on race, *Troublesome Inheritance: Genes, Race and Human History*, is a best seller; moreover, as Seth Shulman of the *Washington Post* observes, although "Wade's argument [is] that the subject is routinely ignored," his claim "is seriously undercut by the fact that much of his book is composed of reporting about genetic research on precisely this subject."[145] In other words, adoptees are occupied not merely with ghosts from the past but also with a discursive present that remains as engaged with the bio-genealogical imperative and its appurtenances as ever.

In adoption discourse, the origins of adoptee identity problems are deemed to be the result of the absence of the biological tie, which undermines the adoptee's ability to meet the need for bio-genealogical knowledge. Whether adoption experts appeal to nature or nurture or enlist both/and approaches, the idea that normal identity *essentially* turns on the presence of the biological tie and the individual's access to bio-genealogical knowledge can be shown to remain intact in the context of past and present adoptee identity theories. Even when adoption experts depict this need as an effect of social forces, their theories nevertheless implicitly and/or explicitly reinforce a nature bias given their conclusion that, just like a biological need, this socially constructed need, because it is experienced as real, is also only met with and through the experience of biological ties and/or bio-genealogical knowledge, which are commensurate in very important respects. In other words, none of the nurture theories espoused seriously explore the real possibility that this social need, and the real experience to which it gives rise, could be met with a new knowledge, one that refuses to accommodate any bio-bias and that emphasizes *only* that bio-genealogy or the presence of the biological tie does *not* alleviate adoptee identity problems out of any inherent necessity. Fundamentally, entailed in the idea that bio-genealogical knowledge is *any* kind of balm for adoptee identity conflicts is the idea that the biological tie, from which this knowledge solely originates, is essential to normal identity formation.

On what basis, therefore, is the resistance against *knowing* the biological bond as *wholly* irrelevant to identity formation fundamentally founded? What wider social-political-historical fears are reflected in the construction of an adopted subject who is pathologized and differentiated relative to the "normal" experience of the biological family? Why is there such widespread acceptance of the idea, even among poststructural and critical adoption theorists, that bio-genealogical knowledge sheds some fundamental light on the question "Who am I?" Is there a historical tradition for addressing this question in this way, and is the basis upon which it rests sound? To answer these questions, the next chapter considers certain implications of Judith Butler's ideas about materialization and Michel Foucault's theories of power/knowledge for adoption. It also examines some central themes in nineteenth- and twentieth-century individualist and naturalist thought to illustrate how a modern association between the question "Who am I?" and bio-genealogical knowledge may have emerged and its role in the production of the adoptive subject.

2

Adoption, Power/Knowledge, and the "Materiality" of the Biological Tie

The idea that we can uncover the truth about who we really are, and that in doing so we will be liberated is almost ubiquitous in our culture.
                    Daniel E. Palmer, "On Refusing Who We Are"

Discovering herself to be "adopted" at the age of twenty-two, a student – I will call her Celina – told me that she had completely lost all sense of who she was. She felt utterly betrayed by the people who were now her "adoptive" parents. In fact, she joked bitterly that she did not know whether she would be able to regard them as *her* parents again. Her adoptive parents had taken extreme measures to protect her from the knowledge that she was adopted. They had left their hometown for close to a year, returning with her as an infant and telling friends and neighbours that she was born to them in their time away. But at twenty-two, and unbeknownst to her parents, a close relative revealed her adoption to her. She began to fall behind in her studies. She felt immense grief and could barely function. The shock of knowing herself anew as "adopted" had genuinely left her immobile, depressed, angry, and fearful. No longer sure that she could predict her self or the people whom she had known all her life as her "biological" family, she was struggling with sudden and intense feelings of loss, rage, loneliness, and alienation.[1] Thrust upon her as it was, the truth of her adoption made her prior experience and knowledge of herself as a "biological" child feel false. Thus, as the truth of her adoption was uncovered, she found herself not liberated but lost, lonely, and confused about her sense of self.

Since the 1950s, there has been a general move toward what is now a consensus among North American adoption experts that adoption should be revealed and that late-adoption revelation must be avoided at all costs precisely because it is so traumatic, painful, and self-altering.[2] For instance, the impact of late-stage revelations on identity that has occurred for adopted children at or following the age of ten is characterized dramatically by the research of John Triseliotis: "Revelation at this late stage had a stunning effect, shaking their entire life and self-image, leaving most of them confused and bewildered. They felt the need to reassess their whole life and to start 're-discovering' themselves. The later they were told, the greater the distress and confusion ... The revelation shook their whole being and appeared to upset both the physical as well as the mental image of themselves."[3] Although adoption or bio-genealogical alienation, as shown in chapter 1, is understood to lead to identity conflicts in adoptees, actively hiding adoption from adoptees is deemed to be even more problematic because it leads to a (seemingly) false or impermanent sense of self that can be shattered if and when the truth of adoption is discovered. For this reason, and because the possible discovery of secret adoptions is deemed to be so great, "telling" has become the dominant practice within the contemporary institution of adoption.[4]

To tell or not to tell was a central pivot of adoption debate as late as the 1950s and 1960s. The debate would fundamentally shift away from *whether* to tell and toward *when* to tell by 1971. Indeed, as Ellen Herman suggests, in the 1970s the "adolescent psychiatrist Joseph Ansfield ... stood virtually alone in suggesting that children never be told" of their adoptions.[5] In spite of the shift toward telling, however, it remained an overarching assumption that "[n]ot telling and telling were *both* associated with psychological trouble."[6] In fact, according to Herman, "[b]y 1970, telling had emerged as a leading therapeutic issue in adoption," and "the association between adoption and trauma became ever more fixed," which is to say that the association between telling and trauma was fixed as well.[7] The irony, therefore, is that even though the no-tell stance is rejected wholesale by today's adoption experts, the key assumption behind the no-tell stance still fortifies the move in support of telling theories; this assumption, which Ansfield articulated in defence of not telling, is that whether it comes early, later, or late, "'the knowledge [of adoption] will hurt.'"[8] Essentially, revelation or telling at any age continues to be understood by adoption experts as traumatic, although more or less so depending on the age of the child when told. Thus telling is not currently understood to eradicate adoption trauma so much as it is thought to mitigate it by degree, or in comparison to the much greater trauma associated with *late* and inadvertent revelations like that experienced by Celina. It is ultimately a lesser of psychological or developmental evils with respect to questions of adoption, identity, and self-knowledge, even though adoption experts might not like to put it this way.

The contemporary therapeutic debate over revelation turns on when to tell children they are adopted in order to avert as much trauma as possible. And there are two main stances on "whether early or late telling is less traumatic for the child."[9] As Lois Ruskai Melina explains, most experts advise "'early telling'" or revelation as soon as possible, usually by the age of one or two, whereas others argue in favour of "'later telling'" when the child is between five and seven.[10] The main defence of early telling is that it averts the "risk that the child will hear about her adoption first from someone other than her parents or in anything but a loving atmosphere," as parents cannot ultimately prevent relatives, friends, teachers, neighbours, or strangers who deduce or suspect adoption from inadvertently exposing it to their child.[11] Telling early is also supposed to prevent feelings of "deception that could work against the parent-child relationship," an outcome that is thought to be likely if and when parents wait until a child is five or older to tell.[12] The scales are also tilted in favour of early telling in the context of international and transracial adoptions: "Parents of internationally adopted children or children who are racially different from them have little choice but to tell their children as soon as possible" because even if "children don't comprehend enough about genetics [or race] to realize that children usually resemble their parents, other people will comment on the physical difference and ask if the child is adopted in the child's presence."[13] Conversely, the main argument in favour of later telling is that "early telling is disruptive to psychological development" insofar as "to label children 'adopted'" too early "may cause them to think there is something wrong with them."[14] For instance, as Herman notes, the idea of telling early and repeatedly, or "reminding children that their belonging need[s] constant reinforcement," was vehemently rejected as early as the 1960s by such important experts as Daniel Schechter and Lili Peller, who favoured telling only during adolescence.[15] Psychiatrist Herbert Wieder also advised that, to avert problems in development, "'the longer the communication can be put off the better,'" although E. Wayne Carp compares this

stance to "practically advocat[ing] not telling, *ever.*"[16] Since the late
1980s, however, adoptive parents have been advised primarily, if not
solely, to tell early because adoption, as it is now normatively believed, will "likely shape every stage of ... children's development."[17]
In effect, "'early telling' theory is the prevailing philosophy on
revealing adoption" today.[18]

For the most part, contemporary adoption experts agree that adoption or "'being adopted'" is "a lifelong process," and they thus argue
that revelation, as a central part of that process, should not be
approached as a one-time event; parents should repeatedly discuss
the aspects of adoption that concern a child throughout her childhood, adolescence, and young adulthood so that she may ultimately
"resolve each normal developmental task" in light of her "adopted
status."[19] David Brodzinsky explains that adoptees who succeed in
achieving a stable identity "tend to be those whose families allow
them to discuss adoption and help them come to a resolution about
how being adopted does or doesn't fit into an overall sense of themselves."[20] So even as telling is thought to be (more or less) psychically traumatic at any time, early and repeated revelation is the method
that diminishes trauma to the greatest degree, again because it prevents identity crises of the magnitude illustrated by Celina's story.
With early and repeated revelation, adopted children are thought to
be better able to integrate the knowledge of adoption into their
sense of identity at the earliest stages of development; the longer a
child is allowed to develop an identity on the basis of what is regarded as a false knowledge of self (i.e., a belief that she is biologically
tied to her adoptive parents), the more powerful the trauma and/or
identity conflicts will be following revelation. As a result, the fundamental assumption built into the question of *when* to tell is that
adoption or the child's knowledge of it is something that must be
psychologically and therapeutically managed in relation to the self's
identity and development.

Even as experts have shifted support from *later* to *earlier* telling,
the threat of *late* revelation and its potential impact continues to
exist for any number of adoptees – for instance, because their (adoptive) parents made decisions to hide adoption prior to, or in spite of,
the advance and dominance of early-telling theory. Moreover, where
late revelation is concerned, the causes of trauma are really on the
same continuum as those associated with later telling; the main difference is that the traumatic effects are thought to be even more

extreme. For instance, Margaret Watson describes the effect of her revelation in midlife:

> With the telling of those two words – *"You're adopted"* – my life descended into a hellish roller coaster ride with feelings of terror, fear, disbelief, betrayal, rage, confusion, anxiety, powerlessness, impotence and a myriad of others. I went from being a very capable wife, mother, business partner and high achieving social welfare professional, to someone crippled with anxiety and fear who had to sit on the side of the bed each morning, willing myself to stand upright ... My known sense of self had disappeared, I had no idea of who I was, what I was doing in this life, and was totally afraid of every day and what it would bring.[21]

As telling or revelation theories argue, and Watson's personal account illustrates, there are two main sources of trauma associated particularly with late revelation. One turns on the discovery of the (adoptive) parents' *deception* about one's status as an "adoptee," a deception that leads to profound feelings of betrayal; indeed, Watson's story depicts the worst fears associated with late revelation in that her betrayal was compounded; in the midst of divorce, her husband revealed not only that she was adopted but also that her (adoptive) father had divulged her adoption to him, not her, at the start of their marriage.[22] In effect, the trauma of late revelation is distinct from that generally associated with adoption and early telling because through late revelation a person discovers not only that she is "adopted" but also that her (adoptive) parents and any family members "in the know" have lied to her throughout her lifetime. The second source of trauma in late revelation pertains to the reorientation of self and identity that the knowledge of adoption elicits; a new bio-genealogical "truth" or knowledge of biological origins, whether accessible or not, displaces and disrupts the prior "truth" of self or identity that revelation renders false to consciousness. Although revelation trauma may be accompanied by a range of other feelings, such as abandonment, anxiety, reduced self-worth, genealogical bewilderment, and so on, these feelings, ultimately, are already thought to accompany telling at any age, as we saw in chapter 1. Primarily, the trauma of late revelation is distinguished from regular adoption trauma as it relates to the magnitude of both the betrayal and the existential identity crisis into which an adoptee is suddenly pitched.

There is a problem, however, with the characterization of late-revelation trauma as a kind of shocked consciousness that is caused by the
(adoptive) parents' betrayal *and* the self's sudden reorientation toward
a new "truth" of origin: it obfuscates the underlying fact that the
causes of trauma that adoption experts normatively isolate always and
already boil down to a presumption that bio-genealogy or the biological tie is the truest "truth" of self, a presumption that further
entails the idea that the biological tie is ontologically superior *as* the
real, even primordial, basis of normal identity and family bond formation. These causes of trauma that experts identify conceal the
uncritical assumption that the adoptive tie is always an insufficient
basis upon which a "true" knowledge of origin can or should be
secured for the self. They veil the belief that only the presence of bio-
genealogy, and thus the biological tie, facilitates a "true" basis for normal identity formation. They obscure the uncritical belief that *being* a
"biological child" turns absolutely on the presence of bio-genealogy
or the biological tie. In other words, the joint cause to which experts
usually attribute the trauma of late revelation obscures the fact that
bio-genealogical "truth" is never seriously questioned *as a truth about
the self* at all.

Moreover, these uncritical beliefs are fostered by the ongoing treatment of not telling as a *deception* that, as such, is traumatic in and of
itself. To be precise, the idea that not telling a child of her adoption is
necessarily cause for concern because it involves *a lie* is never reconsidered as something that operates as a smokescreen for the uncritical
beliefs of experts in that, where experts focus on *the lie* as the cause of
trauma, they set up bio-genealogy as *the truth* of identity or self. They
also obscure important onto-epistemological questions of identity
and self-knowledge with psycho-ethical ones that presume one particular mode of knowledge (i.e., bio-genealogy) is the (only) truth of
self or origin.[23] For instance, an uncritical focus on the role that
(adoptive) parental deception plays in the trauma of revelation diminishes our ability to observe how adoption discourse effectively sets up
bio-genealogy as the "truth" that matters most in the constitution of
self and identity. Consider that parents of all kinds lie to their children, often repeatedly and either overtly or by omission, about many
different things, the facts of which, when revealed later in life, do not
elicit identity crises.

For example, as a child, I knew and experienced it to be true that
my parents were deeply devoted and monogamous. In my mid-twen-

ties, however, they both revealed that they had had a number of affairs during my childhood; it was the 1970s, after all! Although I was profoundly shocked and, obviously, had been deceived along with my siblings as to who my parents were in an important sense, neither I nor my siblings experienced identity crises or began to question our family bonds with our parents or each other as a result of this newly revealed "truth." The reason, or so I suspect, is that by the time we were all adults, the discursive *content* of our parents' lies could no longer be understood by us to reflect on our identities normatively speaking – although it might have reflected on theirs – and as their relationship remained intact, the revelation that they had lied to us for years also failed to threaten our sense of cohesion as a family. In effect, perhaps adoption experts place too much significance on the impact of (adoptive) parental *deception* in late revelation, when really it is the uncritical belief in the bio-normative "truth" of the content behind the lie that ultimately matters most in the maintenance of adoption revelation trauma. In other words, instead of focusing on deception as a cause, a red herring of sorts, we should really parse the question of whether the trauma emerges because the self discovers she is an "adoptee" or because the self realizes she is an "adoptee" located within a bio-normative context that always and already constitutes real "family" subjects in proximity to their bio-genealogy.

To drive this point home, consider the peculiar adoption story of Judy Lewis. Lewis was the "illegitimate" daughter of Loretta Young and Clark Gable; Gable was married to Maria Langham when he had an on-set affair in 1935 with Young, his co-star in the film *Call of the Wild*.[24] Young, who was twenty-two, unmarried, a devout Catholic, and concerned with the continuation of her film career, went abroad to hide her pregnancy, returning in the end to secretly give birth to Lewis in California.[25] Lewis remained in her mother's care until she was eight months old, at which time Young placed her in a Catholic orphanage, where she remained until her mother brought her home at nineteen months. And in order to do so, Young announced in the Hollywood press that she had "adopted" a little girl. Lewis was raised to believe she was "adopted."[26] At the age of twenty-three, on the verge of marriage, Young describes an experience of terrible panic very like an adoptee identity crisis wherein she felt she could not wed her fiance Joe Tinney, telling him "'I don't know who I am,'" to which he replied, "'Judy, don't worry about it. I know everything about you.

You're Clark Gable's daughter,'" a revelation that left her completely stunned.[27] Although it took Lewis eight more years to confront Young, her mother would acknowledge only in private that Lewis was not adopted and that Gable was her father.[28] In 1994 Lewis published her memoir, *Uncommon Knowledge*, which detailed these facts and caused a deep rift between herself and her mother, who publicly denied them. Lewis and her mother would not reconcile until shortly before Young's death in 2000.[29]

Lewis's story is enlightening because it suggests, even illustrates, that the *knowledge* of adoption, not the *fact* of it, is at the root of adoptee identity crises. Lewis's genuine bio-material proximity to the biological tie did not secure a sense of identity for her so long as it was coupled with the knowledge that she was "adopted," as falsely promulgated by Young and those around her. Moreover, Lewis's experience, as it relates to the question of identity, appears to be just like that of an adoptee, yet the truth revealed to her was that she actually was her mother's biological child. Oddly, in this respect, she and Celina are alike, despite the fact that what was revealed to each woman was completely different: Lewis's identity *is* in question until her biological tie is revealed, whereas Celina's identity *is not* in question until her adoption is revealed, but in both cases, an identity crisis is manifested only to the extent that Lewis and Celina are situated as subjects within the knowledge of adoption. When situated within a knowledge of family that is "biological," Celina's sense of self is intact (i.e., prior to revelation) and Lewis's premarital panic over her identity is resolved (i.e., following revelation). In both cases, it is the *knowledge*, not the fact, of a biological tie that operates as the basis upon which the stability of identity is secured, whereas the knowledge, not the fact, of adoption leads to the instability of identity.

Arguably, the idea that adoption experts and discourse explicitly or implicitly set up the biological tie as the most authentic or superior basis for stable identity and family bond formation is a straw-person argument in that it is borne out less and less by contemporary adoption literature: there is literature that suggests the new aim with respect to adoption psychology, identity formation, adoptee subjectivity, and the minimization of trauma is to encourage the adoptee to acknowledge and integrate *both* her bio-genealogy *and* her adoptee experience. Indeed, a growing body of adoption literature supports the idea that the adoptee should be encouraged to explore and determine the meaning of both her biological and adoptive ties for her self and identity; this idea is often coupled with the idea that the adoptee's sense of self is often more fluid, mixed, hybrid, and myriad because adoption invokes unique questions in relation to notions of family, culture, nation, race, gender, sex, and class, a fact that is celebrated within adoption literature that is poststructuralist, feminist, postcolonial, and/or queer, as chapter 1 observed. Its emphasis on the idea that adoptees need to acknowledge both kinds of ties does not appear to privilege biological ties over adoptive ties. As a result, my idea that even contemporary poststructuralist, feminist, postcolonial, and/or queer adoption literature does set up the adoptive tie, albeit implicitly, as an inferior basis upon which to secure a stable sense of self and/or family experience does appear to be false. But is it? Partial as I am to such theories, "post" and queer approaches to adoptee identity and subjectivity, which situate adoptees in "disparate and multiple worlds" (e.g., relative to family, culture, nation, race, gender, sex, and class) *because* of their biological *and* adoptive ties, are not really a sign of meaningful normative change. Instead, they are just a sign that the bio-genealogical imperative has reinstituted or adapted itself to what is merely the appearance of "[f]amily-making [that] has burst out of a rickety frame that assumed the need for blood ties and heterosexuality."[30] The idea that adoptees must integrate the knowledge or experience of *both* their biological *and* adoptive ties entails a de facto bias in favour of the biological tie that continues to differentiate the ontological status of adoptive ties. It is an adaptation of the bio-genealogical imperative because this both/and logic applies solely to adoptees: there is no dominant, complementary imperative in new or old adoption or family literature that suggests children situated within biological families need to forge, acknowledge, and integrate their experiences of (even informal or chosen) adoptive ties. As a result, the superiority of the biological tie or bio-genealogy as the best basis for self-knowledge and family bonds is left unchallenged at a deep onto-epistemological level. The bio-genealogical imperative is no less potent as a totalizing force, ontologically speaking, when it is conjoined with (but cannot be replaced by) a need to integrate adoptee experience as an equally normal, independent, and self-defining origin.

What the dominant discourse on adoption revelation trauma means for someone like Celina, therefore, is that in spite of twenty-two years of experience as such, she cannot in any "true" or ontological sense of the term be a "biological child" without a biological tie to her (adoptive) parents. Yet this is a strange conclusion, especially when so much adoption discourse and theory that arrive at it, explicitly or implicitly, take nurture-based or, increasingly, poststructuralist and/or postcolonial feminist and/or queer approaches to the problem of adoption. Thus neither historical nor contemporary adoption discourse meaningfully questions, or decentres, the explicit or implicit bio-normative logic that informs adoption and adoption revelation discourse. It refuses because it neglects the kinds of questions that are raised by experiences such as Celina's: it does not deeply probe how and why the "truth" of self that is conflated with bio-genealogy must necessarily render Celina's prior experience as the "biological" child of her (adoptive) parents unreal or false. For instance, what if the discourse of adoption and revelation was taken up seriously as the cause of Celina's trauma in that the contemporary "truth" of adoption, not the fact of it, is what is so alarming. Is it the web of bio-normative beliefs within family and adoption discourse or the factual absence of a biological tie that actually renders Celina's experience of herself as the "biological child" of her *adoptive* parents unreal or unintelligible for both her and us? If it is possible that the biological tie's presence or absence is merely set up to function existentially as a hard fact that is a self-defining or self-diminishing truth, why do adoption experts typically fail to critically interrogate whether conflations of biological fact with the truth of being are, or should be, treated as necessarily suspect relative to questions of self-definition and experience?

Late revelation is fascinating because it raises philosophical questions about whether or not there is a natural and essential ontological difference between being an "adoptee" and being a "biological" child. Yet adoption experts tend to regard the effects of late revelation on identity axiomatically: the effects are a clear sign that the difference is natural and essential. I say this simply because experts do not seriously ask *whether* the experience of being a "biological" child turns on the factual presence of the biological tie or on the belief that the tie is factually present. They do not deeply entertain the idea that if a person believes and thereby experiences herself *to be* a "biological" child for twenty-two years, the revelation of her adoption does not necessarily make her prior self-experience of *being* a "biological" child any less real or a lie, even if that belief was originally founded upon a lie that was effectively maintained as the "truth" by that person's adoptive parents. The possibility that *experiences* based on the self's false beliefs about its (biological) ties *are* nonetheless genuine and authentic experiences of that belief is not one with which adoption experts engage; they do not consider, because they do not advise, that the experience of self as a "biological child" need not be made unreal if and when the belief that informed it is revealed to be false. They do not suggest that *being* a "biological child" is not essentially commensurate with access to bio-genealogy or with the tie's actual presence, nor do they entertain the possibility that if a person's adoption is completely and forever hidden, she not only *experiences* herself to be a "biological" child but actually *is* one.

It is no small point that if Celina had lived her whole life in the absence of adoption revelation, she and those who knew her as a "biological child" would never have doubted, known, or experienced her experience of herself as a "biological child" as inauthentic or false. In other words, there is a profound sense in which the truth or falsehood of a biological tie *as* an experience or mode of being lies precisely and only in *knowing* that it is present or absent, not in its factual/material presence or absence. Contrary to what adoption experts would lead us to believe, therefore, a *real* experience of being a "biological child" need not be determined by the tie's factual presence at all. Arguably, there are good reasons to believe that Celina's self-experience as a "biological" child is undermined solely by her *knowledge* of the tie's absence as opposed to its factual absence. For instance, even though a tie was factually absent throughout Celina's first twenty-two years, her self-experience as a "biological child" changed only when she knew of the tie's absence. To what extent, therefore, can we understand the effects of late revelation not as a proof that the biological tie makes the "biological child" but as an illustration that a belief in the biological tie's presence and, in particular, the ongoing "reiteration" of that belief are sufficient conditions for *being* a "biological child"?[31] In effect, perhaps it is the reiteration of the knowledge of the biological tie that "materializes" the tie, and perhaps this can be so in spite of the tie's factual absence.[32]

How can a person *be* a "biological child" in the absence of a biological tie, and what are the implications of this idea for adoptee subjectivity and identity crisis? The idea that the presence of a biological tie is both a material fact and an essential condition of *being* a biological child is one that needs to be carefully scrutinized. Doing so, however, entails that we get at a more basic idea that pervades Western science and culture: biological facts are objective facts essentially

devoid of social trappings. For instance, science and medicine historically and currently take for granted the idea that material facts pertaining to things like a person's biological ties, sex, and/or skin colour
are just that: socially unadulterated facts, or *brute facts*, about a person's body "for which no further explanation (reason, account) need
or can be given."[33] This is not to say that science has not and does not
try to examine how sex or colour develops and manifests relative to a
body's physiological development. Instead, it is to say that once these
qualities are manifested in a body, science and medicine treat them as
plain factual truths about that body. But science and medicine also do
something else: they too often conflate biological fact with being, and
they treat *being* "male," "black," or a "biological child" as something
that is inextricably tethered to the bio-material fact of sex, race, and/or
the presence of the biological tie.[34]

What does it mean to say that a biological fact about a body is not
necessarily relevant to that body's being or its ontological status?
In *Bodies That Matter*, Judith Butler suggests that sex, like gender, is
socially constructed. This idea is highly provocative, especially within
the context of feminisms, philosophies, psychologies, sociologies, and
social sciences that clearly distinguish sex and gender as biological
fact and social construction respectively. Butler's idea that sex is a
social construction is important because it opens the door to questions of whether a person is or can be understood *to be* "male," rather
than being merely masculine, in a body that is bio-anatomically
female and vice versa.[35] Butler investigates how a biological fact, such
as sex, is conflated with a social meaning of sex (not gender), both of
which function together singly as a plain, material fact. She considers
how a sedimentary meaning of sex surrounds the biological fact of sex
in such a way that the element of the fact that is a product of the
social escapes notice; the social element of sex and the biological fact
of sex are socially constituted *as* one and the same and thus solely as
an irreducible material reality.

The sense in which sex is socially produced, for Butler, lies in the
way that sex, indeed the body, is typically "posited as prior to the
sign."[36] By this, she means that the "materiality" of the body is most
frequently taken for granted as something that is essentially "irreducible" or as something that "only bears cultural constructions and,
therefore, cannot be a construction."[37] In other words, the body is
typically regarded as a material "surface" upon which social constructions are founded and as something that is itself not affected by

the social constructions for which it serves as a foundation.[38] Yet, insofar as the body is posited as prior to the sign, it is, according to Butler, nonetheless "always *posited* or *signified* as *prior.*"[39] What this means is that the irreducible body, the plain fact of its materiality, is always "bound up with signification from the start."[40] For Butler, therefore, an important question is "how and why 'materiality' has become a sign of irreducibility."[41] By raising this question, Butler is by no means suggesting that there is no *real* material body: she is suggesting only that the material body is not outside the reach of the social and, indeed, that it is socially constructed *as* outside the social or as an exclusion precisely to facilitate further social constructions that depend on an outside in order to be intelligible. In other words, implicit in the social construction is the idea that there is something more fundamental outside the social upon or out of which the social is constructed. Thus, where gender is typically viewed as a social construction, sex is already set up to function as a fundamental matter that is essentially outside intelligibility and, as such, that which makes the very constructedness of gender, as opposed to sex, intelligible. In effect, sex and gender are constructed as binaries that ironically pivot on an assumption that there is an inside (gender) and an outside (sex) to language and signification, both of which, Butler argues, work together and make the signification of gender *as* social possible.

The materialization, or irreducibility, of sex is accomplished by means of what Butler refers to as "performativity." Performativity is "always a reiteration of a norm or set of norms."[42] It is also "the vehicle through which ontological effects are established."[43] Sex materializes through performativity simply by means of the constant reiteration of normative ideals about the body or sex *as* irreducible matter. It also materializes in relation to the body itself, insofar as the body's form, within a matrix of power relations pertaining to sex (and gender), already serves as an occasion that reiterates its own sexual difference.[44] Butler concludes that it is as "a sedimented effect of a reiterative or ritual practice" that sex also "acquires its naturalized effect."[45] In a deep sense, therefore, sex is a normative ideal that is repeatedly produced and prescribed socially, politically, and historically through discourse; it is not ahistorical or static – it is a construct that materializes on and in the body over time – and it is not a "pure" or transcendental fact about the body that escapes the impact of social forces.[46] But even as sex, as a normative ideal, materializes, governs, and regulates bodies, it maintains the ontological guise of a naturalized entity or irreducible biological fact about a body.[47]

The materialization of the naturalized ontological status or the brute facticity of biological sex is illustrated by Butler relative to the female body and its capacity for reproduction. In a discussion about this capacity as a real biological difference that separates the sexes, Butler observes that, although reproductive ability is treated as such a difference, it is not an innocuous biological fact about the female body.[48] It is a fact about some female bodies that is generalized to all female bodies – many of which cannot or do not reproduce – in order to define them within a matrix of heterosexual power relations. Butler's point is that all females, including female children, post-menopausal women, women who choose not to reproduce, and women who are infertile, are defined and measured against the capacity for reproduction. All women, therefore, are measured against a standard of reproductive ability because reproduction is set up as a truth or essence of the female sex, regardless of whether a given female has or uses this capacity.[49] The sex of a given "female" body, therefore, materializes insofar as it is systematically defined as fully or partially functioning, nonfunctioning, or pre- or postfunctioning relative to the biological fact of reproductive capacity and its social treatment as the foundational nature and essence of the female sex. In this way, we can see how "irreducible" biological facts, such as reproduction, can and do function socially in ways that create ontological effects. Butler elaborates: "But the real question here is: to what extent does a body get defined by its capacity for pregnancy? Why is it pregnancy by which that body gets defined? One might say it's because somebody is of a given sex that they go to the gynaecologist to get an examination that establishes the possibility of pregnancy, or one might say that going to the gynaecologist is the very production of 'sex' – but it is still the question of pregnancy that is centaring [sic] that whole institutional practice here."[50] Reproduction, treated merely as a biological fact, bestows upon bodies ontological effects that materialize the female, even if reproductive capacity is an irrelevant and/or false fact about bodies that are signified as "female" through the discourse of reproduction. The important question for Butler, therefore, is not *Does matter exist?* but how does the sex of the female body materialize because reproduction is treated as an "absolutely salient or primary" feature of the female body?[51] Her goal, therefore, is not to get rid of matter but to suggest "that matter has a history," to ask what sorts of power relations are served by the construction of an "unconstructed materiality," and to consider "what kinds of constructions are foreclosed" by the treatment of sex *as* irreducible matter.[52]

The idea that ontological effects materialize through the social treatment of sex as irreducible matter has implications for other kinds of biological facts, the irreducibility of which science and medicine take for granted. The biological tie is one such fact. The difference between a biological and an adoptive tie is that the former is fundamentally presumed to be irreducible and material and that, on this basis, it is also treated as the most salient feature of *being* a member of a family. Considered in relation to the biological tie, Butler's ideas about sex imply that the ontological difference between a biological and adoptive tie is not simply an issue of irreducible materiality but also something that is produced through discursive practices; the biological tie, insofar as it is a material difference, is also a social institution that treats this kind of tie as the most important element when thinking about the family.[53] The biological tie is a normative ideal of family that is founded upon an understanding of the tie as primarily and fundamentally a material difference; but the ontological effects of this understanding are obscured by the tie's sole appearance as irreducible matter. In effect, the difference between a biological tie and an adoptive tie is one that functions discursively *as* an ontological difference that is incontestable because irreducibility is the former's core meaning.

The notion of "continuity," taken up as it is by adoption experts, illustrates how ontological effects occur through the discursive treatment of the biological tie *as* irreducible matter. In the context of adoption discourse, continuity refers to the child's unhampered ability to bind the past and present through identification with forebears. As we saw in chapter 1, adoption experts assume explicitly or implicitly that continuity is best achieved and sustained via a child's proximity to the material presence of the biological tie; they assume that the tie's presence creates the best foundation for the self's acquisition of bio-genealogical knowledge, which is key to normal identity formation. Again, this is the reason why adoptees are said to be prone to identity crisis: they grow up in the material absence of biological ties and thus without sufficient access to the bio-genealogical knowledge that confers a strong sense of identity.

Therefore, insofar as continuity holds that normal identity formation and proximity to the biological tie are essentially interdependent, it sets up the biological tie as a necessary and irreducible material grounding for normal identity formation and/or a complete
sense of self. What adoption experts overlook, however, is how the
assumption of interdependence effectively conflates the tie's materiality with the normative idealization of the tie as the ontological
source of a true or normal identity. The belief that the firmest identities necessarily occur in conjunction with the biological tie's presence discursively produces the idea that there is a direct material,
causal relationship between this kind of tie and normal identity.
When adoption experts fail to identify or acknowledge this conflation, as they tend to do, their normalized usage of "continuity" to
explain adoptee identity crises produces and reinforces the ontological effects that this concept is initially put in place merely to understand or explain. If ontological effects, as Butler suggests, occur
through the reiteration of norms, which are made intelligible due to
what are assumed to be irreducible, but are nevertheless constructed, material facts, the reiteration of continuity as the source of normal identity gives rise to ontological effects that impact "adoptees."
The reiteration of "continuity" as the normalized ideal of identity
formation produces identity crises in individuals who grow up without biological ties.

To explore how ontological effects are produced by a normalized
ideal of continuity, let's try and make strange the idea that a complete
sense of self turns on continuity *as* the biological tie's material presence. Uncovering this strangeness will show, among other things, how
the biological tie becomes confused (e.g., by adoption experts) with
the discursive effects that surround it.[54] What is most peculiar about
"continuity" is the idea that the presence of the biological tie per se is
essentially a bondstone between the *self* and a *history* of forebears that
gives rise to a complete sense of self. Indeed, this notion entails an
almost mystical belief in the biological tie's materiality as an ontological entity that tangibly delineates an absolute surety that a particular history (one that grants a normal identity) is one's *own*. Continuity treats the biological tie as the positive proof that a family history
and, ultimately, an identity are authentic. Indeed, that is precisely why
Celina's identity was thrown into question by the revelation of her
adoption: the surety that a particular family history was indeed her
own disappeared.

The notion of continuity is underpinned by two basic uncritical assumptions: the biological tie grants the self ownership over a history, and bio-genealogical history is a necessary *kind* of history with which a self should identify in order to be "normal." By exploring how the biological tie's material presence is understood to grant the self ownership over a history, we can begin to critically interrogate the idea that bio-genealogy is a kind of history that is necessary relative to the self's development of a "normal" identity. Toward this end, therefore, I would like to ask in what sense my biological grandmother's experience is *my* history insofar as the events and happenstances of her life, recorded however (in)accurately in my biological mother's memory and passed down to me, do constitute a history. Certainly, the events and experiences of my grandmother's life themselves are not events and experiences in my life; they are not *my* history in the sense that the events and experiences I live in my day-to-day life are my history. Nor are my mother's memories and experiences of her mother *my* personal, historical memories and experiences. In relation to me, my mother's memories and experiences of my grandmother, which have been told to me, are really a series of "family" records, narratives, and/or stories. At most, therefore, *my* history as it pertains to my grandmother is a record or narrative of events and experiences in her life; the *record*, however incomplete and/or inaccurate, is what is mine.

Still, what precisely makes this record *my* record? Perhaps it is my record because of my biological tie *and* the fact that the events of my grandmother's life are of little or no interest to anyone outside my family. Indeed, if my grandmother were terribly important outside the context of my family, a bigger audience could legitimately lay claim to this record too, perhaps as a record belonging to Canadians or women or both. For example, if Sue is a Canadian and my grandmother had been an important Canadian, Sue arguably would have good grounds for laying claim to this history in order to identify with it. Certainly, national identities are founded on such bases all the time; we look to famous Canadians to give us a sense of what it means to be "Canadian." Alternatively, if my grandmother had been an important and inspiring Canadian woman, Sue as a "Canadian woman" would also have good grounds for making a claim to my grandmother's history; the recuperation of women's history from a feminist perspective is very important, as it gives women positive historical images of women with which to identify. In Sue's instance, however, the condition for ownership of my grandmother's history has shifted: her legitimacy as a claimant of this history is that she is a "woman" or a "Canadian" or a "Canadian woman." Nonetheless, the reach of Sue's claim to this record is more limited than mine: she can have neither free nor exclusive access to my record of my grandmother, nor to legally protected artifacts relevant to this record, such as my grandmother's belongings, letters, and pictures, without my family's permission. The difference between Sue's claim to my grandmother's record and mine, therefore, is that my biological tie grants me legal rights and privileges that Sue, who is merely a "Canadian woman," is denied. Yet it is not entirely accurate to say that my biological tie is what grants me these rights, for these *rights* are legally, socially, politically, and historically made and linked to the fact that the tie is mine. The biological tie sustains my rights and privileges over Sue's through the meaning it is given socially and legally.

In part, the idea that the biological tie is materially irreducible is already embedded within its social and legal meaning, and as a result, this meaning also ensures that an individual, such as myself, has an apparently concrete ground upon which the claim "this is *my* historical record" is made intelligible and can be made at all. Therefore, it is inaccurate to say that the biological tie in and of itself is what grants me the right at all; the strategic social, political, and historical *use* of the biological tie *as* an irreducible material fact or positive proof by institutions of law is what grants me a right over Sue, for instance, to control or disseminate aspects of my grandmother's record that are not already public knowledge.[55]

The idea that a legal right to a record is not intrinsic to the biological tie, but is an effect of the strategic social, political, and historical use of the tie as an irreducible materiality, is not too far removed from what I ultimately think is amiss in the idea that normal identity is best founded upon proximity to the biological tie. The social use of the biological tie by law parallels its use by adoption psychology. Adoption psychology is very like the law in that it utilizes a *social* meaning of the biological tie that is reiterated *as* the tie's material irreducibility. As in law, the biological tie functions in adoption psychology and search literature as the concrete foundation upon which an individual "rightfully" claims a particular history as one's own and as the most authentic basis for her identity. Adoption psychology also relies on a socially reinforced meaning of the biological tie *as* a material irreducibility because it is only as such that the tie functions as an incontrovertible proof that one history, as opposed to any other, is the one true history with which a self should and needs to identify in order to attain a normal and/or authentic identity.[56]

The Western imperative of normal identity is that the self must identify with bio-genealogical history, but the idea that a self must identify with one kind of history, either in part or in whole – the bio-genealogical kind – over other kinds in order to achieve a normal and/or authentic identity is nonetheless very strange. Indeed, the strangeness of this idea can be observed in the fact that there are many nonadopted selves whose bio-genealogy serves only inadequately, partially, or not at all as a foundation for identity. This situation is demonstrated increasingly by selves whose experience is transnational. For instance, in the context of a diverse city like Toronto, many first-generation Canadians desire to identify with a social environment in which their life experience occurs either in conjunction with or at the expense of a need to identify with their bio-genealogy. This desire can arise simply because the identity commanded solely on the basis of a bio-genealogical identification may actually contradict a preferred identity established on the basis of lived or personal experience. Many first-generation Canadians are encouraged by their parents to exercise their birthright as it pertains to identifying with bio-genealogy, partly because doing so links them to their parents' culture (which is not to say that multigenerational Canadian children are not similarily encouraged for the same reason). Indeed, parents may strongly encourage, compel, or oblige their children to identify with their original birth-culture experience and identity, whereas children may push to identify with the extra-familial culture in which a central part of their everyday experience occurs. Thus, even though first-generation Canadians are bio-genealogically linked to their parents' histories, many selectively and/or completely reject their right to identify with that history, especially if and when this identification contradicts their lived experience, as opposed to that of their parents.[57] That many nonadopted people can and do choose between histories and/or deeply identify with more than just one suggests that bio-genealogy is merely one kind of history, among other possible kinds, that can, but need not necessarily, be used to establish a solid sense of identity. It also suggests that something is amiss when adoption experts characterize the adoptee identity crisis as a phenomenon that is due to the absence of a *necessary* quotient of bio-genealogical knowledge, in that this idea necessarily displaces the signifignace of the "adoptee's" situatedness as such within a bio-normative discursive field that conflates a meaning of lack or inferiority with that of the adoptive tie and/or being adopted.

Ultimately, migration worldwide has raised all sorts of new questions about what constitutes a "normal" identity. Particularly as a result of cultural studies, identities based upon dual or multiple world experiences are described as "in-between," "transnational," "rhizomatic," and/or "hybrid."[58] And even though people who describe their identities in these terms often acknowledge an experience of internal conflict, this conflict is regarded as positive rather than pathological; hybrid and transnational experience is valued as a productive opportunity by postcolonial and cultural studies because it provides an opportunity to "move away" from a "dependence on ontology," which reinforces the essentializing effects of what amounts to state-sanctioned "identity politics."[59] "Hybrids" embrace the tension of being from two or more worlds and the identities that are formed on the basis of a person's variegated and discordant histories. Transnational and hybrid identities make strange the idea that "normal" identity is necessarily founded upon bio-genealogical history because they suggest the self has no inherent need to identify with bio-genealogy, at least not one that supersedes an equal or more powerful need to identify with a "lived in" context that gives rise to experiences that contradict a would-be identity delineated solely through identification with bio-genealogical history. In important ways, hybrid and transnational identities exemplify the fact that the self can and does experience bio-genealogical history as literally foreign if and when a child's lived experience in a present cultural context utterly contradicts her parents' prior experience of another context. The positive reality of "transnational" and "hybrid" identities suggests there are many children who can and do develop "normally" even though their desire or need to identify with bio-genealogical history can be less, and even nonexistent, compared to these needs in children who consistently share a cultural context and experience with their parents.

The uncritical assumption that bio-genealogy is a kind of knowledge that is key to a complete sense of self is also challenged by some adoptees' experiences of search and reunion. For instance, in an article that looks at adoptee identity, Kimberly Leighton, a philosopher and adoptee who reunited with her birth family, observes that "[r]ather than resolving my questions about 'who I am,' finding a

new family complicated my identity, problematized some of my relationships, and encouraged all kinds of re-definition of my family and
its identity. Knowledge of my birth family has indeed made the
impossibility of definitively answering the question 'who am I?' ever
more clear."[60] In passing, Leighton also points out that even an identity developed in the context of a biological family is no guarantee of
a "true" identity. That is because biological family secrets can also
pose real problems to the self with regard to the question of "who I
am." In short, much like the threat associated with late-adoption revelation, the revelation of secrets to "biological children" within the
context of the biological family can, depending on the content of the
secret, undermine a self's sense of identity too; this fact exposes the
extent to which "a true definitive narrative of ... family and identity
[is] itself an ideal, if not a fiction."[61] Leighton is right in this observation, yet it does not quite capture the extent to which identity
crises in adoptees are theoretically located first and foremost in adoption as the *absence* of bio-genealogy, which is also code for the
absence of biological ties and the normative experience that their
presence is assumed to secure. For instance, putting aside the question of genetic anomalies, identity crises in children within the biological family are rarely, if ever, coded in family psychologies and
discourse as ontological crises rooted in the biological tie's *presence*.
Instead, these identity crises are coded differently: they are the
unqualified result of abuse, broken trust, or long-term parental
neglect and so forth, all of which can impede normative identity formation. So whereas the origins of identity crises in adoptees are located first and foremost in their *adoptions*, the biological child's crises
are not located first, if ever, in their presence within the *biological*
family. To put it another way, biological children are not thought to
suffer identity crises because they are denied adoptive ties or adopted genealogies. Indeed, the idea is so foreign that it sounds silly, yet
the adoptive tie certainly can be preferable to a biological tie because
the latter is not, out of necessity, a protection against the abuse and
neglect of children.

As a variation on the theme of revelation in biological as opposed
to adoptive family contexts, consider that Ann has only ever experienced her biological father to be a tender, loving, and humane person toward herself and others. Imagine further that on the basis of a
deep identification with her father, Ann is, and understands herself
to be, a tender, loving, and humane person. Now consider that, in

middle age, it is revealed to Ann that her father is a former Nazi war criminal who actively participated in mass murder, torture, and genocide.[62] Given the idea that Ann's father's history is her bio-genealogy, which aspect of her father's history is – or should be regarded as – the "true" or real basis for her identity? Does the new knowledge of Ann's father *as* a "war criminal" falsify the reality of her *personal* knowledge and, thus, identification with him as "loving and humane"? Should the truth of this history now be understood as the "truth" of her identity out of any necessity? Similarly, does the fact that Ann's father's history *is* her bio-genealogy logically entail that her identity, prior to this revelation, was essentially false, incomplete, and/or abnormal? Or is it the case, and should it generally be regarded as such, that it was really only Ann's sense of her *father's* identity, as opposed to her own, that was necessarily incomplete? If the revelation of her father's history initiated an identity crisis in Ann, it is worth noting that the crisis would occur in spite of the fact that Ann grew up in the presence of a biological tie to her father. Ironically, the tie's presence would be the source of the crisis because its materiality is what links (or is what is *known* to link) Ann and/or her identity irrevocably to a "war criminal."

Ultimately, if we assume that Ann's prior identification with her father *as* loving and humane is "normal" and firm, it appears there is no real ground for her identity crisis unless this unknown aspect of her father's history becomes *known* to her. In other words, Ann's bio-genealogy, *as* the biological tie's material presence, is not central to the possibility of her crisis. Indeed, the crisis would occur in spite, or even because, of the fact that she grew up in the context of her biological family. What is now central is her *knowledge* of her father's history. The result is that her crisis would really occur only out of her own use of a strategic knowledge that utilizes the tie's material irreducibility as a basis that makes intelligible to her the idea that she necessarily *owns* her biological father's history. Although Ann's "self-knowledge" might be conflated with bio-genealogy *as* the biological tie's materiality, her crisis is really a crisis in knowledge; it is essentially independent of the biological tie itself. To put it another way, her crisis is dependent on two things: the tie's irreducible materiality *as* a social, political, and historical strategy that links the meaning of her father's history as a "war criminal" to her self, as well as the treatment of this meaning by herself and others as reconstitutive of her prior identity.

Another critical point is aimed at the idea that identity is something that is or can be "complete," especially because adoption discourse, psychology, policy, and law so often construe adoptee identity as prone to being incomplete. As chapter 1 suggested, adoption discourse often characterizes the adoptee's need to know bio-genealogy as a "'search for something tangible, something whole and something legitimate. We beg to know our complete stories, to know our past.'"[63] Similarly, the dominant move by experts away from secrecy and toward open adoption is informed by the fact that "'[p]sychology recognizes that an individual cannot have a healthy sense of self-esteem without complete identity formation.'"[64] Add to this notion that in the service of complete identity formation, contemporary adoption experts and policy treat access to open records as a basic legal or human right wherein "the right to a complete identity ... encompasses knowledge of genetic origins; the right to stability through a clear determination of parentage; and the right to continuing information about medical history."[65] In effect, the idea that the "biological child" *can* achieve a *complete* sense of identity because of her proximity to the biological tie's materiality as the most wholesome conduit of bio-genealogy is the flip side of the idea that the adoptee is prone to experiencing identity as incomplete. However, both sides of the "(in)complete identity" adoption narrative entail a blind spot. A "biological child's" ability to develop a complete sense of identity by virtue of her proximity to her bio-genealogy is, at best, merely increased as a possibility because even a biological child's bio-genealogical knowledge, as I have argued above, is necessarily partial and incomplete, albeit perhaps less so than in the case of the adoptee. At worst, however, the inherent incompleteness of any person's bio-genealogy *as* a history of oneself is evidenced by the fact that human memory, which is further clouded by interpretation or hindsight, is often selective and/or false. The result is that no child's knowledge of her bio-genealogy, even as it may be gleaned in proximity to the biological tie itself, can necessarily be said to be complete, or even true for that matter, as the story of Ann above suggests. Thus even the self that has complete access to the tie's materiality cannot access a complete and/or accurate knowledge of its bio-genealogy, a fact that the adoption narrative surrounding "complete identity" obfuscates. Still, "biological children" might be said to enjoy an *increased possibility* with respect to the development of a complete identity, but even this proposition – which risks a new bio-centric assumption that should not go unchallenged (i.e., if one's chances in the game of normal identity formation are *increased* because one is a "biological child," the "biological child" still remains in a superior position relative to the "adoptee") – throws the idea of bio-genealogy as a guarantor of a "complete identity" into question. It also demonstrates the earlier suggestion that bio-genealogy is not key to either complete or normal identity formation insofar as its *increased* possibility as a basis for identity could still depend utterly on a bio-normative social context.

Adoption experts believe that the self's natural and essential need to know bio-genealogy in order to establish a "normal" identity is demonstrated by the adoptee's need to search and by her desire for reunion. Arguably, the desire for reunion underlines the extent to which either the implicit or explicit conflation of bio-genealogy with the materiality of the biological tie makes sense; if bio-genealogy *as* mere historical knowledge of one's "biological" family were enough to alleviate identity crises in adoptees, many adoptees who already have this knowledge would not continue to experience a deep desire for reunion with biological family members. This idea is called into question, however, by *Return to Sender*, a documentary about an adoptee's search and reunion story that aired on CBC Television. What is unique about this adoptee's story is that her deep desire to reunite with a biological brother is accompanied by what appears to be an equally powerful desire to reunite with her "adoptive father."

Briefly, the film tells the story of a transnational adoption: a brother and sister, Christian and Alexandra, aged two and nine, are adopted separately by two Canadian families from a poor Romanian widow who has more children than she can feed. Christian's adoption is successful, but Alexandra's breaks down within nine months, apparently because the adoptive mother becomes pregnant. Alexandra, who has only landed immigrant status in Canada by this time, is sent back to her biological family in Romania by her adoptive parents. As a result of various bureaucratic citizenship laws in both countries, Alexandra ends up with no legal identity in either country. The final result is that now as an adult living in Romania, she is impoverished because she is not allowed to work. She is also unable to acquire identity papers for her own daughter, without which her daughter cannot utilize state services, such as school or healthcare, in Romania.

The documentary traces Alexandra's journey back to Canada, her reunion with her biological brother and adoptive father, and her attempt to address the psychic trauma and pain she continues to suffer due to her "adoption breakdown." Her reunion with her brother is emotional and conflicted; she is happy to see him and also angry that his adoptive parents adopted him separately from her. In a CBC Radio interview, the Toronto-based filmmaker Mary Anne Alton explains that Alexandra's anger during the reunion is due to her poverty, the loss of her upper-middle-class lifestyle, which she only briefly enjoyed before being returned to Romania by her adoptive parents, and the fact that her brother continues to enjoy this lifestyle with his adoptive parents.[66] Prior to her reunion with her adoptive father, Alexandra is characterized in the film as having a strong sense of "justice," perhaps to explain both her conflicted feelings about her reunion with her biological brother and her desire to reunite with her adoptive father.

The reunion with Alexandra's adoptive father, who has been located by the film crew, is quite painful. With no advance warning, she knocks on the door of his home and asks whether he remembers her, which he does not by sight. She affirms that he is her "father," which he denies and then concedes. She then asks him why she was returned to Romania. He uncomfortably and unconvincingly explains that during the nine months she was with him and his now ex-wife, she was inconsolably miserable and homesick. Alexandra strongly and confidently asserts that she recalls no such feelings on her part and, instead, affirms that she remembers being very happy living with her adoptive parents; this memory is also confirmed by other people, such as her primary school teacher, who knew her while she was an "adoptee" in Canada. The encounter with her adoptive father ends fairly quickly. He gives her his phone number and asks her to contact him the next morning at nine o'clock. When she calls, she is initially met with an answering service and later finds the number no longer in service.

As painful and heart-wrenching as it is, the reunion story in *Return to Sender* is very interesting in that Alexandra's powerful desire to search for her biological brother *and* her adoptive father suggests the need to search should not be conflated uncritically with a need for bio-genealogy that is understood essentially to be rooted in the materiality of the biological tie. Alexandra's need to reunite with her *adoptive* father appears in the film to be genuine and psychically urgent. Indeed, the psychic urgency surrounding her reunion also appears to be very much like the urgency adoptees are said to experience with regard to the need to reunite with birth parents. At the beginning of the film, Alexandra is depicted as psychically troubled and angry. She is very angry that her adoption and separation from her biological brother initially took place at all, but she is also very angry and hurt that her adoption failed and that she was sent back to Romania. In fact, in spite of a tone that is obviously critical of the adoptive father, the film makes it clear that Alexandra was and is deeply and emotionally attached to her adoptive father. During the reunion, she adamantly claims he is her "father," she is very hopeful at the prospect of their contact the next day, and she is visibly injured when she finds he has lied to her and disconnected his phone.

So what can be gleaned from Alexandra's need and/or desire to reunite with her *adoptive* father? Ultimately, her story opens up the possibility that the materiality of the biological tie is not the etiological core of adoptee identity crisis *as* the need to search. Instead, her story suggests that the need to search is spurred on by something else, particularly the experience of *loss* itself. In adoption discourse, the loss of bio-genealogical knowledge is implicitly or explicitly understood to drive the adoptee's need to search: this knowledge is said "normally" to manifest on the basis of a child's immediate proximity to the biological tie both because (in a bio-centric context) it grants "complete" and/or material access to bio-genealogy as the basis for (physical) identification and because it serves as the child's anchor in her *birth* culture, nation, language, and/or race. Conversely, Alexandra's story suggests the lack of proximity to the biological tie is not what drives the need to search. Her story suggests that the import adoption experts place on proximity overlooks the effects of *loss* itself in that adoption discourse sets up the *loss of* the bio-material tie as the inherent motivation behind the adoptee's need to search. To put it another way, when adoption discourse focuses attention on the *loss of* the biological tie instead of on the experience of *loss* itself, it ends up treating the psychic losses of adoptees as a natural kind of loss: the breakdown of psychic loss in general into multiple kinds, of which adoptee *loss of* the biological tie is purified as a kind in particular, obscures how the "interests of, or facts about, the classifiers" (i.e., adoption experts) arguably render this classification of *loss experience* arbitrary in important respects.[67] Adoption discourse's constitution of the adoptee's identity crisis as a loss that is essentially different or *other in kind* disguises the loss's similarity to identity crises that occur due to the self's loss of a nonbiological family member, a friend, or a lover or loss of a home, a homestead, or a homeland. Indeed, the fact that all of these losses can lead to what is arguably the same kind of psychic pain or experience, wherein the self's sense of itself as complete is thwarted or undone, suggests that these losses, although seemingly different at the start, are actually no different in kind *as losses* in the end. The trouble is that when the *loss of* the biological tie's (material) proximity is treated as a differentiated kind of loss, so too is the "adoptee's" experience of loss because it opens the door to her loss always and only being (mis)read or pathologized through the lens of adoption and to her attachment within the adoptive family being (mis)read or pathologized as inferior or lacking by others and even herself.

At the very least, the biological tie is not the only material thing that can be treated as a cause of identity crisis or the experience of an incomplete sense of self; it has no necessary and/or exclusive relationship to this experience. Indeed, many people suffer deep and disturbing crises of identity in relation to the loss of all sorts of things. For instance, in the context of a war, the painful, abiding desire or need of many people dispossessed of personal belongings or property to reacquire them is a kind of search for a traumatically lost part of the self that is identified and/or associated with the material things lost. Kerry Lynn Moore iterates this idea in "Mourning Loss," wherein she explores the relationship between subjectivity and material objects. She argues that

> objects are "displaced places," that is, how the character/subject constitutes itself partially in the world by the gathering of material things. These things are the loci of memories for the subject, so our past is imbued in them, and we constitute our present by making narratives of our past. Objects, then, are the place makers of our narratives. As the place makers of our narratives of subjectivity, objects are forever marking our sense of isolation, our sensation of disconnection, that perhaps is constitutive of subjectivity (insofar as we seem to be forever in pursuit of always already lost objects). Present objects are, therefore, interdependent with lost or absent ones in memory.[68]

She further observes that "[i]f the subject constitutes itself through objects, it is also worth noting that the subject can be undone by its tenuous hold upon them or by its hysterical dependency upon them."[69] If Moore is right, the materiality of the biological tie can hardly be understood to be unique as a thing that can cause identity crises in human beings; any (material) object that the self imbues with memory or narratives of the past can elicit such an effect upon the subject if and when it is lost.

Here, as with the adopted subject, however, a question still remains about whether the *thing* lost or the experience of *loss itself* is the real cause of identity crisis in general. Although unobserved by adoption discourse, the fact is that even within the context of Freudian psychoanalysis, material things or objects that are external to the self, which can take the form of either people (mother) or inanimate things, are not themselves the necessary and/or essential cause of the self's first and most enduring experience of loss and incompleteness. As Adam Phillips reminds us in a discussion about love and sex, "[t]he individual's first and forever-recurring loss, in Freud's view, is not of the object but of the fantasy of self-sufficiency, of being everything to oneself."[70] A loss of self *as* a loss of self-sufficiency, therefore, is an immaterial loss, and it is this kind of loss that ultimately informs all future experiences of loss, even those that appear to be triggered directly by the loss of material things. Phillips adds that "[f]or Freud, development was a process of substitution in which there were no substitutes, merely necessary alternatives."[71] Under the rubric of psychoanalysis, therefore, the self seeks out material objects – which can take the form of people or things, including the self's own body – only *as* substitutions. However, each substitution that is sought out to reinstate in the self its original sense of completeness is inevitably going to be a disappointment in this regard because the self simply is incapable of re-establishing its original experience of self-sufficiency or completeness in relation to any *external* object.[72] External things or objects, even if they can function *as* psychic substitutions for an original but now past experience of self-sufficiency, will inevitably trigger the self's earliest sense of loss or incompleteness because the self cannot ultimately and infinitely deny the object's externality. Whenever there is a conscious recognition of the object's externality, such as when it leaves or is lost, stolen, or broken, the self will re-experience its primary experience of incompleteness. According to the logic of psychoanalysis, therefore, lost external objects in and of themselves should not be (mis)construed as the *real* causes of identity crisis; rather, the object, when lost, merely elicits a memorial experience of incompleteness that is both originally immaterial and a permanent condition of the nature of self.

From the perspective of psychoanalysis itself, therefore, something is amiss if and when the biological tie's materiality is construed as the ontological source of a complete and/or stable identity. Instead, the tie should be regarded only as an impoverished substitute that is utilized by the self as a strategy to thwart deep and essential feelings of incompleteness. Furthermore, insofar as the self does experience the biological tie's materiality as the ontological source of a complete sense of self, the self should be understood to *give* the tie both its role and meaning *as* "ontological cause" in the context of an essentially unattainable fantasy of completeness. Correspondingly, insofar as the "adopted" self wishes to and/or does experience (via reunion) the biological tie's materiality as the ontological source of a complete sense of self, the "adopted" self should also be understood to *give* the tie its role and meaning *as* ontological cause in the context of an essentially unattainable fantasy of completeness.

The question is how and why does the self make such a fantastic mistake with regard to the biological tie's materiality? The answer is that the self, along with adoption experts, currently conflates or associates the biological tie's materiality, and access to it, with a meaning of "complete self-knowledge" and/or a "complete self."[73] Indeed, this point can be illustrated by looking at how other kinds of material objects may figure in the self's identity. In a discussion of Frantz Fanon's existential psychology and the effects that Fanon observed with regard to an "Algerian" sense of national identity under French occupation, Renée T. White writes that "[t]he self-hood of Algerians, whether as individuals, or as members of a nation with its own national identity, also depended on social life and social organization. Being Algerian had particular social meaning which was defined within the context of Algeria's self-determined national identity. Once national identity was devalued and denied, Algerians became *strangers* in their own land."[74] She also writes that "to occupy people, you occupy their land."[75] Although White does not directly explore the idea of land as a lost (substitute) object that initiates a crisis in the self's sense of national identity, her observations imply that people literally associate their experience of national identity with their homeland in a material sense. Thus, if and when land is lost in the sense that self-determining power or ownership over it is lost as a result of occupation, it can elicit an experience of estrangement that is akin to a *crisis* in (national) identity. Self-determination over land, due to the deep social meaning of national identity that is associated with it, leads to an experience of alienation or estrangement in the self's national identity if and when that land is lost. The material loss of the land can alter, or at the very least complicate, the meaning of the land. In turn, this alteration can undermine the self's ability to wholly identify with the land in the same way that it once did, which is what can be understood to produce something akin to a crisis in the self's sense of national identity. The material occupation of the land necessarily elicits a change in its meaning, which denies the self unfettered access to an original social meaning that was previously conflated with the land itself. Identifying with "occupied" land surreptitiously extracts a partial, but nonetheless unwanted, identification with the occupier insofar as new meanings associated with the occupier now occupy the land alongside old meanings. A kind of identity crisis can manifest, therefore, if and when the land itself can no longer function as an immutable foundation for a formerly unadulterated meaning (e.g., "Algerian") with which the self normally identified prior to occupation.

Fundamentally, a parallel can be drawn between crises in national identity and adoptee identity: the experience of being a "stranger" in one's own land mirrors characterizations of "adoptee" subjectivity *as* the experience of being a stranger in one's own (adoptive) family. Initially, these two experiences appear to be different in kind insofar as they seem to be caused by two different things. In the case of national identity, the crisis appears to be caused by the material *loss of* land, whereas the adoptee's identity crisis appears to be caused by the material *loss of* the biological tie. There is one way, however, in which both types of crisis are essentially alike in kind. Both are an effect of deep social values and meanings that the self associates with the *materiality* of the land and/or the biological ties that have been lost. Crises in national and adoptee identity are alike in that each necessarily depends on a social meaning with which a given material thing is impregnated. In the absence of this social meaning, therefore, the *loss of* the given material thing is or would be essentially meaningless to the self and thus does not or would not create any crisis. In this sense, the material object lost is arbitrary and inessential. It is not an absolute and necessary cause of identity crisis, even though social meanings associated with the object set its materiality up as an absolute, necessary, and naturalized source of a stable identity or as a cause of identity crisis.

Assuming, therefore, the ontological status or identity of the self is not fundamentally determined or linked to a given materiality out of any necessity, how does the self come to experience the relationship between either identity crisis or normal identity and the biological tie as causal? The answer is that, like adoption and family experts, the self tends to conflate a dominant knowledge of "real family" with the tie's materiality, which is also currently imbued with the meaning "cause" as it pertains to identity. In doing so, the self participates in the understanding and/or creation of itself as either a "biological" or "adopted" subject, and the mode of adoption, whether infant, late-stage, monoracial, transracial, and/or transnational, is irrelevant; insofar as any subject *knows* she is "adopted," she will experience a share in the meaning of adoption *as* bio-material loss, a meaning that binds (different) adoptees to multiform discursive continuums that produce a diversity of adoptee experiences or identity crises through dominant, bio-centric discourses of family, culture, race, nation, and/or language as vestiges of the knowledge of adoptee origins at birth. It is through the act of *knowing* that the self creates the differentiated ontological status that it experiences as either a "biological child" or "adoptee." Indeed, this is precisely what happened to Celina. Actively (re)knowing or (re)interpreting herself to be adopted, she is complicit in the erasure of what was previously a twenty-two-year experience of "real family" ties because, like most people, she too conflates the meaning of "real family" with the biological tie's material presence. Interestingly, the result of now knowing she is adopted is that Celina has directly experienced the differentiated ontological status of biological and adoptive ties personally and in relation to only one set of parents. That this is even a possibility has powerful implications with respect to the biological tie as an essentially arbitrary basis upon which to confirm the reality of "biological" or "real family" ties, let alone a "normal" identity.

To explore the idea that all identities, even "problem" ones like Celina's, are ultimately an effect or product of knowledge, let's turn to the work of Michel Foucault. Foucault understands identity, and really the subject upon which intelligible identities depend, to be (re)produced in and through external and internal interpretive acts, which are the foundation of knowledge production.[76] He does not understand identity formation to be rooted in causal, bio-deterministic, bio-materialistic, and/or structural origins but in knowledge and discourse itself. He rejects the idea that identity is caused by a totalizing and universalizable essence, or by anything that smacks of Platonic metaphysics; he disputes the idea of "human nature" and argues that there is no resolute, originary point upon which human *being*, experience, and identity turn.[77] Foucault demonstrates many of these ideas in *The History of Sexuality*, wherein he considers the relationship between a massive production of knowledge that surrounds sex in the modern period and the simultaneous emergence of the sexual subject. He critiques both the dominant eighteenth- and nineteenth-century view of sex as an instinct or essential drive and the idea that this instinct is an objective basis upon which the individual can gain "access to his own intelligibility ... to the whole of his body ... to his identity."[78] He argues that the modern Western experience of sex and sexual identity occurs not only in relation to, but also as a result of, this dominant discourse on sexuality, one that is socially, politically, and historically specific. He suggests that this discourse functions as an interpretive matrix or grid through which meaning is read into, imposed upon, and thereby limits the individual's sexual being, experience, and identity both from without and from within.[79] Therefore, "sexuality is a historical construct, not an underlying biological referent" that essentially determines the self's sexual identity and experience.[80] For instance, the "pervert" exists only as long as her "irregular" sex is read through a discourse of perversion, one that coexists and is interdependent with a discourse of "regular" or normal sexuality insofar as each is inherently contrasted against the other; each pervert's existence is also realized to the degree that she understands and accepts this reading of her sex as one that is accurate.[81] Ultimately, Foucault's idea that the modern Western individual's experience of sexual identity is produced through external and internal acts of interpretation has implications not only for sex and sexual subjects but also for adopted subjects, as well as for the idea that it is the biological tie's material lack that is the fountainhead of adoptee experience and identity.

Identity theories that target adoptees are like those that give rise to the sexual subject because they are primarily rooted in the same modern Western psychologies that take sex as their object. Like early modern sexologists, adoption experts implicitly and explicitly rely on totalizing essences and causal origins to explain "adoptee" identity formation, and on this basis they produce a powerful discourse that surrounds the identity problems to which the adoptee is said to be prone. The force of this discourse, as Foucault would likely suggest, has something further to do with the particular posture that modern modes of psychology and social science (e.g., biological psychology, psychiatry, psychoanalysis, social psychology, sociology, and anthropology) take up: they pose as "human sciences."[82] They attempt to approach or understand human being, the self, and identity in the same way that natural sciences and medicine approach organic diseases like cancer (e.g., insofar as a particular carcinogen is identified as the cause of a certain form of cancer). As powerful as this posture is, and precisely because it capitalizes on the influence of the natural sciences as sources of objective truth, sciences that take human being as their object are nonetheless mistaken when they seek universalizable causes in answer to questions about the self and identity.[83] For Foucault, the main problem with this kind of an approach to the self is that human being is not in the purview of something like a natural science because the self is not irreducible to a thing in itself: "there is no human nature for the human sciences to be right about," and so "although there can be a science of the body there can be no science of the self."[84] If Foucault is right, family and adoption psychologies are also highly problematic: the knowledge of biological family and adoption that they produce is what gives rise to the adopted subject and, thereby, an "adopted" sense of self and identity, which operates further as the object of family and adoption psychologies.

How, then, does the knowledge that adoption experts produce give rise to the adopted subject and her identity problems or to experiences like Celina's? If modern Western family and adoption psychologies are not arbiters of objective truth concerning the adopted self's origins because "[n]othing in man – not even his body – is sufficiently stable to serve as the basis for self-recognition or for understanding other men," how can we begin to rethink the production of "adoptee" experience and identity?[85] Coupled with the idea that "human beings are always self-interpreting beings," the instability of all bases for self-recognition indicates that the self is not, nor can it ever be, infinitely fixed in the manner that traditional notions of identity suggest.[86] Every identity or mode of being is only ever stable contextually because its course, via interpretation, will parallel social-political-historical norms and/or change.[87] Being and subjectivity are coextensive with, and subject to, thought in that being modifies and further (re)interprets itself in accordance with thought or the production of knowledge.[88] Like all human experience, therefore, adoptee experience is arguably an effect of thought, or knowledge, because "[w]hatever it [thought] touches it immediately causes to move ... causing man's own being to undergo a change."[89] So at the same time that human being thinks or produces knowledge, it (re)interprets itself through such knowledge and conforms with it.[90]

Paradoxically, it is the self-interpretive and transformative nature of human being that subjects the self to particularized or limited modes of being and experience. The production of experience through knowledge encloses or forecloses the possibility of other experiences in a given time because thought, in particular, is always limited and finite. As a result, human experience, including adoptee experience, is "the correlation between fields of knowledge, types of normativity, and forms of subjectivity in a particular culture."[91] Experience, or the experience of any and all identity, is produced, disciplined, framed, and particularized through knowledge. Tied to a finite social-political-historical context, the range of human experience that pertains to a given person's identity or sense of self – her sensations, emotions, and identity problems – is circumscribed.

In light of Foucault, the adoptive subject is a function and effect of discourses that pertain to adoptee identity and the biological family. The origin of adoptee identity is not the absence of the biological tie or the lack of bio-genealogical knowledge that this absence is said to entail; instead, the discourses that surround adopted selves "systematically form the objects of which they speak" (i.e., the "adopted" subject).[92] Furthermore, the conflicted "adoptee" is not some pre-existent object that adoption experts simply happen upon. She is not an a priori impetus that motivates adoption experts' search for the cause of adoptee identity conflicts. On the contrary, the institution of adoption's search itself, via the knowledge that emerges from it, produces and grafts onto the self (who grows up in the absence of the biological tie) the "adoptee's" identity conflict or experience. So although Foucault would agree with adoption experts that being adopted is certainly a "process," he would argue that it is a process of subjectivization; it is the result of discursive practices such as the institution of adoption's scientific or causal models of identity formation. Where adoption experts locate the origin of the adoptee's identity, and her identity problems, in the absence of the biological tie, Foucault would further suggest that the self emerges as an "adoptee" through relations of power/knowledge – relations of which the search for origins itself is a part. This situation implies that neither searching nor the obtainment of bio-genealogy on the part of either the adoptee or any self is what gives rise to a *complete* sense of self because the search for the self's "history will not discover a forgotten identity, eager to be reborn, but a complex system of distinct and multiple elements, unable to be mastered by the powers of synthesis."[93]

Assuming Foucault's ideas do facilitate a rejection of the origin that adoption experts attribute to the experience of adoptee identity, how can we begin to explain the adoptee's *real* feelings of being conflicted about her identity, or of being lost, lonely, and incomplete – feelings that in some sense are the result of her lack of access to bio-genealogical knowledge? Timothy H. Wilson explains that, for Foucault, "[w]hat we think of as 'things' or 'entities' are merely the functions of relations of forces."[94] Thus the "adopted" self can be understood to function as one of the "nodes through which institutionalized power relations are transmitted," particularly the power relations of the institution of adoption, which is inhabited by biological family discourse, as well as by the discourse of other institutions, such as law or heterosexual union and marriage.[95] Foucault's ideas about "disparity" are also useful here. He writes that "[w]hat is found at the historical beginning of things is not the inviolable identity of their origin; it is the dissension of other things. It is disparity."[96] By disparity, he means the unequal values in meaning that are attributed to things or entities on the basis of "piecemeal" and arbitrary reason, which is born out of a "will to knowledge," or what is really the injustice of the competition to know, order, contain, or control human being.[97] In relation to adoption, this situation means that the real experience of the adoptee identity conflict is produced by the disparity in meaning between the values placed on the absence as opposed to the presence of the biological tie in a given social-political-historical context that differentiates these ties materially. It is the disparity between the *meaning* of the "adoptive" tie and the "biological" tie, not an ontological presence embedded in the apparent materiality of the biological tie, that ultimately produces adopted and nonadopted subjects.

The production of adoptee subjectivity can now be elucidated even further if we return to Celina and my earlier questions concerning both what it means *to be* a "biological" child and the conditions necessary for determining whether her *experience* as such can be true and real in the absence of a biological tie. Given that Celina's crisis occurs only at the point of her adoption revelation, her self-experience arguably is altered only when the disparate meaning of the (inferiorly valued) *knowledge* of adoption is imposed upon her; it effectively interrupts and (eventually) eradicates her former relation to a (superiorly valued) *knowledge* of herself as a "biological child."[98] This outcome suggests that the material fact that a person does not share a biological tie with her parents, in and of itself, is not sufficient as a test for the truth and reality of that person's *experience as* a "biological child" because the *experience* of all "biological children" is also predicated only upon a *knowledge* of the presence of the material biological tie. Therefore, it is only in the absence of the *knowledge* of a biological tie that the criteria for *being* or experiencing oneself as a "biological child" are *not* met.

Finally, Foucault's notion of "problematization" allows us to think about how knowledge, as opposed to the materiality of the biological tie, shapes "adoptee" experience through discursive practices. Primarily, that is because being "adopted" can ultimately be understood to exemplify a particular mode of being insofar as all human "being is historically constituted as experience; that is, as something that can and must be thought."[99] Problematization refers to the emergence of a concern as a practice of knowledge that instigates and/or abrogates attention and power being drawn toward or away from possible objects of knowledge, such as the "adopted" self. Foucault writes that "problematization doesn't mean the representation of a pre-existent object, nor the creation through discourse of an object that doesn't exist. It's the set of discursive or non-discursive practices that makes something enter into the play of the true and false, and constitutes it as an object for thought (whether under the form of moral reflection, scientific knowledge, political analysis, etc.)."[100] Objects of thought, therefore, appear, disappear, and reappear multifariously in history. They are problematized as they become causes for concern in social, ethical, scientific, and political discursive practices. Thus problematization is not a cause of experience or a dictate for a set of practices for knowing the self; it is the result and a signal about the value that current discursive practices give to particular modes of experience because the self's relation to itself is mediated by the meaning that accrues through discourse. It is thus a (re)configuration of knowledge or thought on the basis of already existent practices, which creates new effects with regard to experience.[101] Regardless of phenomena, then, things, entities, or experiences do become *real* or *true* precisely when they become problematized or emerge as concerns or objects of thought.[102]

Consider that prior to the emergence, event, or "particular configuration of forces" that produces today's "adoptee," a phenomenon somewhat like adoption did occur but not as we know and/or experience it.[103] For instance, nonbiological families have legally adopted children at least since Roman times. But the Roman laws of *patria potestas* and *adrogation* functioned solely to create heirs in order to maintain the continuity of family names and to control fortunes.[104] In fact, prior to the nineteenth century, adoption law was always a mechanism that addressed the needs of parents. In the 1800s, however, concerns emerged with regard to the "preservation of children" and the "welfare of the child," and by the mid-nineteenth and twentieth centuries, these concerns were central in adoption and family law.[105] E. Wayne Carp observes that one of the first "modern" adoption laws originated in Massachusetts in 1851.[106] Unlike Roman-based adoption laws, it entailed "new conceptions of childhood and parenthood, which emphasized the needs of children and the contractual and egalitarian nature of spouses' rights of guardianship."[107] Furthermore, the Massachusetts law is a foundation of the social infrastructure of the modern Western institution of adoption. By "establish[ing] the principle of judicial supervision of adoptions" against a measure of "'the best interests of the child,'" it combined principles and practices that had never before converged in adoption law: scrutiny of parental ability, biological parents' "written consent" prior to relinquishment, legal dissolution of ties and responsibilities between biological parent and child, and adoptive parents "assuming the responsibility and emotional outlook of natural parents."[108] Clearly, social and legal mechanisms for adoption existed in premodern eras. Nevertheless, their design, which focused solely on the interests of individuals seeking heirs, would have constituted adoptee experience in ways that were distinct from that of a modern adoption law system and psychology because the latter problematize adoptee experience in new ways due to their focus on the best interests of the child. For instance, perhaps the Roman adoptee experienced himself less problematically as a means to an important social and political end, whereas the modern adoptee experiences herself as a "chosen child" who is prone to identity problems.[109] In effect, modern adoption law and psychology are modes of knowledge that (re)shape the being or experience of adoptees and adoptive families in ways that simply would not be *true* or *real* under Roman law.

In this light, we can begin to see how adoption revelation and the systems of knowledge that support it, such as adoption psychology and adoption law, produce the experience of the adoptee. When the knowledge of adoption is revealed to a self, not only does *she* begin to know herself *to be* adopted, but so do her parents, siblings, relatives, friends, social workers, therapists, lawyers, teachers, and anyone else who knows of her adoption. This experience is also regulated through biological family knowledge insofar as the child's knowledge of her adoption emphasizes for her that she is not privy to the experiences of the biological family. Thus knowing herself or being known by others to be adopted is not something the adoptee or other individuals accomplish in a vacuum away from pre-existent social forces of institutionalized knowledge. Instead, the meaning that being adopted entails is produced through a system of knowledge that has already considered the fact of adoption to be one that is worthy of scrutiny, and it is to this system that all those who are involved in knowing "adoptees" are hooked up. The adoptee's being therefore is known through the problematization of adoption that has emerged out of a set of discursive practices that already surround the material absence of the biological tie within the family and have manifested as the institution of adoption. These practices sustain the process of adoption – for instance, through the signifier "adopted," adoption law, the adoption experts who counsel adoptive parents, and in turn adoptive parents, who further facilitate these practices as they repeatedly reveal what it means *to be* adopted to the child. Once the knowledge of adoption is revealed to the child, these practices function in the child through her self-knowledge, her belief in the accuracy of others' knowledge of her, and/or her inability to prevent others from knowing her to be "adopted."

So another way to look at the experience of late-adoption revelation is as an important phenomenon that illustrates how adoption, or the material absence of the biological tie, is not an essential or natural cause of being but a powerful mode of knowledge that transforms an interpretive plasticity that is being. For instance, as long as Celina *knew* herself to be a "biological" child, she also genuinely experienced herself *to be* a "biological" child until her adoption was revealed. The crisis that revelation foisted upon her, however, was that the knowledge of her adoption dismantled her ability to ever experience herself *as* a "biological" child again because the *knowledge* now made this impossible. What this late-revelation story depicts therefore is an extreme instance of what is already entailed in the process of adoption generally; that is, the process of adoption, beginning with early and reiterative revelation, structures the experience of the adoptee or contours her being through a discourse on identity that is produced by the institution of adoption on the basis of the claim that the material absence of the biological tie is the causal origin of adoptee identity conflicts. In short, the trauma of late revelation does not speak to the material absence or presence of biological ties as an ontological origin, as many adoption experts believe. Instead, the trauma of late revelation is a profound example of how thought or knowledge can and does dramatically alter the form that being can take. As Celina's adoption was revealed to her, her being had to be rethought, and her present experience of herself was altered in conformity with the new knowledge of her adoption. But this outcome does not imply that her past experience of herself as a "biological" child was unreal or even false; it was merely transformed through a new interpretation of self that was initiated when her adoption was revealed and when she accepted this new knowledge as the accurate account of her being, which she did insofar as she was compelled by a social-political-historical context that devalues the meaning of the adoptive tie *as* "real."

Celina's experience raises highly provocative questions. It prompts us to consider more seriously the role that is played by the meaning, as opposed to the fact, of the biological tie's materiality in adoptee identity and experience. It bespeaks the possibility that the adoptee's experience of bio-genealogical alienation has less to do with the *loss of* the biological tie itself and more to do with *loss* as an experience that is prompted by the meaning with which the tie's material absence is currently and arbitrarily imbued. It is an appeal to us to examine more closely how an institutionalized knowledge of adoption, one that problematizes the adoptee and devalues her ties, shapes her identity and experience. It is a clue that there are good reasons to be skeptical of family and adoption psychologies that uncritically assume it is the self's lack of proximity to the materiality of the biological tie and, ultimately, to bio-genealogy that is the true source of "adoptee" identity. It suggests that both the idea that adoptee identity problems are best prevented and mended in proximity to the biological tie and the perpetual reinstantiation of the bio-genealogical imperative are high-

ly suspect. It urges us to reject family and adoptee identity theories
that implicitly or explicitly assume that the materiality of the biological tie is a resolute, originary point upon which human being, experience, and identity turn.[110] It suggests that access to bio-genealogical
knowledge does not give any self, adopted or not, a genuinely "solid
identit[y]," simply because no such thing exists.[111] Finally, it asks us to
consider that all identities, not just that of the "adoptee" and "biological child," are best understood as a subterfuge of knowledge itself, one
that unifies and orders being within a set of limits that further conceals the complexity and multiplicity of human being.[112]

3

The "Adoptee"
and the Event of the "Individual"

A person's identity is derived from knowing what he is and what he is
not.

Keith C. Griffith, *The Right to Know Who You Are*

All the practices by which the subject is defined and transformed are
accompanied by the formation of certain types of knowledge, and in the
West, for a variety of reasons, knowledge tends to be organized around
forms and norms that are more or less scientific. There is also another reason, maybe more fundamental and more specific to our societies. I mean
the fact that one of the main moral obligations for any subject is to know
oneself, to tell the truth about oneself, and to constitute oneself as an
object of knowledge both for other people and for oneself.

Michel Foucault, *The Politics of Truth*

If "one of the main moral obligations for any subject is to know
oneself," as Michel Foucault suggests, then the subjectivity of the
"adoptee" is an effect of the self's attempt to fulfil this obligation *and*
the inability to do so.[1] Like any self, she is produced by this obligation
broadly speaking, and she is produced by it in the more pronounced
sense that it is reiterated and reimposed upon her as an adopted subject by the institution of adoption. The pathologization of adoptee
identity by adoption psychology, experts, and discourse, as we have
seen, re-emphasizes the self's need to meet this obligation to the extent
that it makes bio-genealogical knowledge essential to the self's development or identity. Furthermore, the "adoptee" is produced by an
inability to meet this obligation because adoption psychology, law, and
social work – not mere circumstance – splinter, mediate, and/or with-

hold the adoptee's bio-genealogical knowledge by various means, such as through a file system that is incomplete, partial, regulated, and/or closed, all of which makes it impossible for the adoptee to know herself to the same extent that nonadopted people can. Still, it is the generalized obligation to know oneself that creates the conditions of knowledge that initially make the adoptee's subjectivity possible. It is only as the self gives meaning to an (in)ability to know oneself that the modern "adoptee," *as* the experience of incomplete self-knowledge, emerges. The modern institution of adoption and the human sciences through which it composes its ordinances are founded upon the wider obligation to know oneself. But to what events or emergent discourses in modern Western knowledge could this imperative be attributed and in what ways are these events relevant to the possibility of adoptee subjectivity? What conditions of knowledge make the modern Western adoptee's experience of bio-genealogical alienation possible?

Today, adoptee experience is largely administered and maintained by adoption as an institutionalized force that exerts itself powerfully upon a family through, among other things, the legal act of adoption. Legal adoption entails that the family, by means of a social work system, is introduced and integrated into the psychology of adoption – a psychology that, once it is impressed upon the now "adoptive family," differentiates that family's experience from that of the biological family. But what events in knowledge made this experience possible? Although there likely are many, the two events we will consider are individualism and (Darwinian) naturalism. Taken together, they produce particular conditions under which it is possible for the "adoptee" to be differentiated from nonadopted people in modernity and, ultimately, postmodernity. Fundamentally, individualism places an imperative on the self to know the truth of *who* and *what* it is in relation to *other* individuals, and naturalism emphasizes that biology or genetics is a fundamental constituent of the self's identity, relations, and destiny. But it is at the crossroads of individualist and naturalist discourse that the self is prompted to seek the truth of its being in her bio-genealogy. This is not to say that bloodline or ancestry is never important before this time but that the meaning of biology, connected as it is to the "individual" as a means of self-knowledge that informs the individual's autonomy, is unique to this period. The imperative that these conditions of knowledge produce is what makes the adopted subject's *proneness* to an experience of bio-genealogical alienation possible and frequent. In a profound sense, the nature of modern adoption is such that the "adoptee" *is* a lack of self-knowledge because she cannot obey the generalized bio-genealogical imperative with which each modern self or "individual" is addressed.

The origins of modern Western individualism – and the "individual" subject it enframes – have been located variously by historians, philosophers, and human scientists in Ancient Greek and Roman philosophy, Medieval Christian thought and the Reformation, Renaissance and Enlightenment philosophies, the social and political history of the French Revolution, and nineteenth- and twentieth-century Euro-American social and political philosophies. Thus Louis Dumont is surely accurate when he writes that "previous authors have seen the origin of 'individualism' nearer or farther back in time, no doubt according to the idea they held and the definition they gave of it."[2] Moreover, scholars who seek the origins of individualism typically emphasize the range and disparity of meanings that surround it. For instance, Steven Lukes cautions that there is a diversity of meanings with which individualism can be associated, a warning he derives from Karl Mannheim, who writes that "the same word, or the same concept in most cases, means very different things when used by differently situated persons," and from Max Weber, who claims that it "embraces the utmost heterogeneity of meanings."[3] Indeed, Lukes identifies eleven key ideas or themes of individualism that are neither exhaustive nor categorically its sole ingredients in that some are mixed and matched or isolated at the expense of others, as well as expanded or omitted depending on the historical moment and its proponents.[4] Therefore, identifying the genuine and exclusive social, political, and historical origins of the ideas that give rise to individualism is a daunting and improbable task. And the same can be said of the origins of naturalism, which this chapter also explores shortly as a discourse integral to the "individual" as an idealized bio-family subject. Herein, therefore, the question of either individualism's or naturalism's origins is simply set aside to consider the "individual" more particularly as a discursive "event," one that is interchangeable with the formation of the modern, Western, family subject and that gives rise to the modern adopted subject. On the basis of a brief discussion of individualism's and naturalism's dominant tenets, therefore, this chapter considers how the contingent admixture of these two modern Western discourses can be understood to elicit a bio-genealogical imperative that demarcates contemporary (biological) "family" experience, which is an experience that also sets up as it depends on the adopted subject as a foil.

The critical idea of "event," drawn as it is from Foucault, is applied herein for my own purposes. It is enlisted precisely to undercut the "individual" as an "ideal continuity – as a teleological movement or natural process," one that descends from a traceable origin, or meta-bio-ontology, that obliges only particular formations of the "family" subject.[5] To approach the individual or family subject in this manner is to greet the "discontinuities" or the "radical events beneath the apparent continuity of a discourse that upset human perception and practice" and, in this instance, to interrupt what is the largely unchecked bio-logic of family and adoption discourse.[6] The difference between questions of origin and questions of event, for Foucault, is that "only a metaphysician would seek its [history's] soul in the distant ideality of the origin," an observation that is analogous to the topic of family at hand: "family" subjects are would-be metaphysicians or meta-bio-ontologists insofar as they are the outcome of a bio-genealogical imperative.[7] Origins operate as totalizing and primordial truths, not only as origins relate to history, knowledge, and subject formation broadly speaking, which was Foucault's point, but more particularly within the family from which the "individual" emerges as a bio-family subject, which is my point. Conversely, the idea of the subject as an event interrupts the uncritical and "constant correlation between an increasing individualization and the reinforcement of this totality" or "the way, in modernity, that individuation and totalizing go hand in hand."[8] It suggests instead that there are "accidents that accompany every beginning," among which the birth of the bio-family subject as the "individual" is but one.[9] (Re)read through the unpredictability of event, the family subject can be rethought as the offspring of chance and contingency, not bio-genealogical destiny, and thereby the totalizing meaning of (biological) origins can be disrupted to allow for a "disintegration of the subject" that otherwise delimits and differentiates, implicitly or explicitly, our possibilities of family experience as, for instance, either biological and superior or adoptive and inferior.[10] As Lynne Huffer observes, "Deleuze reminds us that the subject in Foucault is not so much a person as a 'personal or collective individuation,' 'a sort of event.'"[11] Moreover, it is events, not metaphysics, "that have led us to constitute ourselves and to recognize ourselves as subjects of what we are doing, thinking, saying" as individuals, a recognition that I suggest is generated also in and by means of the self's location relative to the bio-family.[12] The critical significance of the "individual" reimagined as an event is that it exposes the role of accident in "family" subject formation and the power relations that inform it, as well as the limits and determinations of biological or adoptive family experience within a social-political-historical context that is enframed by the bio-genealogical imperative.

Only as an event can the individual recoil from the yoke of a bio-genealogical destiny because the idea of event renders visible the fabrication of such a destiny as merely, not necessarily, something that happens. As a bio-family subject, the individual is a (re)cycle that has been ongoing for some time now but not for all time. It is a repetitive discursive outcome that, regardless of its possible initiates, is a particular and contemporary (re)presence or (re)iteration of family experience, connection, and intimacy, as well as a cloaked dependence; "[i]ntimacy in the late modern world has thus been massively shaped by the development of a society ruled by an individualist ideology" and, I would add, by a naturalist ideology for reasons that relate to the family and thus to adoption.[13] It is a moulded formation of human being that emerges in the modern Western period, one that has enjoyed a long run but need not be an endless run in our thought and experience of family. As an event, the "individual" is explored in this chapter specifically as a "family" subject, one that is generated in and through the social-political-historical impact of individualism and naturalism on family and adoption discourse. As such, the "individual" is examined critically as a limit on the current range of possibilities that human being, within biological and adoptive families, is able to engender.

Although "'individualism' ... is a nineteenth-century word," it signifies multiple meanings in various contexts in that it is ultimately a network of themes about the self that occur in diverse philosophical, social, political, scientific, and economic trends in thought that crystallized throughout the eighteenth and nineteenth centuries to form the modern "individual" subject, a formation that continues to shape our contemporary senses of self.[14] As it concerns this work, however, the event of individualism can be characterized as a change in modern Western-European thought about the self's relationship to truth. The abrupt start of this change is attributed most often to René Descartes and the influence of his seventeenth-century philosophy of self, which prepares the ground for what emerges eventually as a modern sense of self. As Jerome Levin suggests, Descartes has been "widely influential" in that "his theory of the self resonates down the centuries to find a strong and unique response in, and attunement to, the thought of our time."[15] In discussing individualism as a new "philosophical doctrine about the nature of knowledge" and the self's relationship to it, Lukes too considers Descartes's *cogito ergo sum* to be the primary impetus for what will become the modern individual.[16] For Lukes, the upshot of Descartes's question "Do I exist?" is that it creates a distinct climate that enables the self to understand itself as an independent arbiter of truth for the first time because this question is one that only the self, by turning to itself, can answer; Descartes is at the source of what is an epistemological shift, one that gives rise to "the individual's certainty of his own existence" and to the idea "that the source of knowledge lies within the individual."[17] Thus Descartes facilitates what Lukes characterizes as an "epistemological individualism" wherein the self develops a sense of certainty through its relationship to itself; the significance of this shift is that it displaces, for the first time, the church or state as the fulcrum upon which all knowledge is ascertained, and it inserts the self into this position.[18] Béatrice Han, in a discussion of how "philosophy became epistemology," makes a similar point, invoking Foucault, to affirm that "'by taking Descartes as reference point ... there came a moment when the subject as such became capable of truth.'"[19] As Huffer notes, "the Cartesian moment is the moment 'philosophy' denies the possibility of 'spirituality,'" and thus it is the moment that metaphysical notions of truth that merely possess the self from on high or externally via the church and state are and can be rejected.[20] In effect, "[a] decisive transformation in the metaphysical model occurs with the 'subjectivistic turn' of Descartes"; the self individuates itself in relation to God, and "human being (*Dasein*) is transformed into a subject," such that "'to be' means to be the object of a self-certain subject."[21] Therefore, Cartesianism epistemologically, according again to Han, "guarantees for all individuals a universal and a priori access to the truth."[22] Daniel Shanahan reiterates a version of this idea as well. He suggests that Descartes allows the self to adopt an internal sense of authority in relation to truth and thereby plants the seed for "what is arguably the core of individualism, the fundamental premise upon which it is based: the belief that the pursuit of truth is a wholly individual matter."[23] The outcome, as Levin suggests, is that the "radical subjectivism that is so central to Descartes's thought has become so characteristic of modern thought that we don't recognize how much of who we are, and of how we conceptualize who we are ... we owe to him."[24] Insofar as "he was adumbrating the inwardness of modernity – anticipating the self-conscious self-absorption of our own time," Descartes's thought is an event that provokes the possibility of what will become the "individual" and really an inward-turning subject.[25]

Following Descartes, Immanuel Kant reinforces the event of the "individual" through his investigations into the boundaries of self and the self's capacity to reason. Although Kant did not accept Cartesian philosophy holus-bolus, Jonathon Glover explains that "[w]hat Descartes and Kant have in common is the belief that 'I' refers to a self, or ego, that is not reducible to anything bodily, or to my experiences, or to any combination of the two."[26] Kant's exploration diverges from Descartes's in that he is more interested in mapping out the self's intrinsic qualities, the most important of which is *the will* and its ability to reason, a characteristic that makes the autonomous subject possible because, as Lukes puts it, "Kant's autonomous individuals were 'rational wills.'"[27] Kant is also said to have "reflected, embodied and in part created" what became "the great 18th-century intellectual revolution that planted the seeds of tolerance, democracy, reasonableness, and liberalism," all of which depend on a self that is rational and, thereby, autonomous.[28] As an Enlightenment philosopher, Kant is significant because his work secures the modern self's autonomy insofar he characterizes the will as the part of the self that "can intervene to motivate decisions independently of any desires the person may have."[29] Kant's rethinking of the self, particularly the relationship between reason and desire, inculcates within the Enlightenment and modernity what eventually becomes the individualist notion of autonomy, an idea that is the marker of the self's individuality and freedom. As Kant argues, "to 'the idea of freedom there is inseparably attached the concept of *autonomy*.'"[30] Kant's investigation of the will's freedom to reason, coupled with Descartes's establishment of its independence to arrive at self-evident truths, facilitates the emergence of an autonomous self because it enables the self to understand itself as self-determining in relation to the world around it. Kant's prompting of a new "critical attitude," as it is put by Foucault, creates the possibility of a new moment in which "the principle of autonomy can be discovered."[31] Or as Shanahan suggests, Kant's investigation of what is "'not self'" – the realization that the self is distinct from the "noumenal" (real) world and the "phenomenal" (perceived) world – gives rise to the self's autonomous sense of being.[32] Moreover, Georges Canguilhem argues, Kant not only "raised the question, *What is man?*" but also "prosecute[d] the *cogito* before the critical tribunal of the *I think* and den[ied] it all substantialist import"; as a result, "modern philos-

ophy could adopt the habit of referring to the *cogito* as the philo-
sophic event that inaugurated it" – *it* being the cogito.[33] In many
important respects, therefore, the autonomous self emerges because
Kant transforms Descartes's question into "*what*, rather than *whether*,
the self is, and though he does not end the discussion of whether the
self can know anything, he opens the door to the whole range of modern psychological inquiry: speculation about the self by the self."[34]

If the emergence of the modern Western "individual" turns on these
events and others like naturalism, as we are about to see, the significance of individualism for adoptee subjectivity is the onto-epistemological phenomenon it elicits wherein the self turns in upon itself in
a search for truth.[35] The autonomy of the individual demands,
because it depends on, the self's repeated *internal* search for truth; the
act in itself is what reinforces the individual's experience of itself as
autonomous – for instance, as opposed to a self that earlier conducts
an *external* search for truth, turning outward to the church. Within
individualism's modern domain, "individuals," adoptees included,
must participate in the self-search for truth if their autonomy is to be
*real*ized. Thus, as the self's inward search for truth is imperative to
being fully an "individual," the adopted individual is immediately
confronted with a problem: the adoptee simply cannot access the
same internal truths, or access them in the same ways, if at all, that
nonadopted people can. Adoptees must rely on unreliable institutions, such as adoption, social work, medicine, and the law, for the
disclosure of many truths that are already manifestly evident to
nonadopted people. Nonadopted subjects evade bio-genealogical
alienation to the extent that the self-truths in question are already
embedded in their self-knowledge as a result of their proximity to the
biological family. Clearly, the event of the "individual" produces an
imperative wherein the self begins to know itself as a source of truth,
but naturalism appends to this inward looking self a further need to
seek the truth of its being and identity in its biology and so too in its
biological relations.

Like "individualism," the word "naturalism" can refer to a broad
range of themes across a fairly long history in the context of art, literature, philosophy, politics, and science.[36] As Pamela H. Smith
observes, it "emerged in many diverse and specific social and political
circumstances, and it could take many forms and possess a multitude
of meanings."[37] With respect to modern science, culture, and knowledge production more specifically, naturalism is understood typically

to involve "new attitudes to nature and to the pursuit of natural knowledge that formed a crucial part of the Scientific Revolution."[38] J.F.M. Clark claims that in "the historiography of nineteenth-century science ... the defining feature of the latter half of the century is taken to be the rise of scientific naturalism."[39] Increasingly "[c]ommitted to the creed of 'scientific naturalism,'" early modern scientists fundamentally "believed that all phenomena in the material world could be reduced to naturalistic explanations; revelation had no explanatory role in the realm of scientific investigation."[40] According to Clark, naturalism provoked a paradigmatic shift wherein, among modern scientists, "Dalton's atomic theory, the law of the conservation of energy, and evolution were [the] holy trinity."[41] Naturalism, in line with individualism, becomes a cornerstone of modern culture as it rejects transcendental metaphysics within the context of science; throughout the nineteenth century, it posits "a universe devoid of transcendental, metaphysical or divine forces" and replaces them with nature as the force that determines all life and thereby the self because "man" is included among the natural objects or outcomes that it investigates.[42]

Naturalism can be understood fundamentally as an event that gives rise to the self's understanding of itself in relation not only to its natural environment but also to its social, political, and economic environments. It does not materialize in isolation or exclusively within the institution of modern science because it is also a social and cultural phenomenon. It operates well within existing social, political, and economic discourses that already entreat modern individuals to comprehend themselves apart from metaphysics. Similarly, modern social, political, and economic discourses operate with ease within the naturalistic discourses of modern science. In important respects, the emergence of scientific naturalism is as dependent on the social, political, and economic discourses of liberal individualism as the latter come to be on it. For instance, Clark unreservedly locates "scientific naturalism within a liberal, centre-right, 'generalist,' intellectual culture."[43] It has a liberal, political history that supports individualistic social reforms in Europe and North America, such as in the form of eugenics, which was an offshoot of scientific naturalism; Sir Francis Galton, the founder of eugenics, "opposed aristocratic privileges and supported a liberal individualism according to which only personal talents and accomplishments ought to determine social status ... and his proposals for eugenic reform all reflected a political standpoint consistent with the interests of the profes-

sional middle class of the Victorian age."[44] Another case in point is
Alfred Russell Wallace, the purportedly silent co-author of Charles
Darwin's theory of natural selection. He made repeated "attempts to
integrate evolutionary naturalism with an increasingly left-wing
political commitment"; although he rejected eugenics as "a biological solution to ... social problems," he "tread carefully between an
unacceptable substitution of biological excuses for social problems
on the one side, and the total collapse of his evolutionary synthesis
on the other."[45] From the outset, therefore, scientific naturalism was
no strange bedfellow to the social, political, and economic goals of
individualism. Its epistemological bond with individualism is obvious in the work of Darwin, to which I turn now, particularly because
Darwin's theories of evolution continue so profoundly to shape our
contemporary notions of self and self-knowledge, as well as family
subjects. As will become apparent, in an already individualistic
social-political-historical context, the influence of Darwin's naturalism, initiated as it was with the publication of *On the Origin of Species*
in 1859, has unique implications for adoptee subjectivity.[46]

Darwin's theory of evolution caused a rupture in people's understanding of themselves, not simply in relation to nature but also in
relation to the role that heredity and survival would quickly come to
play in people's social world; it is only in "the middle of the nineteenth century" and "especially in the works of Charles Darwin and of
his cousin Francis Galton" that "biological 'inheritance'" and the concept of "'heredity' in this sense ... emerge as one of the central problems of biology."[47] Darwin's ideas and vocabulary were (and remain)
pervasive. As Adam Phillips explains, this influence meant that even
people who rejected him "couldn't help but be suspicious about what
they themselves believed, and how they had come to their beliefs."[48]
Furthermore, Darwin's emphasis upon and "anxiety" over the relationship between the biological and the social, which subsequently
inspired Galton's theory of eugenics, made biology intrinsic to the
self's understanding of itself.[49] His notions of heredity and survival
functioned outside of the natural sciences, producing the self's understanding of what was *naturally* internal to its being and experience –
an effect that retains its full, if not greater, force today.

Darwin's thought flows out of the domain of the natural sciences,
as Robert Young observes, particularly because he annexed the principles of heredity and survival to common lay knowledge, such as that
concerning domestic breeding.[50] For instance, in *On the Origin of*

Species, where Darwin introduces the universal principle of heredity, he writes,

> Any variation which is not inherited is unimportant for us. But the number and diversity of inheritable deviations of structure, both those of slight and those of considerable physiological importance, are endless ... No breeder doubts how strong is the tendency to inheritance; that like produces like is his fundamental belief ... [W]hen amongst individuals, apparently exposed to the same conditions, any very rare deviation, due to some extraordinary combination of circumstances, appears in the parent – say, once amongst several million individuals – and it reappears in the child, the mere doctrine of chances almost compels us to attribute its reappearance to inheritance ... If strange and rare deviations of structure are really inherited, less strange and commoner deviations may be freely admitted to be inheritable. Perhaps the correct way of viewing the whole subject, would be, to look at the inheritance of every character whatever as the rule, and non-inheritance as the anomaly.[51]

For Young, Darwin's analogy makes new ideas familiar on the backs of old. Ideas that originally pertained primarily to animals he now universalizes to human nature: *all* characters of *all* species are effects of heredity. Therefore, familiar new tenets such as like begets like and inheritance is the rule rather than the exception – tenets that already are deemed to be manifestly obvious in animal breeding – are easily interpolated by the self because it too is the *offspring* of parents. And as Darwin universalizes the idea that *"any variation which is not inherited is unimportant for us,"* he minimizes the extent to which the self can or should know itself to be the effect of forces outside of heredity.

Richard C. Lewontin also discusses reasons why Darwin's biology is so easily adapted to the social self. He explains that Darwin's theory of "natural selection" was admittedly modelled on Malthusian social-political-economic theory. Natural selection entails that all "organic beings" are engaged in a universal struggle for existence because, as Darwin notes, "many more individuals are born than can possibly survive."[52] Given the odds, individuals who enjoy hereditary advantages over others are most likely to survive and thus to produce (more) offspring who, because they likely inherit these same advantages, are again more likely to survive – all of which brings about evolutionary change.[53] In comparison, Lewontin discusses the relationship between the theory of natural selection and Thomas Robert Malthus's views of economics:

> Darwin himself was conscious of the source of his ideas about the struggle for existence. He claimed that the idea for evolution by natural selection occurred to him after reading the famous "Essay on Population" by Thomas Malthus, a late-eighteenth-century parson and economist. The essay was an argument against the old English Poor Law, which Malthus thought too liberal, and in favor of a much stricter control of the poor so they would not breed and create social unrest. In fact, Darwin's whole theory ... bears an uncanny resemblance to the political economic theory of early capitalism as developed by the Scottish economists ... What Darwin did was take early-nineteenth-century *political* economy and expand it to include all of *natural* economy.[54]

Much like Young, therefore, Lewontin is struck by the way that Darwin's "scientific theory is a direct translation of social experience," a translation that he argues plays a pivotal role in what has become a powerful biological view of the self that claims "we will understand what we are when we know what our genes are made of."[55] Darwin's biological translation of the social is such that the universal struggle for survival in nature is easily transposed, by the self, back into the individual's social struggle for survival under capitalism. Thus Darwin's biological view of the self speaks so readily to the "individual" that the self hardly need be convinced of the import of heredity for survival in social-political-economic life.

Still, the propensity of Darwinian naturalism to reach beyond biology or the self as a determined *animal* in a struggle against nature and toward the self as a free *individual* pitted against other individuals in the struggle for social survival, in some respects, is very odd. That is because individualist freedom, at first glance, is incompatible with the determinism of heredity in survival or natural selection. Yet Darwin's theories were used early on to justify the rise of industrialization and capitalism.[56] For instance, in *Individualism Reconsidered*, David Riesman observes that even though Darwin's notion of struggle was "completely misinterpreted" in relation to the individual's struggle versus that of the group, "Victorians, who had freed themselves from external restraints on economic competition and who were at the same time still sensitive ... to anti-moneymaking ethics, welcomed their interpretation of Darwin as a support in their continuing polemic against restraints – a polemic carried out also within themselves."[57] Given the contradictory nature of the notion of a self who is socially free and biologically determined in the race for survival, how does the self reconcile within the knowledge of itself the sanctity of a marriage between individualism and naturalism? Individualism and naturalism are reconcilable because the type of restraint that heredity is understood to pose to the autonomous individual's success through competitive struggle is in relation to the self's *internal* ability to survive. Conversely, individualist freedom demands only that there be no *external* barriers in order for the individual to be free. Any restraint internal to the individual's will, or biology, simply is irrelevant to his freedom if he is externally free (socially, politically, and economically) to compete. And because heredity is internal to the self, it also functions well as a truth that the self must ferret out in order to meet the "individual's" obligation to know oneself, to experience his autonomy, and ultimately to maximize his potential for competition and survival in a free market.

According to Lewontin, individualism and naturalism are not merely compatible: individualism is fully *intrinsic* to Darwin's idea of survival. That is because the nature of being an "individual," of being free, is such that it automatically forces the self into a mode of survival. Lewontin explains,

> Before the eighteenth century, European society placed little or no emphasis on the importance of the individual ... [P]eople were not free to move in the economic hierarchy. Peasants and lords alike had mutual obligations and were bound to each other by those obligations. There was no freely moving competitive labor force where each person had the power to sell his or her labor power in a labor market. These relations made it quite impossible to develop the kind of productive capitalism that marks our own era, in which freedom for individuals to move from place to place, from task to task, from status to status, to confront each other sometimes as tenants, sometimes as producers and sometimes as consumers, is an absolute necessity.[58]

Thus it is only when originally inescapable *external* restraints on the self's social-political-economic mobility disappear that the "individual's" *freedom* can appear. And as competition is a derivative of a free labour market, the self is automatically enlisted in a game of survival – a game that also demands that the self, as an "individual," seek out his heredity among the truths internal to him in order to realize his freedom. In a free social-political-economic market, the self's *internal* inventory is integral to his freedom to compete. That is because individualist freedom simply cannot tolerate the idea that what is internal to the self will threaten or undermine the freedom of other individuals. The active discovery of internal truths is itself an expression of the individual's freedom. So to say that an internal truth, even one that is a deterministic human biology, undermines freedom is to contradict the fundamentals of autonomy or the inward-turning motion upon which the self's understanding of himself as an "individual" depends. Thus, where heredity *is* understood to be a truth internal to the self, the excavation of this truth (regardless of any determinism it entails) not only avoids interference with the self's autonomy; it also acts as an expression of it. In other words, the self who succeeds in uncovering the internal truth that is manifested in the knowledge of his heredity more fully realizes his individuality.

The intersection of naturalism with individualism produces the modern experience of being "adopted" because it underlays or couples the "individual's" ability to exercise her freedom with a need to know and use her bio-genealogical knowledge. Where the appearance of the individual causes the self to look inward for truth, naturalism gives a direction to this motion that is relevant to being adopted because it emphasizes that a profound truth about the self, which is relevant to her individuality, as well as to her competitive success, lies in her heredity. Knowing this truth is an exercise of autonomy; knowing who and what the self is and has the potential to be, or to avert becoming, as an individual facilitates autonomy. Thus, in the context of individualist and naturalist discourse, the subjectivity of the individual who knows her bio-genealogy is differentiated from that of the individual who does not. In other words, if bio-genealogical knowledge is experienced by the self as a truth toward which the self must turn to realize her individuality, the adoptee is clearly going to experience the lack of this knowledge as a lack of a sense of herself as an "individual" and, ultimately, as a lack of a sense of identity.

Adoptee subjectivity is realized to the extent that individualism and naturalism also reinforce the superiority of the biological family. This is the case not only because the idea of bio-genealogical knowledge as a self-knowledge that is relevant to being an "individual" is a powerful endorsement of the biological family but also because the structure of the modern Western family itself is inseparable from individualism and naturalism. As Jon Bernardes explains, "'family ideology' requires and legitimates the inculcation of extreme individualism" because a group, like the family, "with an internally structured differentiation actually depends upon individualism to function as a group."[59] The ascriptions "father," "daughter," "mother," and "son" are necessarily individualized and naturalized locations, without which the structure of the modern (biological) family disappears. For Bernardes, this is the paradox of family ideology: the functioning of the family *group* is an individualistic affair. He also suggests that by emphasizing the child's need to grasp the concept of the "self" or "I," modern theories of child development generally insinuate tenets of individualism into the family; the concept "mine," a concept fundamental to individualistic notions of private property, ownership, and privacy, turns on the "self" or "I." Furthermore, he argues that the childrearing process is inscribed with the individualistic "spirit" of competition and achievement because, it seems, the child functions as the legacy of parental success and failure.[60]

Naturalism is intrinsic to the family, according to Bernardes, because "[t]he assertion of the biological bases of 'The Family' underpins the debates about the universality and functionality of 'The Family.'"[61] As a consequence, this basis facilitates state control of "individuals" through institutions like law, science, medicine, psychology, and social work that already tend toward a naturalist view of the family. The family functions as a social-political-economic mechanism for the control and regulation of individuals because relationships, alliances, and roles between individuals are determined by their biological relationships to one another. Incest laws are an obvious example of this reality. And, as Bernardes notes, women's roles are too. Women's roles in the family are designated in relation to their biological ability to give birth, for instance, where science and psychology argue that this ability underpins the uniquely female "maternal instinct."[62] Obviously, naturalist or causal explanations of mothering also call the feasibility of nonbiological families into question because implicit in the idea that family roles are naturally determined is the idea that nontraditional families are prone to being "problem" or abnormal families. As a result, state interventions in nontraditional families are made easier because they can be justified on the basis of a naturalized normal-abnormal dichotomy. And as interventions in these families, as compared to biological families, become more normalized, the social treatment of them as inferior is compounded.

The integral relationship between individualism, naturalism, and the belief in the superiority of the biological tie as a basis for family is also illustrated by Jacques Donzelot in *The Policing of Families*. He observes that in the eighteenth century the natural family was used by the state to support modern Western-European interests in production. The state imposed upon the family, specifically the mother, new responsibilities for the physical and social health of individuals. The state did so by supporting discourses that increasingly linked social order to the medical welfare of the biological family.[63] As a result, the social acceptance of women placing their children in the care of *other* people or wet nurses was diminished because it was treated as a threat that led to a "drifting social species."[64] Elisabeth Badinter corroborates this point. She employs her research on the historic use of wet nurses to challenge the modern concept of "mother love" – the idea that women's mothering of their biological children is both a good in itself and a natural inclination. Much like Donzelot, she argues that the role of the mother changed in the eighteenth century and that, as a result, women bore new responsibilities in relation to the *personal* management of their biological children's health and tutelage. Specifically, mothers who left the care of their children to wet nurses or servants began to be condemned socially.[65] As Donzelot notes, the event of discourses pertaining to social and medical welfare, especially as they impacted women, furthered the state's interests in production because they concurrently aided in the minimization of costs accrued in the care of the poor and unhealthy.[66] So as the state began to "intensify ... production to a maximum by restricting consumption," it arrived at the *biological family* as the answer to the question *Who is responsible for the needy?*[67] In this light, the biological tie is integral to the interests of the state as a mechanism that deflects away from governing powers their responsibilities for the individuals they nonetheless rely upon as producers.[68]

If Donzelot is right about the natural family's use in relation to new interests in production, a use that is facilitated through state-sanctioned discourses of social and medical welfare, it is not hard to imagine how this shift impacts the subjectivity of the modern "adoptee." Where the "individual" is freed from external restraints, his experience of being obligated to others (such as he was in a feudal system) is diminished, but so is his experience of others being obligated to him. In this naturalized state of freedom, therefore, the "natural" family is made responsible for the individual because the biological tie is interpreted to be one of the few tangible and immutable connections left between what are now free individuals. Put to such uses, the significance of the biological tie manifests in such a way that individuals without "natural" family cannot experience nonbiological connections to be nearly *as* tangible and immutable as, perhaps, they may have once been or as biological ties have become. Furthermore, in a context where the "natural" family is known to be the guarantor of the individual's health and education, the biological tie, or lack thereof, plays another role in that it functions as a measure against which the subjectivity of the individual is determined. Compared to the self who can lay claim to people who are responsible for him through the biological tie, the self who cannot do so is less of an "individual" because he is less "free" in certain ways. For instance, individuals without "natural" families are subject to more controls that are imposed by institutions like medicine, social welfare, and, of course, adoption. Furthermore, being an individual, as we have seen, depends on the self knowing himself or his bio-genealogy in order to fully realize his experience of autonomy. Thus the lack of the biological tie compromises the self's experience of himself as an individual both externally because it justifies more and different institutional controls over his person and internally because autonomy dictates that to know oneself is to know one's bio-genealogy. Where individualism and naturalism intersect with the biological family, therefore, they produce the modern adoptee's subjectivity because they produce conditions for being an individual that simply cannot be met by people who have little or no knowledge of their biological ties.

Ironically, however, the subjectivity of the individual is perhaps as dependent on the "adoptee" as it is on the biological tie. That is because the "adoptee" is much more than some inert effect of individualist and naturalist modes of knowledge. She is instead an active metaphor for the "individual." The adoptee's subjectivity, characterized by her proneness to the pathology of bio-genealogical alienation, functions as a warning and affirmation that to be fully an individual, to know oneself, is to bind oneself to the "natural" family. Therefore, she is also a touchstone, a foil, against which the current ontological status of the biological family is affirmed. At the same time that the individual is centre stage, modern Western culture is fascinated with themes of adoption, search, and reunion. For instance, thanks to Sigmund Freud, modern psychology has largely been founded upon the ultimate reunion story: the myth of Oedipus. Furthermore, search and reunion form an important and popular literary theme, one that Julie Shaffer discusses as the "*cri du sang* – the cry of blood that enabled unacquainted blood relatives to recognize their relationship."[69] For example, many influential works in the modern Western literary canon, such as Daniel Defoe's *Moll Flanders* (1722), Charles Dickens's *Oliver Twist* (1838), and Oscar Wilde's *The Importance of Being Earnest* (1895), involve protagonists who are reunited, often accidentally, with biological family members. In many such texts, the biological tie is a driving force behind the story. It is depicted as immutable, regardless of immense separations in time and space or whether its presence is consciously unknown; naturally or unconsciously, it draws relatives together by some inner compulsion. Even the monster in Mary Shelley's *Frankenstein*, an archetypal modern text, can be interpreted to reflect the concerns to which the adoptee *as such* gives rise. Consider the monster's greatest sorrow: "But where were my friends and relations? No father had watched my infant days, no mother had blessed me with smiles or caresses; or if they had, all my past life was now a blot, a blind vacancy in which I distinguished nothing. From my earliest remembrance I had been as I then was in height and proportion. I had never yet seen a being resembling me, or who claimed any intercourse with me. What was I? The question again recurred, to be answered only with groans."[70] The monster is very much like the biogenealogically alienated adoptee insofar as he too searches out Victor Frankenstein, his creator, as his "father" to glean some knowledge of origins that will provide him with some distinct sense of self.[71] And as a *monster*, he is, in a sense, an extreme manifestation of the fate that awaits those who lack biological ties.

The theme of search and reunion is also compelling as a *human* interest in contemporary film and media, one that is exemplified in the popular acclaim of films such as Mike Leigh's *Secrets & Lies* (1996), Chris Columbus's *Harry Potter and the Sorcerer's Stone* (2001), and Robert Altman's *Gosford Park* (2001). Search and reunion stories are also a frequent topic of television talk shows, the news, documentaries, and dramas. For instance, in *Adoption, Identity, and Kinship*, Katarina Wegar notes that of the family-related issues (i.e., abortion, pregnancy, divorce and separation, birth control, and infertility) discussed by American media in 1994, adoption was only less talked about than abortion and pregnancy.[72] The significance of this finding about the frequency of adoption as a topic is that the act of adoption occurs much less frequently than other family- and pregnancy-related events. Given that comparatively fewer people experience adoption personally, Wegar suggests that popular interest in

> the search serves as a compelling symbolic drama that both tests and clarifies their own, often unformulated questions concerning identity and the nature of family bonds. In a time of high divorce rates and unstable relationships, media stories about adoptees and birth parents in search of their unknown biological relatives might function to calm deeply harbored anxieties about the meaning and strength of the blood relation ... Popular culture depicts adoptees and their quest for genealogical knowledge as familiar yet different: adoption stories are compelling to the extent that the audience can identify with them.[73]

In effect, the desire to search confirms the superiority of the biological tie and the idea that identity turns on the self *knowing* its bio-genealogy. Thus it is not that nonadopted people identify with the adopted as such but that they identify with what the adopted's search and reunion stories affirm: bio-genealogical knowledge is essential to the self's identity. In other words, the adoptee's search simply embodies what "individuals" already take to be true; that is, the answer to the question "Who am I?" is "You are your bio-genealogy." The adoptee's search is familiar to nonadopted people simply because she too wants to answer the question "Who am I?" in the same way that they do.

Where the adoptee's search captures the popular imagination, she acts as the differentiated meaning that confirms it is the biological tie, as a conduit for a knowledge of self, that completes a person's sense of identity. However, the adoptee's anxiety over her identity also serves as a metaphor for the individual because her search is equally a search for internal truths – truths that not only promise to complete her sense of identity but also make the "individual's" experience of autonomy possible. Unlikely to be a mere coincidence, search and reunion discourse, as much as it is concerned with identity, is also brightly coloured with discourse that is characteristic of individualism. For instance, Florence Fisher, the founder of the Adoptee's Liberty Movement Association, argued in 1971 that adoptees should have political and individual "rights" to unfettered access to their origins – a notion that has been fundamental to the success of challenging laws or legal practices that entailed the sealing of adoptee birth records in North America.[74] Betty Jean Lifton, who was also a formidable figure in the adoption rights movement, characterizes search and reunion as a form of "liberation."[75] She writes that the search "is an act of will; a new dimension of experience. It is the quest for the intrinsic nature one was born with before it got twisted out of shape by secrecy and disavowal. It is a way of modifying the past, of living out the script that might have been. It is a way of taking control of one's own destiny, of seizing power. It is a way of finding oneself."[76] In this light, the adoptee's need to know her origins appears to be as much about an experience of individuality as it is about attaining a sense of identity. Of course, identity is arguably inseparable from individuality, at least in some Cartesian sense, in that the self experiences itself to be marked off and distinct from other selves and the world around it. Furthermore, Lifton seems to say that to know one's *"intrinsic nature"* is to know one's potential, or the self *"that might have been,"* and that this knowing is an exercise of autonomy insofar as it involves *"taking control of one's own destiny,"* all of which implies that the experience of individuality is central to identity. Thus, in her capacity as a kind of anti-individual, the adoptee and the institutions of knowledge that produce her play a reifying role in the subjectivity of the individual. Her pathology, her lack of identity, and her intrinsic need to search simply breathe more truth into the modern Western imperative that to know oneself is to know one's bio-genealogy.

Today, the confluence of individualism and naturalism continues to throw up an "individual" and family subject whose sense of identity as such is completed through her observance of a bio-genealogical imperative. Even though the landscape of family is changing in that "individuals" may not necessarily need to emerge from traditional, nuclear, monoracial, and bio-heteronormative families, this change has by no means displaced bio-genealogy, its experience, as the immutable source of self-knowledge and identity. In all likelihood, it has merely exacerbated its dominance as an imperative. For instance, the next chapter examines the impact of twin studies, genetics, and epigenetics on family discourse, but let us briefly consider here that advances in human genetic and genomic sciences are on a continuum with the past and that they effectively move contemporary culture to be more, not less, invested in bio-genealogical meanings of self and identity simply because fears about the decline of the nuclear family are on the rise. In effect, the trade in bio-genealogy as self-knowledge is scaling up because of the particular values our culture places on the "truths" these sciences "uncover": we are now "consuming genomes" from companies such as 23andMe and Navigenics, which peddle "direct-to-consumer (DTC) genetic testing for a variety of diseases and traits" despite these tests' "technical reliability [being] far more readily available than truth, owing to the inherent difficulty of tracing traits to genotypes in the highly variable human population."[77] Moreover, where genomics is distinguished from genetics historically because it is represented as a more "holistic" and "less reductionist" approach that both moves away from "'genetic determinism'" or "monogenetic causation" and moves toward "a 'systems' approach emphasizing the interplay of large numbers of genes" and "complex networks of gene regulation," the bio-genealogical imperative is not fundamentally altered within science and culture.[78] Its discursive project has merely adapted its bio-logic to encompass the genome, alongside the gene, heredity, and/or bloodlines, which is to say that the latter three do not play lesser roles in our imaginings of self, identity, and family. Genomics contours meanings of self now drawn from what was the Human Genome Project and what has become genomic science and research. In other words, the idea that "we will finally be able to know and explore ourselves" via the genome, as opposed to any other avenue of bio-genealogy, is not really a significant paradigm shift with respect to the formation of present-day "individuals" and "family" subjects.[79]

The genomic brand of naturalism also maps onto (neo)individualism very easily, both because of its metaphors and because of the ethical, social, political, and economic concerns it elicits. The Human Genome Project as a venture in "self-knowledge" production, from the outset, was also associated with "immense *power*" and "competition" even as it depended a good deal on "collaboration"; world leaders such as Bill Clinton and Tony Blair characterized what is arguably its individualistic promise as a "*map*" that grants us "the ability to read 'our own instruction book'" and as "'the working *blueprint* of the human race.'"[80] Since the completion of the Human Genome Project, genomics research has burgeoned along with ethical and legal questions surrounding its social, political, and economic purposes and utility. Genomics has as much to do with issues of property, capital, competition, and markets as it does health; the "[u]se of the information for the development of therapeutic and other products necessarily entails consideration of the complex issues of intellectual property (for example, patenting and licensing) and commercialization."[81] Genomics, therefore, is a naturalistic arm of individualism not only because of its utility as self-knowledge but also because it pivots on questions of rights and freedoms. For example, it is a potential threat to individuals' rights as an external barrier to freedom in the form of "genetic discrimination"; potential employers and insurance companies have obvious investments in genomic self-knowledge as risk (i.e., disease) against which employability and insurability could be measured.[82] As a question of self-knowledge, property, rights, and freedom or discrimination, genomic naturalism is a mode of individualism that reproduces the bio-genealogical imperative; it is an affirmation of the individual's need for bio-genealogy to rule out risk, to lay claims to rights, and to be better able to compete. As a result, it further reproduces the adoptee's difference and inferiority; although adoptees can acquire it as readily as any bio-family subject, genomic self-knowledge is ambiguous, it is equivocal in the prediction of health and disease, and it does not determine the truth of causes, primarily because it is holistic or systems-based. As Christine Hauskeller puts it, "genomics seems to open up an unlimited horizon of vague knowledge about susceptibilities, as well as the potential need for individuals to constrain their behaviour to minimize risks. The uncertainty of genomic knowledge actually makes it more difficult to cope with."[83] It is only in conjunction with an individual's knowledge of her bio-family's history of lived health and illness that genomic susceptibilities come into focus not as sureties but as distinct possibilities. In effect, genomic self-knowledge is only one such kind of knowledge – a new one – among many extant kinds of bio-genealogical knowledge that continue to shape us as "family" subjects. As a result, its possession alone will not alleviate the individual's need or, therefore, the adoptee's desire for bio-genealogy because family discourse always places the adoptee at a distance from the biological family. Like genetics and epigenetics within the context of twin discourse, to which the next chapter turns, genomics compounds the formulation of bio-genealogy as an inherent need within all "family" subjects, a need that is further materialized through its differentiation and pathologization in adoptees.

4

Twin and Adoption Studies and What They Tell Us about "Family" Experience

In sum, we don't know who twins are or how twins happen. We only presume to know what they tell us about who *we* are.

Lawrence Wright, *Twins: And What They Tell Us about Who We Are*

The way twins differ from the rest of us, and the way they are treated as a result, may help them to think of themselves as a special unit. This could be the basis of a bond.

Peter Watson, *Twins*

In the modern Western context, twin and adoption studies are used by the human sciences to debate whether genes drive personality, experience, and, so too, familial ties. By examining behavioural geneticists', psychologists', and psychoanalysts' use of twins and adoptees in this debate, the discourse on biology to which their use gives rise is made apparent. This discourse, in turn, (re)produces the bio-genealogical imperative that I have argued (re)produces adoptee subjectivity. In other words, neither the twin nor the adoption study is merely an innocuous apparatus that facilitates the discovery of objective truths about the role of nature and nurture in human experience: the emergence of these studies is a social-political-historical event that in and of itself determines human experience. Lawrence Wright ruminates that "[t]wins pose questions we might not think to ask if we lived in a world without them. They are both an unsettling presence, because they undermine our sense of individual uniqueness, and a score-settling presence, because their mere existence allows us to test certain ideas about how we are the way we are."[1] In other words, the questions that the genetic similarity of twins is typically understood to raise about their own identities and bonds facilitate their discursive use or treatment as a standard of comparison for other *kinds* of ties. Much like "adoptees," therefore, "twins" function as a touchstone against which modern Western subjectivity is evaluated, constituted, and determined.[2] Furthermore, the events of both twin and adoption studies, and the discourses to which they give rise, are an instrument of the modern Western bio-genealogical imperative: they produce a limited and determined knowledge about biology or genetics *as* a necessary and indubitable human experience. As a result, the discourse on twins is germane to the adoptee's subjectivity even where it generally limits and determines modern Western subjectivity. That is because the modern idea of "twins" produces a perceived qualitative distinction between experiences that pertain to ties that are *more* or *less* biological. And through a concern with the "twin bond," the twin study constructs biology *as* an essential basis for familial *kinds* of bonds; this effect is reflected in the behavioural geneticist's and psychologist's belief that the experience of a bond is an inherited genetic predisposition *and* in the psychoanalyst's belief that these bonds are a psychic response to an environment of genetic similarity. In short, examining the debate surrounding twins and the twin bond exposes the sense in which the nature-nurture dichotomy itself generally serves and (re)produces the modern Western bio-genealogical imperative and thus the superiority of the biological tie.

Twins have a long history in mythology and philosophy, but in the late nineteenth century the meaning of being a "twin" changed because twins became a valuable "research tool."[3] The twin study had been invented and developed by Sir Francis Galton by 1875.[4] He published two works that addressed the scientific uses of twins: "The History of Twins, as a Criterion of the Relative Powers of Nature and Nurture" and *Inquiries into Human Faculty and Its Development*.[5] He correctly hypothesized that twins from the "same ovum," or identical twins (monozygotic, MZ), share a larger common genetic makeup than either nonidentical (dizygotic, DZ) twins or nontwin siblings (singletons).[6] Working with this assumption, he proposed that the study of monozygotic and dizygotic twins could be used to distinguish between inherited and environmental traits in individuals.[7] Since Galton, behavioural geneticists, psychologists, and psychoanalysts have drawn conclusions about nature and nurture in relation to the individual's personality, psychology, and relational bonds on the basis of twin research. Twins are used to determine any number of questions pertaining to human experience. For instance, twin studies claim to measure the origin of traits in individuals ranging from criminality to IQ to health to homosexuality to socio-economic status.[8]

Without delving too deeply into the science, we can see that the basic mechanics of twin studies have generally continued to adhere to Galton's model, which now forms the basis of behavioural genetics, or the "part of psychology built around the statistical comparison of identical and fraternal twins."[9] For instance, Elizabeth A. Stewart describes the *classic twin method* and the scientific value that is attributed to the use of reared-together identical and fraternal twins:

> [S]ince the heredity or genetic factors are the same or similar for monozygotic twins and different for dizygotic twins, the twin method is based on the proposition that one can distinguish the effects of heredity and environment by comparing these two types of twins. The classic twin method ... assumes that while heredity differs, the influences of the environment are the same or equal for the two types of twins. Thus any differences between monozygotic twins are due to environmental or at least non-genetic functions; the corollary to this is that the greater degree to which MZ twins resemble each other (in comparison with DZ twins) mirrors the impact of the hereditary contribution to any particular characteristic.[10]

Conclusions about heredity and environment are drawn, therefore, on the basis of correlations identified between the similarities and differences that occur among different types of twins; notably, Galton "invented the method of correlation" in 1888.[11] Correlations among reared-apart twins are also measured.[12] Indeed, in the context of behavioural genetics, the most compelling twin studies are those that link personality traits to heredity through the measurement of similarities that occur between people who share more or identical genes (DZ and MZ twins) but do not share an environment. These studies are further enhanced if and when they are compared and contrasted with studies of the similarities between people who share an environment but only some or no genes (DZ twins and adoptees).[13]

By no coincidence, the adoption study, a method also invented by Galton, plays an integral role in relation to twin studies.[14] As Wright explains, "adoption studies are a natural complement to twin studies, since the one investigates genetically unrelated people raised in the same environment, and the other examines genetically identical people raised in the same or (in the case of separated twins) different environments."[15] Where adoption and twin studies converge especially is in relation to twins reared apart because these twins are usually adoptees. Adoption studies are generally pertinent to twin studies too. In behavioural genetics, the adoption study is thought to allow the researcher to "separate the effects of heredity from those of the environment."[16] For instance, adoptee studies are used to examine the role of environment, as opposed to heredity, with regard to a range of traits. Specifically, adoptees are measured against their adopted nongenetic siblings. Similar or dissimilar IQs between nongenetic siblings imply a relationship between IQ and environment. Or the IQ of an adoptee can be measured against that of her adoptive parents *and* a sibling who is the biological child of those same parents: because both children share an environment, the degree to which the adoptee's IQ is unlike the IQ of her adoptive parents and their biological child is interpreted to speak of genetic difference. A variation on the adoptee study is the "virtual twin" study; virtual twins can be two adopted children or an adoptee and a birth child who share the same parents and environment and are very close in age. As Nancy L. Segal explains in an interview, this type of adoption-twin study is thought to "give us a really pure estimate of the shared (home) environment."[17] Virtual twins' environmental experience is more twin-like than that of differently aged, genetically unrelated siblings, or so it is assumed, because development and the parenting style to which each virtual twin is subject are more simultaneous. But it is the study of reared-apart adoptee twins that is most significant. Identical twins are understood to be two people who are as genetically alike as is possible, and thus the study of identical twin adoptees is considered the most accurate test of genetically determined traits. Wherever significant similarities occur between reared-apart identical twins, they are attributed to genetics, whereas differences are attributed to the environment.[18]

If we put aside the basic mechanics of twin and adoptee studies, what is eventful in Galton's invention of the twin study is the unique meaning of sameness that it confers upon the twin and the biological tie that she represents in the modern Western context. For instance, Peter Watson observes that the concern with twins' *similarities* is a recent social and scientific phenomenon that occurs when Galton turns his attention to twins primarily as scientific tools.[19] Prior to the nineteenth century, religious and cultural beliefs about twins more often revolved around a concept of *difference* largely because they were looked upon either as inherently different from each other and/or as inherently different from singletons.[20] For instance, compared with the human sciences' view of twins *as* similarity, wherein, as we shall see, their relationships are treated as symbiotic, twins in mythology and the Bible connote difference because they are associated with the idea of *conflict*.[21] In both the Roman legend of Romulus and Remus and the biblical story of Esau and Jacob, twins serve *as* difference because these stories tell of struggle between a good and a bad twin. Abandoned at birth, adopted, and raised by wolves, Romulus and Remus quarrel so fiercely about where the city that becomes Rome will be built that Romulus murders his twin, founding the city in his own name. And Jacob, who loses his birthright to Esau in the womb because he is the second born, later deceives his father into giving him that birthright over his elder twin by disguising himself as Esau.[22]

Various premodern, religious, and cultural beliefs about twins have also signified their difference *as* good or bad omens. According to many cultural superstitions, the birth of twins is considered a bad omen – one that has justified the killing of one or both twins and sometimes their mother. This belief has operated in parts of Asia, Africa, and Australia, where twins were thought to be signs of either a woman's infidelity or her impregnation by an evil spirit.[23] Conversely, Stewart observes that twins have signified rain and fertility, such as among the Mohave and Yuman tribes of North America.[24] In other instances, twins have represented difference in that they have been regarded as subhuman beings or evolutionary throwbacks akin to the idea of "the litters of lower animals."[25] These examples show that twins have a history of functioning *as* difference. The fantastic meanings with which twins are historically associated outside the modern Western context place them at a distance from the meaning of the singleton birth, with which no comparable associations are made. So even though twins have a long history as a social-political-historical object of concern, the idea of sameness that currently enframes their existence and experience is a relatively new event.

Although they remain a unique phenomenon in the modern Western period, the concern with twins changes in that they come to be thought of as a powerful resource, one that begins to determine, even as it might clarify, the meaning of human experience, relationships, and personality insofar as these things are understood to be dependent on genetic similarity between selves.[26] In effect, Galton's invention of the twin study initiates a discourse about the possibility of certain experiences of similarity between selves being commensurate with the degree of biology they share.[27] He produces conditions of knowledge wherein shared heredity means shared experience, conditions that facilitate the modern Western view of biology as a basis for a special bond. Today, behavioural geneticists assert that a "trait" refers not simply to a genetic predisposition toward physical attributes or diseases but also to a genetic predisposition toward types of experience.[28] On this view, individuals with the same genes are prone to share traits and thus experiences, whereas people with different genes are prone to different traits and experiences. In fact, behavioural genetics contends that the most important part of each individual's character, interests, psychology, personality, and relationships is rooted in one's genes. Thus, as psychology and personality traits are thought to determine the outcome of human relations, the success or failure of ties between selves is accepted as heritable in a profound sense. Given their identical genes, monozygotic twins function as the ultimate litmus test for the role that biology plays in experience, including the experience of familial ties between self and other.[29]

The role of twin studies in determining the boundaries of experience with regard to *kinds* of familial experience is illustrated by behavioural geneticist Thomas J. Bouchard Jr's claims about adoptive ties – claims that are deemed credible because they are founded upon the science of his famous and ongoing work in the Minnesota Study of Twins Reared Apart.[30] For instance, he argues that ultimately "heredity tends to predominate over environment" and that people with common genes do share more in terms of mannerisms, personality, IQ, psychology, and experience than those with common environments but unrelated genes.[31] He further claims that exclusive to each family is a "biological milieu" that is produced and circumscribed by genes.[32] He also arrives at the idea that adoptees and adoptive parents cannot be encompassed by such a milieu because they lack the genetic similarity that makes this encompassing possible. Therefore, as a propensity for similarity is lacking in adoptive families because adoptive parents and adoptees have different genes, the adoptee's experience of family ties is essentially different from that of biological children. At an ontological level, therefore, the adoptee's experience of family ties is treated as though it were inevitably different from that of the biological child because her dissimilar genes break "up a kind of biological system" that otherwise is the (biological) family.[33] Although Bouchard Jr makes no overt value judgment about adoption as a family form per se, he concludes that the adoptee's *difference* from biological children is inescapable, even where the adoptee has no knowledge of being adopted. In a fashion, Segal, who was a collaborator on Bouchard Jr's Minnesota Study of Twins Reared Apart, reiterates this idea. She does so, perhaps inadvertently, when she says that "in virtually every adoption study I've looked at in which parents have a biological child and an adopted child, the adopted child has a lower IQ."[34] She goes on to say that this is the case in spite of the fact that "adoptive children are wanted children" and the fact that "research shows greater maternal warmth toward, and emotional involvement with, adopted children than naturally conceived children."[35] Minimally, what is implied by Segal's pairing of questions about IQ with questions of adoptive maternal love is that no amount of adoptive, familial love and warmth can make up for the biological tie's lack. The nature of adoption is identical, therefore, with difference because, inherently, the adoptee's genes are unlike those of her adoptive family. She is genetically incapable of sharing in a particular *kind* of familial experience – one of sameness or similarity – because this experience is embedded solely in the presence of similar genes and ultimately in the presence of biological family ties. So where the twin study underpins determinations about the ontological status of the "biological" child *as* a kind of sameness that is genetically determined, it simultaneously determines the "adoptee's" ontological status *as* a kind of difference.

Given the significance of reared-apart twins, twin studies can also be understood to inadvertently determine kinds of bonds or familial experience to the extent that they neglect adoption as a force that produces the experience of many twins. Obviously, "twins" are the subjects of studies on reared-apart twins, but reared-apart twins usually are "adoptees" too. Still, twin experts pay little or no attention to the role that reared-apart twins' adoptions may play in producing their shared experience. Instead, the studies on reared-apart twins consider only the implications of the twins' similar experiences in relation to either the environmental or genetic impact of their being twins. Thus these studies' conclusions are already predeterminations of their hypotheses; the hypothesis that genetic similarity gives rise to similar experience functions not simply as a prediction but also as an edict because "twinship" is the sole grid of interpretation through which the shared experience of twins, regardless of their adoptions, is interpreted.

Consider that in 1960 Peter Neubauer, a prominent psychoanalyst and past director of the Freud Archives, began a long-term study of identical infant twins (Amy and Beth) who were reared apart in significantly different adoptive homes. As Wright notes, however, a full account of the study has not been published because there were some questions about Neubauer's ethics.[36] Still, what is known about it retains importance because although other kinds of studies on reared-apart twins had occurred since 1922, Neubauer's study was the first to look at families that each had an adopted twin with no knowledge of the other twin during childhood and into adulthood, if at all.[37] Prior to Neubauer, these studies had looked only at twins raised in extended family units, separated twins who nonetheless knew of each other, and twins who were reunited before a study began.

On the basis of psychoanalysis, Neubauer hypothesized that the identity development of twins reared together is hindered because the presence of a twin, as opposed to a singleton sibling, can interfere with identification – a process that is said to underpin the normal individuation and separation of self. In line with this assumption, he also proposed that when twins are adopted, they *should* be raised apart without any knowledge of each other precisely to prevent such problems.[38] So as Amy and Beth grew up in different homes, Neubauer predicted they would develop distinct personalities regardless of the fact that they, as identical twins, were two people who were as genetically alike as is possible.

Contrary to his nurture hypothesis, however, Neubauer's findings ultimately appeared to side with nature in that Amy and Beth, although reared apart, shared strangely similar psychological profiles. For instance, as Judith Rich Harris explains, Neubauer's study indicated that "Amy's [adoptive] parents regarded her as a disappointment."[39] They valued education a great deal, but as Amy had a learning disability, their aspirations and appreciation for her were diminished. Amy was also found to have been rejected by her parents in favour of a brother, and the environment she was brought up in was generally cold and unsupportive. In contrast, Beth was found to be "her mother's favorite," and although she developed the same learning disability as Amy, her parents, very little concerned with academic achievement, remained "empathic, open, and cheerful" toward her throughout her childhood.[40] But given the striking differences in their familial environments, it was odd that Amy and Beth still shared so many important psychic similarities. As Wright tells the story,

> In nearly every respect ... Beth's personality followed in lockstep with Amy's dismal development. Thumb-sucking, nail-biting, blanket-clenching, and bed-wetting characterized her infancy and early childhood. She became a hypochondriac and, like Amy, was afraid of the dark and of being left alone. She, too, became lost in role-playing, and the artificial nature of her personality was, if anything, more pronounced than Amy's ... [O]n psychological tests she gave vent to a longing for maternal affection that was eerily the same as her identical sister's.[41]

Therefore, Neubauer's results implied that the genetic similarity between Amy and Beth determined the personality traits they had in common. Certainly, within the context of behavioural genetics, the fact that Neubauer's nurture hypothesis was contradicted by his findings is treated as a compelling proof that personality and experience are driven by genes.[42] And as Harris reports, even Neubauer gave a nod to behavioural geneticists when he later "admitted that if he had seen only one of them it would have been easy to fetch up some explanation in terms of the family environment."[43] So as Neubauer's study showed that these twins grew up in different environments *and* shared matching symptoms, this finding was taken to mean *only* that their similar experiences and personality traits must be due to their matching genes.

Remarkably, neither Wright, Harris, nor seemingly Neubauer consider Amy's and Beth's symptoms in light of the fact that they are both adopted subjects; nor do studies of reared-apart twins do so in general. If we assume, then, that both children were aware of their adoptive status, each child was a self who interpreted herself and was interpreted by others to be "adopted."[44] So if adoption experts observe any number of the symptoms suffered by Amy and Beth in many adoptees, perhaps these symptoms should be considered by twin experts not only, if at all, in light of the twin's matching genes and different environments but also, or even solely, in light of their adoptions. For instance, as we have seen, adoption experts argue that the adoptee's desire to search for her biological parents is motivated precisely by *a longing for maternal affection* – a longing that is said to be quelled only when biological ties between mother and child are present. Perhaps therefore all that is *eerily similar* about this symptom in Amy and Beth is the extent to which their experiences echo what the human sciences identify and arguably produce as the adoptee experience of loss, loneliness, and grief due to the discourse of bio-genealogical alienation.[45] Apart from the correlation of their psychological profiles with their matching genes, rather than with their environments, which arguably only appear to be completely different, there is a correlation between Amy and Beth *being* "adopted" and therefore being bio-genealogically alienated or troubled *as* adopted subjects within a social-political-historical context that devalues their adoptive ties. In other words, twin experts seem to be selective about the correlations they will contemplate or to which they are liable to grant meaning.

Furthermore, physical symptoms such as enuresis, perhaps due to genetics in some cases, are associated with the psychic impact of traumatic experiences or posttraumatic stress in other cases.[46] It is often "expected" in relation to adoption.[47] For instance, enuresis as an "unconscious conflict" is treated as an issue that adoptees and foster children may face.[48] So correlating it with Amy's and Beth's adoptions is as likely to point at the cause of such a symptom as is the correlation made between it and their genes. And given that adoption and adoption revelation are constituted as trauma in this social-political-historical context, "adopted" children will develop physiological symptoms of trauma, which is not to say that they are excluded from other traumatic experiences or losses not normally associated with adoption but that, as they are known and know themselves to be "adoptees," *adoption trauma* will be a, or the, central lens through which their experiences are and will be read. In other words, where Amy's and Beth's matching symptoms are accompanied by their knowledge of adoption, this knowledge may provoke real sensations in the body. Thus their shared symptoms need not originate in their matching genes. As Michel Foucault suggests, knowledge or "power relations can materially penetrate the body in depth, without depending even on the mediation of the subject's own representations."[49] As a result, even if the adopted self resists the *knowledge* of her adoption, she remains subject to its power relations when she thinks of herself as adopted or when her parents, the institution of adoption, or anyone else exercises the knowledge of her adoption over her by means, for instance, of adoption revelation. In short, she cannot totally efface her subjectivity as an "adoptee" in a modern Western family context that does and will not recognize her as a "biological" child. Thus Amy and Beth may be prone to many matching symptoms associated not with matching genes but with the effects of being socially, politically, and historically constituted as "adoptees." Indeed, as "adoptees" *or* "twins," Amy's and Beth's similar symptomologies are as likely to mean *adoption* as *genes*: twin *and* adoption experts can easily read them as meaning either one in a social-political-historical context that is overdetermined discursively to read twins, adoptees, and twins separated and adopted at birth in these ways.

Ultimately, it is irrelevant *within the context of the human sciences* whether the origins of Amy's and Beth's matching symptoms are assigned to "twinship" or "adoption" or both. Simply, where the human sciences address twins and adoptees, their investigations are already informed by the modern Western bio-genealogical imperative. In other words, the adoption expert's claim that because adoptees are bio-genealogically alienated they are prone to experiences of trauma is coextensive with the twin expert's claim that because twins have matching genes they are prone to matching experiences. These two views essentially reflect each other because they locate both the adoptee's and twin's experiences in the biological tie. At a fundamental level, the only difference between each claim is that the experience that is shared by adoptees is said to be the result of the *lack* of the biological tie, whereas that which is shared by twins is said to be due to its *presence*. But either way, both discourses locate the origins of personality, identity, and experience in a relation with biology that is causal. As a result, twin discourse does not simply complement adoption discourse but also actively reinforces it and vice versa.

The interplay between twin discourse and adoption discourse in maintaining the superiority of the biological tie, however, is most pronounced in the concern with what is known as the "twin" or "twinning bond" – a special relationship that is thought to occur primarily between identical twins.[50] Although there is debate over the origins of the twin bond, its existence is not largely contested. The main question is whether the origins of the bond lie in the genetic material or in the environment that twins share. For instance, Barbara Schave and Janet Ciriello describe the twin bond and the questions it raises concerning the nature-nurture debate:

The twinning bond has been described as a psychological thread between twins. It may manifest itself as a similar response to the environment and may include a heightened sense of telepathy or extrasensory perception. An accurate description of the twinning bond necessarily includes its development: Why do twins have a psychological thread that serves to connect them?

The most obvious reason for the existence of a bond between identical twins is their similar genetic and constitutional beginnings. Further, among identical and fraternal twins the impact of the environment and parental style serve to make their experiences very similar; thus their resultant responses are also very much alike. These genetic, constitutional and environmentally similar experiences serve to establish very early in the twins' lives what has come to be called the twinning bond.[51]

The twin bond can also be characterized by phenomena such as the development between twins of a private language, uncanny likenesses in character and lifestyle, and overwhelming feelings of attachment and deep loss brought on by twin separations and death regardless of age.[52] And although the literature on twins acknowledges that not all identical twins experience this bond, it warrants and receives serious investigation because a significant number of twins do.

Generally, the study of the twin bond is conducted from the two perspectives that speak to the nature-nurture dichotomy. Of course, the central question as it concerns nature is the extent to which the twin bond is due to the genes that twins have in common. As we have seen, behavioural geneticists and psychologists argue that twins' identical genes determine the psychic similarities between them. But they also argue that this genetically produced similarity is the basis for the *special bond* between twins. Here, then, studies that uncover uncanny similarities between reared-apart twins are interpreted to suggest not only that genes produce common experiences but also that, by virtue of having so much experience in common, twins will be closer to one another than are people with fewer experiences or genes in common. So if the twin bond were not genetic, twins reared apart should experience little or no psychic similarity nor any special affinity toward each other. Yet important studies like the Minnesota Study of Twins Reared Apart do seem to show that reared-apart twins, upon the discovery of each other, do share unusual psychic similarities and are magnetically drawn to each other following their adoption reunions.[53] All of this implies that the twin bond is the result of twins' common genetic material.

With regard to nurture, the question surrounding the twin bond is the extent to which the twin bond is an environmental effect. For example, psychoanalysts focus on whether the twin bond is due to primary narcissism or "primitive identification," which in the context of the twin's environment pertains to how the presence of a twin can undermine the other twin's ability to identify normally with her parents.[54] On this view, each twin is susceptible to relating to her twin as a "surrogate symbiotic object."[55] The presence of a twin is said to impede the normal process of identification with the mother as the primary love object in each twin. Indeed, psychoanalysts suggest that the mother may sometimes be wholly rejected by the twins *as* a disturbance to their symbiotic relationship.[56] Where the mother is displaced by the other twin, the twin will fail to achieve "separation-individuation," which underpins the normal development of a fully separate sense of identity.[57] That is because the twin does not experience the pain and loss that singleton children experience in unavoidable separation from the mother. Therefore, the experience integral to separation-individuation is avoided by the twin because her twin is most likely present even when the mother is not. These environmental forces cause the twin bond, which can be "so satisfying and necessary that it excludes others and interferes with individual growth."[58]

The detrimental effects of the twin bond are that it can lead to pathological attachments and loneliness in twins, the experience of which will arise as twins begin to experience unavoidable separations from each other in adolescence and adulthood. For instance, a profound loneliness may be brought on by the marriage or death of a twin, one that may threaten the surviving twin's sense of self. As Elizabeth A. Bryan explains, a twin death "can undermine the survivor's basic sense of identity" because "[m]any twins have never even imagined, let alone risked, life without their twin. They assume they will share their old age together."[59] In such instances, the intensity of the twin bond is deemed to be an environmental barrier, one that earlier inhibited the mother-child bond that is necessary for otherwise normal development. In contrast to behavioural geneticists, therefore, psychoanalysts, like Neubauer, will use the study of reared-apart twins to test whether psychic abnormalities arising from the twin bond can be averted when twins are reared apart and, if so, what this possibility implies about the relationship between environment and personality. If abnormalities are averted among reared-apart twins, the twin bond is assumed to be an environmental effect – one that arises solely out of each twin's physical proximity to the other.

Needless to say, within the context of the human sciences, the nature perspective of the twin bond is treated as though it is opposed to that of nurture. This is not to say that behavioural geneticists and psychologists who attribute the twin bond to nature do not acknowledge nurture's role in personality at all or vice versa. For instance, as Harris explains, even behavioural geneticists claim that the average correlation for similarity in personality traits among reared-together monozygotic twins is only 0.50; and their *differences*, it is conceded, are due to the environment.[60] And behavioural geneticists do struggle with the observation that if experience is genetically determined, the correlation for personality and experience between identical twins, because they have identical genes, should be much higher than 0.50.[61] Nonetheless, behavioural geneticists attribute the *cause* of the twin bond itself precisely to nature, whereas environmental psychologists, if you will, attribute the *cause* of the bond itself specifically to nurture. For the behavioural geneticist, nurture in and of itself, although it may contribute to personality and experience, is not sufficient as a *cause* of the twin bond. Matching genes, or matching genetic tendencies toward certain types of experience, are necessary even if it is acknowledged that nurture does complement nature. For example, if parents dress and treat twins as though they are alike, this shared environment merely reinforces an already genetically determined experience of similarity; treating two singleton children in this manner would not produce the degree of likeness in personality and experience that makes the twin bond possible. Thus, in children with different genes, the same environment is as likely to give rise to different experiences because inherent in the difference of genes are different responses to, and thus experiences of, the same stimuli. For instance, behavioural geneticists believe that this fact explains why nonidentical twins and singleton siblings who share the same environment, but fewer genes, have fewer experiences and traits in common than identical twins who also share an environment.[62] In response to the behavioural geneticist, however, the psychoanalyst might suggest that the visceral similarity between identical twins is a significant factor in creating an environment of similarity that makes the twin bond possible. Thus nonidentical twins or singleton children growing up together in the same family are not sufficient as an environmental point of comparison. For example, the visceral differences in the latter case might mean not only that nonidentical twins and singletons will be treated differently, albeit in the same environment, but also that they are less prone to the narcissism that undermines separation-individuation in identical twins.

Still, the human sciences' generalized focus on the twin bond is arguably more significant than the internal debate about either the bond's nature or nurture, for regardless of the debate, the fact that the bond in and of itself is a central focus suggests that among the individual human sciences there is nonetheless a pervasive investment in the presence of the biological tie. It is also as a result of this focus that twin discourse can be said to play a role in producing the subjectivity of the adoptee and/or in making the experience of adoptive ties inferior. In effect, the nature *and* nurture discourse surrounding the twin bond is very much like that surrounding adoption in that it reinforces the bio-genealogical imperative, which constitutes the biological family bond as superior in the modern Western context. Quite simply, immanent throughout twin discourse is the idea that biological similarity must be *present* for a qualitatively different bond to exist between two or more individuals. From the view of nature and nurture, the twin bond is unique to twins *as* individuals who share more genetic similarity than nonidentical twins, singleton siblings, or individuals who share no genetic ties. So although there is some debate concerning the kind of *cause* genetic similarity is, it nonetheless functions to cause the same *kind* of bond between biological family members insofar as the *presence* of genetic similarity is always essential to the bond. Regardless of nature or nurture, the basic assumption embedded in twin and, by extension, adoption and family discourse is that *the more alike individuals are genetically, the more they will share psychically and experientially and thus the greater their propensity will be to bond with one another*. Moreover, within twin and adoption studies that, in their turn, feed twin, adoption, and family discourses, the uncritical operation of this assumption, via its inversion – *the less alike individuals are genetically, the less they will share psychically and experientially and thus the lesser their propensity will be to bond with one another* – automatically elicits a meaning of inferiority for adoptive ties.

For instance, although it is true that twin experts examine the twin bond as an "abnormal" bond, the social intrigue with the abnormality of this bond is very interesting in the ways that it parallels the social intrigue with (the normality of) the adoptee who searches and wants to be or is reunited with her birth family. Twins who claim to be very different are like adoptees who claim to have no desire to search: both are regarded as more uncommon and not quite believ-

able compared to twins who claim to be very much alike and
adoptees who desire to search. Indeed, *there are* identical twins who
purport to be very different from one another, as Barbara Klein's
most recent works, *Alone in the Mirror* and *Not All Twins Are Alike*,
suggest. *Alone in the Mirror* examines "twins themselves who are on
the opposite side of 'public opinion'" because they claim to be different, and it admonishes behavioural geneticists because they "are
another source of humiliation that is possibly equally as demeaning
to twins who struggle to find and define themselves as unique individuals."[63] It also challenges twin experts who would normally
appear to side with nurture: Klein argues that "research psychologists
are so invested in the genetic determinants of life that they are blind-
ed to the real-life emotional issues of being a twin" – for instance,
insofar as being a twin, although not perceived as such, can and does
pertain to being different.[64] Moreover, in *Not All Twins Are Alike*,
which presents the results of a study of thirty pairs of twins, Klein
offers the "unique perspective" that "twins are distinct individuals."[65]
She argues that "[t]wins long to have their own 'perfect' identity separate from their co-twin," which is a complicated objective because a
twin's "search for self is overdetermined by the reality of twinship"; it
is undermined by characterizations of twinship "as the ideal intimate
relationship," one that treats twins as a unit, a pair, or two parts of a
whole, instead of as individuals.[66] Although Klein's theoretical position is at odds with my own because it is more or less psychoanalytic (i.e., I argue that psychoanalytic identity theories conform with the
bio-genealogical imperative), the impetus behind her books (i.e., to
show that identical twins are not the same) is very instructive: it
demonstrates that as objects of scientific and popular intrigue, twins
are pressured discursively *to be* the same, even if abnormally so,
because human science and culture are so deeply invested in only
particular meanings being attached to (identical) genes, or genetic
similarity, as determinants of self, identity, and bonding. From my
perspective, the social provocation behind her work is evidence, at
least, of a *will to sameness* being imposed on twins, and by extension
on biological family members, in spite of their differences, the flipside of which is the *will to difference* that, in spite of likenesses, is
imposed on adoptees within their adoptive families and culture at
large. The intensity of scientific and popular interest in the abnormality of twins' bonds and the normality of the adoptee's desire to
search is fuelled by the social-political-historical function of each as

a foil against which people with profound investments in the biological tie reinforce it as the superior basis for a bond.

From the perspective of nature, twin experts assume that the existence of a high density of genetic similarity in and of itself creates the
basis for mutual understanding and experience because having the
same genes means that twins are hardwired for similar experiences.
Thus, where uncanny likenesses in character, personality, lifestyle, and
preferences – ranging from attire to hobbies – are found to exist
between reunited reared-apart twins, behavioural geneticists will
argue that these likenesses are due to matching genes.[67] The biological bias of this view, therefore, is that as genetic similarity is the causal
basis for similar experience and thus the twin bond, individuals who
lack this degree of similarity cannot experience this bond, at least not
to the same degree or with the same intensity.

From the perspective of nurture, twin experts assume that the environmental presence of so much genetic similarity between twins
accounts for the twin bond in a different sense. As we have seen, twins'
psyches match insofar as each twin functions as the other's symbiotic
object or is undistinguished as separate and distinct from the twin's
self. Thus genetic similarity increases the likelihood, intensity, and
complexity of non-separation-individuation and narcissism, thereby
determining the self's psychological development. For twins, the possibility for a highly reciprocal experience of sameness is created environmentally because their biological similarity is highly and mutually tangible, which increases the shared and reifying experience of self
as other. For instance, these environmental circumstances could
explain why identical twins, during the course of "language acquisition," often use what is known as "twin language"; twins may use "me"
to refer to oneself and one's twin, or they may use "we" in place of
"me" to refer to oneself.[68] It might also explain a recent study of other-
sibling variance in twins' environments, which "found that twin pairs
who didn't have an older sibling, who showed frequent nonverbal
play and who didn't attend preschool were more likely to have a twin
language" as an alternate side of the same coin.[69] And beyond questions of language, for example, it could account for why twins who
lose a twin through separation or death suffer higher rates of "psychiatric morbidity" than singletons who lose either a parent or sibling.[70]
A surviving twin's susceptibility to a heightened sense of loss might
signal that losing one's twin, as opposed to one's singleton sibling, is
experienced more fully as a loss of self because the twin bond, as psy-

choanalysts argue, is the result of "only partial differentiation of their ego structures," which are environmentally determined.[71]

Furthermore, the revival of primary narcissism that the twin bond is said to entail can be intensified by the ways that twins provoke similar responses to their genetic similarity on the part of others in their environment. Thus twins' environments react similarly to their genetic similarity and thereby grant them the same experiences. This situation means that, contrary to nature arguments, twins are not genetically preprogrammed to experience their environments similarly. Instead, they have similar experiences because they are raised in similar environments and are externally acted upon equally – for example, by what Schave and Ciriello call a similar "parental style."[72] In other words, since twins are more often treated as though they are the same, they become more alike than individuals who are more often treated as though they are not the same.[73] The unique bond between twins is rooted in their shared treatment, which in turn elicits their shared experience and further enables them to over- and interidentify with each other. And where twins are reared apart, they may still be treated the same insofar as their genetic similarity, reflected as it is in their physical appearance, can elicit the same treatment even in different environments. For instance, Harris observes that there is evidence to suggest that children are treated better or worse depending on their looks; therefore, since identical twins look the same, they will elicit the same treatment, in many important respects, due to their looks regardless of being raised in different families.[74]

However, in the context of nurture, as in the context of nature, the condition for the possibility of the twin bond is still genetic similarity. Therefore, nurture arguments participate in nature's discourse because they accept the idea that twin bonds occur *only* in conjunction with genetic similarity – for instance, as opposed to any other sort of similarity that is not genetic. The only difference is that in nurture arguments the twin bond is usually based on the twin's *knowledge* and *experience* of her twin's genetic similarity, but the bond is still wholly determined by the *presence* of genetic similarity, just as it is in traditional nature arguments. So although genetic similarity does not determine twins' psychic likenesses in some sense that is genetically a priori, this symbiotic relationship is utterly and thus essentially *dependent* upon it, for it is solely the palpable experience of this particular *kind* of similarity that creates the possibility wherein the twin may experience a near total lack of difference between herself and her twin.[75] Thus a kind of argument from nature is implicit in nurture arguments about the twin bond. To the extent that neither perspective considers the possibility of twin-*like* bonds arising outside the *presence* of genetic similarity, nurture arguments simply are like nature arguments. Whether genetic similarity is treated solely as an extra-environmental cause of the bond or as the sole thing internal to the environment to which the psyche will respond by developing the bond, genetic similarity still functions categorically as a *necessary condition* for both the purported nature and nurture of the twin bond.[76] And as a necessary condition, genetic similarity can be only a natural condition because this *kind* of similarity is always and only the product of nature.

The significance of the nature bias in nurture arguments about twins is that it says something about what dominates the knowledge, and thus the experience, of biological bonds generally. Where nurture arguments accept nature or genetic similarity as the necessary (environmental) condition of the twin bond, they let slip their wider social-political-historical investment in the experience of family being one of sameness, a sameness that is coextensive solely with the *presence* of the biological tie. That the human sciences do not examine the extent to which the twin bond or an experience of similarity does occur in relation with or is founded upon genetic difference is arguably a glaring omission in the study of the phenomena of sameness in personality and experience.

In other words, it is possible for two individuals who share no genetic similarity to be very much alike in terms of connectedness, personality, and experience, or to share a twin-*like* bond. For instance, a close friend and I are constantly told by other friends, family members, and our respective romantic partners that we must be twins separated at birth because we are uncannily alike in terms of posture, attitude, personality, sense of humour, worldview, and taste. We have no genes in common, and we look nothing alike. She was born and spent her formative years in Newfoundland in a working-poor family, whereas I was born and raised in Toronto in an initially middle-class family. Still, we frequently finish each other's sentences, irritate our partners for similar reasons, and buy identical pairs of shoes or items of clothing when we shop apart. We also seem to have the extra-sensory ability to read each other's minds or know when something is wrong even when we are not in touch. The point is that people do have profoundly similar experiences in the absence of genetic similarity all the time, but the implications of this occurrence with regard to what, *other* than natural and/or environmental genetic similarity, might cause this sameness do not meaningfully or ever capture the attention of the human sciences.

Twin and adoption studies focus only on correlations between similar experience and similar genes *or* similar environments. As Harris points out, "for the typical behavioral genetic study, only adoptees and twins need apply."[77] As a result, these studies do not look for or speak of correlations between people with deeply similar identities or experience and different genes if those genes also happen to mature in different environments. So even as the adoptee study might appear to measure the relation between genetic difference and similar experience, it still measures *only* the relation between a similar environment and shared experience. As a result, the supposed function of the adoptee study as the ideal differential control for the twin study is foiled by the extent to which it already serves the twin study's embedded bio-logic; the adoptee study is also based upon the assumption that *sameness manifests only out of sameness*, albeit the sameness of the environment as opposed to genes. In other words, subjects who share personality traits and experience are of interest *only* when they share genes and/or an environment. The question is why? Why is there little or no interest in conducting a twin-*like* study? Why not examine subjects who share no genes *and* no environment *but* do share experience and personality traits? Why is this not even an interesting question for the human sciences in this social-political-historical moment?

Remarkably, the twin-like portraiture of Quebec photographer François Brunelle in his collection *I'm Not a Look-Alike!* speaks to this question insofar as it focuses on unrelated doppelgänger pairs. The work "explore[s] the intimate relationship between subjects and how they approach their remarkably similar appearances" in spite of being (genetic) strangers.[78] The portraits, which also cross boundaries of gender and nation, are intriguing as visceral and uncanny illustrations of the idea that genetic difference is a real basis for profound similarities occurring between selves, even if modern and postmodern subjects are bio-normatively directed against such thought and experience. Although Brunelle's photographs bring the *physical* similarities of genetic strangers into relief, they are also emblematic of the idea that twin-*like* similarities and intimacies do occur between genetically different strangers, friends, and family members. They are also a reverse metaphor for the idea that genetic and environmental similarity is a basis for difference, which is what Klein's work on identical twins ultimately implies too. They can be interpreted to query the analytic inertia of human sciences that refuse to direct a critical lens toward a taken-for-granted equivalence between genetic similarity and socio-familial similarity and between genetic difference and socio-familial difference, an inertia that signifies the ongoing stability and operation of the bio-genealogical imperative. In effect, the fact that *twin-like* bonds can occur in conjunction with genetic difference suggests that we need to reconsider our investments in this imperative as the truth of our family bonds and identities.

Arguably, the reason that twin-like behaviour on the basis of *difference* is not theorized is that no hypothesis that explains it is currently available; and the hypotheses that are available, genetics and environment, do not apply or may conclude only that twin-*like* bonds are anomalies from the perspective of the established paradigms of sameness. This is also true of epigenetics, or "the missing third element, alongside nature and nurture," which has recently appeared as a new hypothesis and a possible third way in the research of twin experts; "epigenetics – meaning in Greek 'around the gene'" – is the study of how "genes [are] literally being switched on and off by a new mechanism," or a newly recognized mechanism, that allows genes to respond to their environments.[79] Essentially, epigenetics refers to the idea that environments can alter genes, that these alterations are heritable, and that genes, in later human generations, can reverse any alterations depending on subsequent environments. It encompasses the idea of "acquired inheritance" or "'soft-inheritance,'" which is a prior notion that, until very recently, was rejected by contemporary genetic science.[80] Historically, the idea is typically attributed to Jean-Baptiste Lamarck and, fifty years later, to Charles Darwin, who was "an admirer of Lamarck" and "accepted as possible" his idea; indeed, Darwin proposed a somewhat similar concept known as "pangenesis."[81] According to genetic epidemiologist and twin expert Tim Spector, who is the founder-director of Twins UK Registry (one of the world's largest), epigenetics challenges those who take "the gene-centric view of the universe for granted," as he once did, to rethink the nature-nurture debate.[82] It disrupts "[s]cientific dogma [that] has long stated that genes are fixed entities and cannot be changed," or the idea that genes are "immutable," "our 'blueprint,' the 'code of life,'" because it suggests that more impact should be attributed to environment as the stimulus for the activity of this genetic mechanism.[83] Conversely, it also challenges traditional epidemiologists "who study the environmental causes of disease" because it implies that more can be attributed to what is now perceived to be the active and no longer static nature of genes.[84]

According to Spector, epigenetics entails a paradigm shift that side-steps the nature-nurture debate because it makes the debate irrelevant: "There are few if any examples of environmental factors without a genetic component, and conversely genes don't work alone and are usually dependent on the cells they live in and their environments. So in a world where hundreds of genes are working together to influence a trait or disease, the old distinction between nature and nurture is simply no longer relevant."[85] Although Spector argues that epigenetics renders the nature-nurture debate irrelevant, I suggest on the contrary that his construal of epigenetics as a paradigmatic change really just conceals the debate, or more precisely its discursive effects, which nonetheless continue to operate in the service of the bio-genealogical imperative. Conventionally, the nature-nurture debate is a question of either/or, but in the context of epigenetics, as Spector depicts it, the question is newly framed as one that essentially takes a both/and per-spective wherein genes *and* environments, ultimately, are set up as the cause of traits, bonds, and identity. However, the apparent shift of twin experts like Spector away from an either/or approach that sided with nature over nurture and toward a both/and perspective that posits the influence of nature and nurture, which he claims renders the former debate irrelevant, is deceiving because the actual terms of the debate have not really changed but continue to remain in play. What has changed, merely, is the extent to which the same terms – genetics and environment – are considered to be more *or* less relevant by twin experts like Spector. This result is evident in the fact that even though the terms of relevance favoured by epigenetics may be different on some fronts compared to those favoured by traditional behavioural genetics, the concepts, practices, and tools of epigenetics, characterized as they are by Spector, have not changed much at all relative to behav-ioural genetics and research psychology: twin and adoption studies, given the biologic baggage they contain, along with the threats and promises of inheritance overall, continue to figure just as large. As a both/and position, epigenetics does not meaningfully transform the either/or nature-nurture debate into a novel debate or no debate but into a *more or less* version of the old debate (i.e., more genetics and less environment *or* more environment and less genetics), wherein what are now really just twin experts' *more or less* stances largely fall in line with the side they preferred in the old either/or debate.

Epigenetic both/and approaches to nature and nurture are also problematic in that epigenetic theory, metaphorically speaking, is really just a nature amalgam, wherein nature is the base alloy or stable pivot of (genetic) change and nurture is the capricious element of (genetic) change that, as such, is less easily understood and less reliably reproduced; irrepressible nurture stimulates an epistemic desire to direct attention back to nature, or the changeable but nonetheless predictable gene, as the more reliable, or more reliably understood, cause of traits, bonds, and identity. A case in point is a discussion of epigenetics and Bayesian learning models by Alison Gopnik wherein her goal is to reject notions of "innateness" outright. She argues that together epigenetic and Bayesian theories indicate "that almost everything we do is not just the result of the interaction of nature and nurture; it is both simultaneously. Nurture is our nature, and learning and culture are our most important and distinctive evolutionary inheritance."[86] However, there is something striking about her discourse in that it betrays her position: she appears to want to suggest that nature and nurture are mutually important forces, but her discourse inadvertently appropriates nurture within the logic of nature. It does so because she poses nurture *as* our nature, not the other way round, even though there are many good reasons to think, hard as it is, that nature really is our nurture. Without being too hard on Gopnik, to say or even think that "nature is our nurture" is (almost) nonsensical, but that it is nonsensical is precisely the point: it is a sign that our concepts of nurture, epistemologically speaking, are already dominated by the logic of nature within (and without) epigenetic thought. Ultimately, what poses more neutrally as the balance of a both/and position in epigenetic thought is just an adaptation of the bio-genealogical imperative.

To return to twins, the problem with these paradigms, if indeed they are distinct, is that none prove or negate the fact that the presence of environmental and genetic *difference* does not preclude the possibility of twin-*like* bonds occurring between genetic and/or environmental strangers. Indeed, that such bonds do occur, in and of itself, is an important critique because it raises questions about whether genetic and/or environmental *sameness* is a necessary condition for twin(-like) bonds at all. To be precise, if sameness is a false necessary condition for twin(-like) bonds, monolithic paradigms founded upon the assumption that genetic and/or environmental sameness *is* a necessary condition for twin(-like) bonds become highly problematic. This problem is especially significant in the context of this work because these are the paradigms that inform the experience of biological ties and hierarchically differentiate them from adoptive ties on the basis of the value attributed to the presence or absence of sameness.

Ultimately, I suspect the reason that difference is neglected as a possible basis for twin-*like* bonds is that the guiding principle of twin and adoption studies is informed by and serves the wider modern Western imperative discussed in chapter 1; explicit in the edict that to know yourself is to know your bio-genealogy is the further assumption that I know myself only in relation to that to which I am most similar. Perhaps that is why the twin study and its complement, the adoption study, can be shown to begin with the assumption that there is a necessary causal connection between similarity that occurs in the presence of similarity, be it genetic or environmental, but not between similarity that occurs in the presence of difference. And perhaps it is also precisely the reason why nature and nurture arguments that concern the twin bond can mutually be shown to assume that this unique bond occurs only in the *presence* of genetic similarity.

With this in mind, we can see that the wider social meaning of biology as the superior *kind* of familial bond is mirrored in the logic of both nature's and nurture's discourse on twins. For very much like the twin bond, the family bond is thought not to exist outside of the presence of genetic similarity.[87] The only difference between these two bonds, if there is one at all, is where each is located on a continuum of meaning that correlates the degree of genetic similarity with the degree of connection that is possible between individuals. For instance, the human sciences' juxtaposition of twin studies with adoption studies speaks to this continuum because it produces a spectrum wherein being bound as a twin is at one end and being bound as an adoptee is at the other. What this juxtaposition further implies about the meaning of bonds between these poles of the spectrum is simply that they too are distinguished relative to the presence of *more* or *less* genetic similarity. For example, "twin sister," "sister," "stepsister," and "adopted sister" all entail distinct meanings about bonds and thus about the kinds of experience and connection to which they are expected to give rise. If this were not the case, an unqualified "sister" would assuredly suffice as the signifier for all sisters. But imagine the chaos that would be created in relation to the experiences we currently have of bonds if the signifiers and therefore the meanings we give to them were changed. For instance, imagine how this change would alter the narrative of *Cinderella*, where the reader arguably depends on knowing that Cinderella's sisters are her paternal "stepsisters" in order to meaningfully reconcile both the evils they perpetrate against her and ultimately her complete rejection of them once she is married to the prince. If it were now a tale of evil "sisters," would Cinderella's desire to leave them behind without a second thought once married be so completely understandable? Or might she now as a "sister" be expected to turn the other cheek and love her "sisters" even in spite of not liking them? Food for thought.

The story of Cinderella makes sense because it reflects extant knowledge about what the presence of more or less biology means to experience. In the same fashion, the human sciences' fascination with the twin bond makes sense only because it reflects an existent social investment in the idea of the biological tie *as* a distinct and irreplaceable experience. This point, of course, is simply a variation on Foucault's ideas concerning the modern "objectivisation of sexuality," his argument being that "sexuality, through thus becoming an object of analysis and concern, surveillance and control, engenders at the same time an intensification of each individual's desire, for, in and over his body."[88] Like sexuality, the twin bond as an object of knowledge is a force, among others, that increases each individual's desire to experience the sameness of connection that the discourse on the twin bond, as the ultimate incarnation of the biological bond, promises. In contrast, the adoptee, as an object of that same knowledge, increases the desire not to experience the difference and lack of connection promised by adoption or the discourse on the lack of the biological bond.

Finally, there is simply no objective means by which to measure what are said to be essential and qualitative differences between *kinds* of bonds as conduits for experience. That is because the human sciences cannot make distinctions between kinds of bonds in the way that the natural sciences can measure differences between kinds of conductors of electricity (e.g., rubber as opposed to copper). For instance, claims about the twin bond or the adoptive tie being conduits for an experience of sameness or difference are based on a science of correlations that relies first on the reported experience of twins, adoptees, and their families (i.e., largely by means of questionnaires and interviews). These data are then merely correlated against the absence or presence of genetic similarity. So if the twin bond is *known* by twins *as* the conduit for their bond or if the adoptee *knows* her ties to be inferior at the same time that this knowledge produces that experience, the correlation between twins' or adoptees' reported experiences of their ties is not meaningful relative to the essential quality of their ties. The *subjectivity* of the twin or adoptee (or the singleton for that matter) cannot be a ground for *objective* truth claims about kinds of bonds if the knowledge of adoption and twinship that is inscribed upon "adoptees" and "twins" already obscures what is purported to be the essential nature of these bonds.[89] Imagine, then, that the nature of the twin bond and the adoptive tie is essentially and qualitatively the same but that the (*known*) experience of these ties by twins and adoptees is one of opposition because "twins" and "adoptees" and the experts attending to them *know* their ties to be diametrically opposed. The result is that their subjectivity is a testament only to the experience, not the nature, of their bonds. And, as long as the juxtaposition of the twin study with the adoption study depicts an adoptee experience that is in absolute contrast with an experience of twinship, a function of the event of twin and adoptee discourse is the production of a bio-hierarchy that debases the experience of adoptive ties.

5

Under the Influence of Psychoanalysis: Family Experience and Adoptee Subjectivity

I watched her thinking. Waited. "This just occurred to me," she said. "When your brother expresses pride in your intellect, pleasure about all the books in your house," she said, "he may be celebrating the achievements of his mirror image – the part of himself that is free of the burden of his disease. Do you think that's plausible?"

I shrugged. "Couldn't tell you."

"In a sense, as your identical twin, he is you and you are he. More than most siblings, you are each other. No?"

Wally Lamb, *I Know This Much Is True*

Dr Rubina Patel is a psychiatrist. Her client, Thomas Birdsey, is a paranoid schizophrenic and an identical twin. In Wally Lamb's popular novel *I Know This Much Is True*, Dr Patel asks her client's twin, Dominick Birdsey, to help her with respect to Thomas's treatment. She asks Dominick to give her an account of Thomas's childhood, which involves recounting abuses Thomas has suffered at the hands of their stepfather, Ray. Clearly, Dr Patel's approach is somewhat unorthodox. She turns to Dominick to understand and elucidate Thomas's childhood experience because Thomas's mental illness makes this knowledge and history inaccessible to him. The danger of Dr Patel's approach, of course, is that she runs a risk of treating Dominick's voice as one that is either commensurate with, or more accurate than, Thomas's voice with respect to the retelling of his childhood experience and self-knowledge. Yet Dr Patel's use of Dominick also makes a lot of sense with respect to a narcissistic popular imagination and twin discourse: as Thomas's twin, he is unlike other kinds of human beings in that his identical genes and the childhood environment he shared with Thomas constitute him as a unique, alternate hold for Thomas's self-knowledge and (childhood) experience.

Dr Patel, Thomas, and Dominick are all characters who are deeply engaged in (biological) narcissism, or the idea that, as twins, the two brothers are profoundly self-same. In her role as psychiatrist, Dr Patel is seduced by this idea, as evidenced in her unusual decision to use and, further, trust Dominick's memory as a kind of substitute for his brother's in order to better treat Thomas's mental illness. Thomas's engagement with this idea manifests, as Dr Patel suggests, in his attempt to hold onto his sanity by "celebrating the achievements of his mirror image," Dominick, whom he regards as "the part of himself that is free of the burden of his disease." Finally, Dominick's attraction to the idea is depicted by his terrible fear that the biology he shares with his brother also fates him to a future personal destiny of mental illness: "My old fear: that I was as weak as Thomas. That one day, I'd look in the mirror and see a crazy man: my brother, the scary guy."[1]

In many respects, it is the bio-narcissistic logic enlisted by Lamb's characters to understand their relationships, experiences, and circumstances that makes the novel a popular success; *I Know This Much Is True* reached number one on the *New York Times* best-seller list and was singled out as a must read by Oprah's Book Club. Bio-narcissism as the romanticism surrounding the intensity of the twin bond is a theme that engages and fascinates a large audience. Lamb's fiction captures the popular imagination because it effectively trades on the reader's readiness to understand or identify with the narcissistic experiences, assumptions, wishes, and fears of his characters about the nature of the twin bond and, therefore, biological ties.

Myths and stories about twins are popular because bio-narcissism is already a mode of being in modern Western culture; it is a central and common aspect of modern and postmodern Western experience. Furthermore, the logic of bio-narcissism and the bio-genealogical imperative are integral to each other because the idea that familial love is inherently predicated upon narcissism affirms the self's need to know the individuals it is most and least like. If we accept this idea as true, how does the modern Western self come to identify with experiences that are determined by the logic of what I call "bio-narcissism"?

One answer is that the experience of bio-narcissism is due to the influence of psychoanalysis: the intelligibility of psychoanalytic discourse that elicits a logic of the self-same, or narcissism, is realized through its emergence in a social, historical, and political context that is already permeated with individualist and naturalist discourses. As psychoanalysis gains influence, narcissism becomes a key component of the human psyche and family relations. In effect, psychoanalysis produces the self's love of the self-same when it "discovers," in the myth of Narcissus, the universality of narcissism; the existence of the Ancient Greek myth functions as evidence that narcissism is a timeless attribute of the human psyche. Although the myth might be evidence of narcissism's universality, I explore the alternate idea that the experience of narcissism is evidence of the pervasive influence of psychoanalysis: it is a sign that psychoanalysis has successfully imposed the knowledge of narcissism upon modern Western human experience.

On the surface, I focus in this chapter less on the explicit "problem of adoption" as a social and political question and more on the actual theory of psychoanalysis as a key rationality that makes adopted and biological family subjects intelligible as subjects who are at odds. I consider psychoanalysis, particularly its influence *via* the concept of narcissism, to be a central discursive field that inculcates in us, be it as moderns or postmoderns, our senses of ourselves, or the lack thereof, as *family*. To do so, I introduce the psychoanalytic concept of narcissism primarily to address the question of how psychoanalysis purportedly "discovers" and, thereby, determines what for too long has posed as the human psyche's inherent propensity for narcissism. I argue that psychoanalysis successfully maps out the phenomena of narcissism simply because it maps the conventional meaning of the myth of Narcissus *as* a love of the self-same *onto* human experience and attachment. Contrary to psychoanalytic theory, therefore, I do not assume that psychoanalysis actually "discovers" a genuinely universal truth about the human psyche when it concludes that human beings are prone to narcissism. Instead, through theoretical analogies, I show how the influence of psychoanalytic discourse institutes narcissism within us as a pervasive mode of family experience and desire. I consider how the influence of psychoanalysis is perpetuated by its advent within the modern Western context because the ground of that context has already been prepared by the logic of individualism and naturalism. Indeed, I suggest that the influence of psychoanalysis is propelled precisely by its share in this logic. I also examine how psychoanalysis garners objective truth status for its claim that the human psyche and, by implication, family relations are essentially narcissistic. With respect to adoptee subjectivity, I ultimately suggest that the critical accomplishment of psychoanalysis is that its role in the production of the modern Western self *as* a narcissistic subject further produces "family" experience as a mode of being that conflates love and intimacy with the presence or experience of (biological) sameness. In other words, the influence of psychoanalysis – the logic it has embedded in our onto-epistemologies of family bonds – plays a very important role in maintaining the bio-genealogical imperative.

In the modern Western context, psychoanalysis employs the conventional meaning that is drawn from the Ancient Greek myth of Narcissus: Narcissus dies at the edge of a pool because he suffers an overabundance of self-love. This meaning is the basis for Sigmund Freud's psychoanalytic concept of narcissism – a concept that enjoys great influence with respect to "family" psychologies, as evidenced by "twin" and "adoption" psychologies.[2] Narcissus's symbolic desire to form an exclusive bond with himself characterizes the original state of desire Freud claims is experienced by the human infant prior to its conscious realization that it is both absolutely dependent on and separate from its primary love object (mother). Unaware of its dependence and separateness, the infant is like Narcissus because it is completely consumed with itself, its own needs, and its own desires at the expense of all others.

In its simplest terms, the psychoanalytic concept of narcissism involves the idea that every child experiences a primary, infantile phase of self-love or concern in the normal development of an identity and/or an individual sense of separation.[3] Narcissism is also regarded by psychoanalysis as a "normal" part of all child development, as it pertains to the interdependent realization of both an identity and family bonds. A strong sense of identity depends on the family bond. The family is the context in which a normal sense of self or identity is developed through identification, which assumes an experience of (biological) sameness between the self and the other.[4] Furthermore, narcissism is central to the self's identity and experience of family ties at every stage of development, including adulthood, because it both underpins the psychic workings of the family romance and is the "precondition" of the Oedipal complex.[5] Moreover, narcissism does not merely affect a child's experience of "family" but also shapes a parent's experience of the child as "family." For example, Freud characterizes parental love as a form of self-love that is directed toward a self-same image that the child reflects back to the parent: "Parental love, which is so moving and at bottom so childish, is nothing but the parents' narcissism born again, which, transformed into object-love, unmistakably reveals its former nature."[6]

Narcissism, family experts suggest, can also play an important role in abnormalities associated with identity and/or "family" experience. For instance, when the primary narcissistic phase of a child is prolonged or prematurely shortened, it may lead to abnormal identity formations in the adult. As discussed in the previous chapter, twin experts often suggest that identity problems associated with the twin bond are the effect of a prolonged narcissistic phase, and adoption experts may attribute adoptee identity crises to an abnormally foreshortened narcissistic phase; these family experts may also use the concept of narcissism to explain how and why the twin bond achieves its intensity and the adoptee experiences a deep need to search for bio-genealogy.

Psychoanalysis, therefore, takes it for granted that the self is essentially narcissistic and that (family) intimacy and shared experience are intensified or diminished by narcissistic identifications or a lack thereof. Under the influence of psychoanalysis, many "family" psychologies take narcissism for granted, a truism that is clearly evidenced by the discourse surrounding "twins" and "adoptees." So how has psychoanalysis and, therefore, narcissism acquired this powerful position of influence over the psychology of the self, "family," "twin," and "adoptee"?

Unquestionably, psychoanalytic ideas about human psychology are part of our everyday language, and they actively influence our understandings of ourselves as human beings. According to Joseph Schwartz, psychoanalysis is "comparable to the theory of evolution in the controversy it has caused and continues to cause," and at the same time, it "informs part of our daily discourse in a way that evolution has never done."[7] Psychoanalysis permeates Western culture. Its associated "[t]erms such as unconscious, repressed, ego, ambivalent, complex, projection, denial and double-bind enter into conversations in every walk of life whenever people talk about mental states and the reasons for human actions."[8] Its reach is far beyond any select group of people who engage with it academically as a theory or medically and therapeutically as a psychology. It directly addresses "lay people" and popular culture because its assumptions and conclusions about human nature occur frequently in popular films, plays, poetry, and fiction, like that of Lamb.[9]

Popular interest in dream analysis is a powerful example of the widespread impact of psychoanalysis on people's everyday lives. Many lay people and mental health professionals believe that dreams are a reasonable source of symbolic meaning or truth about the self. They find meaning in their unconscious dream life that they assume has direct implications for the self in waking life.

The now popular idea that there is a "logic" embedded in dreams, or the unconscious, one that bears on conscious life and conveys empirical truths about the self, can be linked directly to psychoanalysis.[10] The "logic of the unconscious" with respect to dreams was first identified and examined by Freud in *The Interpretation of Dreams*: "[E]very dream reveals itself as a psychical structure which has a meaning and which can be inserted at an assignable point in the mental activities of waking life."[11] This idea initiated by Freud does not mean that dreams were never popularly regarded as meaningful prior to psychoanalysis; indeed, Freud observed that dream symbols and dream dictionaries had long existed and been used to predict future events.[12] The psychoanalytic approach to dream life is distinct, however, in that its location of logic in the unconscious establishes a previously irrational dream life within the realm of reason and, ultimately, science. It constitutes the dream as a source of objective truth about the self's quotidian psychic life, and it is this interpretation of the dream that continues to enjoy widespread popularity in the West today.

Although frequently unaware that the source of this idea is psychoanalysis, many people do regard the dream as containing truths that illuminate both conscious experience and often repressed childhood memories by means of association. The popular observance of the idea that the unconscious is intelligible in this manner demonstrates the influence of psychoanalysis on human subjectivity: insofar as the self knows and experiences itself through the logic of its unconscious dream life, psychoanalysis *is* effectively intrinsic to self-knowledge and experience.

Psychoanalysis, therefore, is not simply a theory of psychology. It is a basis upon which we understand ourselves, even when we have never read psychoanalytic theory or visited a psychoanalyst. Michel Foucault argues that it is a core aspect of modern subjectivity and experience. As John E. Toews explains, the ubiquity of psychoanalysis means that "the archaeology and genealogy of the modern subject could virtually be reformulated as the archaeology and genealogy of psychoanalysis."[13] To put it another way, psychoanalysis is a modern and, ultimately, contemporary state of being and experience. What, however, does that mean and how does psychoanalysis achieve this influence with respect to our experience generally or specifically as family subjects? It means that modern experience cannot be *had* "outside" of psychoanalysis because it cannot be *understood* outside of psychoanalysis, just as it cannot be had or understood outside of other formidable modes of knowledge, such as naturalism and individualism.[14] Thus psychoanalysis *alone* does not constitute subjectivity in the twentieth century; the subject is affected by any number of forces, which may compete, contradict, and/or cooperate with each other in a given social-political-historical moment. For instance, psychoanalysis's impact on the subject is facilitated precisely by its ability to work well with and through naturalism and individualism and vice versa. That, in part, explains how and why it is able to dominate the self and family experience so well. Nonetheless, the widespread influence of psychoanalysis with respect to the subject is also realized because so many of its key assumptions, such as those regarding the unconscious, ego, repression, and trauma, still serve as a foundation for contemporary and mainstream psychologies. Add to this state of affairs the fact that psychoanalysis is a mode of knowledge that takes the self within the family as its object, and we can begin to see why it is such a powerful force that effectively shapes multiform "family" subjects (e.g., as "twin," "adoptee," and/or "biological child").

The force of psychoanalysis is perpetuated by the social-political-historical context in which it emerged. At the end of the nineteenth century, the influence of naturalist and individualist discourse was already well established. In this context, psychoanalysis sprang forth, in part, because it shared in, and reiterated, the logic of individualism and naturalism. Consider, for instance, Christopher Badcock's observation that psychoanalysis is a "fundamentally individualistic approach to social psychology."[15] Consider also that much of the sense of psychoanalysis is realized through a dependence on the intersection of naturalism with individualism.[16] For example, in psychoanalysis the psychic self – comprised of the inner workings of the id, ego, and super-ego – which is what determines the individual's place in civilization, bears a striking resemblance both to Charles Darwin's notion of adaptation, or "survival of the fittest," and to the idea of the individual as a competitor in a free political and economic market. In psychoanalysis, the individual's ability to function or *succeed* in a social environment centres on the self's psychodynamics; the individual's psychic happiness is threatened, as is her viability as a full participant in civilization, whenever the ego fails to mediate properly between the competing demands of the id and super-ego.[17] The individual whose ego cannot restrain the id or meet the appropriate demands of the super-ego cannot participate fully in civilization because she will fail to sublimate enough libidinal energy for the purposes of work; and work, for Freud, is core to an individual's successful participation in civilization.[18] The logic of psychoanalysis, naturalism, and individualism, therefore, is alike: naturalism understands a maladaptive biological inheritance to hamper the success of an organism, such as man, in nature; individualism understands what amounts to a maladaptive (bio-genealogical) self-knowledge to impede the individual's autonomy and, therefore, social, political, and economic success; and psychoanalysis understands the maladaptive psyche to impede the individual's success in civilization.

Psychoanalysis, therefore, obtains its influence over modern subjectivity by sharing in the rationality of naturalism and individualism. It easily capitalizes on the social currency of these discourses; the notion of what might be called the "survival of the fittest psyche" exudes a strong scent of the familiar in a context that is already inscribed with naturalist and individualist discourse. In effect, the force of psychoanalysis over modern subjectivity is essentially *pre*confirmed and (re)inscribed prior to its event because the stage upon which it is set is already furnished with naturalism and individualism. Furthermore, once it is established, psychoanalysis, in its turn, reinforces the same discourses that sustain it. The impact of psychoanalysis on modern subjectivity, therefore, is intensified through what is now a combined set of forces.

The idea that the logic of psychoanalysis combines easily with the logic of naturalism and individualism and the idea that this combination facilitates the momentum of its influence are evidenced in parallels that Freud draws between psychoanalysis and Darwin's theory of evolution. Freud rightly observes that the impact of psychoanalysis is comparable to that of Darwin's theory of descent in regard to the modern Western knowledge of the self. He compares psychoanalysis with Darwinian naturalism when he argues that each "science" uncovers a similar kind of truth about the mysteries of human psychology and human biology respectively. He writes that "Darwin's theory of descent ... tore down the barrier that had been arrogantly set up between men and beasts ... I showed how the psychoanalytic view of the relation of the conscious ego to an overpowering unconscious was a severe blow to human self-love. I described this as a *psychological* blow to men's narcissism, and compared it with the *biological* blow delivered by the theory of descent and the earlier *cosmological* blow aimed at it by the discovery of Copernicus."[19] Essentially, Freud draws an analogy between his ego psychology and Darwin's biology, which suggests that the logic of psychoanalysis is modelled on, and is benefited by, the already pervasive influence of Darwinian thought. Freud originally trained to be a natural scientist prior to developing an interest in psychiatry, a fact that also gives credence to the idea that psychoanalysis gains influence through its share in the logic of naturalism. Indeed, Freud closely studied Darwin's work, and although he abandoned the natural sciences to pursue psychiatry, he did not abandon Darwin's thought.[20] This influence of Darwin is evident in the degree to which the latent and often unpredictable unconscious, which can adversely impact conscious life, is like a beast that threatens man in nature; the unconscious and beasts are alike because the individual must overcome them to survive in civilization and nature.

The influence of psychoanalysis is not simply enhanced by a pervasive Darwinian logic but is also deeply dependent upon it. As Catherine Ann Gildiner observes, Freud's ideas about female psychology are completely intelligible only in light of Darwinian theory.[21] This observation is also relevant to Oedipal psychology in general. For example, Freud bases the central psychoanalytic hypothesis, which underpins the Oedipal complex, on "Darwin's conjecture that men originally lived in hordes, each under the domination of a single powerful, violent and jealous male."[22] Specifically, Freud locates the origins of Oedipal desire in the idea that the primal father of an original horde, who takes all women for himself, sparks the jealousy and desire of his sons for the mother, which leads the sons to kill the primal father.[23] This original patricidal event, Freud contends, is both real and what gives rise to a universally *inherited* sense of guilt that now resides within the human psyche and manifests itself as the Oedipal complex, which each individual must resolve if he is to be happy in relations with other individuals.[24]

Given that the influence of psychoanalysis is secured through the logic it shares with naturalism and individualism, how does it produce the modern subject, particularly a biologically narcissistic subject? In *Darwin's Worms*, Adam Phillips observes two important things about Darwin and Freud that help us to address this question: Darwin's "language" changes the self's understanding of the body's relationship to the physical environment, just as Freud's "language" alters how we understand the self's relationship to itself, the family, and the social world; the idea of inheritance, whether it is biological or psychological in nature, is pivotal to these changes. As Phillips writes,

> [T]he new languages of Darwin and Freud have been immensely influential. Their versions of nature – that is to say, their versions of what we are really like – have had a pervasive influence. A lot of people now think of childhood and sexuality as the sources of their suffering, just as many people tend to think of themselves as virtual animals struggling competitively for survival. What we inherit from the past is now a cultural obsession; and the nature of inheritance itself informs our most compelling fictions. Whether or not we read Darwin and Freud, they read us; we speak a version of their languages.[25]

Additionally, we speak their languages because Darwin and Freud speak so well to each other. They do so because the language or rationality of *inheritance*, as Phillips observes, informs both naturalism and psychoanalysis – and, I would add, individualism.

The significance of these languages for subjectivity, or these "discursive relations, and their interplay," as Foucault would put it, is the common or tripartite rationality that they not only share but also realize in the form of bio-family discourse; they are "modes of objectification of the subject" that make today's family subjects appear.[26] Naturalism, psychoanalysis, and individualism are allied by virtue of the idea that inheritance plays an important role in the biological, psychological, and/or social-political-economic success of a human being.[27] A consequence of their easy interplay with respect to subject formation is that the rationality to which these discourses subscribe now encompasses the self more completely. Unlike a single discourse, the alignment of these discourses allows them to operate from a number of (institutionalized) vantage points at once, which more fully limits and determines the subject or forms of experience that are open to the self. Where psychoanalysis, naturalism, and individualism are allied, therefore, these vantage points are biological science or medicine, psychology, and socio-politics; and where naturalism, psychoanalysis, and individualism are allied by the logic of inheritance, this logic is more totalizing in its ability to effectively inform self-knowledge and experience.

The biological narcissism of the modern subject is produced by an alliance founded on the logic of inheritance. The psychoanalytic idea that the self is narcissistic easily grips the subjectivity of the "family" because it reiterates this logic in a context already saturated with the logic of inheritance as an effect of naturalist and individualist discourse. The idea that the human psyche is inherently narcissistic is palpable in a social context that conceives the self's independence to be driven by a *heritable* set of traits, personality, and identity. Furthermore, the self who seeks independence in and through his inheritance must be narcissistic out of necessity; he must look for himself – the truth of his being and potential – in those to whom he is biologically related. Psychoanalysis's treatment of the biological tie as integral to "family" experience, identification, intimacy, and connection, insofar as it understands narcissistic identifications to play a central role in the self's identity and family relations, is cradled by an extant concern with heritability, which has already been produced by individualism and naturalism.

Additionally, psychoanalysis's impact on family subjectivity is served by individualism where state interests emphasize the value of *independence* in order to decrease the "individual's" and, therefore, his family's *dependence* on state resources. That is because independence is one of psychoanalysis's inherent values. At a time when the modern Western family bears greater "social responsibility" for its sick and poor, psychoanalysis's perspective on the individual's psychic life offers him and his family a new means by which to be independent.[28] For instance, as psychoanalysis links the "individual's" mental health to the family, it makes the individual and his childhood family independently responsible for his mental health and well-being, and it makes him, as the head of a family, responsible for the mental health of his own offspring. It accomplishes this feat because it understands each "individual's" abnormal behaviour to originate in a previously unknown and unconscious history of his desires and instincts, which are unresolved primarily because of childhood experience within the family. Psychoanalysis thrives on the value of independence because it offers itself to the individual as a balm that will eventually enable him to heal his own symptoms, all of which are rooted in his unresolved desires and instincts. It gives him the tools with which he can reinterpret latent and misunderstood self-truths and family dynamics that are the source of his abnormal or neurotic behaviours.

The erection of the instincts, narcissism, and the Oedipal complex – which are on a continuum in human psychic development and neurosis – *as* universals gives psychoanalysis a central role in providing the "individual" and the "family" with the ability to meet the individualistic imperative of independence.[29] Where narcissism and the Oedipal complex are inherent features of a universal human psychology, the family *is* the independent cause of mental health or illness. That is because, with psychoanalysis, the realization of the always potentially tragic fates of Narcissus and Oedipus in the "individual" is located in the milieu of child-parent relations. In a context where an "individual's" mental illness reflects on the failure of a family to meet the demand of independence, psychoanalysis makes itself indispensable. It offers the family the knowledge that enables it to independently thwart the potential of psychic tragedy, which might lead to its dependence. Psychoanalysis's "discovery" of narcissism and the Oedipal complex reinforces individualistic demands made on the family. The discovery of what is universally a potentially menacing psyche implies that the family is ultimately responsible for the mental health of its members simply because the menace is best addressed in the context of early child-parent relations. All in all, the family that embraces psychoanalysis as a panacea for mental illness, which threatens its independence, is one that meets its duty with respect to the demands of an individualistic civilization. Psychoanalysis increases its influence, therefore, through its bond with individualism: a dutiful family depends on psychoanalysis to remedy its narcissistic and Oedipal conflicts and, thereby, realizes its independence.

Psychoanalysis is further reified through its easy intercourse with individualism and naturalism because it shares with these discourses the assumption that the individual, to know himself, must uncover his family history.[30] However, the contribution that psychoanalysis makes to the modern Western idea that self-knowledge *is* family knowledge is unique because it makes sexuality function as a form of self-knowledge.

For instance, Foucault observes that Freud plays a distinguished role in the history of sexuality because he gives "a new impetus to the secular injunction to study sex and transform it into discourse."[31] And although psychoanalysis appears along a continuum "of a general deployment of sexuality," it is unique because it constructs "around and apropos of sex an immense apparatus for producing truth."[32] Specifically, psychoanalysis gives a new value to the truth of sex by aligning itself with the natural sciences and by transforming the Christian pastoral strategy of confession into therapeutic analysis as a strategy for uncovering that truth in the self. Psychoanalysis also gives a truth value to sex that makes it very, very hard for the self to understand or experience its sexuality in the twentieth century outside the confines of that truth.[33] In effect, the psychoanalytic discourse on sex structures modern sexuality and, ultimately, subjectivity. Sex at present is unknown and cannot be experienced wholly outside of the knowledge and power that are psychoanalysis; again, that is why "the history of the deployment of sexuality, as it has evolved since the classical age, can serve as an archaeology of psychoanalysis."[34]

The significance of sexuality for the idea that self-knowledge is family knowledge is that it is through this deployment that psychoanalysis deploys another truth: the individual understands himself in the present only when he uncovers what is a largely unconscious history of a childhood and/or family sexuality. Although psychoanalysis does accept that this project cannot be completed because consciousness can tease out only fragmented memories from the unconscious, it insists that the self, to know itself, must embark on this project. That is because the self will really understand itself only in the present if and when it knits the fragments of a formerly infinite unconscious history into a finite, continuous narrative of desire that is essentially narcissistic and Oedipal.[35] Psychoanalysis, therefore, not only imposes a continuity on the self's psychic history but also creates a continuity between self-knowledge and family history.[36] Where self-history is tantamount to an inherent and universal desire or sexual instinct that is both narcissistic and Oedipal, the family as the site of self-sameness, and incest is necessarily invoked as the "true" source of self-knowledge. Given that the modern Western self places a high value on self-knowledge *as* family knowledge because of the influence of naturalism and individualism, psychoanalysis more easily contours modern Western subjectivity by treating self-knowledge *as* a universally repressed sexuality that simultaneously is a narcissistic and Oedipal family history or knowledge.

The longevity of psychoanalysis's influence with respect to subjectivity and the idea that self-knowledge is family knowledge can also be attributed to the fact that the child, as opposed to the adult individual, eventually becomes an object of its focus. According to Nikolas Rose, since the 1950s psychology has increasingly intervened in the life of the child. In *Governing the Soul*, he writes that "[p]sychology has played a key role in establishing the norms of childhood, in providing means for visualizing childhood pathology and normality, in providing vocabularies for speaking about childhood subjectivity and its problems, in inventing technologies for cure and normalization. Through the connections established between the norms of childhood and images of family life, parenting, and motherhood, the psyche of the child and the subjectivity of the mother have been opened up for regulation in a new way."[37] Obviously, psychoanalysis is a central axis along which the subjectivity of the child and the nature of child-parent relations are forged both in the context of modern psychology generally and in the context of adoption psychology and discourse. For instance, the work of psychoanalysts Anna Freud (who takes up the psychology of adoption in her work directly) and Melanie Klein from the 1930s to the 1950s gave rise to a productive new strategy in the regulation of childhood and family life: child analysis. Prior to the development of child analysis, psychoanalysis focused on childhood history but solely on its repression in the adult unconscious, which, when uncovered in adult life, is used to alleviate and give meaning to neurotic symptoms.[38] As a natural progression of psychoanalysis's grip on modern subjectivity, which occurs through its use of the adult's repressed childhood history, child analysis now allows psychoanalysis, and psychology generally, to develop an even firmer hold by intervening in earlier and earlier stages of the self's psychic life and/or childhood development; "professionals (physicians, nurses, and workers) in the psychology and psychopathology of human relations" have become increasingly involved in the "treatment of children and the giving of expert advice to parents, especially mothers of young children" who may be biological *or* adopted.[39]

A key aspect of the power of psychoanalysis is realized through its posture as a science that uncovers objective truths about the human psyche or self as it develops within a family. Within Freud's lifetime, psychoanalysis gained widespread influence. And arguably, it did so in part because of Freud's reiterative strategy; he insisted, as we have seen, that the fundamental nature of his theory was akin to that of a theory like Darwin's. In other words, psychoanalysis's success, at least according to Freud, lay in the *objective truth* of its discoveries: the sexual instinct, the unconscious, narcissism, and the Oedipal complex are posited as and thereby become real and universal aspects of the human psyche. Indeed, Freud frequently affirmed the "analytic work" of psychoanalysis as a project that "brings forward nothing but observed facts, almost without any speculative additions."[40] However, Freud's invocation accomplishes something else for psychoanalysis too. It creates the appearance of objectivity and thereby capitalizes on a particular kind of influence that is already established by and for the natural sciences on the same basis. Nonetheless, even though Freud assumed that the popularity and controversy surrounding psychoanalysis was provoked by the truth that it discovers about the self, it is also possible that the *truth status* of psychoanalysis's "discoveries" is merely a product of its popularity and the controversy it has caused. This is an idea that ultimately has implications for the meaning of family or narcissism as a core aspect of child-parent love and intimacy, as well as for the uncritical idea that this kind of intimacy thrives best in the presence of biological sameness. It implies that the experience of the family tie, which psychoanalysis does claim is rooted in the psyche's inherent propensity for narcissism, is a product of the influence of psychoanalysis. To explore how psychoanalysis produces the bio-narcissism of the modern subject, therefore, the *truth* of its discoveries needs to be distinguished from the *effects* of its discoveries.

The real accomplishment of psychoanalysis, according to Foucault, is that it is a highly productive mode of knowledge. This productivity is the source of its influence. Its greatest success, therefore, is not its discoveries or universal truth claims about the human psyche but its impact on subject formation in the modern Western context. Psychoanalysis realizes its influence through the production of a sexual subject that is concomitant with and incomprehensible outside of its now pervasive discourse. Foucault illustrates this idea by explaining that

> Freud's originality was taking all that [i.e., Jean-Martin Charcot's work on sexual hysteria] literally, and then erecting on its basis the *Interpretation of Dreams*, which is something other than a sexual aetiology of neuroses. If I were to be very pretentious, I would say that I'm doing something a bit similar to that. I'm starting off from an apparatus of sexuality [psychoanalysis], a fundamental

historical given which must be an indispensable point of departure for us. I'm taking it literally, at face value: I'm not placing
myself outside of it, because that isn't possible, but this allows me
to get at something else.[41]

Psychoanalysis, therefore, cannot be escaped. It is a mode of knowledge and/or being that dominates the twentieth century – for
instance, *as* narcissism, incest, unconscious desire, or human enact-
ments thereabouts in discourse and deed; that is why Foucault readily admits to its inscription upon his own being and thought.

The contemporary and modern truth of human psychic experience
is particular to the discourse of psychoanalysis because of its influence,
not the other way around. Truth and experience are realized through
knowledge in relation to the influence or dominance of psychoanalysis; in effect, the subject's repertoire of thought and experience changes
if and when there is a change in the social-political-historical dominance of a mode of thought. So, just as important linguistic constructions are unique to a specific language, which can result in meaning
being "lost in translation," human experience is unique to discursive
fields, such as psychoanalysis, which inform the social-political-historical context in which the self is situated. The objective truth of psychoanalytic discoveries, therefore, is ultimately irrelevant to its influence; its influence is determined by its ability to subject the self and/or
experience to the limits and determinations of a bio-narcissistic discourse, regardless of whether its discoveries are objectively true. Still,
psychoanalysis's influence *is* bolstered by the objective *truth status* that
is also attached to its discoveries. Psychoanalysis effectively secures its
grip on modern subjectivity because it emerges in a social-political-
historical context in which the natural sciences, informed as they are
by individualism and naturalism, dominate knowledge production
and because it models its approach to mind on the natural sciences. To
be specific, the psychoanalytic approach to mind and mental illness, as
Foucault suggests, mirrors the approach of the natural sciences or
organic medicine to the body.[42] So just as the natural sciences attribute
cancer to what are organic causes, such as the malfunction of otherwise
normal cell growth, psychoanalysis roots mental illness in universally
inherited drives and instincts, which, when controlled abnormally by
the ego, elicit a psychic malfunction.

Regardless of the discursive currency leveraged by psychoanalysis,
its posture as a natural science that objectively discovers the self's

narcissism and Oedipal desire is problematic not only because it is *really* a human or social science but also because there are good reasons to doubt the objectivity of the natural sciences too. At least since Thomas Kuhn's *The Structure of Scientific Revolutions* – "an important stimulus to what has since become known as 'Science Studies'" – the natural sciences' claim to objectivity has become suspect.[43] As Kuhn demonstrated, even the objective truth claims and hypotheses of natural scientists are rooted in "paradigms" or ideological systems of belief that a *community* of scientists shares. Thus it is a community of scientists, not truth itself, that grants authority to the paradigms that scientists set up as the truth about the natural world; a paradigm's truth is irrelevant to its epistemological influence and merit because these things manifest only if there is a community of scientists to subscribe to it. The paradigm fosters a collective consciousness among scientists that obfuscates objective truth, and as scientists are educated by other scientists who subscribe to the paradigm, it subjects their research to "a strenuous and devoted attempt to force nature into the conceptual boxes supplied by [their] professional education."[44] Thus beliefs that may be true, partially true, and/or false are intelligible and treated *as* truths only insofar as they are in accord with a given paradigm; as a result, even "[n]ormal science ... often suppresses fundamental novelties because they are necessarily subversive of its basic commitments."[45] For our purposes, the significance of Kuhn's work is that although the instantiation of psychoanalysis *as* a natural science does not actually ensure its objective truth status, this instantiation does enhance its paradigmatic influence and intelligibility in a modern, Western context that already strenuously naturalizes (bio-)narcissism as the universal basis of family bonds and identity.

Another important problem with the idea that psychoanalysis's influence is realized by virtue of its objectivity relates to the object of its study: the mind. The mind, and this is a Foucaultian point, cannot be approached in the same way that the natural sciences (or human sciences modelled upon them) set out to approach the natural world because the mind, particularly the imagination, unlike the body, is not organic. To be precise, psychoanalysis takes an organic approach to the mind and mental illness when it treats the mind as an object that is structured and ordered by universally inherited drives and instincts. This idea, rooted as it is in philosophy *as* existential psychology, throws into question the objectivity of the psychologies that any *sci-*

ences offer up, and it is a reason why psychoanalysis's influence cannot be the result of "discoveries" about the mind that are objectively true.

The critical value of rethinking the truths of psychoanalysis, such as (Oedipal) narcissism, as the truths of family bonds and identity is also evident in Foucault's criticisms of psychiatry and in his existential investigations into the nature of human existence, imagination, and mental illness. At the vanguard of the existential "anti-psychiatry" movement (in which *Madness and Civilization* plays an obvious part) and influenced by Martin Heiddegger's philosophy of being, Foucault's thought, according to Keith Hoeller, shared with R.D. Laing's and David Cooper's the idea that "so-called 'mental illness' is not ... an isolated, intrapsychic entity existing merely within the individual patient. Rather ... one must put the patient back into a world" both because "human beings are always constituted by the concept of 'being-in-the-world', and [because] 'madness' is a societal event which occurs *between* people who may in fact have conflicting values and goals."[46] At the risk of abstraction, Foucault's early explorations of mental illness pose it as a problem or stagnation in the relationship between human existence and imagination. It is a form of alienated freedom wherein "existence comes to inscribe itself in this determinism of its illness."[47] It occurs when the imagination develops a "fixation" through which it imagines, and thus *becomes*, a singular or limited number of images that impact being's freedom of existence.[48] These images are static "view-points" on a nonlinear continuum of imagery that is the dream, whereas imagining is a traversing of the dream's manifold imagery, a traversing that is being's freedom or the experience of its radical movement through and among infinitely variform and different worlds.[49] On this view, the nature of the human mind or being, as imagination, is such that mental illness is best averted through the possibility of freedom of existence. Freedom of existence is the idea that the human imagination, particularly the dream or unconscious, affords the self experiences of "breaking with the objectivity [that] fascinates waking consciousness."[50] Freedom from mental illness is realized, therefore, in the labour of imagining, a labour that entails the profuse, as opposed to static, imagining of new imagery, which is how new possibilities for experience or being are created; additionally, the dream, as a traversal of new imagery, presents the self with its freedom to experience new possibilities or worlds in which the individual *as* being can partake. The problem that any image can pose to our imaginations as freedom of existence, however, is that an image *is* fixed: "The image as fixation upon quasi-presence is but the vertigo of imagination as it turns back toward the primordial meaning of presence. The image constitutes a ruse of consciousness in order to cease imagining, the moment of discouragement in the hard labor of imagining."[51] Albeit the spawn of imagination, the image negatively impacts the freedom *to be* because the self stops the movement of imagining if and when it rigidly or repeatedly fixes upon a particular image.[52] The individual's worlds or possibilities for being become finite when the imagination is constrained by a finite image or finite set of images; fixation on an image imposes a limit on being that essentially alienates the self from the experience of its freedom of existence. To abandon an image, or illness, that can "envelop," "immobilize," or "crush" human being, therefore, the imagination can and, really, must attract the self's attention to the nonorganic nature of its own being as freedom and imagination.[53] And although all individuals are subject to fixation to greater and lesser degrees because "wakefulness can reach the dream only mediately" or through an image, those suffering from mental illness fixate longer and upon fewer and perhaps different images.[54] The result is that some individuals are less free because they experience fewer and different worlds or images for longer durations than other individuals with whom they share a social context; prolonged fixation on any world, even a different one, alienates being from the freedom of existence.

Obviously, the existential psychology behind the image as psychic fixation that engaged Foucault prefigures (perhaps inversely) his later ideas on the regulatory effects of knowledge that fix a subject within the sights of discourse. His work on freedom, imagination, and mental illness implies his subsequent ideas about the possibilities of being and resistance generally; indeed, his suggestion that resistance to dominant modes of knowledge that socially, politically, and historically restrict and limit the self's possibilities for experience can be realized in "the search for styles of existence as different as possible from each other" is very like the idea that imagining can thwart the image as fixation, which can culminate in mental illness.[55] The object lesson, for our purposes, is that if the mind, imagination, and mental illness are inorganic (i.e., are misconstrued through the lens of universally inherited drives and instincts), then the mind is not a tangible thing or positivity that can be objectively and finitely known in the manner that psychoanalysis suggests.[56] If the infinite possibility of being, realized through the nature of imagination, makes an objective knowledge of the mind impossible, there can be no necessary or causal relationship between the objective truth of psychoanalytic claims and their widespread influence; the nature of the "object" of psychoanalytic study contravenes access to the kind of truth about the mind that psychoanalysis claims to discover.

Assuming, therefore, that the truth status of psychoanalysis's discoveries is not inherently relevant to its influence, how is its influence explained? When Kuhn's and Foucault's ideas about our access to objectivity and the mind are combined, the influence of psychoanalysis simply depends on a widespread willingness of both a community and the self to think its truths into existence – for instance, insofar as a community and the self participate in, or fixate on, a knowledge or subjectivity that is bio-narcissistic. Kuhn provides us with an understanding of how *communal thought*, such as among adoption and family experts and among "family" subjects, sustains the influence of psychoanalytic reason as the truth of family bonds and identity, whereas Foucault provides us with an understanding of the role of the *self's thought* in its own familial fixations, or subjection, *as* the realization of the bio-narcissistic truths that psychoanalysis claims to discover about the family.

Ultimately, the self – whose subjectivity is limited and determined because it interprets itself and is interpreted by a community that subscribes to the discourse of psychoanalysis – is a human being whose freedom, world, experience of intimacy, love, and connection are limited by a fixation on a bio-narcissistic image (or paradigm) of self and other. A universally true experience of the self *as* bio-narcissistic is not discovered by psychoanalysis; rather, a bio-narcissistic subject or image of the self is realized because human being and human communities fixate on and/or (re)interpret the self through a pervasive discourse of psychoanalysis. Psychoanalysis does not acquire influence because it discovers the objective truth that bio-narcissism is a core aspect of the self or its familial bonds. On the contrary, its discourse perpetuates a dominant interpretation of self and, thereby, self-experience, such as within and through communities of adoption, twin, and family experts, that is bio-narcissistic.

The *influence* of psychoanalysis poses an inherent danger to human experience. The danger is that psychoanalytic answers to questions about self and family experience can and do have totalizing effects; these effects are realized through its role in the "overproduction" of our "socio-cultural knowledge of sexuality," a knowledge that shapes modern and postmodern "family" subjectivities insofar as family dynamics have become psycho-sexual dynamics that are narcissistic and Oedipal.[57] Under the rubric of psychoanalysis, which informs family, adoption, and twin psychologies, sexual subjectivity and (biological) family subjectivity are one and the same: human sexuality *and* child-parent relations are Oedipal or incestuous. As such, they are also bio-narcissistic because Oedipal love, as incest, signifies love objects for the self that are biologically self-same initially and that continue to be so metaphorically in the context of "normal" adulthood.[58] Read through an interpretive grid of narcissism, which underpins the Oedipal drama and logic of the family romance, the ontological status and, therefore, experience of the adoptive tie is impoverished by an extant biological family order that is realized by dint of the interplay between the discourses of individualism, naturalism, and psychoanalysis.[59] The adoptive tie is impoverished by the truth claim to which the influence of these discourses gives rise, namely that the self is inherently narcissistic, a truth that is employed widely by adoption, twin, and/or family experts.

The influence of psychoanalysis on modern Western subjectivity *as* the sexual etiology that it attaches to family relations determines that authentic "family" experience *is* narcissistic, which invests the self, or ourselves as family and/or adopted subjects, deeply in the experience of the biological tie as the most "real" family tie. The construction of the self as narcissistic, or as something that inherently tends toward a love of the (biologically) self-same, has clear implications for the bio-genealogical imperative in that the self who loves the (biologically) self-same essentially abides by this imperative. It also has implications for the ontological status of different kinds of "family" ties. Insofar as psychoanalysis has successfully set up narcissism as a psychic reality of human being, the experience of (biological) narcissism, especially as it plays out in the context of Oedipal desire, functions as a reality test for "family" ties; family ties become indubitably real *only* to the extent that they facilitate narcissistic (i.e., biologically self-same) and, ultimately, Oedipal (i.e., incestuous) love, an accomplishment, by definition, that belongs solely to the biological tie, which is an idea that continues to be explored in subsequent chapters.

To challenge this current reality, the following chapter interrogates how and why the psychoanalytic concept of narcissism logically conflates the presence of biological sameness with the possibility of modern Western "family" experience. The conventional meaning of the Narcissus myth, as it is applied to the self and family ties by psychoanalysis, is also critically examined and challenged; *other* meanings of the myth are explored to denude the possibility that real "family" experience can occur in adoptive families, an experience that otherwise is foreclosed by the myth's conventional meaning.

6

Scientia Familialis:
Psychoanalysis, Bio-Narcissism, and
the Constitution of the Adoptive Subject

Narcissus is the son of Liriope. Following his birth, his mother asks the "seer" Tiresias whether Narcissus will live a long life. Tiresias assures her, "He will live long, if he does not know himself."[1] As he grows, Narcissus becomes a beautiful, arrogant youth who spurns the love of female nymphs and male youths alike. But when he rejects the overtures of the lovely nymph Echo, he humiliates her. For doing so, he is punished by yet another of his scorned suitors, who implores the gods to make him suffer the same pain of an utterly elusive love. Narcissus finds himself forever unrequited in love, much like Echo is in relation to him. The difference is that Narcissus's love is for his own immaterial reflection, which he first encounters when gazing into a still pool. His reflection immediately enchants him and fills him with desire. Deeply and spontaneously attached, Narcissus lies down on the bank of the pool to be with his love. With every physical advance he makes toward the object of his desire the water stirs and his reflection fragments, eliciting in him the torture of an infinitely retreating love. Once Narcissus realizes the youth in the pool is a reflection of himself and thus knows that the object of his desire is merely his own image, or *the same*, it is too late. This self-knowledge gives rise to an excruciating consciousness of a love that must remain forever unreturned. The young and beautiful Narcissus, utterly bound to an inaccessible, because immaterial, love object, dies of self-obsession at the edge of the pool.

In psychoanalysis, myth is generally understood to be a true "reflection of psychic elements and processes of growth."[2] For this reason, Sigmund Freud turned not only to Oedipus but also to the myth of Narcissus in order to understand the human psyche. He modelled his psychology of human attachment and love on the Ancient Greek myth as it is told by the Ancient Roman poet Ovid in *The Metamorphoses*. Freud regarded the myth as a universal narrative that essentially mirrors the human infant's original state of desire: the human infant is like Narcissus in that its unconscious, initial state of self-absorption renders it incapable of recognizing or addressing the other's needs and desires. Freud also believed that Narcissus's failure to redirect his love and desire away from himself and toward others mirrors an ongoing psychic threat with which every self wrestles through the course of development. Narcissus's social isolation, loneliness, and death symbolize a failed human psychology, one that occurs when the primary tendency toward self-love is not psychically curtailed.[3] Still, Freud did not think that narcissism in and of itself was all bad. On the contrary, he believed that it plays a key role in all stages of the self's development; it is the psychic foundation of all forms of love and identification. Freud, therefore, drew a *psychology*, rather than a morality, from the Ancient Greek myth of Narcissus, one that informs twin, family, and adoption discourses through the continued influence of psychoanalysis today.

In this chapter, I examine how psychoanalysis indelibly marks our knowledge and experiences of identity and family through its treatment of narcissism as the force that brings each fragile self, ego, or identity into being, protecting it from dissolution. I investigate how it does so through the institution of narcissism, particularly biological narcissism, as the first principle of both an identity and "family" relations that are normal. Freud argued that "the 'double' was originally an insurance against the destruction of the ego, an 'energetic denial of the power of death,' as [Otto] Rank says; and probably the 'immortal' soul was the first double of the body ... Such ideas, however, have sprung from the soil of unbounded self-love, from the primary narcissism which dominates the mind of the child and of primitive man."[4] And at least since Freud, the double has operated as a main medium through which the self is construed to understand itself and its family bonds. The use of the double or the same by psychoanalytic modes of family knowledge incites a narcissistic mode of subjectivity that, coupled with the bio-genealogical imperative, operates as human psychology. The aim of this chapter, therefore, is to critically address the institution of narcissism as the truth of human psychology by psychoanalytic modes of family knowledge. It questions the location of a narcissistic desire for the "double" in the self and reconsiders the idea that this desire necessarily enables the self to experience self-knowledge in and through its bio-genealogy. It thinks critically about how the implantation of this desire limits the possibilities of experience within biological and adoptive families. It does so as it denudes the narcissistic rationality that drives the four key psychoanalytic concepts that continue to inform "family" experiences and psychologies today. It examines the role of *childhood history*, *the unconscious*, *narcissism*, and/or *identification*, all of which remain key constructs in contemporary knowledge about human development. To challenge this logic, finally, this chapter offers a re-examination of the Narcissus myth not as a psychology but as a critical epistemology. It also investigates an alternate version of the myth, as told by Pausanias, to challenge this logic even further. It does so in order to facilitate a better understanding of how and why the idea of difference, which is and can be a basis for family bonds, remains largely unintelligible to us today.

As conduits of psychoanalysis, contemporary twin, family, and adoption psychologies all subscribe to some semblance of the idea that narcissism, or a love of the self-same, is intrinsic to the human psyche, its development, and its relationships. Where these psychologies treat narcissism as a core characteristic of the psyche, one that is at the root of the self's identity and family ties, the universality of the self's need for its biological doubles or twins is made inevitable. As I suggested in the previous chapter, the psychology of the same that dominates the self and family today is clearly demonstrated by our widespread fascination with twins – for instance, in the context of popular myth, literature, media, science, and psychology. Typically, however, family experts read this fascination as a sign that narcissism is an inherent, psychological longing for understanding between the self and other. Lawrence Wright illustrates this idea when he writes,

Being genetically identical with another human being encroaches on our sense of being unique in the world, of having thoughts and desires and experiences that no one else knows about or can possibly share ... It is the most narcissistic encounter imaginable – to be able to stand aside and really look at your almost-self, to talk to someone else who is inside the same physical package, to experience your almost-self as others must experience you ... Perhaps there is an element of the uncanny in your new relationship; you may have always thought there was something uncompleted in your life that now is resoundingly answered and fulfilled. The power of this widespread fantasy is a testament to how much we long to be understood on a deeper level than ordinary love and friendship can provide.[5]

Certainly, most of us can and do identify with these sorts of fantasies, as Wright suggests. Where the double's or twin's ability to attract so much attention from singletons satiates an extant need for the same, however, it also validates and stabilizes the reality of the self's intrinsic biological narcissism and, as a result, the biological family's superiority as *the* site for gleaning self-knowledge. Although the double's ability to capture the popular imagination is a sign that the self's biological narcissism is widely experienced as both real and inherent, it is also a sign that the discourse of narcissism (re)produces subjects for whom it is imperative that the biological tie be experienced as an exclusive, material bond that grants one a complete sense of self. Where love of the double is located in the self by family experts, therefore, it accomplishes many things: it wards off loneliness and the longing for understanding that threatens the "individual's" success; it reinforces the normality of the biological family tie; it incites the intensity of the twin bond in particular and biological bonds in general; and it (re)produces the inferiority of the adoptive tie as a basis for self-knowledge and/or family.

Hillel Schwartz writes that "[a]cts and images of doubling start here, at the root of our lives: our flesh, our blood, our coming to be."[6] Imagine, however, that the popular fascination with the biological double reflects less a narcissism that is a universal characteristic of the human psyche and more a narcissistic or psychoanalytic logic that is intrinsic to the bio-genealogical imperative, one that (re)produces the double's function as a repository of bio-genealogical knowledge. This idea suggests that the self's imagination is captured easily by the biological double simply because there is a social-political-historical imperative that both commands and enables her to realize her "individuality," a "normal" identity, and the exclusive love and connection of a "family" bond. Intrigue with the double, therefore, is a sign that, today, sameness alone is intelligible as the essential foundation of normal identity formation and family bonds; it signals our widespread doubt about the reality of family bonds that are not biological.

Prior to the emergence of psychoanalysis, the bio-genealogical imperative, as we have seen, entailed a bio-narcissistic logic that had already appeared in and through the influence of naturalism and individualism: to know oneself, or the truth of one's being, was to know those whom one was most like at the level of flesh, blood, or genes. The confluence of psychoanalysis with naturalism and individualism, however, has made the imperative even more formidable. Each discourse elicits bio-narcissism as a need and thereby affirms the self's need to know her bio-genealogy and, consequently, the need to remain in proximity with others who are biologically or genetically similar. Still, as these discourses share a narcissistic rationality, they each do so in their own way. Naturalism employs bio-narcissism where it assumes that the self's need to know her potential as the genetic offspring of her parents is met by her access to bio-genealogical knowledge. Individualism does so through its supposition that the self needs to know both who bears a responsibility for her and for whom she bears a responsibility, a need that is also met with bio-genealogical knowledge. But psychoanalysis's role in the production of the bio-narcissistic subject lies in its assumption that it is the self's (in)ability *to be* the child of her biological parents that will dictate her psychic success as an individual. It is in this way that psychoanalysis conforms to a narcissistic rationality that is already intrinsic to the bio-genealogical imperative: it presumes that the acquisition of self-knowledge and the promise of love, which underpin normal identity formation, turn on *being* the biological child of one's parents. It regards the biological child, not the adoptive child, as the most capable of resolving psychic conflicts that can undermine the family bond and a firm sense of self.

The impact of narcissism *as* psychoanalysis on modern Western family psychologies and subjectivities is inestimable. Indeed, Stephen Frosh critically contemplates the extent to which modern Western subjectivity is predicated upon (psychoanalytic) narcissism "as an emblem for cultural experience" partly because "it has been employed as a tool of cultural analysis" with such frequencey.[7] Today's families are contoured by a bio-narcissistic logic because family, twin, and adoption discourses do not yet transcend the effects of psychoanalysis or the effects of naturalism and individualism. To understand the adoptive subject, therefore, is to understand that she is just like the biological child in that she too is as an effect of psychoanalysis; the difference is that she is reared on a knowledge that psychoanalysis has determined she lacks. The idea that narcissism is a universal aspect of human psychic life, with all that it implies for "family" bonds and identity formation, is instituted by psychoanalysis in a number of important ways. Specifically, the universality of bio-narcissism is realized by psychoanalysis wherever family experts emphasize its fundamental assumptions and concepts. In particular, family experts today also regard childhood history, the unconscious, narcissism, and/or identification as key components in human development. It is, therefore, the family expert's ongoing use of this knowledge that is (originally) psychoanalytic that constitutes the experience and knowledge of genetic similarity as the primary foundation of a normal childhood and normal development within the family. And it does not matter if family experts affirm the biological tie's presence as the best basis for familial identification explicitly or implicitly because they begin uncritically (i.e., normatively) with the biological family as *the*, not *a* (i.e., an undifferentiated), site of normal identity formation and bonding in both instances; the effects of psychoanalytic knowledge that experts enlist are the same because the inherent logic of this knowledge is always and already bio-normative. That is how psychoanalysis *as* bio-narcissism sustains the bio-genealogical imperative and differentiates the "adoptee" from the "biological" child. Therefore, to understand psychoanalysis's part in the production of the adopted subject and its role in rendering difference unintelligible to us as a basis for family ties, we need to examine the inherent bio-narcissism of these four most basic psychoanalytic concepts that continue to inform family psychologies today.

In *The History of Sexuality*, Michel Foucault argues that Freud is instrumental in the deployment of a "*scientia sexualis*" that since the nineteenth century has located in the heart of Western civilization the "'interplay of truth and sex.'"[8] Freud's science imposes on individuals the idea that "the secret of their truth lies in the region of their sex," a truth that is discovered in the therapeutic confession of wishes and experiences that originate out of what psychoanalysis has said is a childhood sexuality.[9] The pivotal role that psychoanalysis plays in the general deployment of sexuality, therefore, makes the modern subject inseparable from the history of his sexuality, a history that begins, first and foremost, during childhood within the confines of the biological family. To the degree that psychoanalysis is a *scientia sexualis*, it is even more so a *scientia familialis*. It is a *scientia familialis* because it locates the origins of the *normal* individual's sexuality in a childhood history that is incestuous, which determines that it must take place within the biological family.

Freud consistently argued that the origins of neurotic symptoms are discerned by unearthing the individual's childhood history – the meaning of which is uncovered when the individual's child-parent relations are measured against what psychoanalysis deems to be normal relations. So convinced of the import of childhood history was Freud that he retained this proposition from his early theory of neurosis, the seduction theory (1886), which he would reject in 1887. In the "The Aetiology of Hysteria" Freud argued that, ultimately, repressed or unconscious infantile *"sexual experience"* is "an aetiological precondition for hysterical symptoms," or neuroses.[10] Neurotic symptoms, which usually arise in relation to adult experiences of sexual desire, are rooted in the patient's childhood history. In light of his early work with "hysterics," all of whom reported childhood memories of sexual abuse, Freud initially suggested that neurotic symptoms are linked to repressed feelings and memories of *real* abuse, which was frequently perpetrated by the biological fathers and/or uncles of his patients. For a brief time, therefore, Freud did believe that child sexual abuse, largely as it pertains to incest, is the universal cause of neurotic symptoms.[11]

By 1887 Freud had rejected the seduction theory, but this change did not diminish the import he gave to childhood history.[12] Childhood history remained a central component in his new theory, introduced in *The Interpretation of Dreams* (1900), which later became known as the "Oedipus complex."[13] Invoking the myth of Oedipus as evidence of a universal complex among men, Freud now claimed that "[i]t is the fate of all of us, perhaps, to direct our first sexual impulse towards our mother and our first hatred and our first murderous wish against our father."[14] With this idea, Freud universally granted children a sexuality that is absent in the seduction theory. In 1905, in *Three Essays on the Theory of Sexuality*, Freud further proposed the idea of "infantile sexuality."[15] What were once repressed feelings about *real* abuse now became repressed erotic *fantasies* that all children experience in the course of normal psychic development. As a result of the new assumption that children universally experience erotic (Oedipal) fantasies about their parents, Freud concluded that adult neurosis arises from unresolved childhood wishes and feelings that pertain to these fantasies. Whereas the seduction theory proposed the child's innocence in the face of an abusive and incestuous adult sexuality, infantile sexuality replaced this innocence with a precocious, incestuous sexuality that was now located in the child as an Oedipal subject.[16]

Regardless of whether the childhood history that is unearthed by psychoanalysis is treated as real or imagined experience, it clearly remains the fundamental avenue by which sense is made of the adult psyche, even today. Of course, this is not to say that psychoanalysis was the first to emphasize the import of *knowing* childhood history. As I have shown, a generalized idea that self-knowledge turns on knowing bio-genealogy was already operative within the context of naturalist and individualist discourses, both of which informed the context in which psychoanalysis emerged. The idea that childhood *should* occur within the biological family because it ensures the individual's access to bio-genealogical knowledge was normalized prior to Freud. But as psychoanalysis entered into a dance that was already choreographed by force of this idea and unquestioningly assimilated it into psycho-analytic discourse, Freud's emphasis on childhood history essentially (re)affirmed the individual's turn toward the biological family for self-knowledge. One of Freud's unique contributions to the intrinsic narcissism of the bio-genealogical imperative, therefore, is the extent to which he makes the unearthing of childhood history integral to understanding the normal (as opposed to abnormal) psyche.[17] Anoth-er obvious corollary of psychoanalysis's (re)inscription of the individ-ual's need for the biological family is that it necessarily marks off as different the adoptee's "family" experience from that of the biological child. The psychoanalytic association between childhood history and a firm sense of self necessarily hinders adoptee identity because the meaning it attaches to extra-bio-familial history is categorically *abnor-mal* as a basis for identity formation. Within psychoanalysis, the bio-logical difference is the psychic abnormality because the meaning of this difference makes incest in the form of Oedipal desire *as* narcis-sism impossible, along with the desire's normative resolution.

Certainly, the psychoanalytic logic embedded in contemporary family psychologies also realizes abnormalities in any family as a bio-narcissistic (Oedipal) drama that is interrupted at key moments of development by childhood histories of divorce, family blending (i.e., stepfamilies), single parenthood, or the death of a parent, and so on; psychologies, pathologies, and family experts are deployed to prob-lematize these kinds of interruptions as abnormalities too. Neverthe-less, the adoptee's differentiation and marginalization and the social-political-historical suspicion through which she is constituted as an inauthentic "family" subject within the adoptive family are unique; her otherness is mediated not by meanings of *divorce* or *death* and so on but by the meaning of adoption as a lack of identity and connection, for which bio-genealogy, not dispute resolution or grief counselling, is the central cure.[18] Moreover, the influence of psychoanalysis – its adaptability – within bio-heteronormative family and adoption discourse has ensured that the meaning of adoption as lack has stood the test of time.

For example, in *Kinship by Design: A History of Adoption in the Modern United States*, Ellen Herman demonstrates this point about the meaning of adoption. She discusses the history and impact of "psychoanalytic narratives" as a powerful force that has sustained the inferior meaning of adoption within adoption psychologies.[19] In a historical discussion about the move from secrecy to openness (i.e., the prevailing adoption practice prescribed today wherever possible), she points to the adaptive capacity of psychoanalytic discourse. She observes that adoption experts have employed psychoanalysis both to advocate secrecy and to reject it in favour of open adoption. As she elaborates, by 1978 "clinicians had started to advocate search and reunion – the antithesis of anonymity and confidentiality – on the basis of the very psychoanalytic perspectives that had earlier justified anonymity and confidentiality."[20] In effect, she draws our attention to the apparently strange contradiction that psychoanalysis nonetheless transcends with respect to its own centrality in adoption discourse: in different eras of adoption, psychoanalysis is enlisted in support of two wildly different adoption practices (i.e., secrecy and openness), even though its goal, which is to aid normal identity formation and bonding within adoptive families, is the same in both instances. Herman dispels the contradiction, however, when she writes that "[t]his change suggests that the *view* of adoption embedded in psychoanalytic narratives was pliable," although I would add that *the bio-narcissistic logic of psychoanalysis is not*; in other words, psychoanalysis does not alter the logic of bio-narcissism that diminishes the adoptive tie but adapts only its view, or formulation, of the adoptee's and adoptive family's needs and desires to fit this logic in order to respond to new trends in adoption theory and practice.[21] In the final analysis, Herman concludes that the fundamental *meaning* of adoption as lack remains intact even as the view, or enframing, of adoption by psychoanalysis changes: adoption *as* kinship by "[d]esign and deliberation proved again to be at odds with realness," and thus adoptees can "never take belonging for granted precisely because they were adopted."[22]

In conjunction with the value that psychoanalysis places on childhood history, the discovery of the unconscious as the key to self-
knowledge also reinforces the narcissistic turn of the self. The unconscious is a repository for repressed childhood wishes and/or experiences that repeatedly resurface not only in dream life but also in the
adult's conscious life as neurotic and hysterical symptoms.[23] Important
aspects of the self's present and conscious life are known through the
return to childhood history or to past wishes and experiences that are
repressed in the unconscious, the archive of the mind. The unconscious reinforces the self's narcissistic need of bio-genealogical knowledge; it functions as a source of truth to which the individual *can* and,
therefore, *must* turn to unearth his family history. It promises to unrav-
el the secret truth of his psychic present, which in turn *real*izes his ability to exercise his autonomy as an arbiter of (self) truth. The unconscious is implicated in the narcissism already entailed in the need for
childhood history because it *is* the repository of that history. The
deployment of narcissism, therefore, is supported by the purported discovery of the unconscious. The unconscious is what facilitates determinations about the self *as* "normal" or "abnormal" because its con-
tents are compared against the psychoanalytic model of *normal*
childhood – a model that assumes imprimis that to be normal the self
must first be located within the biological family. The discovery of the
inner workings of the unconscious, relative to the meaning that psychoanalysis attaches to childhood history, fundamentally (re)institutes
a turn toward the biological family as the bedrock of self-knowledge,
self-affirmation, and identity. In effect, this is one of the important
ways that both the adoptee's ontological status as *other* and the adoptive tie's inferiority are realized and fortified.[24]

Narcissism is further constituted as the basis of modern Western
subjectivity insofar as psychoanalysis explicitly sets it up as the universal and original condition of the self. In "On Narcissism" (1914),
Freud suggests that narcissism "might claim a place in the regular
course of human sexual development."[25] He understands narcissism –
a concept modelled on the traditional meaning of self-love that is normally drawn from the Ancient Greek myth of Narcissus – to be essential to normal psychic life and to self-preservation through self-
regard.[26] As a psychic process, narcissism is the extent to which the
libido (i.e., sexual energy, desire, or impulse) is "withdrawn from the
external world and has been directed toward the ego" (i.e., the part of
the self that mediates between internal and external experience).[27]

Freud generally understands psychic abnormalities to arise in relation to narcissism whenever the self directs too much libido toward or away from the ego. For example, if a normally occurring narcissistic phase in a child's life is either prolonged or prematurely shortened, it can cause abnormal identity formations in the adult. Twin experts often suggest that identity problems linked to the twin bond are due to a prolonged narcissistic phase, and adoption experts tie adoptee identity crises to a narcissistic phase that is abnormally foreshortened by adoption; as we have seen in earlier chapters, these experts also enlist the concept of narcissism to explain how and why the twin bond achieves its intensity and the adoptee experiences a deep-seated need to search for bio-genealogy.

Overall, Freud assumes that every individual experiences a phase of psychic life known as "primary narcissism."[28] Primary narcissism, or the "original libidinal cathexis of the ego," is the earliest period in life when the individual's libido is directed solely toward the ego rather than toward external objects.[29] This stage is experienced as a "self-contained state" into which the self is born, which he is reluctant to give up, and to which he repeatedly attempts to return throughout ego development.[30] It occurs because each individual emerges from the womb oblivious to the external world and its objects. As a result, "narcissism is the universal and original state of things, from which object-love is only later developed."[31] The external world remains unknown to the ego until objects that originally satisfy all immediate desires (particularly the mother) are experienced as separate for the first time. Initially intolerable, the ego's first experience of separation conveys to the self his utter dependence upon external objects for satisfaction. This dependence causes the ego to yearn to return to its primary stage of narcissism, a yearning with which the self struggles in the course of development.

Realizing its dependence on external objects for satisfaction, the ego begins to move the self through primary narcissism by directing libido away from the self. The first external object to bring satisfaction, usually the mother or person who *first* cares for the child, is the libido's first (i.e., "'anaclitic'") object-choice.[32] Normal as opposed to abnormal object-choices are not due to the self's dependence on a given object per se but are due to the *degree* to which the self is (or is not) dependent on a given object for satisfaction. For instance, by making an exaggerated anaclitic object-choice, the self can overvalue the object to such a degree that his love of it undermines his ability to love himself. Thus the loss of an overvalued object can result in the experience of a complete loss of self. Indeed, as I have already discussed, variations of this psychology are used by family experts to explain adoptee identity problems and the drive behind the adoptee's need to search. The search is a manifestation of the self's need to complete itself through reunion with what is always, originally, an overvalued object (the biological mother). According to Freud, the anaclitic object-choice most commonly occurs in the adult as "the peculiar state of being in love."[33] In love, the beloved is overvalued above the self to such an extent that he experiences himself as nothing without his love object. Other types of anaclitic object-choices that Freud suggests the self can make are "the woman who feeds him," "the man who protects him," or their "substitutes."[34]

Conversely, the self can react in the opposite fashion toward external objects and choose himself as his own first object-choice. In doing so, he is said to make a narcissistic object-choice. In the extreme, this choice can subject the self to an abnormal narcissism that depends on the degree to which his self-love excludes the possibility of libido being directed toward external objects.[35] To exemplify abnormalities manifesting from this choice, Freud points to the "hypochondriac." In the hypochondriac, the concern with health is magnified to such an extent that it diverts overly large portions of "interest and libido ... from the objects of the external world" and toward the ego.[36] In the main, narcissistic object-choices made by the self generally pertain to "what he himself is (i.e., himself)," "what he himself was," "what he himself would like to be," and "someone who was once part of himself."[37]

As the individual passes through primary narcissism, he will normally tend toward one type of object-choice. It is, however, possible for the self to make both anaclitic and narcissistic object-choices. Furthermore, because different kinds of social restraints are imposed upon the sexes, Freud concludes that males tend toward anaclitic object-choices, whereas females tend toward narcissistic object-choices. Still, neither choice need be made exclusively by either sex.[38] Both choices can be made by males and females, and doing so is detrimental only to the degree that the tendency to make opposite-sex choices is magnified. Only in such a case does Freud think that the male's or female's ability to function normally will be impeded because of the social constraints they face in the external world. So, as the difference between normal and abnormal narcissism is only one of degree, the abnormal self is merely an individual whose libido is exclusively self-focused or is directed toward a single external object, as opposed to a series of objects that conform to one type of choice.

In his discussion of primary narcissism, Freud suggests that there is some danger entailed in the (narcissistic) ego-libido being too fully transformed into an (anaclitic) object-libido; narcissism, therefore, serves an important overall role in normal development. To be normal or function successfully according to social and ethical constraints, the self must repress primary narcissism by transferring it onto what becomes the ego-ideal. The ego-ideal is the self's best concept of itself as it would like to be, which is modelled on some external authority, such as the father. It is toward this ideal that the self, to be normal, must begin to extend love.[39] The ego-ideal emerges when the self is faced with social and ethical criticisms from the external world, such as from parents and authority figures. These experiences show the self that he is not as perfect as primary narcissism would have him believe. Thus the self adjusts behaviour and desire in a manner that balances the greatest satisfaction against the external world's social and ethical demands. To the extent that the self is unwilling or unable to give up self-love, the ego-ideal is inserted in place of the ego as the object toward which love is now directed precisely in order to sustain the inclination toward self-love; the ego-ideal is a substitute for primary narcissism. For Freud, therefore, normal psychic life and development are essentially infused with narcissism, whether it be primary narcissism or the repressed form that is the ego-ideal, and it necessarily facilitates the individual's success in the external social world.[40]

Where psychoanalysis is commensurate with modern Western subjectivity, the self is embroiled in narcissism to the extent that a version of self *as* narcissistic is central to psychoanalytic discourse; the interpretive grid of narcissism that psychoanalysis imposes upon the self is an imperative *to be* narcissistic. For this reason, the self *as* either "parent" or "child" becomes essentially narcissistic. In fact, narcissism is regarded by Freud as a vital characteristic of parental love:

[T]he attitude of affectionate parents towards their children ... is a revival and reproduction of their own narcissism, which they have long since abandoned ... Thus they are under a compulsion to ascribe every perfection to the child – which sober observation would find no occasion to do – and to conceal and forget all his shortcomings. (Incidentally, the denial of sexuality in children is connected with this.) Moreover, they are inclined to suspend in the child's favour the operation of all the cultural acquisitions which their own narcissism has been forced to respect, and to renew on his behalf the claims to privileges which were long ago given up by themselves ... Illness, death, renunciation of enjoyment, restrictions on his own will, shall not touch him; the laws of nature and of society shall be abrogated in his favour; he shall once more really be the centre and core of creation – "His Majesty the Baby," as we once fancied ourselves. The child shall fulfil those wishful dreams of the parents which they never carried out – the boy shall become a great man and a hero in his father's place, and the girl shall marry a prince as a tardy compensation for her mother. At the most touchy point in the narcissistic system, the immortality of the ego, which is so hard pressed by reality, security is achieved by taking refuge in the child.[41]

As it turns out, therefore, the child is not the only one subject to primary narcissism within the family context. To commandeer parental love, the child must, in fact, revive the parents' primary narcissism.[42] And the (biological) child is able to draw out the primary narcissism of his parents because it has already been set up by psychoanalysis as the universal original condition to which every self retains a repressed desire to return.

Psychoanalysis's constitution of parental love in this way (re)inscribes a narcissistic turn toward biology *as* "family," a turn that is already intrinsic to the modern Western bio-genealogical imperative. It further precludes the intelligibility of biological difference as a solid basis for "family" ties. This conclusion is evident in the idea that the child is loved only insofar as he is an external object who represents and replaces for the parent a version or part of the *self* that once was, and still is, loved. Parental love, therefore, is primarily derived from the parent's ability to experience the child *as* an extension of the self. Given the logic of psychoanalysis, however, this experience is treated uncritically as one that is commensurate with being in the presence of genetic similarity. This idea is implied, for instance, in the way that psychoanalysis interprets the twin bond as it pertains even to a nurture perspective; the intensity of the twin bond occurs through each twin's overidentification with the other insofar as the environmental experience of the presence of their genetic similarity convinces each that he is more like his twin than any other human being.

It is also evident in Freud's discussion of maternal narcissism; motherhood, he explains, is a significant opportunity for a woman to pass through primary narcissism into (narcissistic) object-love.[43] Mothers are granted this opportunity because "[i]n the child which they bear, *a part of their own body* confronts them like an extraneous object, to which, starting out from their narcissism, they can give complete object-love."[44] In effect, a child is loved because he is experienced *as* an extension or *part of* the mother, not *as* an object that is fully recognized as separate and distinct. Love originally reserved for the mother, now directed toward the child, becomes object-love only insofar as the mother *initially* experiences her child/object to be part of her (biological) body.[45]

Freud does discuss the mother's love for her child apart from and prior to parents in general, but he still seems to indicate that there is little difference between the sexes *as* "parents."[46] For instance, as we have just seen, he clearly characterizes a mother's love as a narcissistic object-choice and describes a parent's love as "a narcissistic stigma in the case of object-choice" wherein that love "is nothing but the parents' narcissism born again ... transformed into object-love."[47] He also makes it clear that his discussion of parental love is addressed to fathers and mothers. Thus a father's love, as much as a mother's, is the result of a revival of primary narcissism to whatever degree the child reflects the father and/or the father as he wishes to be.[48] Furthermore, psychoanalysis's general determination that "parental love" is narcissistic can be understood to imply that parents, regardless of sex, do love their children more or less to the degree that they experience their children as physical or biological *parts* of their bodies.[49]

In a modern Western social-political-historical context where biological narcissism is operative, biological children provoke *parental* love because this context equates genetic similarity with self-sameness to greater and lesser degrees. So if being a "parent" currently means that parental love is extended insofar as a child is experienced as a body *part*, rather than as an incidental and external *by-product* of bodily processes, the experience of the adoptive tie is necessarily made different and inferior by virtue of a psychoanalytic logic that is bio-narcissistic, one that continues to inform modern Western meanings of family and identity. The effect of the narcissistic turn that psychoanalysis imposes upon the self *as* "parent" is that adopted children are categorically effaced as objects of *parental* love in the full sense of the word because they are not *parts* of their *adoptive* parents' bodies. Psy-

choanalysis's narcissistic "parent" essentially precludes an interpretation of the adoptee as anything but difference or a fully extraneous
object. Failing to function as a (biological) narcissistic object-choice,
the adoptee cannot be understood – or, therefore, experienced – to
instigate normal *parental* love either to begin with, to the same
degree, or in the same way as the biological child in the modern Western context.

The logic of psychoanalysis that operates within the modern Western context makes the love of *adoptive* parents other and inferior
because the possibility of "real" family ties occurring on the basis of
biological difference is discursively unintelligible within it. An explicit demonstration of this logic is Stanley Schneider and Esti Rimmer's
analysis of hostilities expressed toward adoptees by infertile adoptive
parents; infertility is popularly understood to be a central reason for
adoption among adoptive parents. They argue that adoptive parents
experience latent rage or grief over infertility and that this emotion
gives rise to the adoptee's "sensitivity in the narcissistic realm."[50] The
adoptee, they claim, is a child who suffers "a deficit in 'narcissistic sup-
plies.'"[51] They further claim that the adoptee is "not ... able to truly
represent" the mother and that the adoptee, as "an extension of the
parent's ego, [is] in a conflictual bind" because "[t]his child isn't a biological part of the adoptive parents, yet is to be an emotional part of
them."[52] In effect, their analysis evidences the bio-logic of psychoanalysis because it requires that to be an emotional part of one's parents *without conflict* is to be a biological part of one's parents.

I have argued that due to the influence of psychoanalysis, the logic
of bio-narcissism and its onto-epistemic effects repeatedly (re)order
bio-normative family experience and the production of the adoptive
tie's inferiority. Moreover, adoption discourse perpetuates this logic
because it implicitly or explicitly affirms a dual-edged notion of bio-
narcissism: adoptees are unable to serve as extensions of the self for
adoptive parents, and they are also unable to properly identify with
adoptive parents, all of which renders adoptive ties inferior to biological ties. Notably, Charlotte Witt and Jean Keller, two feminists who
theorize adoption, claim that adoptive parent-child relations *can* elicit self-same experiences from which the adoptive family is normatively understood to be barred. On this basis, Keller's and Witt's arguments are seemingly unique in the field of adoption discourse, but we
will nevertheless see that this tack can still be shown to capitulate to
the bio-genealogical imperative.

Charlotte Witt critically examines "family resemblances" as "relational properties that are important for the self-understanding of persons as members of families."[53] She elaborates that "[f]amily resemblances are relational properties which are biological/social hybrids: they exist only as part of a family mythology and hence are social, but the myth tells a story of genetic inheritance, and hence they are biological."[54] Her position is social constructionist: she argues that "there is nothing inevitable about our culture's idealization of families based on genetic ties between parents and their children; it is as much a socially constructed form of life as are other kinds of families – stepfamilies, 'blended' families, adoptive families."[55] Her aim is to show that family resemblances are not exclusive to biological families out of any *genetic* necessity in that, as bases for identity, they can and do occur also within adoptive families. To this effect, she writes that "[d]epending upon the constitution and history of the adoptive family, the language of family resemblances is available to [adoptees], at least in relation to those characteristics that are 'passed on' but not written in the genes."[56] To undercut the significance of genetic similarity among resemblances that are available, she argues that "family resemblances which are heritable via the gene are just one ingredient in a child's self-understanding: many important family resemblances are past on in other ways" due to social relations.[57] In short, Witt's position entails the idea that although a given self, or family, or social context *thinks* that family resemblances are inherited via the gene, *genetic* family resemblances are only one possible kind that may or may not occur in an "'eclectic'" mix of "many different kinds of relational properties [that] might be important ingredients of the self"; that is to say, the possibility of experiencing family resemblances, which is necessary for identity formation, need not turn on genetic resemblance at all or more so than other kinds of resemblance.[58] Witt's ultimate conclusion is that "this means that the significance of family resemblances to a particular child's sense of self can vary from individual to individual – as it surely does."[59] And Witt is surely right that there are individual cases or moments in which adoptive parents and adoptees do share and experience family resemblances. Nevertheless, as it concerns the bionormativity that she intends to thwart, there are a number of problems with this line of reasoning. The main problem is that Witt's argument begins with the uncritical assumption that family *resemblances* of some kind are necessary for the purposes of normal identity formation, which is a de facto reiteration of narcissism as *the* basis for identity and family bond formation and all that it entails, including a tacit turn of the self back into the arms of genetic resemblances. Moreover, Witt does not demonstrate any onto-epistemic equality, even if there is a constructed equality, between possible kinds of family resemblances, which effectively leaves the genetic family episteme intact. Witt's demonstration of a stripped-down equivalence of one construct to another does not effectively undercut the inequality of the social-political-historical meanings that are attached to each construct; it shows a parity between resemblances only as *constructs*, not as *kinds* constructed. So even if Witt is right that all kinds of family resemblances are equivalent in one sense, she does not resolve the problem that genetic family resemblances are constructed as *the* superior kind of resemblance in the game of "normal" or narcissictic identity formation – a game she validates because she affirms the family's need of resemblance – no matter the eclectic tastes of selves. There is one further inequity rooted in Witt's position: it entails that adoptive families have onto-epistemic access to *social* family resemblances *alone*, whereas biological family members enjoy onto-epistemic access to social *and* biological resemblances. In a social-political-historical context that idealizes resemblance, families and selves that are barred access to the same number and same kinds of resemblance are going to be found wanting, yet again.

In the end, the real problem is Witt's presumption that family resemblances "are important for the self-understanding of persons as members of families."[60] Not only does it preclude the critical question of whether *genetic* resemblances are resemblances that *any* self should strive toward as *family* experience; it also precludes the larger question of *whether* resemblance should be a family value at all, simply because its affirmation on any such front, given the contemporary state of family and adoption discourse, is bound to recentre genetic resemblance as the most important kind of *family* resemblance. Indeed, why not avert the effects of the bio-genealogical imperative by newly iterating that personal identity is just as much or more a matter of differentiation as it is a matter of resemblance because every affirmation of what "I am like," inside and outside the family, is equally a simultaneous (albeit unsaid) affirmation of what "I am unlike" – so why not completely interrupt family and adoption discourse and refocus as much or more on difference, and on the existential equality it elicits, as the best basis for identity formation?

Jean Keller discusses her own experience as an adoptive mother and suggests that adoptive parents can experience the adoptee as an extension of the self not merely in the social sense but in the biological sense too. Her position builds on Sara Ruddick's rejection of feminist and essentialist overvaluations of biological bonds – although she rejects Ruddick's problematic "birthgiver/adoptive mother distinction" because "birthgiver" unfairly sets birth mothers apart from "mothers," just as the term "*birth* mother" arguably does too.[61] Notably, Keller does not argue that biological and social bonds are different but equal. Instead, she suggests that social bonds can actually be or become biological bonds. In support of this idea, she enlists evolutionary psychology – which, like epigenetics, turns on an interactive "socio-biological" logic, although Keller focuses on socio-hormonal, not socio-genetic, interactions – to show that social or adoptive parenting can occasion biological bonds (i.e., produce prolactin hormonal responses in and between adoptive family members), and by implication opportunities for bio-narcissistic experiences, insofar as there is "*prolonged physical contact* between adoptive parent and child."[62] She further argues that "acknowledging the role of biology in caregiving behaviors need not result in biological determinism, a reinforcement of objectionable gender roles, or a devaluing of adoptive mothers."[63] As evidence of her "socio-biological understanding of maternal instincts," she offers her personal experience of "attachment parenting" as an adoptive mother.[64] She writes, "I *once* found myself within the first year of adopting my son talking about him as if I had been pregnant and given birth to him" because "he felt so much like an extension of my physical body, that I literally *sometimes forgot* I actually hadn't carried him within my body."[65] Clearly, Keller intends to resist bio-essentialism, or to suggest that there is a bio-experiential (e)quality to be had as an adoptive parent, but her words point to how and why conflations of *family* experience with bio-narcissism are a problem. From where I sit, her words actually entail a tacit affirmation of the bio-genealogical imperative, or the idea that adoptive bonds, even sociobiological ones, are not equivalent to unqualified biological bonds. Her revelation that she "once" talked of her son as though he had been born by her and "sometimes forgot" that he had not been signifies that sociobiological bonds, despite Keller's position, are conceptually transitory bonds; they demand "prolonged physical contact" yet still deny adoptive family subjects a reliable, unforgettable, uninterrupted onto-epistemological experience of connection that biological family subjects do take for granted, even in the absence of prolonged or, perhaps just as often, *any* such contact. Contrary to her stated aim, Keller reiterates what goes unobserved as an understanding of adoption that indirectly posits what we might call socio-bio-narcissism (i.e., the *forgettable* and *infrequent* experience of the adoptive child as an extension of the body) as the poor cousin of bio-narcissism (i.e., the *unforgettable* and *reliable* experience of the bio-child as an extension of the body) insofar as the biological, not the sociobiological, bond continues to be the normative baseline that grants bio-family subjects their steady sense of self *as* family experience.

The point of these examples is not to denigrate the work of Witt or Keller. Nor is it to show that adopted people can *never* be experienced, nor experience others, as extensions of the self within the adoptive family. Instead, the aim is to show how, as an arm of the bio-genealogical imperative, the bio-logic of narcissism (i.e., the influence of psychoanalysis) in adoption and family discourse makes the adoptee unintelligible as an extension of self within the adoptive family in any sense that rivals the taken-for-granted certainty and realization of these experiences in biological families. Indeed, even Witt and Keller, who intend to problematize the superiority of biological ties, hold to this troublesome certainty because they do assume that the difference in the (e)quality between biological and adoptive ties is real; that is why their arguments focus on the *social* or sociobiological as the real point of comparison between ties. They show that adoptive families can and do enjoy *some* narcissistic experiences, along with biological families, but their arguments do not escape a logical outcome, inadvertent perhaps, that nevertheless relegates adoptive families to experiential pathways that are fewer, temporary, forgettable, and thus dramatically different, which sets these experiences apart, qualitatively, as inferior.

In broader terms, the adoptive tie remains inferior because family and adoption experts, no matter their stance, are still compelled to identify the difference of adoption in a social-political-historical context that treats the difference as one that it is profound: there is not and never has been a modern Western non-bio-genealogical imperative that grants equal social-political-historical, or onto-epistemological, status to the adoptive tie. Outright disavowals of bio-narcissism, bio-normativity, or the bio-tie as a singular kind of family tie that is absolute and incontestable are taboo or suspect in our culture; experts who speak or write about family and adoption really are expected minimally to pay proper respect to biological ties. But what is the impetus for this phenomenon? One answer is that it is an outcome of the influence of psychoanalysis as a *scientia familialis*, which has shaped family and adoption discourse and instituted bio-narcissism (i.e., a kind of incestuous desire) as the core basis of normal identity formation within the family. Consequently, disavowals of bio-narcissism are as taboo as avowals of incest; they are discursive stand-ins for one another that ultimately reinforce bio-heteronormativity. And that is why obligatory nods to bio-narcissism are quotidian within family and adoption discourse, even among experts, like Witt or Keller, who actually set out to critique bio-essentialism.

The bio-narcissistic current that psychoanalysis fuels broadly throughout adoption discourse, I think, is illustrated nicely by Emily Hipchen's recent examination of the life writing of adoptees, many of whom have profoundly shaped the search movement and, so too, adoption theory and practice (e.g., Florence Fisher, Debra Levy Holtz, and Betty Jean Lifton, a psychoanalytic mother of the movement).[66] Hipchen considers how such "texts deploy an extended sense of the self grounded in the physical" or in the body.[67] The body in these texts, as she explains, is not any body but a "'family body,'" one that is interchangeable with the meaning of biology as the proper touchstone for adoptee identity formation and family experience. Hipchen observes that "[t]he family body in these search narratives is thus privileged, constructed by biogenesis, and visible in resemblance (on the body of the adoptee and her biological family)."[68] She further shows how "relinquishment and adoption are constructed as disrupting that family body."[69] Ultimately, the lesson Hipchen draws from the repetitive narrative in these texts is that "we can begin to notice the global, endemic nature of our preoccupation with the body in all of our discussions about adoption" and "the subtle ways we manipulate the intersections of body and family in *all* our thinking about the way we make families."[70] As a result, Hipchen's discussion also serves herein as evidence of the bio-narcissistic turn that denigrates meanings of adoption, a turn that I suggest is an outcome of the broad influence of psychoanalysis on adoption theory and practice; wherever visible resemblance of the body is treated as a truth that proves a bond is real or that identification is authentic, the bio-narcissistic current of psychoanalysis is at work.

In a social, historical, and political context delimited by bio-narcissism, or by psychoanalysis as an arm of the bio-genealogical imperative, the biological child enjoys the absolute advantage in the game of attracting "parental" love. His bio-genetic similarity is experienced as a true reflection of his likeness to his parents *as* selves or with regard to their selfhood. In effect, the child's bio-genetic similarity guarantees his status as a complete narcissistic object-choice. It does so even when he reflects his parents in no other way. For instance, biological parents often attribute their features and personality traits to newborns even before such conclusions can be drawn by the human sciences if, indeed, they can be confirmed at all: "she has Dad's temper and Mom's laugh"; "she's impatient, just like her brother"; "he gets his charm from my side of the family." Parents are frequently adamant about the truth of these (and even more imperceptible) observations, which exposes the extent to which the biological narcissism of the bio-genealogical imperative operates through them *as* parents. Nor are adoptive parents exempt from this tendency. They can also participate in a kind of reverse biological narcissism when they "attribute" negative features, characteristics, and/or their "child's problems to heredity," even though they may have no knowledge of the personalities of a child's birth parents.[71] Apart from the fact that heredity gives adoptive parents someone to blame for the failings of their children, their recourse to heredity shows that all parents are subject to a bio-narcissistic imperative that ultimately affects the value and experience of adoptive ties. Of course, this is not to say that narcissistic identifications are impossible inside the adoptive family, as we have seen. An adoptive parent certainly can, on the basis of nurture, identify with aspects of her child's personality, or the "adoptee" might do so by pursuing a parent's interests or lost dreams. However, no authentic or mutually *bio*-narcissistic identification – which psychoanalysis treats implicitly and explicitly as necessary to parental love and normal development – is understood to occur between adoptive parent and adoptee in a social-political-historical context that imposes a bio-genealogical imperative on the family in general.[72] The "adoptee" is excluded discursively from the possibility of being a *bio*-narcissistic object-choice and, therefore, from *parental* love that is understood to be experienced solely on that basis.[73]

The process of identification, which "is known to psycho-analysis as the earliest expression of an emotional tie with another person," also perpetuates biological narcissism in the self relative to the family.[74] In the first place, all forms of identification are essentially narcissistic because they occur solely on the basis of experiences of sameness between the self and the other. Even where psychoanalysis finds identifications to be either "ambivalent" or cannibalistic, sameness remains fundamental to them: the self who hates and wishes to devour or destroy the other does so because he further wishes to instate himself in the same place as the other.[75] The Oedipal complex is an obvious example of this idea. The male child's hatred of his father and love of his mother is an ambivalent identification with his father in that he wishes to take the father's place in relation to the mother.[76] Albeit narcissistic in nature, identifications with sameness are perhaps not always identifications with biology.[77] Yet psychoanalysis's use of this concept, when it is applied to the family, can inevitably be shown to emerge from the imperative of biological narcissism.

For instance, we have already seen that psychoanalysis interprets the family tie or parental love essentially to be a series of biological narcissistic identifications with the child. It additionally interprets a child's emotional ties with his parents to be grounded in biological narcissistic identifications. This perspective is illustrated in the role that identification is given in the family romance, a fantasy that is ultimately rooted in the Oedipal complex.[78] Remember, too, that psychoanalysis applies the family romance to the psychology of adopted children. In effect, it is said to be a stage in which the child first experiences his parents' love as inadequate because they no longer attend to his every wish. Convinced his *real* parents would deny him nothing, he fantasizes that his parents are not real, or that he is adopted. The fantasy is resolved only when he accepts his parents are real, an acceptance that emerges out of his identification with them. In the case of the adoptee, however, psychoanalysis concludes that identification is hindered because she is not her adoptive parents' biological child and, therefore, she is always and already aware that her adoptive parents are not her *real* parents. What is implicit in the idea that the adoptee cannot fully identify with her *adoptive* parents is the further idea that the psychic process of identification, *as* an emotional tie that binds the family, depends on the presence of genetic similarity. The reason for this dependence is that the child's main assurance his parents are real, an assurance that supports identification, is his essential status as a "biological" child.

Apart from Freud's assertion that narcissism is the "precondition" of the Oedipal complex, the discursive use of identification as a com-

ponent of this phase further imposes upon the child a biological narcissistic turn that is said to sustain his emotional ties to the parent.[79]
What is at the centre of the Oedipal drama, as we know, is the male
child's incestuous love for his mother and hate for his father, who has
become an obstacle in the face of this desire. Initially, the child's hate
is manifested in an identification with his father that is "identical
with the wish to replace his father in regard to his mother."[80] Where
the Oedipal phase is resolved normally, the male child represses his
incestuous desire or "object-cathexis" for his mother through an
"intensification of his identification with his father," which "consoli-
date[s] the masculinity in a boy's character."[81] Although he would
later change his mind on this point, proposing a somewhat more
involved female psychology (i.e., the girl transforms her initial love
for a once phallic mother into hatred for a now castrated mother and
thereby experiences Oedipal desire for the father), Freud concludes
in the same passage that the girl's Oedipal experience is "precisely
analogous" to that of a boy.[82] She initially hates her mother, desires
her father, and through an intensified identification with her mother resolves her desire for her father and, therefore, establishes her
femininity.[83] In effect, the general identification with the hated parent is internalized at the same time that it is transformed by the normal child's ego into the ego-ideal. To distinguish between these two
modes of identification, Freud characterizes the former as "what one
would like *to be*" and the latter as "what one would like to *have*."[84]
The significance of this distinction with regard to the biological narcissism that I argue underpins family ties, as opposed to adoptive ties,
within a social-political-historical context of psychoanalysis largely
pertains to this first mode. In the Oedipal phase, the idea that the
child imagines himself *to be* interchangeable with his father, relative
to his *mother*, constitutes the nature of this type of identification as
biologically narcissistic simply because it is incestuous. The reason is
that, since psychoanalysis sets up the Oedipal complex as a normal
and essential part of psychic life within the family, the child simply
must have an opportunity to experience Oedipal or incestuous desire,
and resolve it, if he is to be normal. But this outcome is possible if
and only if a child resides *within* the biological family; incest, by definition, demands that the sexual partners in question, whether they
are psychic or real, be biologically or genetically similar. Being a normal child, therefore, demands first and foremost that a child is, or is
able to imagine himself to be, the "biological" child of his parents.

For obvious reasons, being, *as* knowing oneself to be, an "adopted" child makes incestuous desire within the adoptive family, at worst, impossible and, at best, inauthentic, a point that is further illustrated in the next chapter. Thus, insofar as Oedipal desire turns on an ambivalent identification with the father *and* identification is synonymous with the child's emotional ties to his parents, adoptive ties are rendered inferior to biological ties; the bio-narcissistic turn that psychoanalysis imposes on the child results from the fact that Oedipal desire demands children identify with biological parents in order to experience authentic familial ties.[85]

Now that we understand how a bio-narcissistic logic, or a "normal" love of the double, is implemented through the most fundamental of psychoanalytic concepts, let's revisit the idea that the myth of Narcissus, which informs these concepts and the family psychologies founded upon them, is a model for the self's origins, relations, and psychology. As I have said, Freud treats myth, particularly the Narcissus and Oedipus myths, as true reflections of the structure of the human psyche. He understands them to be "signs that represent something belonging to reality that must be de-codified to arrive at the 'real' thing, the fact."[86] And the key fact he takes from myth is that it signifies a real and universal human psychology. For instance, he believes that this signification is evidenced in and by the "tragic effect" of the Oedipus myth, which "is due to the presence of the same conflict in the unconscious of all individuals."[87] Freud defends this idea where he suggests that the Oedipus myth's "profound and universal power to move can only be understood if the hypothesis I have put forward in regard to the psychology of children has an equally universal validity."[88] As with Oedipus, Freud believes that the conventional experience of Narcissus as a tragic figure bespeaks a truth about our psychic lives: the Narcissus myth's ability to evoke an apparently universal experience or meaning of tragedy is a sign that human psychology is narcissistic. For Freud, both myths symbolize the self's original psychic destiny, one with which it struggles throughout its lifetime.

Admittedly, Freud's study of Narcissus did not match in detail his exploration of Oedipus. However, his early integration of narcissism as a "notion into the psycho-analytic theory as a whole, particularly by relating it to libidinal cathexes," did liken Narcissus's significance to that of Oedipus.[89] It effectively determined that Narcissus would be treated like Oedipus by psychoanalytic modes of knowledge that have mapped out the origins of identity formation and family bonds.

Indeed, more than Oedipus, it is arguably Narcissus who serves today as the dominant object lesson in human psychology. The Narcissus myth remains a powerful model that identifies, as real, the danger of self-dissolution that is posed by self-love when it is turned abnormally inward. It is used to reiterate the psychoanalytic truth that self-knowledge *as* self-consciousness relies on a "normal" dose of narcissism and is the best remedy for the kind of psychic tragedy that befalls Narcissus. It is used to demonstrate the psychic import of self-consciousness that appears to be identifiable in Narcissus's woeful relationship to self-knowledge. For instance, psychoanalysis assumes that if Narcissus had come to know himself, or been self-conscious, *prior* to meeting his reflection in the pool, he could have averted his fate; he would have recognized his reflection as immaterial. He would not have mistaken a self-reflection for a self-same *other* or for someone with whom he could properly identify and, thereby, experience a "normal" sort of self-love – the kind that is directed outward and thus away from the self, as opposed to abnormally inward.

The psychoanalytic ideal of "normal" self-love is also represented in the Narcissus myth through the character of Echo. If Narcissus had returned Echo's love, he might have succeeded very well in the achievement of "normal" narcissism. Loving Echo would have demanded that he extend love outward and thus toward a self-same other in that her self-sameness is symbolically manifested in her constant echo of Narcissus's words. Narcissus, however, is unable to recognize and balance his psychic needs and interests against those of others because he lacks the self-consciousness that underpins "normal" self-love. This is the psychological threat that is symbolized by Narcissus's situation from the perspective of psychoanalysis. His inward turning form of self-love makes it impossible for him to bond because he cannot identify in any meaningful or authentic sense with self-same *others* such as Echo or with the youths who are like him in their sex. It is this inability that leads Narcissus to extend love mistakenly toward an illusion and, therefore, toward abnormal narcissism.

Narcissus's untimely death symbolizes the psychoanalytic ideal of balance that must exist between self-love and self-consciousness. This balance does not denounce narcissism so much as it affirms its centrality for bonds of adult sexual love, which Freud thinks are rooted in the same bonds that form the basis of the family: for Freud, as we know, all love is merely an imago of Oedipal love, the precursor of which is primary narcissism. From the perspective of psychoanalysis, therefore, Narcissus does not suffer death – the ultimate form of self-dissolution – because he is narcissistic but because he lacks the psychic balance that would enable him to engage in "normal" narcissism, wherein he would allow himself to be drawn to an *other* in whom he locates value based on a reflection of self-sameness. It is this understanding that psychoanalysis takes from the myth and displaces onto human psychology. Today, Narcissus implores us all to achieve self-consciousness through an exclusive love that takes the other's self-sameness as its object.

Freud's erection of the Narcissus myth *as* human psychology has several effects. It permeates the family sciences (i.e., family, twin, and adoption psychologies) and produces a new tragedy that directly affects the "family" subject. As the family subject is bound to its doubles through its new psychology, the self that is unbound is necessarily subjected to deep loss and trauma. In effect, the psychology of the same for which Narcissus is the model (re)vivifies the bio-genealogical imperative; it renders unintelligible the idea that any meaningful family bonds can be forged on the basis of difference. This psychology, in turn, deforms the adoptee's experience of family, producing it as one that is second-rate. Moreover, family discourses that share in what is originally the psychoanalytic distinction between normal and abnormal forms of narcissism now participate in the eradication of difference as a possible basis for real and enduring bonds. Psychoanalysis's modern adaptation of the Narcissus myth makes the self's ability and willingness to engage in "normal" narcissisms, such as identification with and the desire to unearth a formerly unconscious childhood history that offers the promise of self-knowledge, a central determinant in the self's success or failure as a "family" subject. Consequently, the tragedy is the impact of psychoanalysis on biological and adoptive families, which profoundly differentiates their experiences, ranking one above the other.

In contrast, when the conventional meaning of the Narcissus myth or the source of its tragedy is opened up to reinterpretation, the bio-genealogical imperative literally *as* psychoanalytic modes of family knowledge can be resisted. Given the value that psychoanalysis places on the achievement of self-consciousness, its treatment of Ovid's Narcissus myth *as* human psychology appears to entail an overt contradiction. In the myth, Tiresias predicts that Narcissus "will live long, if he does not know himself."[90] In effect, the literal meaning of Tiresias's words is clearly inconsistent with the symbolic meaning that psychoanalysis takes from them insofar as psychoanalysis insists that self-knowledge is a psychic good toward which each self should strive. Tiresias's assertion that self-knowledge is the cause of Narcissus's self-destruction flies in the face of psychoanalytic modes of family knowledge. It does so because psychoanalysis binds the achievement of a normal identity to the achievement of self-knowledge *as* self-consciousness, which further entails that the self have access to its bio-genealogy. The myth, therefore, upsets the psychoanalytic precept that self-knowledge *as* bio-genealogical knowledge, in the therapeutic sense, will remediate identity problems associated with its lack: Narcissus's existence *is* snuffed out, as Tiresias forewarns, *because* he comes to know himself or achieves self-consciousness. It is odd, then, that in spite of Tiresias's words, psychoanalysis interprets the myth not as a sign that self-knowledge is and can be dangerous and destructive to identity but as a sign that this knowledge will necessarily grant the self a "normal" psychic life and stable identity. The question is how can psychoanalysis, and the family experts who implement its logic, completely ignore Tiresias's words when modelling human psychology on the myth of Narcissus?

Primarily, psychoanalysis can ignore Tiresias because it is an interpretive changeling. Indeed, the real beauty of psychoanalysis is its ability to eradicate the import of literal meanings and contradictions because the object of its inquiry, the unconscious and thus the imaginary, is rarely something that is understood to offer up content that can be taken at face value, given its symbolic nature.[91] Another reason psychoanalysis can do so is that at the same time it uses the myth to determine that human psychology is narcissistic, it effectively maps an inherently narcissistic psychology onto Narcissus himself. Regardless of Tiresias's words, therefore, psychoanalysis's use of the myth as an objective proof that narcissism drives human psychology functions simultaneously as a proof that Narcissus's fate is the result of a primordial, unconscious narcissism that has gone unchecked. Therefore, psychoanalysis can read the myth simply as one that portends the fate of a self that achieves self-consciousness too late to effectively inhibit its inborn potential for abnormal narcissism. The logic of psychoanalysis does not demand an understanding of Narcissus as someone whose fate is caused by self-knowledge in and of itself; he need serve only as a symbolic warning against the self failing to achieve this knowledge *on time* and in order that it might transcend its potential to suffer a narcissistic personality disorder. The main tragedy or threat that psychoanalysis locates in the myth, one that drives the bio-genealogical imperative, is that self-knowledge *as* self-consciousness can give rise to loneliness and isolation only if it comes too late or not at all. It is the timely pursuit of self-knowledge, and thus compliance with the bio-genealogical imperative, that averts the self's original inclination to extend love exclusively toward an immaterial and self-same image, a tendency that, if left unchecked in the course of development, results in what Narcissus's fate symbolizes as an immobilizing state of grief and, ultimately, psychic death.

Psychoanalysis's use of the myth can be further complicated by debate over whether Ovid thought Narcissus was immediately aware that the youth in the pool was merely his reflection.[92] In translations where Narcissus is self-aware and makes no mistake about who he sees in the pool, the literal content of the myth again seems to reject the idea that self-knowledge is the self's best defence against the onset of psychic tragedy. Insofar as Narcissus *consciously* extends love toward an immaterial and unattainable love object, self-knowledge is necessarily suspect as the guarantor of his psychic well-being. Furthermore, if Narcissus extends love toward his noncorporeal image knowingly, psychoanalysis's use of the myth – as a proof that an *unconscious* or primary narcissism is universally characteristic of the human psyche – is undermined because this particular truth no longer appears to be borne out by the myth itself. The myth acts more like a morality tale in that it warns against vanity and selfishness, which Narcissus exhibits because his self-love and neglect of the corporeal other are now intentional. Still, the logic of psychoanalysis remains terrifically adaptable. It can readily accept that Narcissus's recognition of his own image wholly as such need only reflect one end of a possible continuum of narcissism wherein a conscious Narcissus is even more pathological than a Narcissus who is not initially self-aware. Indeed, psychoanalysis would do well to embrace both versions of the myth. If Narcissus, in one instance, knows himself too late and, in another, is caught in a self-conscious obsession with his image, psychoanalytic modes of knowledge can determine the self's susceptibility to both an unconscious primary narcissism and a conscious narcissism. The latter simply broadens narcissism's influence over human being because it enables these modes of knowledge to determine that an intentional preoccupation with the self is a personal, even a cultural, ideal.[93]

On its own terms, as an interpretive psychology, psychoanalysis can respond to most objections that can be raised about the Narcissus myth's literal content, thereby enabling it to maintain the bio-genealogical imperative. Psychoanalysis's highly interpretative and adaptive nature sustains the universal psychology that it draws from the myth and, therefore, the largely uncritical assumption that at the root of normal identity formation and family bonds is a good and necessary dose of narcissism. Still, when the Narcissus myth is read anew as a critical epistemology, as opposed to as a psychology, it flatly refuses the bio-genealogical imperative. Undoubtedly, the myth is a critical epistemology insofar as it offers up the idea that, with respect to its nature, value, and tangibility, self-knowledge is a problem that can lead to tragedy. It can also be understood to throw into question the inflated value that family and adoption experts tend to place on bio-genealogical knowledge. It does so because its equation of tragedy with the acquisition of self-knowledge challenges the excess and necessity of Narcissus's desire for communion with his reflection, a desire that, in turn, mirrors the self's search for the truth of its being in those few others whose biological similarity acts like a pool in which the self sees itself reflected.

The Narcissus myth's merit as a critical epistemology lies not in the potential of its varied and multiform symbology but in its literal content, which is what psychoanalytic modes of family and adoption discourse typically ignore. Once again, the myth's meaning is articulated clearly by the prophet Tiresias: "He will live long, if he does not know himself."[94] Tiresias is warning that self-knowledge is and can be a source of tragedy and even the terminus of being and existence. For Narcissus, tragedy and death do not culminate out of the knowledge that what he loves is an *other* so alike in being that it is identical to his own. They occur in relation to the self-reflection that he, by virtue of his singular being, projects into the pool. In other words, the self-knowledge that Narcissus gleans is that no matter in what or whom he sees himself externally reflected, he is mistaken to think the truth of his being resides outside of himself; he discovers that to search interminably for the truth of his being in the outward appearance of self-sameness is an odyssey of loneliness toward death. That is how the myth resists the epistemology of the bio-genealogical imperative: it problematizes – because it characterizes as very, very dangerous – the seductive and exclusionary pursuit of self-knowledge in and through a superficial appearance of self-sameness in the other. To approach the other in this manner is always a mistake, one that is demonstrated by Narcissus's recognition that the self-same other in the pool is not real but merely the projection of his own image.

In the context of psychoanalysis, Narcissus is regarded as the victim of self-love. But when the prophecy, rather than desire, is treated as the locus of Narcissus's story, the meaning of his tragedy is recast as a problem of self-knowledge. In a philosophical discussion of Narcissus as a metaphor for the push to achieve artificial intelligence, Eric Steinhart depicts Narcissus in just this way. He considers him to be the "tragic hero of the drama of self-knowledge."[95] The question of artificial intelligence aside, Steinhart's characterization of Narcissus enables us to reimagine the myth as a critical epistemology. Now the obvious effect of self-knowledge, Narcissus's fate ignites a critical doubt for us: does the discourse of identity and family that psychoanalysis has instituted in his name accurately reflect a universal human psychology, or is it a manifestation of the intersection of multiform social, political, and historical practices? Where his fate ceases to warn solely against an overabundant self-love, it offers a vantage point from which to critique the value that is generally placed on self-knowledge, particularly on bio-genealogical knowledge, as a personal, social, and cultural ideal. The myth presents the possibility of a new knowledge, one that, at the very least, is skeptical of the social, political, and historical imperative to achieve bio-genealogical knowledge at all costs. As a form of self-knowledge, it is now intelligible as something that is as likely to beget tragedy as it is to thwart it, a possibility that may be evidenced in occurrences of adoption "reunions that break down."[96]

Tiresias warns that Narcissus will experience an early death – the ultimate loss of self – if and only if he knows himself. To understand Narcissus's fate as one that is epistemological, as well as its implications for the bio-genealogical imperative, the nature of Narcissus's self-knowledge needs to be re-examined. In the myth, the moment of truth occurs as Narcissus acknowledges that the object of his love is not real: it is a noncorporeal reflection of himself in the pool. Narcissus's mistake, as Steinhart observes, is his failure "to understand that the reflection in which he recognized himself was only a self-representation, not a self-presentation, not the presence of his double, not the appearance of his other body."[97] This is the tragedy: Narcissus "mistakes a copy for the original, he mistakes a part for the whole. Indeed, he mistakes a partial copy for the whole original. He mistakes a fragmentary representation for an integral presence; he mistakes a counterfeit for the real thing; he mistakes his reflection for his double."[98] Narcissus does not comprehend the *difference* between himself

as an original and his self-image as a copy. He does not understand
that the double, as an integral presence that is identical to his own
presence in body, thought, and emotion, does not exist until it is too
late. The self-image that he thinks he has located in an *other* is "counterfeit," just as a copy of the Mona Lisa, no matter the quality of the
imitation, is always counterfeit.[99] Insofar as Narcissus extends love
toward a counterfeit self, he rejects both the reality of his own and
the other's singular originality and difference. Worse than this, when
he accepts his counterfeit self-image as an original, he "sacrifices himself by accepting a counterfeit self-presence as the truth of his being."[100]
He sacrifices himself and his autonomy with respect to his being,
experience, and identity because he trusts that his self-knowledge is
and can be in the hands of the other who appears as his double and
who, even if he were a real person rather than his reflection, would
reflect, at best, not *an identical self* but merely some identical biological similarities.

Essentially, a self-image is an image that is inseparable from the self
it represents; it is the self's conception of itself. If an *original* self does
not or has not existed, therefore, there is and can be no *self*-image; the
occurrence of the latter is concomitant with the former. In the
absence of a real and particular self, a given image is no more than an
unqualified image of some self that is as imaginary as a unicorn. This
is what Narcissus comes to know about himself: "What you seek, you
have" or "With you it comes and stays, and with you it will go, if you
can bear to go."[101] His self-knowledge culminates in the realization
that the object he seeks and desires, because it is a self-identical *other*,
is actually his self-image, something that is tied already wholly to himself. The very nature of his love object is such that it always comes and
stays with him alone. It does so out of necessity because it does not
exist without or beyond him. Narcissus's self-image is like all *self*-
images, therefore, in that it is bound to the original it reflects. Consequently, the knowledge he acquires is that his double – the one who
has an "innate understanding of every idle thought that crosses [his]
mind," offering him "immediate sympathy and affection," and the one
with respect to whom he feels the "same quick apperception of your
slightest mercurial mood" – does not exist.[102] His double does not
exist because the one true image, or self, or identity of Narcissus is
unique to him. It does not and cannot exist in his absence. This is the
essence of human being, and thus his tragic mistake is to imagine that
an *other* can embody something that he *is* alone and already.

As a critical epistemology, the Narcissus myth challenges family psychologies that are driven by the bio-genealogical imperative. It dismisses the idea that self-knowledge resides unmediated in a corporeal other even if the other appears to be the self's twin or double because of biology. It rejects the imperative because the belief that the other contains Narcissus's self-knowledge is at the core of his tragic fate. As he comes to know himself, Narcissus recognizes his originality and difference, *and* he realizes that his system of knowledge or belief about self-sameness as a basis for love and relationship is fatally flawed. Together, these realizations conspire in the production of his tragedy. He knows himself when he knows that the self-same other in the pool is an illusion, yet he does not forfeit the original system of knowledge that, because it alienates him from the other, also casts him out of the human world. Instead, he commits himself to pine eternally for the self-same at the edge of the pool, thereby choosing to be completely *alone*. It is the knowledge he rejects in favour of a fantasy that leads to his trauma and death! As an epistemology, therefore, the myth challenges the bio-genealogical imperative because it contradicts psychoanalytic modes of family knowledge. Where psychoanalytic discourse treats bio-genealogical knowledge as key to "normal" identity formation and "family" bonds, it presupposes, like Narcissus, that an authentic or unmediated self-knowledge is and can be housed by the other who, because of biology, merely appears to be the self's double. The epistemology of the myth, however, rejects this assumption because it indicates that the cost of making it, which Narcissus does, is trauma and death: his desire for self-knowledge *as* the desire for the self-same is instrumental in the loss, as opposed to the completion, of his self. In the myth, seeking the other *as* someone who is self-identical is a fool's errand rooted in an illusion. The illusion is that the double exists and is a vessel of unadulterated self-knowledge.

The profound and existential cost of a system of knowledge that assumes the other's biological similarity *is* the self-same is that thinking with this system causes the self to lose sight of its originality and difference and all that this existential reality implies for being and identity in relation to the other. To whatever degree Narcissus's inability to commune with suitors who are genuinely *other* (i.e., Echo and the male youths) is a psychological failure, it is also an epistemological failure because he does not, indeed will not, comprehend the powerful opportunity for self-knowledge and relationship that occurs in and through the other's originality and difference. He narrows his existence through a neglect of the world that terminates in his death – the most complete loss of self – because he will not relinquish his belief that sameness is the basis for the self's deepest bonds. Consequently, where modes of family knowledge model human psychology on Narcissus and, thereby, (re)institute the bio-genealogical imperative, they mirror his epistemological mistake and the tragedy it entails. They efface the value of the other's originality and difference as a basis for love and identity because their approach to biological similarity is just like Narcissus's approach to the pool: in biology, they insist, lies an image to which the self is inherently drawn in the course of love as "normal" development. They empathize too deeply with Narcissus and overdetermine that to achieve a normal identity the self must interminably seek communion with its reflections in the bio-pool. The result is a profound neglect of Tiresias's warning; they ignore the meaning of Narcissus's inability to redirect his gaze toward the value of the other's originality and difference. Where family experts insist that the self's lust for bio-genealogical knowledge is inherent, rather than implemented, they fail to comprehend that the existential cost of Narcissus's epistemology is loneliness, grief, and (psychic) death. This is how the adopted subject is produced!

There is another way to upset the bio-genealogical imperative and the discourse of narcissism as a core apparatus for understanding family relations and identity. Where Narcissus continues as a metaphor to inform psychoanalytic modes of family knowledge and, therefore, human psychology, family experts must necessarily consider the polymorphism of his myth, at the very least to avert the pitfalls of being arbitrary. In the different accounts of his story, Narcissus has a great deal more to tell us about family relations. The heterogeneity of his tale offers a range of meanings to which family experts should attend if they are to treat narcissism as the truth of human psychology. As Pausanias discussed in the second century AD, there is "another story about Narcissus, less popular indeed than the other, but not without some support."[103] In this story, Narcissus gazes longingly into a pool as well, but he does so to ease his grief over the death of his twin sister, with whom he was deeply in love.[104] He and his sister looked, dressed, and wore their hair alike. Like many twins, they were inseparable, hunting and sharing together in almost every activity. Unlike in Ovid's tale, however, this Narcissus is immediately conscious of his reflection in the pool *as* a reflection. In fact, Pausanias vehemently rejected Ovid's characterization of Narcissus as unconscious because it is "utter stupidity to imagine that a man old enough to fall in love was incapable of distinguishing a man from a man's reflection."[105] For Pausanias, the use that Narcissus makes of his image is both conscious and strategic. He uses it with intention as a balm for his sorrow, finding "relief for his love in imagining that he saw, not his own reflection, but the likeness of his sister," who was once a bona fide corporeal other.[106]

Pausanias's version of the myth can be appropriated by psychoanalytic modes of family knowledge, at least to some degree. The sexual intensity of Narcissus's twin bond, for example, can be read as a sign that an unrestrained narcissistic psychology leads to psycho-sexual or Oedipal abnormalities, such as incest. Nevertheless, there are also important ways that Pausanias's tale contradicts psychoanalytic modes of family knowledge. Fundamentally, it resists the uncritical assumption that narcissism is necessarily rooted in an unconscious love of the same because the Narcissus we meet at the beginning of Pausanius's story is immediately aware of the powerful role that difference plays in his family relations. The recognition of his sister's difference is signified by the fact that he is *consciously* grieving her loss. It is also evident in the enlistment of his representation as an instrument. He does not engage his image out of self-love, nor does he come to grief over the noncorporeality of his *re*presentation, as is the case in Ovid's tale. He turns to his image with the awareness that he is using it to soothe his grief over the loss of a formerly genuine presence, one he knows was his beloved sister. Where Narcissus is both in a state of grief *and* conscious of his *re*presentation, he symbolizes a concept of self wherein it is possible to be deeply bonded to what is simultaneously recognized to be other. He elicits a crisis in the logic of the same that underpins contemporary modes of family knowledge because, whether or not Narcissus realized this truth before or through the experience of his sister's absence and death, he clearly has done so by the start of the tale as told by Pausanias. We meet Narcissus only as he is face to face with both the indissolubility of his bond and the reality of his sister's otherness. We witness him as a twin for whom being closely bonded *and* being separate and distinct are at the forefront of his knowledge and experience.

Earlier, I suggested that Ovid's version of the Narcissus myth can be read as a critical epistemology about family relations. In a similar way, Pausanias's tale inspires further readings that evoke a critical ontology. It permits interpretations that challenge Narcissus's modern Western positioning as the emblem of a universal psychology of the same. Undoubtedly, the bio-genealogical imperative as twin discourse already predisposes us to read the Pausanius myth retrospectively as a tale that affirms sameness as *the* meaning of Narcissus's twinship (i.e., as a story about the experience of the loss of *a part of the self*). In contrast, I think that it can be read as a tale about twins *and* existential difference (i.e., a tale about an experience of the loss of *an other*). Indeed, there are many ways that Pausanius's account allows for a reconsideration of Narcissus as a self that recognizes existential difference in the face of the same, at least insofar as the same is what twins signify among modern Western family subjects. The Pausanius myth does so from the outset because, as observed in chapter 4, the contemporary fascination with twins' biological similarities as conduits for *being the same* is a relatively recent event in Western history (e.g., because of eugenicist Sir Francis Galton's influence); recall that twins typically signified difference or opposition in Ancient Greece (e.g., Apollo and Artemis) and Ancient Rome (e.g., Romulus and Remus). To assume that Narcissus *as* a twin was intended to signify sameness is likely an interpretive mistake, especially because of Pausanius's remarks about his age and powers of perception. These observations and Narcissus's conscious and strategic use of his reflection to soothe his grief suggest that the meaning of existential difference is reasonably drawn from the Pausanius myth; that Narcissus intentionally invokes a sameness strategy to soothe himself demonstrates that his twin's existential difference is delivered to his consciousness. And even if he intermits the experience and knowledge of his twin's otherness (i.e., her death) by turning to the appearance of sameness (i.e., his image as a substitute for her former presence), he does not, indeed cannot, refuse his twin's otherness if it is true that he is conscious of his reflection in the pool as such. His twin's difference is known to him, and signified to us, by virtue of her death; her death is the visceral reality of her otherness in spite of her being his twin, and it symbolizes the existential permanence of her difference. Insofar as Narcissus is a (psychic) model for the self and insofar as the absence or death of his twin demonstrates the imminence of the double's essential difference from the self, the Pausanias myth suggests that profound "family" bonds, which may or may not be (psychically) incestuous, can and do occur in tandem with the experience and knowledge of otherness.

As a grieving twin, Narcissus presents us with an alternative account of family subjectivity. He betokens a self that experiences a resilient bond at the same time that it does not refuse the otherness of its biological double. The idea that a family bond *is* forged across difference, even on the part of Narcissus *as* a biological twin, or in spite of it, makes the idea that profound "family" bonds *do* occur across difference intelligible in all "family" contexts, not just adoptive ones. The meaning of difference that the Pausanius myth elicits thwarts modern Western family discourse: it contradicts the psychoanalytic logic of the same that is drawn archetypically from Ovid's myth, and consequently it challenges the bio-genealogical imperative. Where it addresses family relations, it suggests that narcissism should not be imagined simply, or uncritically, as an innate human psychology wherein the self and its bonds are understood essentially to be oriented toward a love of the same. It counters the discursive effects of bio-narcissism that dissemble the profound existential differences, and the experiences thereof, that occur between selves both within the biological family and within the adoptive family.

The sexual difference of the twins in the Pausanius myth also speaks to meanings of existential difference. It clearly marks them as distinct. Of course, the meaning of sexual difference is complex. Its social, political, and historical contours are multifaceted; questions of race and whiteness, sexuality, class and ability, as well as culture, nation, and colonization shape the subordination of females and femininity, the operations of heteronormativity, and variegations of heteropatriarchy. In spite of women's subordination, however, the social significance of sexual difference as a sign of alterity is unequivocal. For instance, Brooke Holmes suggests that classical scholars generally tend toward "the influential argument that, in the mythological imagination of early Greece, 'the feminine' functions as the 'Other' to the masculine norm," which is not to say there is no debate about the representational roles of sexual difference in Ancient Greek myths, texts, and culture.[107] Feminists also accept the idea that sexual difference in and of itself is a sign of existential otherness, although they may debate its operations within language, the social, and the symbolic of the psyche, as well as debate "the proprietary claim of 'the feminine' on the position of the 'excluded Other'" – for instance, on the grounds that there are additional excluded others to consider, such as "slaves, children, and animals" in Ancient Greece, or on the grounds of race, class, ability, and nation today.[108] Nevertheless, the meaning of sexual difference as existential otherness is well established in the context of feminist theory. It is the focus of a vast and diverse feminist literature into which only a brief detour is possible here. In particular, I enlist Simone de Beauvoir, Luce Irigaray, and Judith Butler to show that sexual difference in the Pausanius myth is reasonably interpreted to suggest that, in spite of a contemporary habit that misrecognizes the same as the best basis for family bonds, existential difference is the best basis for viable and enduring family bonds.

Famously, Simone de Beauvoir explores sexual difference as existential otherness in the *The Second Sex*, as well as its phenomenology within the inequity of gendered social relations. She enlists a Hegelian logic to characterize how "the Other" is situated by and within meanings of sexual difference and how such otherness is enlisted in the service of the male subject. Beauvoir effectively isolates the qualities of human consciousness that make possible, as Margaret A. Simons puts it, the "determination to respect the differences between self and Other while maintaining a relationship."[109] Beauvoir's ontological analysis of relations between the male subject and female other posits that "once the subject seeks to assert himself, the Other, who limits and denies him, is none the less a necessity to him: he attains himself only through that reality which he is not, which is something other than himself."[110] As Nadine Changfoot observes, Beauvoir exposes the ontological irony that where the male subject dominates the female other "to bend and mould her to his will ... there is a fundamental opposition that leads to failure" in that "man's individual need for recognition cannot be met by an(other), who is already subject to his will."[111] In effect, Beauvoir understands sexual difference to be a true alterity. And she concludes that the difference is a genuine possibility that enables mutual recognition and thereby an ethics wherein the self and the other may transcend the immanence of the master-slave dialectic. Beauvoir sums it up this way: "Thanks to her, there is a means for escaping that implacable dialectic of master and slave which has its source in the reciprocity that exists between free beings."[112]

Luce Irigaray, who reads the "phallogocentric" core of language and philosophy against itself to expose women's "negative assignment as man's denigrated inversion," also examines sexual difference as a basis for ethical relations through mutual recognition.[113] She exposes "the sexuation of language" and "the index of sexedness in speech."[114] She demonstrates how "[t]he subject speaks to himself" and why, historically speaking, there has been "[n]o place for words for the other."[115] Her project is ontological in that she intends to demonstrate the "*being* in the feminine."[116] In this respect, Irigaray is controversial; her ideas about sexual difference stir debate over whether her conception of it is biologically essentialist, politically (i.e., strategically) essentialist, realist essentialist, or post-essentialist.[117] What is not debated is whether Irigaray is right to treat sexual difference *as* existential difference, which she does, such as when she writes, "Certainly, this reality of the *two* has always existed. But it was submitted to the imperatives of a logic of the *one*, the *two* being reduced then to a pair of opposites not independent one from the other."[118] Between the sexes, therefore, and irrespective of "[w]hatever identifications are possible," Irigaray, not unlike Beauvoir, is clear that as it concerns the ontological status of sexual difference, "one will never exactly occupy the place of the other – they are irreducible one to the other."[119]

Judith Butler also articulates a clear understanding of sexual difference as existential otherness in a critical response to Irigaray. Butler lauds Irigaray's "original contribution to ethical thinking" about sexual difference, *but* she rejects any "presum[ption] that it is only the masculine and the feminine who come into an ethical encounter with the Other."[120] She argues instead that these encounters are as likely to be had between others for whom the difference is, or is also, due to "other kinds of social differences," such as those that occur out of racialization and/or heteronormativaty.[121] She affirms Irigaray's project, which "takes sexual difference as its point of departure," only insofar as she accepts the idea that sexual difference is *a*, but not *the*, point of departure for ethical encounters of mutual recognition.[122] Nevertheless, Butler is like Irigaray, and Beauvoir before her, in that she considers sexual difference to be *an* ontological sign of existential otherness, wherein an other, even a subordinated one, makes itself known because it must be recognized – if not wholly, then in part – due to its incommensurability with the subject (i.e., the male subject for Beauvoir, the masculine subject for Irigaray, and the heteronormative and/or white male subject for Butler). As Butler explains,

[T]he ethical relation might be said to emerge between the sexes precisely at the moment in which a certain incommensurability between these two positions is recognized. I am not the same as the Other: I cannot use myself as the model by which to apprehend the Other: the Other is in a fundamental sense beyond me and in this sense the Other represents the limiting condition of myself. And further, this Other, who is not me, nevertheless defines me essentially by representing precisely what I cannot assimilate to myself, to what is already familiar to me.[123]

The import of Butler's discussion is that recognition of the other is evidenced in the subject's desire to repress the other, to absent it, or to deny it recognition (e.g., as in the Hegelian dialectic); this desire is the subject's admission that it intuits the other as an *existant*. Thus to will an other away is paradoxically to demonstrate the recognition by the subject of the other, which is why *the willing* is the threshold for the possibility of an ethical relation, or mutual recognition, on the basis of differences such as sex, race, gender, and/or sexuality.

Referring to Irigaray and Butler, Sara Beardsworth characterizes "the feminist investigation of sexual difference [as] an attempt to recognize and install difference as the prodigious foundation of multiple relations and connections with others."[124] Beauvoir, Irigaray, and Butler go somewhat further, I think, in that they already understand sexual difference, even when it is refused as such, to be an extant foundation and possibility for relations because subjects and others who are sexed are also incommensurable.[125] Therefore, when these ideas about sexual difference are combined not only with the idea that twins historically signified difference (discussed in chapter 4) but also with Pausanius's claim that Narcissus recognizes his reflection as such and, thus, that Narcissus consciously uses his reflection to soothe himself over his twin's finitude, it means that the sexual difference between Narcissus and his twin as told in the Pausanius myth also reinforces the idea that Narcissus is a subject who is aware of the existential differences that bring deep and powerful bonds into being, for what is a bond if not a tether between two separate and distinct beings? Ironically, Narcissus the twin can be understood to destabilize bio-narcissism as the locus of intense family relations by virtue of his differences, a result that challenges the influence of psychoanalysis and the bio-genealogical imperative.

To complicate matters, Narcissus's story also suggests that the absence of a biological tie is not sufficient to preclude the reality of family bonds. The final profundity of the Pausanias myth is that it presents us with a very complicated and messy view of family relations; the sexual love between Narcissus and his twin sister and the possibility that their love was consummated prior to her death throw the meaning and nature of their "family" bond further into question.

Nonetheless, the messy and contradictory nature of Narcissus's bond with his sister/lover also rings true as it concerns the complicated experiences most people have within their families, regardless of whether their ties are biological or adoptive. Narcissus's incest can be interpreted to reiterate an Oedipal truth, one that is rooted in biology and proceeds out of primary narcissism, but it need not be. The temptation to make the myth conform to a *scientia familialis* or *sexualis*, one that iterates bio-narcissism as the precursory Oedipal truth of "family" subjectivity, is averted if incest is refused as the most important meaning of Narcissus's sexual desire. In other words, when the myth is considered in remove from modes of family knowledge that are predicated upon a bio-sexual logic of the same, it is possible that Narcissus's desire for his sister does not signal incest at all but the degree to which the self's experience within the family is always a complex tangle wherein biological relatives are and are not experienced as "family." It is possible that the meaning of incest in the Pausanius myth is less important than the meanings of family that the factual presence of the twins' sexual desire throws into question. Narcissus's experience of his twin sister as his "lover" challenges our uncritical assumption that the biological tie is either a sufficient or a necessary condition for "family" ties. His desire in the presence of a biological tie destabilizes normative meanings of family *as* biology because it produces the twin, contemporaneously, as "family" and "not-family."

Contrary to being an affirmation of a universal love of the same, therefore, Narcissus's desire demonstrates the antinomy of family experience and thus the frailty of the biological tie as the surety of family experience. His paradoxical relations with his sister/lover undercut the idea that family experience is circumscribed by the biological tie or is limited to *the same* because, in the myth, the same (i.e., biology) neither bridles the twins' experience nor subjugates it solely to *being* one of family. They *are*, or were, "lovers," a meaning that clearly contradicts their identities as "family"! Although Narcissus is appropriated by psychoanalysis to reiterate a bio-genealogical imperative that diminishes the intensity of adoptive bonds, he also presents us with the possibility that the limits of family discourse and experience can be reinvented.

This chapter brings to an end my discussion of how psychoanalytic modes of family knowledge institute bio-narcissism as the first principle of normal "family" relations and identity. I have argued that the use of the Narcissus myth as a psychology effectively bars the adoptive tie's ability to function as a *real* "family" tie. When the myth is re-examined as a critical epistemology and as a critical ontology, I have suggested that it makes intelligible the possibility that real family experiences are rooted in difference, despite any appearance of sameness. With this idea in mind, my brief discussion of incest in relation to Narcissus is now an impetus for a broader investigation into the effects of incest discourse upon adoptee subjectivity. In the coming chapters, I investigate the meaning of incest both inside and outside the context of adoption psychology. In doing so, I not only consider the impact of incest discourse on family knowledge and experience today but also challenge and resist it.

7

Genetic Sexual Attraction:
The Place of Incest in Adoption Discourse

It takes the form of an overpowering, almost electrical grip of emotion, associated with an inability to keep away from the other person and an almost primordial sense of having belonged together all their lives. The attraction gives rise to a sense of underlying shame and guilt, together with a feeling of rejection that may prevent effective communication because the emotions are too threatening to share with anyone. This may be compounded by any sexual relationship resulting from the attraction.

"Genetic Sexual Attraction,"
Encyclopedia of World Problems and Human Potential

Due to the momentum of the adoption rights movement, an increase in legal access to formerly sealed records in different provinces and states in Canada and the United States, and thus a rise in reunions, adoption experts have discovered that in the midst of reunions, adoptees and birth parents or siblings may experience intense sexual feelings toward one another. This phenomenon is what is now known as "'genetic sexual attraction'" (GSA).[1] For the obvious reason that reunitees share biological ties, adoption experts primarily conceptualize GSA in two ways: they treat it as a form of incest, or they contend that, although it is not incest per se, acting on it will subject reunitees to the same social and psychological consequences associated with incest.

By investigating adoption discourse surrounding GSA, this discussion sets the stage for the main focus of the following three chapters: how does the relationship between the meaning of incest *as* the biological tie impose limits on the kinds of "family" experiences that are available to the "biological" family as opposed to the "adoptive" family? Currently, the biological tie is socially and legally conflated with the family tie, unless, of course, a child is legally adopted, which transfers all legal rights onto adoptive parents, who are expected both to treat the child "'as if born to'" them and to "assum[e] the responsibility and emotional outlook of natural parents."[2] Given the biological bias already implicit in this idea (i.e., that adoptive ties are or should be mimetic), the social and legal reach of the biological tie, as a "family" tie, is not fully erased when an adoptive tie is put in its place. This reality can be seen in the experience of many "adopted" children who, when they are socially known as such, generally grow up being asked questions about their biological parents, such as what they know about them and whether they know or want to know them.[3] Interrogations like these are a sign that some semblance of the ontological status of the biological tie, *as* a "family" tie, is maintained alongside the adoptive tie, even if the former exists only in the imaginations of those conducting the interrogation. Of course, the desire for search and reunion on the part of an "adoptee" also speaks to how the biological tie remains intact, as a "family" tie, even in the presence of an adoptive tie.

The question of whether the biological tie's onto-epistemological status *can* ever be replaced by that of an adoptive tie in this social, political, historical moment elicits the further question of whether it *should* be replaced? But just like the question of whether incestuous desire or GSA should be acted upon, the question of whether biological ties should be replaced as de facto "family" ties is utterly taboo. Indeed, both questions have monumental implications for a social, legal, and economic order that is governed by bio-family discourse, which is a fundamental reason why family and adoption experts of all stripes, as discussed in chapter 1, explicitly or implicitly refuse or sidestep them, such as with both/and positions.[4] The idealization of biological ties over and above adoptive ties and the prohibition against incest or GSA are two sides of the same coin. They work together to uphold the bio-genealogical imperative as the modern Western truth of family and do so, in part, because they make meaningful consideration of the erasure or displacement of biological ties as de facto family ties practically impossible. They are interdependent facets of a mode of reason that refuses thought about family and sexuality apart from bio-normativity. They are reflected mutually within past and present justifications for secrecy and open adoption, closed and open records, search and reunion, and the use of bio-genealogical knowledge in the treatment of adoptee pathology, whether that pathology relates to adoptee identity, including transracial adoptee identity, or to GSA; as a result, traditional debates about the legal or psychic rights and privileges that should or should not be granted to adoptees, birth parents and siblings, and adoptive parents with respect to bio-genealogical knowledge do not actually rock the boat of a bio-normative social order. Instead, they veil the degradation of family experience that is due not to a lack of biological ties but to a totalizing refusal to question whether bio-genealogical knowledge is, or should continue to be treated as, *self*-knowledge.

Where bio-genealogical knowledge is treated as an inherent need or necessary right of the person in family and adoption discourse, it also plays a symbiotic role in the regulation of the family in relation to sexuality and incest. As shown in this and the chapters that follow, incest discourse, including that of GSA, not only reiterates the self's need for bio-genealogical knowledge but also institutes a set of privileges and pleasures that differentiate and render superior or inferior, to greater or lesser degrees, the different kinds of family subjects upon which they are conferred. It is as a right, a privilege, a pleasure, an identity, a cure, the best basis for experiences of family and belonging, and a bar to sexual relations that the bio-genealogical imperative as incest and GSA discourse also undercuts the authenticity of adoptive family relations. So even as normative constellations of the biological family may be changing – for instance, due to new reproductive technologies, the use of surrogates, divorce, interracial and gay marriage, and/or queer adoption – the overvaluation of bio-genealogical knowledge has not disappeared. For instance, the idea that changing family formations are either a necessary cause or even a correlate of the bio-genealogical imperative's ultimate demise is contradicted by Suzanne Pelka's finding that lesbian co-mothers often experience maternal jealousy when one mother is and one is not genetically tied to the child; "[t]ypically, when these feelings surfaced it was in the context of a non-birth mother feeling jealous of the physical relationship that her partner, the birth mother, and her children shared."[5] It is also evident in Petra Nordqvist's study of "lesbian couples who desired to 'match' physical family resemblances through their donor" in order to "facilitate the construction of a biogenetically connected two-parent family ... which is socially and culturally perceived as a 'normal' family."[6] Still, Katarina Wegar indicates in a discussion of kinship and race that "alternative view[s] of kinship and child-parent bonding" seem to be "more common among already marginalized and stigmatized groups."[7] And no doubt she is right in that when a group is denied normative access to kinship, is isolated, suspect, and under siege, as racialized and/or LGBTQ people often have been, alternative kinship bonds *are* a way to resist and survive. Indeed, LGBTQ people historically have opted for "chosen family," yet as LGBTQ people access rights to marriage, new reproductive technologies, surrogacy, and so on, the queer mantra of "chosen family" is rapidly dissipating in favour of biological ties or bio-homonormativity and bio-homonationalism.[8] In effect, the more that families change and/or the more that marginalized groups are enfranchised, the more that the bio-genealogical imperative adapts *and* remains the same, whether as a product, an object of desire, a superior sense of connection and belonging, or a unique commodity that satiates an ostensibly incontrovertible human right to, or need for, self-knowledge – a point illustrated by the increasing popularity of ancestry research services (e.g., 23andMe, AncestryDNA, and MyHeritage) in and among mainstream *and* marginalized individuals and families.

In the modern Western context, the existence of close biological ties between two people who engage in sex constitutes their sex, by definition, as incest and, further, as a crime if they so acted with the knowledge of these ties.[9] In effect, the meaning of incest is conflated with the presence of the biological tie. At the same time, the dominant meaning of "family" is also conflated with the presence of the biological tie. Furthermore, despite the fact that the legal adoptive tie is said to sever all rights and responsibilities normally founded upon the biological tie, there are important ways that the status of the biological tie remains legally intact, as a "family" tie, because of the current meaning of incest: a birth parent and a birth child as well as birth siblings remain subject to incest law following separation through legal adoption, and adoptive parents and adopted children and siblings, although they can commit sexual abuse, cannot legally speaking commit incest. Two interesting and unusual court cases illustrate these points.

In an American case that went to the US Supreme Court, a biological father by the name of Bohall had sex with his biological

daughter many years after her legal adoption to another family.[10]
Charged with incest, he argued that the sexual encounter did not
constitute incest because his biological daughter, having been legally
adopted, was not his "daughter." Bohall was initially convicted. He
appealed, and although his conviction was overturned, the Supreme
Court later overturned the appeal decision and again convicted him
of incest. The reasoning behind the Supreme Court decision was that
in light of the clear, precise, historical, and legal meaning of incest,
the presence of the biological tie between Bohall and his biological
daughter was sufficient to prove that she indeed was his "daughter"
as pertained to the charge of incest. In effect, the legal status of her
adoptive tie did not negate the legal status of their biological tie in
this instance.

A Canadian case that went to the Ontario Court of Appeal illustrates that incest is not understood to be a committable offence
within the adoptive family. In *R. v. Schmidt*, the case revolved
around the question of whether an accused brother and his sister,
the plaintiff, committed incest because it was unclear whether
Schmidt *knew* he was his sister's "biological" brother; knowledge
of the biological tie is generally a necessary consideration in determining the criminal element of incest.[11] Schmidt was twenty years
his sister's senior, and their parents were not available to confirm
that they conceived and gave birth to both children. Largely,
Schmidt appealed his conviction based on the idea that the evidence against him – which included a claim by his sister that he
was her biological brother, a letter he sent to the same sister that
began "Dear sis," and another letter to her that he signed "Brot
Chris" – could be counted only as hearsay; the evidence did not
show he had direct knowledge of a biological tie to his sister.[12] The
main debate pertained to possible meanings that can be attributed
to "sis" and "brot," as short forms for "sister" and "brother," which
created doubt about whether Schmidt could be fairly judged to
have knowingly committed incest. One of the judge's main observations was that "sister" and "brother" might merely refer to an
"adopted" sibling, and as "there was no evidence to show in what
sense these terms were used," he acquitted Schmidt of the crime of
incest.[13] In this case, the judge's basis for acquittal (i.e., the possibility of adoption) points to the lack of a legal view of incest as a
committable offence between people with adoptive ties.[14] It also

suggests how incest law and incest discourse (of which the law is a part) play a role in maintaining the differentiated status of biological as opposed to adoptive ties.

These examples ultimately show ways that incest discourse does not explicitly demarcate or mediate adoptive ties in any meaningful way. They also point to how incest discourse demarcates people as "family" on the basis of biology even though this might not be how they experience themselves in relation to each other. My aim, in light of these examples and throughout subsequent discussions, is to explore how the onto-epistemic terms that constitute the meaning of incest foreclose the possibility of adoptive family experience being regarded as equal to, or as good as, biological family experience. I also suggest that incest discourse is a strategic mode of the modern Western bio-genealogical imperative to the extent that it currently functions as a litmus test for the individual's ontological status *as* "family." In other words, incest discourse impacts human being in important ways because the biological tie is used to signify people who are both "family" *and* subject to incest prohibition; the self who is categorically capable of committing incest is also produced by incest discourse *as* "family." In limiting and determining individuals *as* "family," incest discourse can be understood to effectively intensify the experience of genetic similarity and (re)produce the superiority of the biological tie simply because the meaning of incest implicitly confutes the authenticity of the adoptive tie *as* a family tie.

It is with this idea in mind that I now turn to the question of how adoption experts' appeal to incest discourse in order to explain GSA essentially participates in the differentiation and degradation of the adoptive tie. If we assume that incest is a test that delineates the boundaries of family in the modern Western context, adoption discourse (re)inscribes this test (and a biologically based notion of family) specifically when it functions *as* incest discourse. Primarily, this (re)inscription is accomplished when adoption discourse utilizes incest discourse, and its implications, to explain and prevent GSA. Adoption experts reinforce incest discourse and its impact on family ties in a number of ways: they utilize it directly; they reinforce the biologically based notion of family, with which the meaning of incest is interdependent, to explain GSA; and they warn that acting on GSA, even if they (as opposed to courts) do not conceive of it precisely as incest, is just as socially and psychologically catastrophic with regard to the true aim of reunion, which is to (re)establish and maintain a (biological) family tie. Finally, adoption experts' utilization or support of incest discourse also (re)inscribes the modern Western bio-genealogical imperative simply because the ability to avoid incest or GSA requires that individuals know their bio-genealogy.

Apart from contexts of adoption and reunion or incest studies in evolutionary biology, psychology, and anthropology, most people are unaware of the phenomenon of GSA. Members of the general public will have encountered it rarely, if at all, in the odd television or radio documentary, such as "Incest: The Last Taboo?" and "Forbidden Love: Genetic Sexual Attraction," or in a one-off, sensational newspaper or magazine article, such as "What's It Like to Date Your Dad?" and "Can You Really Justify Wanting to Have Sex with Your Mom?"[15] For the most part, however, GSA is a focus of concern for adoption experts and people directly affected by search and reunion.[16] Although GSA is normalized as a feeling that may arise during reunion, experts agree that reunitees must be warned not to act on these feelings if and when they occur. The frequency of GSA in reunion is as yet unknown for a number of reasons. It is a relatively new discovery. The taboo around it *as* incest may predispose reunitees to ignore or hide these feelings, as well as any sexual actions they inspire. Occurrence rates of GSA continue to change in line with changes to adoption laws and practices, insofar as such changes increase the frequency of reunion. For these reasons and others, GSA literature is still quite limited and variable. It can also be contradictory. For instance, a 2003 article in the *Guardian* claims that "some agencies estimate that elements of GSA occur in 50% of reunions."[17] In contrast, Julia Feast, a postadoption counsellor with a London "Children's Society," wrote in 1992, "I am aware of four experiences of genetic sexual attraction" in eighty-four reunions mediated by her agency, which gives the impression it is uncommon.[18] The stark difference between these claims could be attributed to the eleven years that divide them, in that today there are perhaps more reunions and/or experts who are better able to identify GSA, but it may also reflect different agendas; the *Guardian* is a mainstream newspaper that could have reason to sensationalize GSA, whereas Feast's article in the journal *Adoption and Fostering*, which briefly mentions GSA in a discussion of outcomes related to mandated adoptee counselling as a provision for birth record access, may reflect a professional's desire to protect reunitees from the stigma of GSA as incest.[19] Overall, however, discussions about GSA are repetitive with respect to the sources, theories, and studies they cite. And in much reunion literature, there is a curious pattern: although GSA is affirmed as a serious concern, it is frequently discussed only briefly, or *en passant*, solely to acknowledge that "possible complications arising from genetic sexual attraction are real and require greater attention from the professional community."[20] In other words, reunitees do not appear to be the only ones who are uncomfortable discussing GSA; many experts are too, even though they clearly feel a responsibility to acknowledge it as professionals.

Apart from Maurice Greenberg's oft-cited 1993 study – based on interviews with seven adoptees and one birth parent who experienced GSA and "supplemented by additional case histories" from "counselors, who reported approximately 40 cases," and by his 1995 study with Roland Littlewood, which surveyed nine self-selected subjects from Greenberg's original study – there are next to no studies that focus exclusively on GSA, or "postadoption incest," as it is also sometimes called.[21] In Greenberg's first study, GSA is said to be "quite common," although "it varies considerably in intensity from a fleeting thought to an intense preoccupation" and can lead to "intense erotic feelings," to "sexualized behavior, such as touching or fondling," or "to actual sexual relationships."[22] His study with Littlewood, wherein the focus is on the possibility of GSA as evidence of "phenotypic matching," includes many of these observations. In his independent and more influential study, Greenberg observes that "[t]he nature of this investigation [i.e., the sample] makes it impossible to state with certainty the frequency with which this phenomenon occurs," a claim that is obviously true of his study with Littlewood too.[23] Indeed, he concludes only that "a number of couples who reunite following adoption experience intense erotic feelings ... and that a proportion of those who experience them proceed to consummation through sexual relations."[24] He adds, however, that his "colleagues [i.e., the counsellors interviewed] estimate that it [i.e., GSA in some form] affects up to half the clients who currently present themselves."[25] In the study with Littlewood, comment on GSA frequency appears only in a footnote that reads, "[S]ome post-adoption counselors reported to us that it was fairly uncommon, others that it was virtually universal when clients were asked sensitively. We would estimate from their reports that over 50% of current clients ... have experienced strong sexual *feelings* in reunions."[26] Although GSA, for Greenberg, refers to feelings that may or may not evolve into sexual action, his distinction between *feeling* GSA and *acting* on it is not always observed in the literature that cites his studies; there is a tendency to overstate the frequency of GSA that leads to sexual action. For instance, Robert A. Paul's 2010 evolutionary anthropological and psychoanalytic study of the Westermarck hypothesis claims that Greenberg's data indicate that GSA "often lead[s] to consummated incest."[27] David Livingstone Smith, who also discusses the work of Edward Westermarck, claims that "[a]ccording to Greenberg and Littlewood this phenomenon, which is called Genetic Sexual Attraction (GSA), occurs in over 50% of relatives reunited after early separation."[28] In effect, the question of frequency is often at issue in literature that concerns GSA.

The theory that is developing around GSA occurs primarily within a matrix of sociobiology or evolutionary psychology and anthropology, behavioural genetics or epigenetics, psychoanalysis (including theories on object relations and on loss and attachment), and socialization discourse.[29] GSA theories are also like adoptee identity and twin bond theories in that they tend to straddle both sides of the nature-nurture debate. Apparently contradictory theories are often mixed and matched by adoption experts, who do not seem to hold one perspective at the expense of the other. Instead, they tend to appeal to nature and nurture, often simultaneously, in order to give a comprehensive view of the origins of GSA. Furthermore, nurture perspectives on GSA also entail implicit, fundamental nature assumptions that, in turn, reinforce a biologically based notion of incest and/or family. In part, that is because adoption and reunion theories assume that to act upon GSA is *essentially* wrong, abnormal, and/or catastrophic, regardless of the fact (which experts fully acknowledge) that reunitees do not *know* each other *as* family and, therefore, are *not* family in a profound sense.[30]

Barbara Gonyo wrote the first known paper on GSA in 1987, and although she is unclear about whether she originally coined the term, she is accredited with doing so.[31] Gonyo's work is informed by her own confusing and painful experience with GSA as a result of a reunion with her relinquished son.[32] Since that time, GSA has been routinely discussed among adoption experts, ranging from search activists to social workers to psychologists, as a potential phenomenon that is associated with adoption reunion. Although subsequent discussions of GSA, as we have seen, suggest as often as not that it "isn't all that common," Gonyo claims from the outset that it is "happening to a great number of newly reunited people."[33] Debates over its rate of occurrence, however, are much less interesting than the theories that have been produced to explain why it occurs.

Genetic sexual attraction is commonly characterized as a "magnetic pull" that culminates in an experience of sexual desire between adoptees and their newly discovered blood relatives.[34] These feelings, it is suggested, can be so strong that it is not unheard of for adoptees and newfound blood relatives to engage in sexual relationships.[35] Adoption experts reassure all reunitees that this feeling is "normal and natural" and, at the same time, forcefully warn them not to act upon it.[36] They also assert that there is a need for "defensive strategies to keep it [GSA] under control," and they warn that reunitees who commit incest, or what is socially and legally perceived to be incest, court natural, emotional, psychological, and social disaster.[37] For instance, Betty Jean Lifton claims that "adoptees who cross the incest barrier forgo ... a natural relationship" with the birth parent and "the chance to become an accepted part of that parent's life."[38] She also warns that reunitees "should be cautioned that intimate physical contact, which is appropriate for a mother and her infant, can be dangerous when the baby has an adult body."[39] Gonyo suggests that reunitees who act on these feelings subject themselves to new experiences of loss because the consequences of their actions, manifested as "strong feelings of guilt and shame," can lead one or both reunitees to cease all contact with one another.[40] David Brodzinsky, Marshall D. Schechter, and Robin Marantz Henig suggest that acting on sexual feelings in reunion can lead "to new distortions" or to problems in "sexual identity" to which it is assumed adoptees are already prone.[41] The psychological and social cost of acting on GSA or committing incest, therefore, is construed to be at odds with the adoptee's true aim in reunion: to develop and maintain a healthy, meaningful, and lasting relationship with her biological relatives.

One of the most extensive theoretical examinations of GSA to date is Robert M. Childs's 1998 doctoral dissertation, entitled "Genetic Sexual Attraction." Although unpublished, his dissertation is noted in contemporary GSA literature, such as that of Carmen M. Cusak, a twin expert who utilizes his work in her discussion of GSA between reunited twins separated at birth by adoption.[42] Nevertheless, it is Lifton's work that is most widely known and repeatedly referred to by adoption experts, Childs included. For instance, search manuals frequently recount the basic thrust of Lifton's ideas in order to promote a general understanding of GSA among possible reunitees. This recourse to Lifton's work is hardly surprising, not only because she is one of the first people to seriously theorize about GSA, doing so from a psychoanalytic perspective, but also because, until her death in 2010, she was a primary and influential figurehead in the adoption rights movement.[43] Generally speaking, however, adoption experts' discussions of GSA are sweeping and brief, especially in the context of search manuals and reunion guidebooks. Furthermore, their discussions take a common sense approach, urging that it is best to hold a "'forewarned is forearmed'" attitude toward GSA and its dangers.[44] Although they do not necessarily agree on all the purported causes of GSA, adoption experts are usually open to the idea that a number of different causes can be at work at once and in one or more reunion participants who experience this phenomenon.[45] Experts do, however, largely agree that GSA is not an expression of adult sexuality, regardless of the fact that many reunitees experience their feelings to be adult and sexual. Instead, experts claim for a variety of reasons that reunitees are mistaken in this regard and, therefore, that they are also wrong or mistaken to act on these feelings.

There are various kinds of origins that adoption experts attribute to GSA. From the perspective of nurture, one reason GSA is said to arise is that reunited adoptees and birth parents or siblings have no psychic experience of each other in light of the incest taboo, which normally informs permissible and barred relations within the biological family.[46] Thus reunion participants are thought to be susceptible to emotions and sexual feelings that normally do not occur within the biological family because they have no historical *knowledge* or experience of each other as sexually off limits or *as* "family" in the normalized sense. Under regular circumstances, the incest taboo, which informs a child's knowledge or experience of her family members *as* "brother," "sister," or "parent," is said to cause the psychological repression of sexual feelings within the biological family in early development. Due to the separation that is adoption, however, adoptees and birth parents or siblings simply do not learn to repress these feelings, and thus sexual desire may occur between them. For instance, Gonyo argues that reunitees "are attracted to each other because they have no bond of brother and sister, or mother and child, [given that] they were not raised together."[47] She understands this lack of a family bond to open up the possibility of sexual attraction where none usually exists because the experience of this kind of bond is normally combined with the experience of the incest taboo, which normally prevents any sexual attraction. In Michelle McColm's *Adoption Reunion*, a social worker explains that "'[i]n your head, you know that there is a biological affiliation, but on an emotional level, you don't.'"[48] Or as Brodzinsky, Schechter, and Henig suggest, "sexual feelings might not be repressed as readily when the incest taboo carries less weight."[49] Unlike parents and children or siblings who learn early to experience each other's biology as sexually abhorrent, reunited blood relatives are said to experience GSA because their experience of each other *as* biological kin is not yet psychically internalized or experienced in relation to the meaning of the incest taboo.

As a fusion that may include many, if not all, of the ideas above, GSA theories also echo the nature and nurture assumptions of twin bond theories insofar as they depict GSA as a human tendency wherein "we're attracted to those who resemble us and with whom we share interests and abilities."[50] The nature assumption in this idea, much as in twin bond theories, is that birth relatives, more than anyone, will be *like* the adoptee both physically and with regard to personality because of their genetic similarity.[51] The nurture assumption is that people are commonly attracted sexually to "strangers" in their environments who appear to be self-similar. And either of these two things or both are said to facilitate GSA, especially during reunion, because environmentally the incest taboo is inactive. Therefore, reunited adoptees can be understood to experience something akin to, but not quite like, a twin bond because, in this instance, the pull between selves is sexual as a result of both an inactive incest taboo and the presence of genetic similarity, which for reasons of nature or nurture, or for reasons of nature that are compounded by nurture, nevertheless create a sexualized sense of self-sameness or narcissism between reunitees.[52]

Further complicating reunions in the *same* vein, but solely from a nurture perspective, are instances where it is said an adoptee reminds one birth parent of the other – be it in body, youth, or manner. Here, the adoptee's genetic likeness is treated as an environmental trigger for old or unresolved feelings that a birth parent may have for the original sexual partner with whom the adoptee was conceived. For instance, Lifton's work reflects this idea to the extent that she suggests that mothers can be "surprised ... that their awakened maternal feelings are merging with the erotic attraction they felt toward the birth father, until the two seem inseparable," and that the father can be too if he "regressees [sic] back to the young lover he once was, envisioning this daughter he has never known as a younger version of her mother."[53] Thus the GSA that a birth parent feels in reunion may really reflect only a yearning for spent youth and/or a past love.[54] However, large age differences may also act as a kind of sexual taboo and mitigate the experience of likeness between reunited parents and children. As a result, GSA is thought to be somewhat more common among reunited siblings than parents and children. It is also suggested that, compared to reunited parents and children, offspring of the same parents who are reunited siblings may be prone to stronger sexual interidentifications to the extent that they experience each other as a kind of "twin."[55]

Although Lifton considers such nature and nurture theories to be plausible, she elaborates largely on the nurture of GSA, especially given that her interest lies in applying a psychoanalytic approach to the phenomenon. Generally, therefore, she reassures reunitees that although feelings of GSA are natural, it is psychologically detrimental to commit incest.[56] For Lifton, GSA is rooted in unresolved psychic conflicts in the adoptee that are due to the trauma of adoption *as* separation. She also suggests that GSA is a manifestation of the Oedipal drama, which is central to Sigmund Freud's theory of human psychic development: "Some male adoptees and their birth mothers relive the scenario of Oedipus and Jocasta, who, after being separated for years, are irresistibly attracted to each other. Some fathers and daughters find themselves in a similar scenario, as do mothers and daughters, and brothers and sisters – although only a few actually consummate their desire."[57] Lifton concludes that it is unresolved Oedipal desire within the adoptee that ultimately leads to an experience of a loss of self.[58] In this light, she depicts GSA as a regression that is an attempt to realize childhood fantasies of "union," rather than sex, with the (newfound) birth parent.[59] Therefore, GSA is on a continuum with the need or desire to search; it is simply a more pronounced or distorted symptom of the adoptee's basic wish to undo the trauma of separation. On the basis of adoptee experience, Lifton argues that GSA is fundamentally a psychic confusion wherein a "primal" or residual childhood desire to reconnect is misunderstood by the adoptee as *adult sexual desire*.[60] The "regressed adoptee, who feels the yearnings of the infant for its mother," according to Lifton, is vulnerable to the "danger" of GSA because of this yearning.[61] To illustrate this idea, Lifton refers to her personal conversations with psychiatrist Alexander Lowen, who explains that normally a (biological) parent and infant physically bond at an "oral level," whereas a reunited birth parent and adult child misinterpret this same desire at a "genital level."[62] A search manual that utilizes the same perspective further suggests that this confusion can occur because adults (as opposed to children) are generally "conditioned to equate physical intimacy with sex."[63] In this way, reunitees mistake what is *really* the pull of a familial bond with sexual desire. Additionally, Lifton indicates that GSA is not sexual in an adult sense insofar as it can also be motivated by Oedipal revenge: "The son's need for penetrating the mother who gave him up can represent revenge and power as much as desire."[64]

Apart from the logic of bio-narcissism, which her use of psychoanalysis to interpret GSA, or adoptees, already entails, Lifton's view is peppered with other important essentialist assumptions.[65] Generally, she argues that GSA is caused by the environmental impact of adoption *as* separation on the Oedipal psyche. Still, she makes the absolutist claim that adoption interferes with the "natural attraction" between biological parents and children.[66] Relying further upon expert and adoptee testimonials to reinforce her psychoanalytic view, Lifton fails to question the nature assumptions with which these testimonials are imbued. For instance, she cites a reunitee's experience of his biological brother: "Intellectually and emotionally, we're stamped out of the same cookie cutter."[67] Although behavioural genetic theories of personality are implicated in this statement, Lifton offers no debate whatsoever with regard to these theories even though they can be construed as contrary to her psychoanalytic view. She simply allows the nature assumptions of such testimonials to speak for themselves. Similarly, in recounting the sentiments of a reunitee who comes "to see this attraction [GSA] as the natural one that a mother and newborn infant have for each other," Lifton makes no mention of the extent to which this reunitee essentially conflates the biological bond with the family bond.[68] Apart from her silences, however, Lifton does raise some questions

concerning the nature of GSA: "Does the unnaturalness of being separated from blood kin drive human beings to unnatural acts when
they are reunited? Is our erotic arousal caused by our 'selfish' genes
seeking out their own kind, or by a psychological need for connection with our kin?"[69] But, again, because she raises these questions
without debating them, their function is rhetorical, which implies
an acceptance of the idea that GSA is rooted in nature.

Robert M. Childs is a therapist in Cambridge, Massachusetts, and
teaches "clinical psychology at the Massachusetts School of Professional Psychology."[70] He specializes "in the psychology of Adoption, including search and reunion issues, identity issues and
Genetic Sexual Attraction," as well as "working with individuals
who are Twins."[71] As noted earlier, his doctoral dissertation, "Genetic Sexual Attraction," is one of the most in-depth theoretical analyses of GSA. His theoretical work enlists a series of nurture and
nature arguments to explain GSA, and he makes an overt point of
incorporating important aspects of behavioural genetics into his
otherwise psychoanalytic perspective. He begins by accepting the
idea that an inactive incest taboo plays a role in GSA.[72] He also
claims that "preoedipal, as well as Oedipal, forces are stirred" in
reunion.[73] Much like Lifton, he argues that GSA is a form of regression wherein reunitees are transported back in time "to psychosex-
ual areas of development that have either remained undeveloped or
in an arrested state of development."[74] He further explains that GSA
is likely to be a pre-Oedipal regression in the adoptee that is relinquished as an infant but an Oedipal regression in birth parents,
especially if they relinquished their child in their teens. Accepting
that adoption can undermine the normal resolution of the family
romance, Childs also suggests GSA is motivated by a "narcissistic
aim," which hampers the repression of incestuous desires that are
triggered by reunion.[75]

According to Childs, both reunion and GSA are important opportunities for the adoptee to begin to heal the trauma of adoption
because they provoke a return to the original experience of separation. In this respect, Childs agrees that GSA is a normal phenomenon
and that it must not be acted upon because the social shame and
secrecy attached to committing incest can rewound reunitees psychically.[76] He also agrees that GSA is not *sexual* but an attempt to communicate a desire for intimacy, union, and identity, as well as an
attempt to undo the psychic effects of adoption, where separation

from the birth parent is experienced by the adoptee as a loss of self.[77] Regardless of whether the adoptee interprets her feelings to be sexual, therefore, GSA is "related to the need to separate from unresolved preoedipal experience in order to develop the autonomy necessary for mature union with another."[78]

In an attempt to account for GSA even more fully, however, Childs also returns to the womb. He argues that the grief and loss commonly associated with adoption are due, in part, to the interruption it causes in the "original mothering culture," or the preverbal, intrauterine relationship between mother and child.[79] Generally, Childs is convinced that the trauma of adoption *as* separation – which gives rise to the adoptee's proneness to identity conflicts and is manifested as a feeling of a loss of self – is due to the destruction of a special mother-child bond that originates out of in utero experience and continues to be experienced following birth. Somewhat akin to Thomas J. Bouchard Jr's idea that particular to each family is a "biological milieu," Childs claims that "self-experience, and the self-boundary, are not derived solely from skin sensation and the interaction of mother and infant but are also derived from an *a priori* foundation that reflects a personal idiom which is genetically based."[80] Simply, the severing of a relationship between a mother and child that is intrauterine in origin is a source of deep personal loss and grief among adoptees, even when they are relinquished and adopted immediately or soon after birth. Notably, Childs's perspective in this regard is controversial, even among some other adoption experts whose approaches to adoption, search, and reunion rely prominently on behavioural genetic assumptions. For instance, Brodzinsky, Schechter, and Henig "strongly adhere" to the "notion that genetic tendencies are more important than environment in determining who it is we become."[81] Nonetheless, they argue that "true attachment to a primary caretaker, the kind that lasts a lifetime, doesn't happen in utero or in the first moments after delivery."[82]

Obviously, Childs's idea of a genetically based personal idiom between mother and child that first manifests in utero has important implications for adoption generally. Under this rubric, there is a genetic component to the parent-child bond and, therefore, to any (normal) psychic development that is founded upon this bond. Thus the psychic development of adoptees becomes essentialized as abnormal given the adoptive tie's nature or lack thereof. Moreover, the trauma of adoption, although it continues to be the result of separation, is compounded insofar as the adoptive mothering culture is now *genetically* foreign. Thus, even when the circumstances of adoption are ideal, Childs's perspective necessarily suggests that adoptive ties are essentially inferior to those that are biological. This idea is illustrated by his claim that "[d]ifficulties in the resolution of Oedipal experience due to the lack of genetic relatedness can lead to adoptive parents holding back from their children" emotionally and physically in terms of love and affection, a withholding that he equates with the lack of a bond that is first and only established in utero.[83] On this view, *to be* adopted, therefore, is to suffer what is a genetically determined psychic wound that prevents the possibility of adoptees and adoptive parents forming a genuinely complete or "normal" family bond. The significance of this kind of wound with regard to GSA is that what reunitees (mistakenly) experience to be authentic sexual desire now becomes a symptom of the adoptee's essential need to undo the *genetic* trauma of separation. Or, to put it another way, GSA is treated as a mismanifestation of the otherwise normal desire to reclaim the genetic personal idiom that Childs argues must first be in place in order "to drive the personality through the Oedipal experience."[84]

Suzanne G. Matson also relies on nature and nurture to explain GSA in that she too blends aspects of psychoanalysis and behavioural genetics together. Her use of psychoanalysis is unique, however, insofar as she completely rejects the idea that GSA is best understood in light of the Oedipal narrative. For instance, she writes that "[g]enetic sexual attraction is not about incest or Oedipus, it is about psychological trauma."[85] Although she still suggests that GSA is essentially a misinterpreted desire to heal the "narcissistic wound" caused by adoption, she does so on the basis of object-relations theory, which is a branch of psychoanalysis that began to part ways with Freudian psychoanalysis as early as 1935.[86] For Matson, the real point with regard to Oedipal theory is that it is too commonly relied upon to explain GSA, which has adverse effects on reunitees. She argues, therefore, that "GSA needs to expand beyond Freud, just as psychoanalytic thought did."[87] The main reason for this argument is that when GSA is characterized *as* incest, which it necessarily is within a context of Oedipal theory, it becomes far too "sensationalized."[88] And this sensation is detrimental because it shames the adoptee into silence and directs important social attention and support away from her basic need to acquire the psychological ability to withstand the shock and grief of adoption *as* separation and reunion, which further facilitates her social and psychological growth.[89]

Also key to Matson's perspective on adoption and GSA are some important aspects of behavioural genetics. She firmly believes that normal "attachment and connection" between mother and child are fundamentally determined at the "bio-chemical level," which in turn fosters normal psychological development and growth in the individual in the absence of interruptions like adoption.[90] On the flipside, where there is a break in attachment and connection between mother and child at the bio-chemical level, she argues, the child will experience anxiety that would otherwise be soothed normally by the biological mother's presence.[91] She goes on to say that "genetic sexual attraction serves *simultaneously*, as a physiological defense mechanism *and* psychological defense mechanism against pain or discomfort associated with grief."[92] In other words, GSA is a natural pain-avoidance response to the repressed anxiety, pain, and grief of adoption that resurface, or are heightened, during reunion.[93] Reunitees can respond in two ways to what is simultaneously a physiological and psychological experience of anxiety and grief resulting from reunion: either with anger or with sexual arousal, but the latter response is often experienced as more self-soothing than anger.[94] Still, both responses are fundamentally "dissociative" because they "work to arrest normal developmental processes – *to disrupt the grieving process* – often before it even begins."[95] So although GSA is a normal physiological and psychological response and, due to its soothing effect, is a highly appealing choice, acting upon it is detrimental, not so much because of its implications *as* incest but because it undermines a more important psychological or anti-dissociative benefit that reunitees achieve if, and only if, they face and withstand the return of the repressed grief and pain caused by adoption.

In light of this cross-section of the kinds of origins commonly attributed to GSA, it is evident that these theories fall on either side of the nature-nurture dichotomy. Yet, like adoptee identity and twin bond theories, nurture perspectives associated with GSA also acquiesce to certain nature assumptions, and arguably, because they do so, the apparent dichotomy between these theories turns out to be false. On the basis of psychoanalysis and socialization, the main nurture arguments above contend the following: the environmental fact of being an *adult* facilitates a misinterpretation of oral *as* genital desire between reunitees, *or* people who share genetic similarity; a "stranger" in one's environment who appears and is experienced to be self-same (because of genetic similarity) can incite sexual desire; the reunited adoptee's genetic likeness to one birth parent can environmentally trigger unresolved sexual feelings in the other, which are misdirected toward, or projected onto, the adoptee; and, finally, reunitees may experience sexual desire because the incest taboo is inoperative between them.

Similar to nurture arguments surrounding the twin bond, the nature assumption that underpins the psychoanalytic idea that GSA originates in oral desire that is merely misexperienced by adult reunitees as genital desire pertains to the implicit manner in which genetic similarity is construed as the *necessary condition* of this phenomenon. On this view, genetic similarity is a necessary condition for GSA because its environmental presence is the sole thing that distinguishes sexual attractions between reunitees as *genetic*. Furthermore, the mere presence of genetic similarity in the context of reunitees' sexual desire is used to preclude the possibility that their attraction is, or can be, authentically *genital*. In other words, this nurture perspective assumes there is no such thing as authentic adult or genital desire in *the presence of genetic similarity* or between reunited adoptees, birth parents, and siblings. Essentially, therefore, this view collapses genital desire into oral desire out of some unnamed necessity that it seems to associate with the so-called *environmental* presence of genetic similarity.[96] Logically, therefore, the environmental impact of *adulthood*, in and of itself, is negligible or even false as any *kind* of cause of GSA. Rather, it is genetic similarity that functions categorically as the real cause of GSA insofar as its presence is essential to the determination that *adult* reunitees' desire is *not* genital desire. Finally, although genetic similarity plays an environmental role – for instance, as a trigger of either a primary narcissistic or Oedipal psycho-sexual response – it plays another more fundamental role as a natural cause. Simply, the concept of *genetic* sexual attraction is entirely dependent upon the presence of genetic similarity, and the fact that genetic similarity is only ever a natural condition or product of nature means that GSA is categorically dependent upon a cause that is rooted in nature, regardless of whether it is depicted as being due to nurture.

The same can be said about the idea of the (seemingly) self-same "stranger" and about the idea that genetic similarity is an environmental trigger of unresolved sexual feelings in the birth parent for the other birth parent that are projected onto the adoptee. Also like twin theories, the main point of these nurture arguments is that the *knowledge* or *experience* of genetic similarity, as opposed to *genetic similarity* in and of itself, elicits many intense emotions that can give rise to GSA. For instance, a reunited birth parent touches on both of these views when she asks, "How do you rebond to a twenty-year-old man who acts like his father, looks like your brother, and is your son?"[97] As this reunitee suggests, environmental genetic similarity evokes a profound sense of sameness between herself, others she has loved, and her birth child on four different fronts that, taken together, are said to undermine her psychic ability to know this other *solely* as a "stranger" (whom she also experiences to be like herself), "former lover," "brother," *or* "son." Instead, she experiences him in all of these ways in different moments or, perhaps, simultaneously because she experiences her birth son's genetic similarity as likening him to her, to her former lover, and to her brother.[98] Nevertheless, even if this birth parent's response is characterized as an *environmentally* triggered psychic response to genetic similarity, the response itself, as GSA, still remains a particular *kind* of response that depends absolutely on the presence of genetic similarity, if only as *the* trigger of the psychic response. In effect, genetic similarity functions as the necessary condition of GSA here too because it is *essential* to creating the kind of environment that causes the profound blurring of boundaries between reunitees that makes these feelings possible. These two views, here combined, entail an implicit nature assumption: genetic similarity, albeit an environmental cause in one sense, is a natural cause in another because *only* its presence, which is determined solely by nature, gives rise to *genetic* sexual attraction.

Finally, the idea that GSA, *as* a form of incest, is due to a lack of socialization in light of the incest taboo capitulates to nature, but this time it does so by treating genetic similarity as a necessary condition of *incest*. As incest, GSA categorically depends on the natural presence of genetic similarity to be incest. A sensational example that speaks to the idea that incest depends on the presence of genetic similarity involves the end of filmmaker Woody Allen's twelve-year relationship with actress Mia Farrow because "he was in love with one of Farrow's adopted daughters, Soon-Yi Farrow Previn."[99] Allen's arguments in support of his sexual relationship with Previn raise important questions about the nature of incest as opposed to child sexual abuse.[100] To thwart the idea that he could be construed to have committed either, Allen, in a *Time* magazine interview, "The Heart Wants What It Wants," discussed both his relationship with Previn and allegations of "child molestation" against his seven-year-old daughter Dylan, who was one of two children he adopted with Farrow.[101] As it pertained to Dylan, Allen flat out denied all sexual allegations on two possible grounds: the allegations were false *or* they were true but he had no means by which to defend sexual activity with a seven year old under any circumstances. Either way, Allen did not face criminal charges. He did, however, lose his custody battle with Farrow and was denied unsupervised visits with Dylan because doctors, social workers, psychologists (including David Brodzinsky), and police who evaluated Dylan were divided on whether sexual abuse had taken place.[102] Conversely, Allen openly admitted to sexual activity with Previn. The strategy he used to elude charges of abuse and, worse, incest, which Farrow attached to his behaviour as soon as she discovered it – she "pointed out that, psychologically, this was incest" – was very different.[103] Allen employed Previn's status as an adoptee, as well as her age and consent (e.g., "She's a sharp, grownup person," "a grown, sophisticated person," "probably more mature than I am"), to prove he had done nothing wrong.[104] To combat the idea that his actions should or could be construed psychologically and/or socially as incest, Allen traded on the literal (i.e., biological) meaning of incest by relentlessly invoking Previn's adoption as the proof that he had no socio-psycho-paternal responsibility toward her; a notorious analysand, transfixed by psychoanalysis, Allen arguably knew his emphasis on the lack of a biological tie was a defence not merely of his sexual activity but also of his sexual and social psychology. Indeed, Allen enlisted adoption in every way possible to distance himself from Previn as a "father" and, thus, from incest as her lover. For instance, he argued that Previn was not just "*Mia's* daughter" but Mia's "*adopted* daughter" and that, *as* a "father," he was "only interested in his own kids," of whom there were three: the two he and Farrow had adopted and a biological child, or so it was assumed until recently.[105] Although he had known Previn since she was nine, he insisted that he was "not Soon-Yi's father or stepfather" (a sentiment Previn corroborated) or "a father to *her* [Mia's] adopted kids in any sense of the word."[106] He claimed that Previn "never said two words to me" when she was a child, that he "never even lived with Mia," "never in [his] entire life slept at Mia's apartment," and "never had any family dinners over there"; he depicted himself, at best, as a distant figure connected meaningfully only to Previn's mother while Previn was a child.[107] He also controverted any family tie to Previn by rendering suspect, as family ties, the adoptive ties of all involved. He asserted that "[t]his was not some type of family unit in any remote way" but just "a collection of kids, [who] are not blood sisters or anything."[108] He claimed that, as concerned him, "[t]he only thing unusual is that [Previn is] Mia's daughter. But she's an *adopted* daughter and a grown woman. I could have met her at a party or something."[109] But of course he did not meet her at a party; Allen met her when she was nine years old and the daughter of his lover.

Nevertheless, Allen's main argument that Previn is only Farrow's "adopted" daughter, and a consenting adult, distances him from any (legal) status or responsibility as a "father"; his manipulation of the social meaning of adoption, which is at odds with the biological meaning of incest, protects him from the characterization of his actions as either incestuous or abusive respectively. Indeed, if Previn had been Farrow's biological daughter, Allen's position would be far less convincing insofar as the meaning of a biological tie between Previn and Farrow could still ensnare him as a quasi "step-father," drawing incest nearer as the meaning of his actions, at the very least in the popular imagination. The overt downplaying of his sexual "relationship with Mia [as] simply a cordial one in the past four years," wherein the "romantic relationship had tapered off," also reinforced his denial as a "father."[110] Discursively speaking, an actively sexual relationship with Farrow *would* biologically bind him closer to her, and thus to Previn, in that sexual bonds do operate as stand-ins for biological ties because of the historical "idea that 'the sexual union makes man and woman one flesh,'" with the consequence that "one's relatives by affinity are transformed into relatives by blood," albeit usually in conjunction with marriage.[111] It is also possible that Allen anticipated that the reiteration of Previn's adoptee status would subtly underscore (i.e., as a stand-in for the meaning of biological difference) Farrow's and Previn's racial difference (i.e., Farrow is white and Previn is a transracial Korean adoptee), which in all likelihood aided his disavowals of incest and abuse insofar as racial difference also invokes meanings of biological difference.

Distasteful as Allen's behaviour is to people who are convinced that he played a real role for Previn as a father, his arguments, discursively, are actually very compelling. This is evident in the fact that, at worst, the media concluded that his behaviour was an unconscionable "abuse of power" or that he was someone who "blurred the lines ... in a parenting role."[112] Notably, some journalists did "raise the issue of incest" – insofar as Allen could be shown to have played a significant *parental role*, even if he had not legally adopted Previn and was not married to Farrow – but all stopped short of calling his relationship incestuous, not because they wanted to but because "[h]e is not the biological father" of Previn.[113] So, even if Allen's sexual relationship with Previn is regarded by many people as *socially* questionable, it is *essentially* acceptable insofar as it is not categorically "incest" in any literal, legal, or popular sense. Whatever the nature of Allen's relationship, it is not incest because the biological tie continues to function as the essential pivot of the meaning of incest, which is consanguinity.

The reluctance by the media to attach the word "incest" to Allen's relationship with Previn illustrates the important sense in which *genetic similarity* continues to operate discursively as an absolute that precedes *socialization* as the intelligible cause of incest. If the meaning of incest really hinged on socialization, Allen could not have used Previn's adoption so effectively to defend his sexual relationship with her. The (ongoing) truth is that Allen is not understood literally, legally, or popularly to have committed incest because where there is talk of incest there is a built-in assumption that those who commit it *must* share not merely a social or psychological tie but first and foremost a biological one. So even if Allen, at the time, conceded to being at least a "father figure" to Previn, he cannot be understood to have committed incest – as opposed, for instance, to some other sexual harm or a betrayal of trust – legally or otherwise.[114] No doubt, that is why Allen, more than twenty years later, feels at liberty to admit that "I was paternal" and that Previn is someone who "responded to someone paternal"; it is also why interviewers no longer raise the issue of "incest," which is not to say none suggest that "from afar – to the general public – it's a bit harder to understand" his relationship.[115]

Similarly, where there is talk of GSA within would-be nurture perspectives that treat it *as* a form of incest, they also depend upon the presence of genetic similarity in order for reunitees to be intelligible as *the* kinds of people who can experience the phenomenon. For example, imagine a man finds himself attracted to his adoptee partner's mother following their reunion because genetic similarity makes mother and daughter appear alike, or perhaps a man is attracted to the identical twin of his adoptee partner upon the twins' reunion for the same reason; obviously, normative socialization, which regulates the avoidance or repression of the desire one should feel or express for a sexual partner's immediate family members, would be absent in both of these cases, just as it is for the incest taboo in relation to GSA.[116] Although there is no genetic similarity between the subject and the objects of his desire in these two scenarios, the genetic similarity of the first object in each case genuinely *is* the environmental cause of his attraction to the second object; that is, he is attracted to the mother *because* she is like the daughter, or he is attracted to the second twin *because* she is like the first twin. Arguably, these examples meet the criteria for the explicit definition of GSA nurture theories, which turn on socialization as cause, but not the criteria for the implicit definition, which exposes their bias. The meaning of GSA, because it is in line with the meaning of incest, prevents either case of desire from being properly understood as GSA because GSA nurture theories *do* assume that the genetic similarity that attracts must be embodied in the subject and the object of desire; it is not embodied in two genetically similar objects that equally attract a subject with whom no genetic similarity is shared. In other words, if GSA cannot be understood to occur between people who are attracted to genetic similarity that is not their own, then nurture arguments about GSA entail an implicit nature assumption. Fundamentally, the nature assumption built into GSA nurture perspectives is that it is the natural presence of genetic similarity, not socialization or the lack thereof, that is really understood to determine whether a sexual attraction is GSA (*as* a form of incest).

Adoption discourse surrounding GSA reinforces the superiority of the biological tie as a basis for family simply because it reinforces incest discourse. Most obviously, it does so when it utilizes incest discourse to explain GSA. By treating GSA as a form of incest, adoption discourse necessarily invokes the implications of incest discourse, one of which is that genetic similarity functions as a test for the authenticity of "family" ties, which is further mediated through the incest taboo. As a necessary condition for both GSA and incest, genetic similarity reinforces, in adoption discourse, the biologically based notion of family that is also intrinsic to incest discourse.

Conversely, where GSA is not regarded as incest but as a genetic or physiological response or as a misinterpreted experience of self-sameness, adoption experts still reinforce incest discourse and its implications for the family because they treat genetic similarity between reunitees as a sign that their desire is not authentically genital or adult. The fact that adoption experts do treat genetic similarity as such a sign is illustrated in their strong warning that reunitees must not act on their sexual feelings, a warning that essentially reduces reunitee desire to a (misconstrued) desire for biological family (re)union. The use of genetic similarity in this way reinforces incest discourse, or a biologically based notion of family, because it is tantamount to saying that reunitees cannot have genuinely *extra*-familial relationships with each other. Being able to have sex is a social-political-historical sign that a relationship is not incest and is extra-familial. Therefore, whether adoption experts treat GSA as incest or argue that it is not incest and nevertheless warn reunitees not to have sex because of the presence of genetic similarity, they reinstate a (biological) family tie between people who are not family in the profound sense that they do know each other as family historically, are not family by virtue of adoption law, and do not experience, know, or choose to know each other as family insofar as they are sexually attracted to each other and do want to act on that attraction.

In the end, the main point of this discussion is not to come down on either side of the question of whether people who experience GSA should be subject to the incest taboo or incest law – although it could be – but to argue that insofar as they are *known* by adoption experts or *know themselves* through the lens of GSA, they *are* regulated by and enlisted in the service of the bio-genealogical imperative. Current perspectives on GSA warn reunitees against acting on their feelings and, in so doing, not only reinforce incest discourse but also essentially reinforce the dominant discourse of the modern Western biological family, which in turn (re)produces the inferiority of the adoptive tie. In effect, adoption experts' utilization or support of incest discourse through GSA theories generally (re)inscribes the modern Western bio-genealogical imperative – an imperative that (re)produces the adopted subject simply because GSA avoidance, like that of incest, demands that the individual know her bio-genealogy. Arguably, therefore, one reason why GSA is so strongly regarded as catastrophic is that reunitees who would or do have sex do challenge the fundamental notion that the biological tie is, by some mysterious necessity, always a "family" tie. By keeping GSA in check, adoption experts and reunitees, whatever else they may accomplish, also participate in securing the foundation of a social-political-historical structure of the biological family that is generated, in part, by the incest taboo.

8

Incest: The Universal
of the Modern Western Family Subject

This much, however, is clear: incest, whether actual or figurative, has been one of the most enigmatic and far-reaching concerns of humankind especially in the modern world. How we ultimately come to understand it, if we ever can, both determines and is determined by the most fundamental concepts of nature, family, sex roles, society and self.

James B. Twitchell, *Forbidden Partners*

In Euripides's play *Hippolytus*, Phaedra is subjected to a terrible tragedy because of her stepson's hubris toward Aphrodite. She is made Aphrodite's instrument to punish Hippolytus. Hippolytus, the son of Theseus, has rejected Aphrodite, who in turn infects Phaedra, Theseus's second wife, with a deep erotic passion for Hippolytus. The increasing burden of Phaedra's secret, her insistent desire for her stepson, quickly renders her ill and tortured. Deeply concerned for Phaedra, her nurse, upon wresting the terrible secret from her, conveys it to Hippolytus in hopes that it will ease Phaedra's suffering. But Phaedra's passion only evokes Hippolytus's horror and disgust: "[T]he thought of physical love for any woman is for him traumatic enough; a sexual relationship with the wife of his beloved father would be an abomination."[1] Humiliated, Phaedra exacts her own revenge. She takes her life and leaves a note for Theseus in which she implicates Hippolytus as both her rapist and, therefore, the impetus behind her death. The loss of Phaedra throws Theseus into a violent fury toward his son, and he utters a curse that brings about Hippolytus's death. Although Hippolytus is innocent, Phaedra's charge from the grave has obscured his loyalty to his father, a fact, to Theseus's shock and grief, that will be discovered only when it is too late.

Today, as in classical times, the meaning and consequence of Phaedra's desire for Hippolytus is of a different order from that of Jocasta and Oedipus in Euripides's more famous play *Oedipus*. As a stepmother, Phaedra is incapable of transgressing the incest taboo through her desire for Hippolytus. The crime of her passion is the betrayal of her husband Theseus. Her failure, exclusively, is as a "wife" who has a duty under patriarchy to love and serve her husband. So although she desires, wrongly accuses, and brings about the death of Hippolytus, she is not commonly understood, if ever, to fail as his "mother" in the terrible way that Jocasta is understood to violate the mother-child bond. Certainly, our inability to comprehend Phaedra as incestuous and a "mother" is due partly to the fact that she married Theseus when Hippolytus was already a young man. Given that Phaedra is unlike a stepmother who raises her husband's child, we have no expectation that she has a duty to Hippolytus as any sort of "son." She has never played the social role of mother in relation to Hippolytus. Nonetheless, we do perceive a duty on the part of Jocasta toward Oedipus even though she and Phaedra are very much alike in this respect. Jocasta never does, nor intends to, perform the social role of mother in relation to Oedipus, for prior to Oedipus's conception, and because of an oracle's prophecy, she is aware of her husband Laius's plan to abandon and expose the child.[2] That Phaedra's crime and circumstance are not so completely unlike those of Jocasta, therefore, raises the question of why Phaedra is incapable of stirring up a degree of disgust and contempt in our collective imagination akin to that provoked by Jocasta. The answer, we too immediately think, is obvious: Phaedra does not elicit our profound horror and disgust because a woman's desire for her stepson and urge to see him dead is not nearly so unthinkable as a woman's murderous intentions and desire toward her *own* son. The knowledge that no biological tie exists between Phaedra and Hippolytus minimizes utterly what it is possible to *think* Phaedra owes Hippolytus, just as the knowledge that Oedipus is Jocasta's biological son amplifies the duties we uncritically think she should observe toward him; the duty exists only where the presence of the biological tie is perceived to exist, and it does so whether or not the social role of mother is performed by the woman in question. Phaedra's and Jocasta's stories of crime and passion mirror one another, yet it is Phaedra who is destined to have the lesser grip on our imaginations. This is the significance of Phaedra's story for our purposes: it demonstrates that incest is not an enigma at all but a familiar knowledge that produces and maintains biological ties as family ties in line with the bio-genealogical imperative. The symbolic failure of Phaedra's desire as incest renders explicit our failure to imagine and experience family bonds as meaningful in the absence of biological ties. The lack of popular affect surrounding her story, as compared to that of Jocasta, is a lesson that demonstrates how our everyday knowledge of family-cum-incest inhibits our ability to *think* and experience the reality of adoptive ties as "family" ties.

Incest is a multifaceted object of concern socially, politically, and historically. Indeed, there is no single definition or set of laws that regulates it throughout the world and history. The meaning of incest is variously determined in relation to nature, age, sex, affinity, genealogy, and social, political, and economic concerns in different places and times. As a phenomenon or practice, it has a history of being accepted, abhorred, normalized, criminalized, and universalized. For these reasons, a comprehensive discussion of the history of incest is not possible in the context of this chapter. What follows, therefore, is a discussion of some of the meanings associated with incest throughout history, as well as the social-political-economic roles these meanings have played in different historical moments. I also investigate changes in the meaning of incest in the modern Western period as manifested through the human sciences.[3] The overarching question that guides this discussion is how the meaning of incest differentiates and shapes the experience of biological as opposed to adoptive ties. To better understand how adoptive ties are made unintelligible as real "family" ties, I consider how thought about incest both broadly speaking and in the context of the human sciences maintains the ontological status of biological ties as family ties.

The idea that incest is an operative of sexuality that "intensifies" the biological family's experience is introduced by Michel Foucault in *The History of Sexuality*, and I would add to it the converse idea that incest simultaneously deintensifies the adoptive family's experience. The intensification of family experience, he suggests, is mobilized through the human sciences' problematization of incest as a *universal*. As we will see, therefore, the relationship between family experience and the meaning of incest as a universal is set up by disciplines such as biology, psychology, and sociology, all of which profoundly influence adoption discourse. For instance, the conclusions that "the incest taboo appears to be universal" and that "incest behavior also appears to be universal" continue to be drawn, usually uncritically, by contemporary therapeutic and research psychologists.[4] Where feminism takes up the subject of incest, it too can be shown to participate because its concern with incest as a social and political issue engages it with the human sciences. Informed by Foucault's and Thomas Kuhn's respective ideas that human being is self-interpretive and that truths contravening the logic of dominant paradigms are largely unintelligible, this chapter examines the idea that the deployment of sexuality, through the interrogation of incest by the human sciences, elicits "the affective intensification of the family space" and its implications for the adoptive family.[5] Combined, these ideas facilitate the critical approach of this chapter: they drive my investigation into the relationship between family experience and the dominant meaning of incest as a universal, which plays a key role in the maintenance of the bio-genealogical imperative; they help us to understand how and why incest is a knowledge that differentiates the experiences to be had in biological and adoptive families; and they make intelligible incest's role not only in the intensification of biological ties but also in the attenuation of adoptive ties.

In *Patterns of Incest*, R.E.L. Masters considers how prominent figures in Western thought answer the question *"Why* is incest prohibited?" He does so in order to establish that there is an array of disparate meanings associated with incest throughout history. Among the answers he recounts are those of Saint Augustine (354–430) and Edward Westermarck (1862–1939), both of whom claim that the origin of incest prohibition is located in a natural instinct against incest.[6] Martin Luther (1483–1586) believed marriages between near kin are prohibited because they are necessarily devoid of love, and Aristotle (384–322 BC) thought they would end in a dangerous overabundance of intrafamilial love.[7] Thomas Aquinas (1225–74) argued that incest prohibition exists "to promote chastity by compelling people to seek mates at a distance."[8] And J.G. Frazer (1854–1941) and Émile Durkheim (1858–1917) claimed the taboo originates on the basis of magic, religion, and superstition, whereas Freud asserted that it arises from a universal sense of guilt that is the result of "primeval parricide."[9] As Masters illustrates, therefore, no hard and fast set of meanings is consistently associated with incest and its prohibition throughout Western history.

The English word "incest" (circa 1225) is derived from the Latin word "incestus," which means "impure or unchaste."[10] Meanings of "blood, contamination or shame" are also historically linked to "incest" as a result of the influence on English by languages such as German, Danish, Swedish, Hungarian, and Czech, all of which are meanings that resonate with us today.[11] But this is not necessarily a sign that the historical meaning of incest is consistent. Indeed, there is a great lack of continuity in its meaning, as illustrated by contemporary definitions that do not clearly specify, or agree upon, the reach of the prohibition. For instance, the *Oxford English Dictionary* defines incest as "the crime of sexual intercourse or cohabitation between persons related within the degrees within which marriage is prohibited; sexual commerce of near kindred."[12] In the *Encyclopedia of Anthropology*, incest "[m]inimally ... refers to mating between father and daughter, mother and son, brother and sister. In various societies it is extended to include larger numbers of consanguineal relatives, especially if the society is organized along the principle of lineages and clans."[13] The *Dictionary of Psychology* defines incest as "sexual relations between individuals of different sexes closely connected by blood kinship, the degree of the kinship being determined by social law."[14] Ashley P. Turner observes that some definitions of incest, such as that used by Elizabeth Janeway, include not only "brother/sister, cousin/cousin, father/daughter, mother/son" but also "relatives of the same sex," whereas James B. Twitchell states that "incest essentially denotes a sexual relationship with a someone who is so closely related that marriage would be forbidden."[15] Although these definitions are generally alike in that they interpret the meaning of incest on the basis of kinship and blood relations, each fails to clearly identify who is and is not subject to the prohibition. In effect, the parameters of the prohibition itself are historically and culturally discontinuous, or fluid, with regard to whom it addresses within the immediate and extended family.

The definitions above also illustrate that the meaning of incest is *social* in an integral sense; each defines incest relative to social structures, such as marriage, or in connection with principles of social organization that regulate heterosexual and less often homosexual sex between blood relatives. As a result, each conveys the idea that there is interplay between the meaning of incest and what it means to be an individual who is accepted as a part of society and culture. By depicting the meaning of incest as inextricably linked to conventions and laws of marriage, these definitions also support the idea that the meaning of incest is social because it serves political and economic aims, such as the regulation of wealth and power. For instance, incest (prohibition) is like the institution of marriage: it not only preserves the family but also controls the individual's political power, wealth, land, titles, and social status by permitting and forbidding legal unions.

The social meaning of incest is discontinuous, however, precisely because it is enlisted to serve various social, political, and economic structures and goals. Its discontinuity is also illustrated in the ebb and flow of the many types of consanguine relationships it regulates. In some historical moments, the application of the prohibition is limited strictly to the immediate nuclear family. In others, it is extended to much more distant blood relatives. There are also historical instances where incest between immediate blood kin is permissible, albeit only among members of a certain class or status, when it facilitates certain political and economic alliances. The inconsistency and malleability of incest prohibition, with regard to who is subject to it, points to its history as a social, political, and economic strategy. For example, in ancient Egypt, Ptolemy II and his sister Arsinoe married to reinforce "alliances between relatives" and to prevent land and wealth from leaving the family.[16] As Robert M. Childs observes, "incest has been the prerogative and privilege of the gods and the ruling families of ancient civilizations"; the exclusive right to engage in it circumscribes their power and sets them apart from those who are subject to their rule.[17] In the Western European context, the "notorious" intermarriage of aristocrats allied royal families, political power, lands, titles, and wealth.[18] Although exceptions to the rule of incest prohibition in many respects, these examples show that the meaning of incest is adaptable, sometimes as a moral or natural concern, depending upon the social, political, and economic context in which it occurs. Increases in the reach of incest prohibition under the guise of its being a moral or natural concern also exemplify how incest is utilized to serve social, political, and economic aims. According to Steve Jones, between the sixth and eleventh centuries, the Roman Catholic Church extended incest prohibition from second and third to seventh cousins. Jones explains that, although this change is justified in relation to God, morality, and natural law, there is good reason to believe that the church's new stance on incest was influenced by economic considerations; people without legitimate heirs often left their property to the church, and harsher incest prohibitions increased this likelihood by decreasing opportunities for legitimate marriage among traditionally small and cut-off medieval populations.[19] Even if incest prohibition is justified with reference to God and nature, therefore, its utility is not negated with regard to the social, political, and economic aims of a given historical moment.

To whatever extent the meaning of incest is influenced by the social, there remains an important sense in which it cannot be understood outside of *nature*. The meaning of incest, particularly its link to the social, is bound up with nature because the biological tie *is* a naturally occurring fact that is used to determine *whose* sexual acts are subject to its prohibitions. For example, however much Paul might wish to, he cannot commit *incest* with Ann if Ann is not in any way biologically tied to him as long as the definition of incest turns on consanguinity. Indeed, this is also why Phaedra's crime as a stepmother is not popularly construed as incest. In this manner, *nature* is an integral aspect of current and historical meanings of incest. The problem of discerning the meaning of incest does not lie in whether nature determines incest and its prohibition, for assuredly it does in the sense above. On the contrary, it lies in determining whether the meaning of incest is natural or socially produced insofar as it is attached to natural facts, such as the blood tie, that in and of themselves are originally meaningless. The tension between the meaning of incest as a natural fact and as a social practice is a central pivot around which the modern Western discourse of incest turns. To illuminate this tension, I examine Foucault's ideas about incest discourse as it relates to the human sciences, and I consider the regulatory effect of this relationship on the family's experience. As I suggest below, it is ultimately this effect that differentiates the experiences of biological and adoptive families, rendering the experience of the former superior to that of the latter.

Foucault's investigation of incest discourse pertains mainly, although not exclusively, to the discourse of sexuality's impact on the (biological) family's sensations and pleasures. Although Foucault explores many of the effects of incest discourse on the (biological) family's experience, he does not consider its impact on the modern Western experience of adoptive ties. Nevertheless, his observations concerning incest and the (biological) family, as we shall see, have important implications for adoptee experience. In *The History of Sexuality*, Foucault suggests that as the human sciences gained momentum and influence in the latter nineteenth and twentieth centuries, *how* incest was known began to change. For example, whereas incest was known by the medieval person or the "pastoral power" to be a question of sin, morality, or divine law, in the context of modern medicine and science, it increasingly became an "organic," "functional," and "mental" question of nature.[20] Prior to the development of the human sciences, incest was known and experienced solely as a crime against natural law *as* God's law. Conversely, as secular and scientific interpretations of the laws of nature emerged, incest and the origin of its prohibitions became a question that was evaluated against new concerns, such as the survival of species in nature and the individual in society.

This change with regard to the question of incest is exemplified by the fact that, in the early eighteenth century, philosophers like Francis Hutcheson and Bernard Mandeville debated whether incest prohibition reflected "that there exists in all of us an inner [moral] sense or instinct telling us whether our conduct is right or wrong."[21] Their concern was with whether the immorality of incest reflected natural law or mere custom, which also speaks to Foucault's observation that incest, prior to the nineteenth century, was problematized solely as a question of natural law and morality rather than of science and nature.[22] By the nineteenth century, the problem of incest had veered away from a dominant focus on its relationship to moral absolutism. For instance, although Charles Darwin does not focus on the meaning of incest or its prohibitions in *On the Origin of Species* (1859), the notion that incest is both a universal and a problem of science, as opposed to morality, is implied in his theory of evolution and natural selection. Darwin discusses how "*close* interbreeding diminishes vigour and fertility" and considers the perils of breeding "*inter se*" in hybrid plants.[23] This discussion set the stage for incest *as* interbreeding to function apart from moral questions and more in relation to questions framed by human sciences, such as eugenics, sociobiology, behavioural or behaviour genetics, and epigenetics, all of which are on a disciplinary continuum and take up Darwinian ideas about maladaptation and survival and apply them to human contexts.[24] Notably, the spread of this effect was further facilitated insofar as Darwin mapped his theory of adaptation and survival onto the logic of already prevalent and familiar social and economic metaphors of the time.

Observing modern Western alterations in the knowledge of incest, Foucault claims that by the end of the nineteenth century, incest or its prohibition was problematized uniquely because, for the first time, it was "posited as an absolutely universal principle."[25] With this idea, he does not mean to suggest that no incidence, knowledge, or regulation of incest existed prior to this period. Indeed, it was often discussed, as we have seen. What he means is that, at this time, it was taken up in a novel manner by the human sciences. He explains that in the nineteenth century,

> [i]ncest was a popular practice, and I mean by this, widely practiced among the populace, for a very long time. It was towards the end of the nineteenth century that various social pressures were directed against it. And it is clear that the great interdiction against incest is an invention of the intellectuals ... If you look for studies by sociologists or anthropologists of the nineteenth century on incest you won't find any. Sure, there were some scattered medical reports and the like, but the practice of incest didn't really seem to pose a problem at the time.[26]

With the rise of the human sciences, therefore, incest was problematized in a way that is unique to the modern Western context. In the words of Vikki Bell, there is "a modern way of speaking [about incest] which suggests that at all times *past and present* there has been a universal incest prohibition."[27] This idea is evidenced in Darwinian biology, where incest functions as a problem that is universally relevant to every individual as a member of the human species because incest as interbreeding is central to questions of survival and adaptation. Foucault generally attributes the reconstitution of incest as a universal to the rise of the human sciences, but feminism also plays an important role in the maintenance of incest as a universal.[28] Radical feminism does so because its critiques of patriarchal incest, as construed by the human sciences, have enjoyed real social influence, especially in legal and therapeutic contexts, and continue to do so, even though the "memory wars" in the 1980s and 1990s against radical feminism over the issue of "recovered memory" have led to fewer instances in which these kinds of memories are treated as admissible in court.[29] And poststructural feminisms, which have enjoyed significant influence since the 1990s, do so as well because their focus on questions of trauma particularly and subjectivity generally has tended to limit discussions to interiority, which leaves the universal and thus its posture as an objective truth intact. As a result, feminism is like the human sciences insofar as it has an impact on family experience. I therefore consider some of the ways that incest prohibition is taken up by biology, psychology, sociology, and feminism in order to demonstrate how the meaning of incest as a universal impacts the family.

Informed by Darwinian reason, modern biological science and, specifically, sociobiology assume that incest is universal. Sociobiology is the central precursor to what is now commonly known as evolutionary psychology, behavioural or behaviour genetics, and epigenetics. Because its logic and fundamental assumptions about nature and the universality of incest have progressed under these newer monikers, or along a continuum, these names are treated as interchangeable herein. Its changes in name have turned on politics as much as they also reflect its scientific evolution as a field. For instance, although "'biological' should not necessarily be equated with 'genetic,'" sociobiology's historical and controversial association with eugenics – and thus racism, sexism, and ableism – from the late 1970s to the mid-1980s, as Edward O. Wilson and Richard Dawkins are noted to have observed, is what ultimately led to sociobiology being "rebranded to make it more politically palatable."[30] That said, it is the main field of biology that takes human being as its object.

Generally, sociobiology is "the systematic study of the biological basis of all social behavior."[31] More specifically, it is the study of the "ways that natural selection has shaped behavior in humans and other animals."[32] It understands human behaviour to be governed by the natural laws of evolution because "humans are part of nature."[33] Incest, or the avoidance of it, therefore, is a human behaviour that is rooted in biology. Sociobiology generally rejects the idea of "social-culture variables as definitive causal factors of incest regulations."[34] It claims, therefore, that incest prohibition does not originate in social causes but in natural causes and that its goal is the survival of the human species. With the exception of epigenetics, sociobiology and its successors explicitly side with nature; epigenetics claims to reject the nature *or* nurture debate through its paradigmatic shift toward a both/and position, or the idea that "[n]urture is our nature," but as I show in chapter 4, epigenetics, which is a discursive outgrowth of sociobiology and genetics, implicitly entails the same nature biases as its antecedents.[35]

From the sociobiological perspective, two main reasons are given to explain how and why social-cultural incest prohibitions occur universally: there is a natural aversion to selecting mates from among those with whom one lives in close proximity, and there is a high probability that the individual lives in close proximity with blood relatives.[36] In 1891 the Finnish sociologist Edward Westermarck proposed the idea that incest avoidance is instinctual rather than social-cultural.[37] As Julie Peakman explains, he thought "that people have a natural biological mechanism to avoid incest."[38] Westermarck's notion of "instinct," which is currently referred to by the name of "genetic preference," addresses the relationship between instinct and the meaning of incest and was fundamental to sociobiology prior to its rebranding.[39] Influenced by Darwin, Westermarck argued that persons living together closely since childhood are naturally predisposed against incest.[40] Specifically, he believed that *any* group of people living together from childhood would have a natural aversion against sexual relations with one another regardless of consanguinity. To explain why sexual relations between *blood* relatives are typically regulated by incest prohibitions, therefore, Westermarck simply claimed that "[p]ersons who have been living closely together from childhood are as a rule near relatives."[41] To clarify, as Allan H. Bittles notes, he effectively understood incest avoidance to "best be explained in terms of negative imprinting against close associates of early childhood."[42] He also suggested that the laws of natural selection determine that species vigour and survival are diminished where there is too much similarity between mates or inbreeding.[43] Furthermore, because there is a higher probability that people who live together are near relatives and thus more similar than those who do not live together, he concluded that the human species selects mates outside the family merely as a matter of course in survival. Westermarck, who was familiar with cases of what is now known as "genetic sexual attraction" (GSA), therefore, did not propose that there is a human instinct that identifies kin versus nonkin but that there is an instinct that identifies near and far proximity.[44]

To support Westermarck's idea that human incest aversion and prohibition are underpinned by natural selection, sociobiology often relies on bird and mammal studies that suggest incest is "relatively rare" or is "usually less than 2 percent" among most species.[45] According to sociobiology, as well as its successors, the strongest proofs that continue to be cited in support of Westermarck's hypothesis are a number of studies that focus on unrelated children who have been raised together.[46] These studies look at unrelated children raised in Israeli kibbutzim and at unrelated children who are raised together with the expectation that they will engage in a form of Chinese marriage known as *sim-pua*.[47] Conducted by Joseph Shepher, the kib-

butzim studies show that unrelated children who live together closely in the same peer group consistently fail to develop any adult sexual attraction toward one another. The only exceptions to these findings involve adults who were separated from each other for some
period of time during their early childhood. To explain these few
exceptions, Shepher argues that "negative sexual imprinting" did not
occur between these adults because, as children, they were separated
during "the first six years of life."[48] In the case of *sim-pua* marriage,
findings are much the same. Here, a girl is raised from early childhood in a family to which she is not biologically related. Furthermore, she is raised by the family of and, therefore, alongside the non-
related boy with whom her ultimate marriage has been arranged.
The goal is to ready the girl for the eventual marriage. These studies
compare the rate of fertility, infidelity, and divorce in *sim-pua* marriages against those in other types of marriage in the same cultural
context. As it turns out, the likelihood of infertility, infidelity, and
divorce is significantly higher in the context of *sim-pua* marriages
than in any other type of marriage, including other types of
arranged marriage where spouses are reared apart.[49] Ultimately,
sociobiologists and their subsequent ilk take the results of both sets
of studies to be evidence of the Westermarck hypothesis; these studies, as Arthur P. Wolf suggests, are key among those that secured
Westermarck's entry into "the twenty-first Century as almost the
only man worth mentioning" with respect to the question of incest
prohibition and avoidance.[50]

Westermarck additionally argued that incest prohibitions existed
long before science began to make sophisticated observations about
the effects of inbreeding.[51] Therefore, from a biological perspective,
the cause of incest prohibition in law or custom is *not* rooted in the
idea that the taboo is preceded by any social-cultural *knowledge* of
inbreeding and its adverse effects. On the contrary, the social-cultural
prevalence of incest prohibition reflects a prehistoric and naturally
adaptive human instinct against the potentially adverse effects of
proximity. In short, the universality of incest within sociobiological
and, later, "genetic" discourses is engendered because humans are
ascribed a natural or "*innate aversion*" to incest.[52] Today, the difference
in discourse primarily is that Westermarck's "instinct" has been re-
framed as the outcome of an epigenetic and thus universal rule: "Most
epigenetic rules are evidently very ancient, dating back millions of
years in mammalian ancestry," and the "instructive example of an epi-

genetic rule is the Westermarck effect, which underlies the instinct to avoid incest."[53]

Among the most formidable modern critics of the Westermarck hypothesis is Sigmund Freud. Freud (1856–1939) was a contemporary of Westermarck (1862–1939) and a competitor with respect to identifying the causal origins of incest prohibition. In terms of his discursive influence, Freud's psychoanalytic theory of incest has undeniably undercut that of Westermarck throughout the twentieth century and into the twenty-first; "the fetishistic quality of Freud as modern icon" retains a significant place in the popular imagination, whereas Westermarck has never had such standing, even though his aversion theory has now gained scientific ground over Freud's Oedipal theory of incest.[54] Moreover, Freud's fundamental assumptions about a universal instinct for incest remain a source of debate within the biological sciences that focus on the social life of humans (i.e., sociobiology, evolutionary psychology, behavioural genetics, and epigenetics), regardless of Wolf's observations about a "Westermarck revival."[55] Larry Arnhart suggests that the "debate between Westermarck and Freud over the origins of the incest taboo manifests a fundamental debate in the social sciences": for Westermarck, "human culture arises as the cultivation of human nature," whereas for Freud "human culture arises as the conquest of human nature" (e.g., via the sublimation of incestuous desire).[56] Nevertheless, it would be a mistake to think that Freud's proposition is treated as one that is necessarily at odds with sociobiology. Whereas Westermarck argues that incest prohibition is the logical social-cultural *reflection* of an aversion instinct, Freud argues that it is a response *against* instinctual desire, particularly against Oedipal desire, or the direction of a child's first sexual desire toward his mother.[57] Freud *is* like Westermarck, therefore, to the extent that he explores the idea that the meaning of incest prohibition is related to a universal instinct. Nevertheless, his ideas about instinct are more variegated in that he characterizes the drive behind incestuous desire as something that is somewhere between what is mental and physical in origin but neither one or the other exclusively.[58] In *Totem and Taboo* (1913), Freud establishes a psychological perspective on incest and claims that its prohibition is universal among primitive and modern societies. That is because he considers incest to be an unavoidable and instinctual aspect of human psychic life. As a matter of psychic health, incest, due to every individual's need to resolve the Oedipal complex, is embodied as a universal in and through psychoanalysis.

In response to Westermarck's idea that incest aversion is an instinct, and in defence of his own position, Freud argues that "[i]t is not easy to see why any deep human instinct should need to be reinforced by law."[59] His point, as James B. Twitchell explains, is "[w]hy should we have an incest taboo ... if the aversion to incest [is] 'natural'? We don't taboo what we don't do."[60] Freud further supported his critique of Westermarck's hypothesis by expanding on the work of Sir J.G. Frazer – an influential anthropologist and also one of Freud's contemporaries. In *Totem and Taboo*, Freud discusses Frazer's juxtaposition of the predominant "horror of incest" against the fact that there is no predominant horror of sexual relations occurring between mere "housemates."[61] This difference might very well explain the fact that Phaedra's desire did not capture Freud's attention, whereas Jocasta's did. Regardless, Freud's point is that if humans are instinctually averse to having sexual relations with all people among whom they are reared, why do incest prohibitions pertain *only* to blood relatives? According to Freud, the most obvious reason a prohibition related to blood relatives exists is that incest is instinctual in that an innate sexual drive culminates in this kind of desire within the family.

Essentially, Freud argues that every individual's earliest sexual desires, which are manifested within the context of the biological family, are incestuous and, therefore, contrary to the aims of civilization.[62] As a result, every individual faces psychic conflict, which is at the root of the widespread occurrence of incest prohibition; this conflict is a universal aspect of normal development, one that is best addressed with the individual's own "psychical energy."[63] Furthermore, in *Civilization and Its Discontents*, Freud argues that social-cultural prohibitions are inculcated and defend against human instinct because of the high demands civilization makes upon the individual.[64] Thus, to avoid unhappiness, to belong, to be loved, and to be able to access all that civilization has to offer, we must "attempt to *control* our instinctual life."[65] Ultimately, this task is achieved by displacing incestuous impulses onto more acceptable sexual objects or by sublimating them.[66] Still, according to Freud, social pressure in and of itself does not explain the extent to which incest is psychically or internally abhorred. In answer to this question, he ultimately arrives at the concept of the super-ego, a psychic structure that emerges progressively in the course of normal human development. Faced with external pressures to abandon all anti-social instincts, the individual psychically internalizes a "sense of guilt" or "'conscience'" in place of what are originally only external prohibitions.[67] In effect, the individual begins to police himself with regard to incest prohibition in order to preserve his place in civilization. Thus, where an individual dares to engage in incest, Freud attributes his actions simultaneously to instinct and to a psychic abnormality that is the result of an underdeveloped super-ego.[68] Unlike in the Westermarckian approach, therefore, Freud argues that incest prohibition reflects the individual's ability and need to utilize his psychic energy against his instinctual or incestuous desires.

Although Freud opposed his theories to Westermarck's, a number of contemporary sociobiologists, or evolutionary psychologists, geneticists, and/or epigenticists, have reconciled their differences.[69] The main reason for this compatibility is that they now acknowledge the late eighteenth century's discovery "that line breeding also produces the opposite of genetic deformities – it produces hybrid vigor."[70] In effect, they do not conclude that Westermarck's hypothesis is eclipsed so much as it is only complicated by this discovery, especially insofar as it lends support to Freud's idea that there is an instinct for incest. Therefore, many now think that the instincts for incest and incest aversion are two sides of the same coin; given that there are advantages and disadvantages to inbreeding and outbreeding, each instinct serves the aims of natural selection and adaptation depending on the environment in which an organism finds itself.[71] For instance, if incest, as a form of "kin recognition," serves survival in some environments, a human genetic investment in incest makes sense. As Richard Dawkins writes in *The Selfish Gene*, "relatives might need to recognize one another for reasons other than altruism. They might also want to strike a balance between outbreeding and inbreeding."[72] Or just as "inbreeding is costly, so is outbreeding."[73] Therefore, what is reflected by the universal social-cultural occurrence of incest prohibition is natural selection's genetic investment in incest aversion, whereas the evidence that incest is accepted historically in a number of different social-cultural contexts reflects natural selection's genetic investment in incest.

Notably, where Freud is appropriated by sociobiology, his ideas about the relationship between experience or nurture and the development of the human psyche are de-emphasized and focus is redirected toward natural selection or adaptation as a causal law that determines psycho-social behaviour or practices in relation to incest. For instance, in *The Red Lamp of Incest*, Robin Fox synthesizes Freud's

views on subjectivity in such a way that instinct or genetic program-
ming is given precedence in all aspects of human psychology. Fox
writes that Freud

> may well have been talking about "recurrent psychic realities," but
> they recurred because *at a crucial period of human evolution natural
> selection programmed them into the creature* ... We go on producing
> the weird combinations of kinship, sex, mating, power, initiation,
> ritual and other games that we do, because these have been pro-
> grammed into us by evolution – like the ankle bone, or the oppos-
> able thumb. The mediating mechanism is conscience – without its
> categorical imperative, the systems would not work. But it, too,
> got there by natural selection.[74]

Contrary to what Freud is understood typically to propose, therefore,
Fox is suggesting that the aims of conscience, or the super-ego, which
keeps the instinct for incest in check, are not in conflict with nature.
Instead, Fox understands these aims to be synonymous with nature
insofar as the demands of survival and adaptation are always and
already tied up in the demands of civilization; put simply, the anti-
social organism is less likely to survive and reproduce in an environment where the likelihood of survival is concurrent with "social
alliances" and "cooperation."[75] Additionally, sociobiologists may enlist Freud's regard of Oedipus as the paradigm of incest not necessarily as the flipside of incest aversion but to reinforce Westermarck's
hypothesis insofar as they suggest Freud got it half right. For instance,
Mark T. Erickson intimates this view in a discussion of GSA, writing
that although it was "not anticipated by Freud[,] Oedipus portrays the
literal truth that early separation undermines a natural adaptation for
incest avoidance."[76] Arnhart explicitly argues that "Freud's psychoanalytic theory might be partially true" because "the myth of Oedipus
that so impressed Freud is the story of a man who had been separated
from his parents at birth, who therefore did not experience the childhood familiarity with his mother that Westermarck believed was necessary to instill a sexual aversion to one's mother."[77] And his additional argument, that "[o]nce the Westermarckian mechanism for
learning incest avoidance is implanted in human nature by natural
selection, then human beings might learn by experience that avoiding
incest has many social benefits," also conforms with Fox's view insofar
as the individual's congenitally emergent super-ego secures his inclu-

sion within civilization.[78] Even Edward O. Wilson's idea that multi-disciplinary evidence in support of Westermarck's theory is proof of "'consilience'" allows equally for appropriations or flipside and half-right nature assumptions about Freud. As explained by Arnhart, Wilson's notion of consilience is the idea that "nature is governed by a seamless web of causal laws that cross the traditional disciplines of study," which means the truth about incest is as likely to be reflected in psychoanalysis "as sociology, anthropology, primatology, genetics, and evolutionary biology."[79] In effect, to say that "Westermarck's argument is, simply, 'the current explanation' of incest avoidance" is not to say that Freud's argument is treated necessarily as false or that it has been rejected by sociobiology and its postliminary fields.[80]

Ultimately, Freud understood his theory to be at odds with Westermarck's. He would also reject the sociobiological idea that *unfettered* incest can be adaptive for at least two reasons. It entirely undermines the "phylogenetic hypothesis which correspond[s] to his theory of individual development based on the Oedipus complex."[81] And the assumption that "'[c]ivilization' requires the relegation of such active wishes to the unconscious, manifested in fantasies and symptoms rather than explicit and self-conscious behaviour," is indispensible to his understanding of human psychology.[82] For these reasons, Freud understands incest to be maladaptive, but he does so apart from any biological question of inbreeding; he argues in *Totem and Taboo* that "the detrimental results of in-breeding are not established with certainty and cannot easily be demonstrated in man."[83] Incest is essentially maladaptive for Freud because the Oedipal complex *and* the individual's need to resolve it (by redirecting sexual desire toward a love object other than the parent) are universal; the complex and its resolution through the emergence of the super-ego (i.e., the psychic mechanism that assures the individual's normal psychic development and thereby his place within civilization) are fundamental to the structure of (normal) personality and the origins of culture.[84]

The sociological perspective on incest is characterized by a number of fundamental principles held by sociologists and anthropologists throughout the late nineteenth and twentieth centuries concerning the origins of modern incest prohibitions. Sociological theories argue that the foundation of the incest taboo is not a derivative of instinct.[85] Indeed, with Émile Durkheim, who is considered a founder of sociology, incest prohibition began to be examined as the primary mechanism that maintains social order and the family.[86] Sociologists alter the landscape of the meaning of incest primarily by focusing on rules of exogamy, the practice of marrying outside the clan and the family, rather than focusing on the prohibition itself.[87] Durkheim, Bronislaw Malinowski, and Claude Lévi-Strauss all argue that incest prohibition cannot be understood apart from rules of exogamy, although they argue this point in different ways.

In *Incest: The Nature and Origin of the Taboo* (1897), which was written prior to Freud's *Totem and Taboo* (1913), Durkheim looks mainly at the question of what constitutes, as necessary, the relationship between incest prohibition and culture. He works with the assumption that incest prohibitions are universal: "[M]ost societies have prohibited incest, and have even classed it among the most immoral of all practices." [88] Observing that incest prohibition is existent among the earliest social groups, Durkheim nevertheless argues that its cultural origin is totally unrelated to biology or natural selection because, prior to the nineteenth century, cultural and scientific knowledge of the physiological effects of incest was nonexistent.[89] All incest prohibitions, therefore, originate precisely in and through the formation of social systems. That is why incest prohibition occurs so early in human history and in the absence of the knowledge of its physiological effects. It also explains the diverse forms it takes across cultures and history.[90]

Durkheim also suggests that the repression of incest is rooted first in the formation of clans.[91] He notes that in primitive domestic societies, "exogamy is the binding force of the clan."[92] He explains that the rule of exogamy originally turned on totems; a totem is a plant or animal being that serves as an "emblem" of a clan and from whom clan members believe themselves to be descendants.[93] Individuals who share the same totem, or belong to the same clan, are barred from marriage. It is a residue of this "primitive form" that, Durkheim ultimately argues, is at the root of modern incest prohibitions that have since become linked not to totems but to consanguinity.[94]

To explain the evolution of the rule of exogamy, Durkheim argues that the incest taboo was a product of social relations and that just as the family evolved out of the clan through the import given to consanguinity, so too did the rules of exogamy evolve relative to the blood tie.[95] He also suggests that modern prohibitions, although different, still share with the earliest taboos a religious nature, which, originally, was linked to totems. The modern incest taboo is essentially a "ritualistic prohibition" that is aimed at "avert[ing] the dangerous effects of a magical contagion."[96] In the same way that priests, chiefs, or kings were thought in earlier cultures to be inhabited by a god, Durkheim argues that the modern home and family maintain a similar type of "religious character."[97] The proof of this character, he suggests, is the profound sense of "duty" and "morality" that is commonly associated with familial love.[98]

Although Malinowski and Lévi-Strauss reject Durkheim's belief that incest prohibitions are necessarily religious in nature, they share his interest in the relationship between the prohibition and exogamy. Bronislaw Malinowski argues that there is a direct correlation between exogamy and incest prohibition and between the clan and the family.[99] Like Freud, Malinowski rejects the Westermarck hypothesis and accepts the idea that the family is subject to incestuous desire. But he does not believe that such desire is due to an instinctual, psychic, sexual attachment to the mother.[100] He explains it merely as a "retrospective," or nostalgic, feeling wherein the individual mistakenly conflates present physical experiences that are erotic in nature with earlier physical experiences of the mother that have no erotic element at all.[101] Of course, Malinowski still deems retrospective incest, as opposed to instinctual incest, to be a threat to the family structure, which he argues is the foundation of all nonprimitive social orders. On this view, therefore, incest prohibition is a universal that maintains social order because it preserves the family.[102]

Claude Lévi-Strauss argues that incest prohibition "is the fundamental step because of which, by which, but above all in which, the transition from nature to culture is accomplished."[103] As a result, "universality" is a "formal characteristic" of incest prohibition. The universality of incest *in nature* is at the root of the universal prohibition against incest *in culture*. And although he does not deny that incest has implications for psychology and biology, the prohibition nonetheless is a "rule," and as such it is undeniably social in character.[104] Primarily, its function is to serve the social order and to enable exchange. Exchange, according to Lévi-Strauss, supports social power structures not simply on the basis of goods but also because it functions as a means of "influence," "security," and "alliance."[105] Therefore, rules of marriage and exchange are coextensive with those surrounding exogamy and incest. Exogamy, particularly the exchange of women, produces alliances between families, which ensures that a given social group remains cohesive, harmonious, and defensive in the face of external threats.[106] According to Lévi-Strauss, therefore, rules surrounding marriage and kinship are not produced by the social state but "are the social state itself."[107] And regardless of the various forms these kinds of rules can take, incest prohibition itself is the fundamental and general structure that underpins all other particular rules.[108]

The function of incest as a universal in the modern Western context is also evident in Anglo–North American feminism; radical feminisms of the 1970s and 1980s have enjoyed real influence within the human sciences of sociology and psychology, especially within the context of social work and child psychology. Like sociologists broadly speaking, these feminisms, and the human scientists they influence, generally reject biological or psychological accounts of incest that treat incest, or its aversion, as instinctual in any sense of the word.[109] They also accept the idea that there is a relationship between incest and social order. Their perspective, however, is distinct from conventional sociological perspectives in that they ask a different question: is incest itself – not its prohibition – integral to social order? Jane D. Atwood, whose contemporary incest research is influenced by radical feminist perspectives, puts it this way: "Perhaps incest signals not chaos in the family but rather an order that is familiar – the order of patriarchy, the gendered power dynamics of the society."[110] Her point is that what the universal taboo really signals is that incest is "a universal behaviour" upon which patriarchy, ultimately, depends.[111] More precisely, therefore, radical feminists, or their scions, examine incest as a fundamental aspect of patriarchy and question the claim that it is solely incest prohibition, as opposed to incest, that maintains social order. As Vikki Bell explains, the argument is that incest "is actually produced and maintained by social order: the order of a male-dominated society."[112] In short, "incest [i]s not a symptom of the failure of a patriarchal law, but rather of its success."[113] Incest, as much as incest prohibition, is considered additionally to be fundamental to the maintenance of patriarchy; it makes women's (and children's) bodies readily available to men within the family, whereas incest prohibition makes women available to men outside the family by supporting social alliances built upon the exchange of women through exogamy.

Radical feminists were the first, but not the only, feminists to argue powerfully that the logic behind Freud's account of female sexuality clearly illustrates the ways that incest sustains a patriarchal social order. That is because psychoanalysis's Oedipal psychology can be understood to assign "responsibility and agency to mother and daughter" and to "divorc[e] the father's actions from any social context," which ultimately maintains patriarchy.[114] In effect, Freud's notion of an instinctual or Oedipal female desire for incest serves a male-dominated society because it allows women (especially mothers) and children (especially daughters) to be construed as the perpetrators, not the victims, of incest, while reinforcing male licence over their bodies. Elaborating on Judith Lewis Herman's 1981 book *Father-Daughter Incest*, Kathleen Coulborn Faller explains that the notion of the "'seductive daughter' and the 'collusive mother'" is intended to diminish incest precisely "because incest is entwined with male hegemony."[115] Rachel Devlin, who is not a radical feminist but builds on what is originally a radical feminist critique, also elucidates the effects of Freud's logic as it is mediated through the human sciences: "Once the psychoanalytic perspective on childhood fantasy, particularly Oedipal fantasy, began to influence social workers and child serving agencies, allegations of incest, historians have argued, ceased to be believed."[116] The idea of an intrinsically psychic female desire for incest, therefore, serves a patriarchal social order in two ways: it can be used to dismiss real incest as fantasy, and/or it can function as a kind of female consent.[117] Elizabeth Ward puts it this way: "Freudianism functions as a subliminal 'psycho-scientific' ideology, reinforcing male desire to believe that women want to be raped."[118] Furthermore, Louise Armstrong suggests that Freud's theory of female sexuality removes the need for overt male violence with regard to incest because if a daughter dares to speak of incest, she admits only to her own blame. The threat of this blame reinforces her silence, passivity, and thus apparent consent to sex with the father.[119] Finally, although she "would not endorse most of the traditional practices of either psychoanalysis or feminism," Jane Gallup – who brings feminism to bear on psychoanalysis (and vice versa) and pursues the critical idea of "a new kind of battle, a feminine seduction/disarming/unsettling of the positions of phallocratic ideology" – manages to elucidate the logic of the "patriarchal law" that is at the crux of the radical feminist's concern with Freud's views.[120] She writes that "the only way to seduce the father, to avoid scaring him away, is to please him, and to please him one must submit to his law which proscribes any sexual relation."[121]

The role of radical feminism in reinforcing the universality of incest ultimately lies in its treatment of incest as a fundamental characteristic of the social order of patriarchy. Indeed, the universality of incest that is elicited by this feminist perspective, and feminisms that borrow from it, seems a subtle variation on Lévi-Strauss' perspective: incest is the fundamental step by which *patriarchal* culture is accomplished. Thus, insofar as feminism does regard incest as fundamental to patriarchy, incest functions as a universal to the extent that feminism also assumes that modern Western culture is essentially a patriarchal culture. As a result, when radical feminism condemns *patriarchal* incest, this condemnation functions not only as a prohibition against incest but also as a *universal* prohibition insofar as it applies across modern Western patriarchal culture and, indeed, across all patriarchal cultures.

Moreover, the social, political, and legal outcome of radical feminisms, as Gillian Harkins notes, is that it "recoded incest as child sexual abuse," thereby "moving it from a marital or sexual prohibition to a criminal form of sexual violence."[122] Although in a sense this outcome was a gain, "incest *as* child sexual abuse" became "grounds for [a] new governmental rationality with the child as its instrument": the "abused child" became a portal through which the state more easily surveils and regulates families, even more so racialized and poor families, in accordance with white supremacy and bio-heteronormativity.[123] In other words, "the state's response to child sexual abuse has not been driven by feminists" but by normative "discourses that reflect existing interests and power relations" that are unaffected by or adapt to the feminist recoding of incest.[124] As a result, the recoding of incest as child abuse fails to disrupt the bio-genealogical imperative; it merely subjects families to the universal prohibition through the new, and additional, lens of criminal sexual abuse.

By the 1990s, feminist poststructural concerns with incest had shifted toward "trauma theory" and questions of interiority and subjectivity, a focus that also maintains the discursive effects of the prohibition.[125] For instance, trauma theory assumes "assault and trauma flourish in the context of male domination, the patriarchal family structure, and larger societal patterns of war and the drive for dominance and control," as Nancy Whittier observes, *but* it does not target these external social forces; its focus is on the interior life of the individual as the subject of trauma.[126] As a result, this turn does not undo, because it does not address, the universal status of *patriarchal* incest. Judith Butler explains that trauma theory examines "relations among memory, event, and desire: Is it an event that *precedes* memory? Is it a memory that retroactively posits an event? Is it a wish that takes the form of a memory?"[127] As a problem of memory, interiority, and subjectivity, incest (again) has become just as elusive and immaterial as a phantasy (whereas radical feminists established that it *was* an event). Where the focus on incest "[t]rauma shift[s] discussions of violation to the aftermath, rather than the cause, of violating events and circumstances," as Harkins writes, it means that feminism addresses the symptom, not the social relations that incest discourse maintains as universal.[128]

Feminism also compounds this effect because of its neglect of incest as a topic of concern. For instance, in her 2016 survey of major feminist sociology journals, Whittier demonstrates that within the twenty years prior, feminists all but abandoned discussions of "child sexual abuse or incest."[129] Additionally, Carine M. Mardorossian argues that in relation to the politics of rape, and by implication incest as a subclass, there is an "extraordinary lacuna that characterizes contemporary postmodern feminism [which] can only be understood ... in the context of the general (re)turn to interiority that animates cultural theory today (of which Judith Butler is the most prominent example)."[130] Although Mardorossian is right that Butler is the most prominent example, Butler's prominence, obviously, is not the cause of feminism's failure on this front overall; feminist incest avoidance, as I see it, is actually the result of feminism's unacknowledged investment in the bio-genealogical imperative, an investment, for instance, that is reflected in the both/and positions poststructural feminists advance within critical adoption studies. Moreover, Butler does directly interrogate "the field of sexual intelligibility" and the "incest taboo" as that which "is supposed to install the subject in heterosexual normativity."[131] She demonstrates that, as it concerns incest, "the form of the norm, however uninhabitable, remains unchanged."[132] Thus, although Butler's particular insight as it concerns incest "is precisely the derealization of lesbian and gay forms of parenting," broadly speaking, it is also that incest derealizes some family relations precisely to realize others.[133] And even if the emergence of homonormativity has rendered Butler's particular point somewhat less compelling – because advances in, and increased access to, a range of fertility services, including surrogacy, means that being "gay," "lesbian," or "queer" no longer precludes incest's realization of bionormative parenting and relations in these kinds of families – her broader insight retains its significance. In effect, the import of Butler's argument herein is that the discursive impact of the incest taboo has continued to derealize, both inside and outside feminism, the adoptive tie's ontological status *as* a family tie. In other word's, feminism's – as opposed to Butler's – real failure with respect to incest and family discourse, historically and presently, is its own ongoing refusal to derealize the bio-genealogical imperative.

On the basis of the preceding discussion, which illustrates various ways that incest is problematized as a universal by central modern Western discourses, I now examine how the universalization of incest intensifies biological family experience and deintensifies the experience of adoptive families. Prior to the deployment of sexuality, Foucault suggests sex and bloodlines are already functioning as strategies of control over experience under the system of "alliance." Alliance is the premodern "system of marriage, of fixation and development of kinship ties, of transmission of names and possessions."[134] It is a system wherein bloodlines and/or marital affiliations are utilized in the distribution and maintenance of wealth and power in an economy that is not yet rooted in industrial capitalism.[135] Alliance safeguards transfers of wealth and power through bloodlines, which define and delimit legitimate heirs.[136] Conversely, sexuality is a system that Foucault describes as "a great surface network in which the stimulation of bodies, the intensification of pleasures, the incitement to discourse, the formation of special knowledges, the strengthening of controls and resistances, are linked to one another in accordance with a few major strategies of knowledge and power."[137] In particular, this network is the human sciences as they manifest in and through medical science and psychiatry. Through them, sexuality emerges as a multifaceted relationship with the body and its pleasures that does not exist under the system of alliance.

Although sexuality undermines the system of alliance in many respects, there is nonetheless an "interpenetration of the deployment of alliance and that of sexuality in the form of the family."[138] In part, that is because both systems connect "up with the circuit of sexual partners" to control reproduction for economic gains.[139] Alliance is concerned with reproduction as it relates to the regulation of heirs through kinship, marriage, and inheritance, whereas sexuality, which emerges alongside industrial capitalism, is concerned with reproduction insofar as it relates to the regulation of "the body that produces and consumes."[140] In effect, the body that is moderate and resists the excesses of sexual pleasure or perversion, such as incest, is also a productive body.[141]

Sexuality utilizes bloodlines to regulate the modern family's sex in new ways. Under alliance, sex is punished and restrained only insofar as a person's "sexual behaviours or arrangements ... threatened the continuation of the system, such as adultery, bigamy and, of course, incest."[142] But in the context of a system of sexuality, the significance of blood *lineages* is transformed into a concern with blood *relationships*. Generally, Foucault attributes this change to the human sciences that take family relationships, as opposed to inheritance, to be a central focus. More specifically, the deployment of sexuality by the human sciences, which problematizes incest as a universal, reframes the meaning of the link between sexual partners as it relates to economy. Now conceived as a universal possibility within all families, incest threatens production because it threatens the health of the individual; production, in the context of industrial capitalism, depends on healthy bodies. The universal prohibition against incest serves production because it controls not only bodies that might otherwise submit to it but also the universal threat that incest now poses to health within the human sciences.[143] Furthermore, sexuality constituted *as* incest by the human sciences reinvents the economic reach of the bloodline strategy along three new axes in the modern Western context. Posed both as a universal threat and as a prohibition, incest is mobilized within the family physiologically, psychologically, and socially through the spread of discourses such as biology, psychology, and sociology insofar as each focuses upon and speaks directly to the family. As a result, it has an effect on the "quality of family life," an effect that does not exist in the system of alliance.[144]

According to Foucault, the discourse of incest, which modifies the bloodline strategy when alliance and sexuality converge, "allows us to understand a number of facts: that since the eighteenth century the family has become an obligatory locus of affects, feelings, love; that sexuality has its privileged point of development in the family; that for this reason sexuality is 'incestuous' from the start."[145] Sexuality is incestuous because the human sciences place the family at the epicentre of the knowledge of sexuality and because the meaning of family under sexuality remains conflated with the blood tie as a result of its convergence with the bloodline strategy that is already operative under a system of alliance. Under a system of sexuality, the family, because it is equivalent to the blood tie, now functions as an incitement to incest. And the universalization of incest, the meaning of which is also equivalent with the blood tie, functions as an incitement *to be* "family." That is why, for instance, Jocasta and Oedipus are intelligible to us as family whereas Phaedra and Hippolytus are not, regardless of the fact that Jocasta's and Phaedra's roles (or nonroles) as mothers are similar. Our revulsion over Jocasta and Oedipus's relationship is a sign that their sexuality incites, on our part, an experience of the pair as family, which we realize as we impose our knowledge of incest on their story. Likewise, in the context of our own families, the deployment of sexuality, or the monitoring of the family through the interrogation of incest, produces a family life or set of familial experiences that are not experienced outside the individual's knowledge that he or she is in the presence of the biological tie.

Incest grants new and exclusionary pleasures to the biological family at the same time that it constitutes the experience of biological ties within the domain of sexual knowledge. Insofar as the experience of family is fashioned by sexuality that is policed by incest prohibition, the experience of the biological tie is sexualized, intensified, and invested with pleasure; the prohibition leads to an "affective intensification of family space," a space that is bound by the biological tie, a tie that is rendered in the push-pull of incest *as* narcissism and/or (frustrated) desire, a desire that "is constantly being solicited and refused" in order to invest biological ties with the exquisite promise that family bonds are indissoluble, outliving all other (sexual) bonds across time and space.[146] The pleasures of family that arise fundamentally on the basis of incest prohibition are necessarily dependent upon, or attached to, the presence of the biological tie. As a result, the biological family currently offers familial experiences that are unavailable to the adoptive family not because of the absence of the biological tie but because of the absence of pleasure that the meaning of incest attaches to the absence of biological ties.

As we have seen, the meanings of family and incest are interdependent at this time. Incest prohibition, which regulates modern Western sexuality, further regulates the boundaries of the experience of family. Through the universalization of incest, the human sciences understand the family to be comprised of individuals who are subject to incest prohibition; the family is made up of individuals who share the knowledge, and thus the experience, that sex and marriage between them are verboten. Through the deployment of sexuality, incest is an experience that is "continuously demanded" by the "family" in order to identify itself as such; it is a foundation upon which the pleasure or the *being* of "family" turns.[147] By interpreting itself either as capable of committing incest or as subject to incest prohibition, the self experiences itself as "family." In this manner, the meaning of incest consolidates the meaning and experience of family with the presence of the biological tie, and thus it excludes the experience of the adoptive family either as a "family" experience or as an experience that is equivalent, which is much the same ontologically speaking and in terms of affect, meaning, identity, and recognition.

In this way, its universalization effectively makes incest function as an imperative that must be met if the self is to experience itself as "family" in the modern Western context. Without the knowledge that incest is possible within a given family, or in the absence of the knowledge of the biological tie, the modern subject is incapable of experiencing herself completely *as* "family." This idea is the twin of my earlier observation that the *adopted* self's experience as an "individual" is undermined because she fails, or is unable, to meet a modern Western imperative that to know oneself is to know one's bio-genealogy. Similarly, the adopted self's experience as "family" is rendered inferior because she fails, or is unable, to meet the bio-genealogical imperative's equivalent demand that to know oneself as "family" is to know those with whom incest is possible. Understood as a mode of the deployment of sexuality, the universalization of incest intensifies the experience of the biological tie at the expense or on the back of the adoptive tie. It is an interpretive grid through which biological ties are differentiated from adoptive ties; the cause of this differentiation relates to the fact that the meaning of the adoptive tie is outside or irrelevant to the meaning of incest, which excludes adoptive subjects from any experiences of family that are conferred by this meaning alone. As an arm of the bio-genealogical imperative, the universalized prohibition against incest has the effect of orchestrating an onto-epistemic failure on the part of the "adoptee," whose subjection as such entails that she *know* her biological ties are absent; whatever else a knowledge of the bio-tie's absence accomplishes for the adoptee (i.e., insofar as experts are concerned), in this social-political-historical moment, this particular *knowing* also realizes a truth, which is that only a paucity of pleasures is to be had within the adoptive family.

Having arrived at the conclusion that the discourse of universalized incest intensifies and differentiates the experience of biological ties, relative to adoptive ties, the next chapter considers the relationship between the meaning of incest and the institution of adoption as it manifests in the discourse of genetic sexual attraction. Examining the

Oedipal narrative, it investigates how adoption experts' conclusions about GSA, rooted as they are in the human sciences, reinforce adverse distinctions between biological and adoptive family experience. Finally, it pursues alternative interpretations of the Oedipal narrative and GSA both to resist the negative impact of incest on the adoptive family's experience and to explore how alternative, and equally valued and pleasurable, experiences of "family" might be maintained in the absence of biological ties.

9

New Oedipal Tragedies,
New Family Experiences

"Oedipus? Never heard of it." A remark, one must agree, that could be made
only in a completely new order of things.

Lowell Edmunds, *Oedipus*

The myth of Oedipus is a touchstone of modern Western incest discourse. Indeed, the historical resilience of the myth is often regarded by the human sciences to be a testament to the universality of
incest and its prohibitions. The Oedipal narrative currently functions as a mode of universalized incest insofar as dominant interpretations of the myth, as a *tragedy*, speak to the truth of incest as it
is told by the human sciences.[1] The tragic fate of Oedipus – his
blinding, dethroning, and exile – is a metaphor for the dissolution
of culture, family, and self. It represents the trauma and isolation
that await all those who fail to comply with the modern Western
imperative that *to know oneself is to know one's bio-genealogy*, an
imperative that is commensurate with the prohibition against
incest. The modern Western experience of biological family is a
problem of Oedipal knowledge, or incest, as is the experience of the
adoptive family, which is equally subject to the bio-genealogical
imperative. In fact, the myth bears a special resonance within the
institution of adoption because it is an inimitable reunion story,
wherein the Oedipal tragedy is manifested through Oedipus's lack
of bio-genealogical self-knowledge, or his ignorance about the true
identity of his biological parents. As we have seen, adoption experts
frequently read the truth of adoptee experience through (the
human sciences' interpretation of) the Oedipal narrative, and they
do so especially in response to phenomena such as genetic sexual

attraction (GSA), search, and reunion. To act on GSA, they claim, is to risk potentially great biological, psychological, and social perils, a warning that is mirrored in the tragic fate of Oedipus as a reuni- tee who sleeps with his biological mother.

Working with the idea that the meaning of incest and GSA is informed by a modern Western meaning of *tragedy* that is attached to the Oedipus myth, I arrive at the final question addressed by this work: what new possibilities for the meaning of family reside in the story of Oedipus if and when the myth's meaning as tragedy is rejected? Some reunitees, as we shall see, embody this question sim- ply because they refuse current Oedipal interpretations of their sex- ual desire, a refusal that rejects the idea that they are "family" sim- ply because they share biological ties. Nevertheless, Oedipus's ongoing resonance as a tragedy signifies the incest taboo's stability. It indicates that the biological meaning of family has yet to change; although adoptive, biracial, transracial, and blended families as well as single, LGBTQ, and step-parented families are posed as evidence to the contrary, these "new" or "alternative" and thus *qualified* fami- ly formations, wherein the value attributed to these bonds is com- paratively inferior, harmonize with the bio-genealogical imperative because the effects of incest discourse remain intact. To read Oedi- pus outside a meaning of tragedy, therefore, is to get at the heart of what the experience of adoption in particular *can* be: in a social- political-historical moment that does not attach arbitrary and hier- archical values to either adoptive or biological ties, adoption is an experience of family that is essentially no better and no worse than that of the biological family. To put it another way, an alternate tragedy emerging out of the Oedipus myth is its use in bolstering the modern Western imperative of bio-genealogy and the incest prohibition, which effectively constitute the ontological reality of family *as* the biological tie.

Although the human sciences disagree on whether the individ- ual's Oedipal experience is biological, psychological, and/or social in origin, they generally regard the resilience of the Oedipal narra- tive as a sign of the absolutism of the incest prohibition. One of the best-known examples of the human sciences' implementation of the Oedipus myth as universalized incest is Freud's "Oedipus com- plex," in which, he asserts, "the beginnings of religion, morals, society and art converge."[2] That is because Oedipus represents "conscience" or the necessary psychic function that enables the individual to join and remain within civilization. Oedipus's guilt "parallels" every individual's psychic destiny with the experience of incestuous desire, a desire that civilization demands must be repressed.[3] The individual who dares to entertain incestuous desire, like Oedipus, is ultimately threatened with exile or the social consequences of breaking the incest barrier. Faced with this threat, the individual psychically heeds or internalizes the warning of the Oedipal tragedy (out of which the conscience or super-ego emerges) by repressing and redirecting all traces of externalized Oedipal desire. Freud models the structure of the human psyche and its development on the universal structure that he discovers in the Oedipus myth, a structure that continues to be cited as evidence of the complex.

For example, Allen W. Johnson and Douglass Price-Williams document 139 cross-cultural tales that meet a set of structural criteria that allow each to be considered an Oedipal myth. Their book, *Oedipus Ubiquitous*, as Jonathon Turner and Alexandra Maryanski note, is so named "because the basic elements of the Oedipus narrative are familiar themes in diverse parts of the world."[4] Once they identify what are apposite Oedipal stories, they further argue that the cross-cultural occurrence of Oedipal tales does not indicate that the myth alone is universal but suggests that the Oedipal complex is also a universal.[5] Robin Fox "integrate[s] ... evolutionary theory, sociocultural theory, and psychoanalysis into a comprehensive biosocial account of incest."[6] Ultimately, his sociobiological synthesis of Charles Darwin, Edward Westermarck, and Sigmund Freud accepts the notion that the Oedipal complex is both real and universal, although he rejects the idea that its fundamental origin is psychic. Instead, he argues that Oedipal complexes manifesting in the psyche are programmed into the individual through natural selection.[7] Joseph Shepher makes a comparable argument to describe the biological origins of the family complex. He emphasizes Freud's use of the phrase "'inherited psychical dispositions'" in *Totem and Taboo* to describe the Oedipal psyche; he claims Freud's choice of words indicates that he believed that psychic life as Oedipal desire and its resolution are rooted in *"genetic inheritance."*[8] Where sociobiology accepts the reality of the Oedipal complex, the meaning of the Oedipus myth as incest prohibition is treated as a reflection of human biology or an articulation of what is initially a human physiological response to the demands of evolution.

Sociobiology and its postliminaries now prioritize Westermarck's incest avoidance instinct, or "early proximity," over Freud's Oedipal instinct, as the basis of the taboo's universality, a perspective, discussed in chapter 8, that enframes GSA as a proximity deficit generated through separations like adoption. Nevertheless, Freud's Oedipal theory has not become a mere matter of history; it retains its discursive significance within sociobiology because it remains a serious topic of debate.[9] In spite of current agreement about Westermarck, there is a deep attachment to Freud and Oedipus within sociobiology, one that psychoanalysis maintains by virtue of its bio-discursive adaptability. For instance, as Lawrence Josephs remarks, "the Westermarck effect does not require an absence of incestuous feelings in childhood: only that awareness of those feelings would dissipate by the time the child reaches sexual maturity."[10] Indeed, the Oedipal narrative is as compatible with Westermarck as it is with Freud because Oedipus's adoption allows his incest to be explained either way, as chapter 8 also illustrates. The imprint of Oedipus and psychoanalysis within contemporary sociobiological discourse is particularly obvious in evolutionary psychology, or the interdisciplinary branch of sociobiology that brings the natural *and* social sciences to bear on human psychology *as* a universal structure that is the outcome of (Darwinian) evolution and adaptation; evolutionary psychology claims to unify, by "reconciling the differences between[,] 'biological,' 'clinical,' and 'social' psychiatry," although its postulation of a universal psychological structure arguably reveals a project that intends to *discipline* clinical and social psychologies *within* biological psychology.[11] "Evolutionary psychology" became popularly known as such in 1992, yet experts in the field, as Richard J. Smith observes, commonly understand Freud to have been writing "about the evolutionary origins of the human mind; that is, evolutionary psychology" in 1913 when he proposed in *Totem and Taboo* his "'phylogenetic theory'" and the "'primal crime'" that "led to development of the Oedipal Complex and subsequently ... the incest taboo."[12] Additionally, Josephs, who echoes this view and considers the Oedipal instinct to be adaptive, contends that "[t]he distal explanations of evolutionary psychology complement rather than compete with the more proximate explanations that psychoanalysis generates."[13] Roland Littlewood also argues that "[a]t a high level of generality, what is described by Freud as 'repression' is equivalent in social outcome to Westermarck's and Fox's 'indifference,'" an observation that also closes the distance between them on incest.[14] GSA, according to Robert A. Paul, is proof positive that "the behavioral pattern of Westermarck's 'propinquity theory' operates according to Freudian dynamics."[15] The genuine reluctance to reject Freud's Oedipal narrative is evident also in Larry Arnhart's suggestion that Freud is not precisely wrong because his analysands were "reared by nurses in isolation from their [biological] parents," a fact that allows Freud's interpretation of his patients as incestuous to be (partly) right *and* in line with Westermarck.[16] Although he "views affiliative and sexual strivings as separate ... and attributes only the former to the mother-child relationship," Mark T. Erickson is also unwilling to completely reject Freud.[17] Instead, he writes that "[c]ontemporary findings indicate that Freud was correct to some extent; understanding kinship is essential to explain key adaptive functions of the unconscious mind and how these functions can go awry" – for example, even in relation to "incest avoidance."[18] Erickson's thought also reflects the discursive endurance (discussed in chapter 6) of fundamentally Freudian concepts because he accepts the significance that psychoanalysis assigns to childhood history, the unconscious, narcissism, and identity. He writes that "[i]ncest avoidance develops at an unconscious level" and that "[u]nderstanding the evolved and largely unconscious underpinnings of kinship" directs "attention to important aspects of a patient's life history that otherwise may be overlooked," including, for instance, adoption history as the cause of GSA.[19] Even denials of Freud's relevance are emblematic of his discursive impact within sociobiology, as David J. Buller's insistence on "deFreuding evolutionary psychology" implies. To combat an assumed congruence between human "motives" and adaptive "functions," Buller urges evolutionary psychology to divest itself of Freud. Regardless of whether "'Freud's emphasis on the sexual origins of human motivation ... is remarkably congruent with the evolutionary psychobiologist's recognition of the crucial importance of reproductive success to human motivation,'"[20] he argues "that evolutionary psychology is not, and should not be seen as, a source of theories about *personal* unconscious motives" but should restrict itself to theories about *"subpersonal"* adaptive mechanisms.[21] The point is that Freud's localization of Oedipal sexuality or incest as the fulcrum of family experience continues to operate, whether as a focus or a foil of sociobiological discourse and debate, and it does so in line with the bio-genealogical imperative.[22]

The resonance of the Oedipus myth in sociology is represented by Bronislaw Malinowski's belief that the *"family complex"* is due to the impact of "a definite type of social organisation" or patriarchal kinship on the individual, wherein the Oedipal complex *as* the structure of patriarchal kinship is merely "the action of a certain type of social grouping upon the human mind."[23] Malinowski accepts Freud's belief that incestuous desire is a threat to the family but does not understand it to be either inherited or essential.[24] Although he argues that Freud's Oedipal complex, as proposed, applies "only [to] the structures of the 'patriarchal' conjugal family typical of Judeo-Christian societies in the West[,] [h]e asked Freud to come up with a broader definition of the Oedipus complex so that it might apply equally to societies with a matrilineal descent rule," which is to say he thinks that the universal complex is real and that the taboo occurs across cultures, although its manifestations are culturally specific (i.e., the players in the Oedipal drama need not be mother and son out of any necessity beyond the structural demands of a given culture).[25] The formidable impact of Oedipus on the individual and culture, on this view, is that the incest taboo is impressed upon the self externally, as opposed to occurring within the self or because it is internal to the mind. Claude Lévi-Strauss also interprets Oedipus to be an external, but nonetheless structural, influence on human experience. He does "not agree that the incest taboo has a biological dimension," believing instead that "it represents the intrusion of cultural norms into the otherwise biological phenomenon of reproduction."[26] In this light, he rejects Freud's thesis (in *Totem and Taboo*) that the Oedipal psyche is an inheritance traceable to a real historical event; he argues that "[t]he magic of this dream [i.e., Oedipal desire], its power to mould men's thoughts unbeknown to them, arises precisely from the fact that the acts it evokes have never been committed, because culture has opposed them at all times and in all places."[27] For Lévi-Strauss, therefore, the structure of the Oedipus myth as tragedy mirrors the structure of culture; that is, as long as culture exists, the truth of the myth as a warning against incest necessarily exists. The battle against Oedipal desire is simply analogous to the meaning of culture. The Oedipus myth essentially parallels incest prohibition, which is first and foremost the necessary condition of culture.

Where feminist perspectives reject Oedipal desire *on the basis* that it is intrinsic to and constitutive of a patriarchal social order, they seemingly stand outside the tradition of the human sciences. But, again, as discussed in chapter 8, given that feminism *rejects* incest, the rejection in and of itself still supports the meaning that the human sciences attach to the Oedipus myth simply because that meaning is also a rejection of incest. Feminism's condemnation of incest operates within the modern Western discourse of incest; it reinscribes the incest taboo and (inadvertently) the structure or experience of family that is produced by the Oedipus myth in its function *as* either a root cause or a reflection of the universal truth of incest prohibition. Similarly, when poststructuralist feminisms treat incest as an interior concern or neglect it as a concern at all, the effect is the same. And where psychoanalysis is recuperated by poststructural feminisms at the crossroads of queer theory, "queer Oedipus looks much like the old-fashioned model" because "queer theory's coupling of Freud with Foucault," as Lynne Huffer observes, entails not only an "investment in a timeless psyche" but also "a psychoanalytic return to the family [it] thought [it] had left behind," which implicates it in the maintenance of the Oedipal narrative.[28] Indeed, queer or queer feminist attempts to "make intimacy strange" within the family fail to disrupt Oedipal normativity if and when they fail to challenge the bio-genealogical imperative.[29] For example, Shelley M. Park is a queer, feminist poststructuralist who argues that "polymaternal" (i.e., more than one mother) or same-sex-led families necessarily disrupt the Oedipal narrative, and thus heteronormativity, because the narrative turns on meanings of *sexual difference* (i.e., between mother and father and between child and parent).[30] What Park's argument neglects however is that the Oedipal narrative still depends first and foremost on *biological similarity* as the initiate of incestuous desire because primary narcissism is the first stage of Oedipal desire! Normatively speaking, therefore, Oedipus can be queer or straight. So, regardless of the number of parents, as long as queer parents, like straight parents, desire biological ties to their children and/or pursue them – for example, through new reproductive technologies or even mitochondrial replacement therapies that can facilitate three-or-more-parent families – their desire will be Oedipal in its reinforcement of the bio-genealogical imperative.

Given the impact of the human sciences on the institution of adoption, adoption experts, as we have seen, also use the Oedipus myth as a touchstone to determine the meaning of GSA. They apply Oedipal knowledge directly and indirectly to explain this experience between reunitees because they apply biological, psychological, and/or sociological perspectives on incest in which Oedipus already functions as a source of meaning. Some experts apply this knowledge inadvertently, such as when they explain GSA as being due to a lack of socialization between reunitees (as "parent" and "child" or "sibling") in light of the incest taboo. This explanation of GSA is complicit in Oedipal knowledge simply because human sciences such as sociology regard the universalized meaning of incest prohibition to be coterminous with the meaning of the Oedipus myth. Specifically, even if GSA is not treated precisely as incest and is regarded as a normal and natural desire for reconnection with a lost self that is embodied by a newfound birth relative, there is a consensus among adoption experts that these feelings must not be acted upon *sexually*, a conclusion that *is* the signification of the Oedipus myth at present: sex between biologically related individuals is equivalent to a courtship with social disaster, the magnitude of which can equal the rejection, loss, shame, guilt, and alienation suffered by Oedipus.

Emily Hipchen, while discussing Kathryn Harrison's GSA memoir *The Kiss* (1997), observes that it "evoke[s] very typical fairy tales and myths – usually and obviously the story of Oedipus."[31] Hipchen's project focuses critically on "how *The Kiss* uses incest to locate fatherhood" essentially in the biological tie, but her reference to Oedipus as the "typical" evocation of adoption narratives like that of Harrison speaks also to the fact that Oedipus is always and already the primary interpretive grid for GSA.[32] Adoption experts, including ones who appear to reject incest as the meaning of GSA, rely (in)directly on the Oedipus myth *as* a tragedy (i.e., by virtue of the warnings they impress upon reunitees not to act on their desire) that is key to understanding the meaning of GSA; Oedipus is the GSA episteme. It is always at work in the background and/or foreground of GSA theories and discourse. For instance, the first speculation about the meaning of GSA by the concept's originator, Barbara Gonyo, is that it is Oedipal.[33] As an episteme, Oedipus is also operative as either a psychological or a biological diagnosis, or both, because GSA is read so frequently either way as a regression to an unresolved Oedipal stage that is triggered during adoptee reunion.[34] To avoid being an Oedipus in reunion is to revisit and properly pass through the normal and natural, but unresolved, Oedipal desire for newfound birth relatives, which is said to be due to the trauma of adoption *as* separation; to establish healthy and normal (i.e., post-Oedipal) relationships, reunitees *must* accept interpretations of their desire *as* GSA and avoid acting on it by instead developing relationships with one another *as* birth "parent," "child," or "sibling."[35] In adoption discourse proper, Betty Jean Lifton's exploration of GSA as a form of unresolved Oedipal desire from a psychoanalytic perspective is as famous an example of this episteme as Gonyo's account.[36] But these applications of Oedipal knowledge are also evident in the extremity of Robert M. Childs's idea that GSA is due to the disruption that adoption causes in the original, biological mothering culture, which partly impacts the subjectivity of the adoptee during the Oedipal phase. And sociobiological theories, like Maurice Greenberg's, that consider GSA within broader discussions of incest phenomena perpetuate the episteme because, although they contend "that Westermarck addresses the behavioral aspects of incest [or GSA] avoidance," they still invoke Oedipus and consider Freud to "illuminate the *psychological* aspects" of GSA through the Oedipal complex.[37]

Ultimately, the discourse on GSA subscribes to the dominant interpretation of the Oedipal narrative, which parallels the biological meaning of incest supported by the human sciences: even if GSA is not incest per se, biological relatives are and remain family in that they must observe the incest prohibition or resist sexual relations, regardless of whether they experience each other as "family." Adoption experts, therefore, never seriously raise the question of whether reunitees *are* "family," even though some reunitees clearly claim they are *not* "family" precisely because they experience each other sexually. The answer to this question is taken for granted by adoption discourse, just as it is by incest discourse: the biological tie between reunitees forecloses the possibility that reunitees are *not* "family"; it also forecloses the possibility that reunitees cannot and should not be subject to the repercussions of committing incest if and when they act upon, as opposed to merely feel and resolve, GSA.

Still, some reunitees do resist the interpretation that adoption and incest discourse would impose upon their experiences of GSA. For instance, in his book on incest, James B. Twitchell discusses a pair of reunited siblings who were married legally but were eventually charged with the crime of incest when the presence of their biological tie was discovered. In defence of their marriage, the couple argued that they were not "brother" and "sister" because "[t]hey had been separated by law, raised by legally appointed parents, and legally belonged to different families."[38] The marriage was legally annulled against their will, but they continued to live with each other in spite of the social spectacle and alienation to which their crime gave rise. Another adoptee describes her feelings for her biological brother: "I find that he's very attractive and that my feelings for him are very comfortable and easy, and we have a very good relationship. I overlook the part about being brother and sister because we were not raised together. My brother, is the kid I took a bath with when I was three years old ... and that I see in my father's home. He is not this man, that I don't even know."[39] Lifton also recounts a reunitee's ideas concerning the meaning of incest: "'I could have sex with my birth father and not feel it is incest,' she told me. 'It would only be incest if I did it with my adoptive father or adopted brother.'"[40] Increasingly, there are also recent media reports, usually sensationalist, about other reunitees who have married (illegally), attempted to evade police or charges of incest, and gone on the lam to be together. At odds with expert or media characterizations of themselves as "victims" of a "devastating affliction," they claim to be consenting adults; there is even an anonymous blogger, Jane Doe, who argues that GSA is but one example of "consanguinamory," or the consensual incestuous relationships to which marriage equality rights should be extended for reasons similar to those in support of LGBTQ marriage.[41] Nevertheless, adoption experts and the media that cite them generally conclude that such cases are merely examples wherein the reunitee misunderstands her self-experience, regardless of the fact that she is fully convinced that her sexual desire is for someone who is not her "parent," "child," or "sibling." The possibility that a reunitee does *not* misunderstand her experience of sexual desire is not in itself seriously examined by adoption experts. Indeed, as we have seen, this possibility is simply discounted in light of the meaning of incest or Oedipal knowledge.

Arguably, to seriously entertain the possibility that GSA is neither Oedipal nor incest is to challenge the family's conflation with the biological tie both inside and outside of adoption. This possibility invites us to explore the question that surfaces in the GSA experience of some reunitees: do reunitees who act on GSA commit incest, and what is the cost to knowledge, the family, culture, the psyche, and the species of allowing these acts to go unmitigated? Currently, the fear is that to affirm that these acts are not incest or are permissible is to facilitate the destruction of the individual, the family, and culture, just as the traditional interpretation of the Oedipus myth predicts. Still, maybe all that need be elicited from this affirmation is a resistance against the dominance of the self by biological family knowledge. In effect, perhaps Oedipal tragedy is not the fate of the reunitee whose sexual desire for a newfound birth relative is taken seriously as an experience of *not* "family." Looking to the family ties of Oedipus, therefore, I now explore *other* meanings of family that, despite currently garnering little or no attention, are invoked by the Oedipal narrative. These other meanings, I suspect, go unobserved because, as they eliminate the threat of tragedy, they also resist the modern Western imperative of bio-genealogy and its twin, the incest taboo, which underpin the experience of the biological tie *as* superior to the adoptive tie.

Antigone is the "daughter/sister" of Oedipus and "daughter/granddaughter" of Jocasta. In *Antigone's Claim*, Judith Butler examines the Antigone myth, more precisely Antigone's relationship, as the progeny of incest, to the meaning of kinship and law. She explores the traditional meanings associated with Antigone in the context of modern Western thought and raises critical questions about the meaning of family and incest in light of the unstable location Antigone holds as the "sister/daughter" of Oedipus. Butler writes that "[i]t is, of course, one function of the incest taboo to prohibit sexual exchange among kin relations or, rather, to establish kin relations precisely on the basis of those taboos. The question, however, is whether the incest taboo has also been mobilized to *establish* certain forms of kinship as the only intelligible and livable ones."[42] To be precise, Butler is interested in how the meaning of incest gives rise to specific forms of kinship that foreclose the possibility of other forms of kinship, forms that are currently unimaginable for precisely this reason. She is also concerned with how the constitution of incest as a crime sanctifies and legitimates some experiences of desire, love, loss, and grief over others.[43] Butler turns to Antigone to explore these questions and to challenge meanings of incest surrounding it and its prohibition as the basis for modern Western kinship because Antigone provides a unique opportunity as a point of resistance against contemporary and normalized notions of family.

Antigone is not only Oedipus's "daughter/sister"; she is also ultimately the only person who does not reject him due to his transgression of the incest taboo with Jocasta, who is his "mother/wife."[44] Thus Butler suggests that Antigone is also an illustration of an important conundrum that kinship *as* the incest taboo has yet to face. Antigone holds an "incoherent, confounding" location as a child of incest both because she is the "sister/daughter" of Oedipus and because she openly asserts her kinship to him in the full knowledge that he has contravened the incest taboo.[45] Antigone defies the rules of kinship in the same moment that she refuses to deny her kinship to Oedipus. For Butler, therefore, Antigone serves as a "productive crisis" in the meaning of kinship.[46] In particular, her ambiguous relation to Oedipus poses an important question to rules of kinship manifesting *as* the incest taboo in a Foucauldian sense. Specifically, "[d]o such rules produce conformity, or do they also produce a set of social configurations that exceed and defy the rules by which they are occasioned?"[47] Paradoxically, Antigone's reality as both the "sister" and "daughter" of Oedipus is produced by the interdependence of rules of kinship and incest, even though an aim of these rules is to make the simultaneity of these realities impossible. It is deeply ironic, therefore, that it is only in the absence of these rules that the possibility of this simultaneous reality ceases to exist. At the same time, however, *biological* family realities cease to exist in the absence of these rules. The ambiguity of Antigone's dual subjectivity, therefore, is an avenue into what otherwise is unintelligible within the confines of rules of kinship *as* rules of incest and vice versa. Utilizing Butler's concerns with how these rules make other forms of "family" largely unintelligible, I now reconsider the universalized meaning of incest, or the meaning of the Oedipus myth *as* tragedy, in order to challenge its function in aid of a modern Western biological family order.

In *Oedipus: The Ancient Legend and Its Later Analogues*, Lowell Edmunds argues that the ending of the Oedipus myth poses a problem to its meaning, which further poses a problem for theorists, such as Freud, who rely on the myth as a source of meaning concerning human subjectivity.[48] Essentially, the problem is that there is no consensus on Oedipus's fate in and among the myth's classical sources. For instance, Edmunds explains that contrary to the tragic outcome of the Oedipus myth in Sophocles's *Oedipus Rex*, or *Oedipus the King*, as it is also known, there are important classical references, such as in Homer's *Odyssey*, to other versions of the myth wherein "Oedipus lives on apparently unscathed after the discovery of his crimes."[49] Similarly, Johnson and Price-Williams agree that, given the different accounts of the myth, the nature of Oedipus's fate is certainly disputable. Although some ancient accounts do depict Oedipus wandering for years blind and in exile, dying a miserable and lonely death that is mourned only by Antigone and Theseus, other accounts tell of his "continued ... reign over Thebes ... until he fell gloriously in battle."[50] Not being a classicist, and unlike the authors above, I do not attempt to trace this controversy in historical texts. Instead, I focus on the salient point that emerges out of the controversy surrounding Oedipus's fate: apart from a standard modern Western reading of the myth as a bio-genealogical tragedy, there are other meanings to be drawn from the story of Oedipus about the possibilities of family.

If we exclude the human sciences' finding of tragedy in the story of Oedipus, a finding that ultimately is recounted as the meaning of incest, the myth lends itself *as* a critique of a biological family order. Similar to the way that Butler suggests Antigone's dual subjectivity is a critique of rules of kinship and incest, Oedipus's precarious location as both the "son" of the king and queen of Corinth *and* the king and queen of Thebes challenges the heightened value that is normally given to biological ties as "family" ties. In his discussion of *Oedipus Rex*, Bruno Bettelheim observes that "[t]he story of Oedipus begins with the incredibly severe psychological and physical traumatization of a child by those who should be his prime protectors: his [biological] parents."[51] The trauma is the violence and rejection that the king and queen of Thebes, Laius and Jocasta, enact upon their biological son, Oedipus. In response to the oracle's prophesy that Oedipus will murder his father and marry his mother, Laius and Jocasta agree to send their son away to be murdered. And prior to doing so, Laius also pierces through and joins Oedipus's ankles. On the basis of these facts alone, Oedipus's biological family, far from loving him in an ideal family way, poses an outright threat to his existence. The threat posed to Oedipus by his biological family is further heightened if Edmunds's observations about why Oedipus is prophesied to threaten his biological father's life are also taken into consideration. According to some versions of the myth from the fifth century BC, the reason Oedipus is fated to kill Laius is rooted in a retributive curse already cast against Laius for his crime of raping a young boy named Chrysippus. As "the inventor of pederasty," therefore, Laius poses a potential danger to his son as either a loving or a rejecting father, all in spite of the protection that the biological tie is normally understood to guarantee.[52] Insofar as Bettelheim's and Edmunds's observations affect the possibility of the meaning of the myth, the myth can be a warning against taking the safety and security of the biological family for granted. The possibility of this meaning is further emphasized by the fact that it is only Oedipus's adoptive parents who do not betray him as "parents." At the very least, these events speak to the idea, as well as a reality extant in many families, that the presence of the biological tie in no way precludes the possibility that a child's familial environment will be dangerous, traumatic, and unloving.[53]

The events following Oedipus's abandonment also lend themselves as a critique of the biological family order. Simply put, Oedipus does not experience the warmth, care, and love of a "family" until he is secretly delivered from harm and given to the queen and king of Corinth, Polybus and Merope, who raise him as their "son." Indeed, even when Oedipus discovers that Polybus is not his father "in blood" – prompting him to ask, "Then how could he love me so?" – he never doubts for a moment that Polybus "loved [him], deeply"; of this experience, he is patently sure.[54] Here, the possibility of the myth's meaning is that the experience of "family" *as* love and connection is not, out of any necessity, an axiom of the biological tie. Furthermore, when Oedipus consults the oracle and is told he will murder his father and marry his mother, but is not told of the (biological) parents to whom the prophecy refers, he quickly leaves Corinth to prevent harming Polybus and Merope, the people he knows and loves *as* his "parents." One thing Oedipus's decision to leave does illustrate, therefore, is that the queen and king of Corinth *are* his "parents." Indeed, in spite of the fact that what originally propels him to consult the oracle is a drunk and taunting stranger's claim that he is "not [his] father's son," Oedipus, when told of the prophecy, believes *or* knows that the prophecy, as it concerns his "mother" and "father" refers to Polybus and Merope.[55] This knowledge about the identity of his parents is further evidenced by his protective decision to leave them and Corinth. In other words, in spite of the fact that Oedipus's (mistaken) assumption is a necessary structural component of the myth, his actions can also be taken as a testament to his experience of the queen and king of Corinth as his "parents"

Upon leaving Corinth, Oedipus meets a stranger at a crossroads whom he quarrels with and then murders. The stranger is his biological father, Laius. Thus Oedipus fulfils the first part of the prophecy. Even so, it is interesting that Oedipus, for all his biology in common with Laius, does *not* recognize him as his "father." What can this mean? Oedipus is warned he will murder his father. He murders Laius, his biological father. But does this murder, in light of the prophecy, really imply that "father" here must refer solely to Laius? In a literal sense, of course, Laius's *murder* combined with his *biology* signifies that he is Oedipus's "father" because the prophecy links each to the other as the sign of Oedipus's parentage. But if a less literal meaning is attached to Oedipus's act, the murder of Laius is also a brutal pun or play on the meaning of "father." Oedipus clearly does not recognize or identify Laius as his "father." Certainly, in his experience, Laius is not a "father," and it is precisely this (lack of) experience that facilitates his ability to murder Laius. This fact concerning Oedipus's nonexperience or nonknowledge of Laius as a "father" leads to a very important question: does Oedipus's murder of Laius necessarily signify "father," or does the murder, regardless of the prophecy and his biological tie to Laius, signify "*not*-father" insofar as Laius has never been a "father" to Oedipus? The same question might be asked of Oedipus's marriage to Jocasta, his biological mother. Does Oedipus's *marriage* to her signify that she is his "mother" because of the prophecy and the biological tie? Or does it signify "*not*-mother" because his experience and knowledge of her is such that she truly is unrecognizable to him *as* his "mother," which is what allows him to marry her in the first place?

The story of Oedipus, Bettelheim explains, is a story of self-knowledge. That is, Oedipus's fate is determined by his neglect of the imperative "'Know Thyself.'"[56] This phrase appears on a temple that Oedipus passes but takes little notice of as he leaves Corinth. According to Bettelheim, the oracle's prophecy is fulfilled primarily because Oedipus fails to acquire self-knowledge before it is too late. Bettelheim elaborates that

> [t]he inscription implicitly warned that anyone who did not know himself would misunderstand the sayings of the oracle. Because Oedipus was unaware of his innermost feelings, he fulfilled the prophecy. Because he was unknowing of himself, he believed that he could murder the father who had raised him well, and marry the mother who loved him as a son. Oedipus acted out his metaphorical blindness – his blindness to what the oracle had meant, based on his lack of knowledge of himself – by depriving himself of his eyesight.[57]

Interestingly, Bettelheim touches here on the idea that Oedipus's real "parents" are the queen and king of Corinth. He also reinforces this idea when he suggests that both Oedipus's murder of Laius and his marriage to Jocasta speak metaphorically to his blindness, or lack of self-knowledge, that he could not harm, through murder or marriage, his real (as opposed to biological) parents. Still, the marriage and the murder that make this conclusion possible are more commonly (mis)read as signs that Laius and Jocasta, as opposed to Polybus and Merope, are Oedipus's "parents." This is especially true if you consider that the central tragedy that is normally associated with the myth in the modern Western context is Oedipus's incest.

Ultimately, Bettelheim does revert to a traditional interpretation of the myth despite his interesting observations. His goal, as it turns out, is not to investigate ways in which the Oedipus myth can be (re)read to challenge the bio-normative assumption that family ties and biological ties are coterminous. Instead, his primary concern is to explain how and why Freud uses the myth as a metaphor for the universal instinct for incest, or the "Oedipus complex." In the context of psychoanalysis, Bettelheim explains that a literal interpretation of the myth is clearly a nonstarter. That is because the psychoanalytic concept of "Oedipal guilt ... make[s] no sense if our father has actually tried to kill us when we are infants; why would we feel guilty for wishing to get rid of such a villain? And the wish to love and to be loved exclusively and forever by our mother, as well as the guilt for wishing to possess her, makes no sense if our mother has actually turned against us when we were young."[58] Given the literal events of the myth, therefore, there is really only one metaphor that supports the meaning of the Oedipal complex, which holds that the (male) child competes with the "father" to possess the "mother." This metaphor is the biological tie between Oedipus, Laius, and Jocasta. In other words, the Oedipal complex, because its central meaning is incest, garners metaphorical meaning from the myth primarily because Oedipus, due to his biological tie, commits incest with Jocasta.

In the context of the Oedipal complex, incest prohibition compels the child to resolve his desire both for his "mother" and to replace his "father." Resolving the complex depends first on the incest prohibition's external application to the child and then on the eventual internalization of the prohibition through the formation of the child's super-ego. Insofar as the meaning of incest is coextensive with the biological tie, therefore, the limit of the meaning of incest is that it applies or is *realized* only between people in the presence of the biological tie. As a result, the complex's characterization of the child's desire for the "mother" as incest simply does not allow for the (complete) signification of "father" or "mother" if the biological tie is absent between the parents and child; the limit of the complex's meaning does not allow mere *desire* for a primary love object on the part of the *adopted* child to truly function *as* incest and, therefore, as a true signification of adoptive parents as either "mothers" or "fathers."

With this in mind, we can see that the only event in the myth that corroborates the meaning of the complex is Oedipus's incest; neither his love for nor his attachment to his (adoptive) parents is relevant as a viable metaphor for the complex. All that is viable is the incest (facilitated by patricide) that Oedipus commits with his biological mother, a woman he is neither attached to nor loved by as a "son." Insofar as the meaning of the complex determines that the biological tie is the relevant metaphor of the myth, the sole possibility of family that it gives rise to is that Jocasta and Laius are Oedipus's "mother" and "father." Freud's complex effaces the possibility that Polybus and Merope are Oedipus's "parents" because the complex's emphasis on universalized incest necessitates that key events of the myth, which speak to alternative possibilities for the meaning of family, be ignored. Effectively, the Oedipal complex illustrates the modern Western moral that is discovered in the myth as a tragedy: *to be* "family" is to be subject to the bio-genealogical imperative of incest. This moral is immanent when the myth as incest tragedy is further coupled with its meaning as a search for truth or self-knowledge, a union that conflates bio-genealogical knowledge with the truth that is self-knowledge.[59]

The possibilities for the meaning of "family" in the Oedipus myth are enlarged, however, if and when the myth is not regarded solely as the tragedy of the self's lack of bio-genealogical knowledge. For instance, if the murder and marriage, rather than the patricide and incest, committed by Oedipus are emphasized, a potential truth implicit in Oedipus's innermost feelings emerges: Laius and Jocasta simply are not his "parents." If one is willing to reject the human sciences' idea that the *only* tragedy surrounding Oedipus is the bio-tragedy that is normatively treated as the meaning of his patricide and incest, then an *other* tragedy begins to emerge: Oedipus's fate is due to his subjection to the bio-genealogical imperative or to his uncritical treatment of self-knowledge as bio-genealogical knowledge. The traditional moral of the story is that if Oedipus were not blind to himself or had *known* that Laius was his biological father and that Jocasta was his biological mother, he would not have killed Laius at the crossroads or subsequently married Jocasta, thereby averting patricide and incest. But outside of the tragedy of patricide and incest, the *other* tragedy to be found in the myth is that Oedipus is alienated from Polybus and Merope *as* his "parents." He is also coerced into identifying with a "family" that pitches him into a profound state of unhappiness, guilt, grief, and shame because he is presented with what arguably is an unwelcome knowledge of his biological ties, which he also accepts blindly as the proof of his family's identity. In this light, the original lack of bio-genealogical knowledge that enables Oedipus to commit his "crimes" is less and less a tragedy – it is actually the realization of this knowledge that gives rise to all of Oedipus's problems. If Oedipus had heeded the knowledge of his experience rather than that of the biological tie, his fate would have been different. The tragedy of his story therefore appears to lie precisely in his subjection to bio-genealogical knowledge, not in its lack. In all ways, apart from biology, Laius's attempted murder and abandonment of Oedipus define Laius as an anti-father, just as Jocasta's part in these acts and her sexual relationship with Oedipus define her as an anti-mother. It is the revelation of Oedipus's biological ties, conjoined with the bio-normative meaning of "mother" and "father" that is drawn from the oracle's prophecy by the human sciences, that effaces Polybus and

Merope as Oedipus's "parents" and erects in their place Laius and Jocasta, "parents" who are anti-parents. In other words, it is possible that Oedipus's revelation story is actually a tale that exposes the injustice of the bio-genealogical imperative as one that can subject and thereby bond the self to a "family" that is an anti-family.[60]

Due to the meaning they give to the Oedipus myth, the human sciences effectively foreclose the possibility of "family" outside the presence of biological ties. This meaning, which makes it impossible for Polybus and Merope to be consistently recognized or recognized at all as Oedipus's "parents," also suggests that the human sciences are incapable of acknowledging adoptive parents fully as "parents," particularly when they invoke Oedipus's story as an adoption narrative or invoke psychoanalysis, and its exports, as adoption psychology. The possibility of such recognition is foreclosed by the human sciences' production of a biological family order. This foreclosure is further reflected in the use of Oedipus that is made by adoption discourse, wherein the myth is read as a tragic reunion story or as the quintessential illustration of the fate awaiting reunitees who act on GSA. Oedipus's marriage, as opposed to his incest, mirrors the resistance among reunitees who claim that their sexual desire is extra-familial, whereas adoption, as a branch of the human sciences, sees only incest and imposes the tragic fate of Oedipus upon them. The institution of adoption ignores reunitees who assert that their (sexual) experience of each other is *not* "familial." Experts assume GSA is Oedipal desire or incest in the same moment that they prohibit sexual relations between reunitees. Adoption discourse, therefore, demands that reunitees experience each other as "family" even if they know that this is not and never will be their experience of each other. Where reunitees fail at "familial" experience or, worse, resist it, their experience is isolated by biology, sequestered by psychology, and alienated by law and culture. In effect, they are subjected to a bio-genealogical imperative of incest that is supported by adoption discourse through its indubitable prescription for GSA, which demands that reunitees abandon their "sexual" experience for "familial" experience; this prescription effectively rejoins the rebel reunitee with the modern Western biological family order.

The idea that some reunitees are right to understand their experiences of GSA as evidence that the person they desire is *not* family should not be confused with an argument in support of incest;

incest *is* a family affair, whereas what is arguably misnamed as *genetic* sexual attraction is a sign that family has nothing inherently to do with biological ties. Ironically, a critical rereading of Westermarck's hypothesis, a poststructural one that divests his (or sociobiology's) proximity thesis of its bio-genealogical bias, is possible and also points to the conclusion that family members are the people you *do not* desire, not because you share biological ties but because you share an immediate or close and enduring proximity to them in their role as your parents, siblings, or children, and so on (i.e., regardless of the presence or absence of biological ties). To put it another way, if proximity displaced the biological tie as *the* onto-epistemological measure of family ties and was made the primary measure of familial obligations and responsibilities, it would destabilize the lack of proximity to biological ties as a discursive force that pathologizes adoptees and normalizes adoption's inferior meaning; a reformulation of incest discourse and law that redetermines familial responsibilities and obligations on this basis also makes the actions of people like Woody Allen fully intelligible as incest. If adoption experts are genuine in their claim that GSA is *not* incest, then it is disingenuous not to advocate for the depathologization or normalization of sexual attraction between biologically related consenting adults who are strangers (i.e., raised apart or unknown to each other as related) by means of the legal and social exclusion of their desire from the category of incest.

The truth that the human sciences attach to what is known as GSA may be the appropriate truth for the majority of reunitees who seek an experience of "family": it is a desire for familial intimacy that manifests as a desire for sexual intimacy and thus is at odds with the ultimate goal of many reunitees but, of course, not all. There are reunitees who wish to, or do, choose sexual intimacy over familial intimacy even when the impetus for their reunion is understood originally to be familial. Yet, in either case, the destigmatization and legal exclusion of GSA from the category of incest *would* benefit all reunitees who minimally experience *or* maximally act on such desire. It would do so by undercutting the catastrophic shame, guilt, and social alienation of those who either feel *or* act on GSA, an outcome that would also facilitate a reunitee's ability to revisit or return to an initial desire for familial versus sexual intimacy and experience, if she so chose. Indeed, if queer experience or theory as well as the AIDS crisis tell us anything, many a familial bond that is authentic and enduring has been forged on the heels of sexual feelings and/or relations between strangers who are consenting adults.

Contradistinctly, it *is* significant that reunion entails the possibility of extra-familial experiences that do occur in spite of the presence of biological ties and that there are reunitees who do not wish to reframe their desires in order to conform to the restraints and demands of "familial" experience solely because a biological tie is present: it is a sign that biological ties are neither a necessary nor a sufficient condition for "family" ties; it is a point of resistance against a bio-genealogical imperative that devalues the differentiated experience of adoptive ties; and it opens up new possibilities for the experience of "family" because it confounds the normative overlaying of family ties with biological ties. Where there is an overt or covert insistence that GSA is universally Oedipal, the human sciences fundamentally diminish the possibility of *other* "familial" experiences. Moreover, when adoption discourse, because of the presence of biological ties, imposes "family" experience upon reunitees by denying the authenticity of their "sexual," as opposed to "oral," experience, it deposes adoption as an equally viable "family" form. Not only is this effect evidenced by the inability of reunitees who resist the pathology of GSA to convince adoption experts that their "sexual" experience is not a misunderstood "familial" experience; it is also evident in the fact that the history, knowledge, and experience of a reunitee's adoptive ties (as "family" ties) are never accepted by experts as the proof that, for her, the biological tie is not "familial." This refusal by experts to take reunitees who make these claims at their word indicates that the adoptive tie has yet to elicit full or equal status as a "family" tie within the institution of adoption itself. Adoption experts' unwillingness in this regard unmasks the institution's complicity in the assumption that to know, value, and experience the adoptive tie as equal to the biological tie is to threaten a biological family order, just as the traditionally obscured value that Oedipus places on his experience of *adoptive* "family" threatens such an order. The human sciences' use of the Oedipus myth *as* tragedy, or the neglect of the nontragic possibilities of the myth, also exposes a commitment to the inferiority of the adoptive tie. Oedipus's departure from Corinth, his murder of Laius, and his marriage to Jocasta all show that he is unequivocal about his experience of Polybus and Merope *as* his "parents." It is no small point, therefore, that it is the tragedy located in the myth by the human sciences that unleashes an *other* tragedy upon Oedipus: faced with the revelation of his biological ties to Laius and Jocasta, Oedipus is presented solely with a mean and vapid experience of "family." The greatest tragedy lies in the insistence that, whatever the cost, Oedipus must *know* his biological relations *as* family!

Conclusion

Vance died just before his forty-eighth birthday. He was the first of eight children, eight years my senior, and the first member of my immediate family to die. Although the days following his death – filled as they were with mourning, reminiscing and wet-eyed laughter, planning, and tending to his funeral – remain hazy and surreal, there is a sharp and lucid memory that continues to haunt me. At the reception, my siblings and I collectively realized that each of one us had been confronted with a version of the same question. People who came to pay their respects – and many did because our brother was politically active in Toronto's community housing movement – wanted to know, "Was Vance your *real* or *adopted* brother?" In my family, the need of others to know whether our ties are adoptive or biological is something with which we are acutely familiar because we are visibly different from each other and other families. We are diverse in race, cultural origin, ability, and, as it turns out, sexuality. So although my siblings and I were startled and hurt to be asked versions of *this* question at Vance's funeral, none of us were surprised by the question itself. We even suspected the motivation behind people's desire to identify the ontological status of our ties was well meant; they (un)consciously wished to reassure us that the loss would somehow be greater, more painful, if Vance were our biological brother. Of course, that was never said, but we felt it implicitly in the concern and self-confidence of those who asked the question and in the quick smiles they flashed that signalled their relief at any suggestion he was adopted.

That so many mourners wanted or needed to know the status of our ties at this of all moments is evidence of the deeply entrenched *idea* – as opposed to the reality – that adoptive ties are inferior to biological ties. It reveals a widespread social preoccupation with the cultural belief that adoptive ties are either unreal or less real than those that are biological. It indicates that this social, historical moment is one when biological and adoptive families are overdetermined by the concepts of "brother," "sister," "mother," and "father," which continue to exclude or diminish the ontological status of "adopted sons and brothers" *as* sons and brothers, "adopted daughters and sisters" *as* daughters and sisters, and so on. It exposes the juxtaposition of the adoptive tie's "inauthenticity" against the biological tie's apparent materiality as a longstanding cultural practice or process that even today, and in ostensibly progressive contexts, sustains a biological family order. It also exposes the fragility of biological ties *as* family ties because the need to reiterate the primacy of the biological tie over and above the adoptive tie is a sign that the biological tie is just as temporal a surrogate as the adoptive tie in terms of real family intimacy and bonding. In other words, if the meaning and experiential intensity of *real* bonds were genuinely guaranteed by biological ties, we would not need to resort to the materiality of biological ties or genetics as the ontological proof of the family bond's existence because the bond, not *as* biology but *as* meaningful family experience and identity, in and of itself, would be its own proof where biology is present.

Here and now, contemporary modes of family knowledge compel us to appraise our identities or family subjectivities against a bio-genealogical imperative. Our (in)abilities to meet this imperative contour the meaning and quality of experience that occurs in and between biological and adoptive subjects and families. The imperative fashions the thought and practices of family and adoption experts, who together, as authors, psychiatrists, psychologists, social workers, counsellors, parents, relatives, self-help leaders, and activists, form an institution of family knowledge and adoption. In its institutionalized form, the imperative shapes the self's everyday life as a series of social and interpersonal experiences that occur *in relation to the other* – an other who resides inside as well as outside the family – to which the self must attach meaning. It manifests historically, socially, and politically out of a *will to family knowledge*. It sustains itself through the discourses of individualism and naturalism, psychoanalysis, and incest. It reinforces itself on the continuum of twin and adoption discourse, which pivots on the binary of nature and nurture. Indeed, the cultural supremacy of bio-genealogism is reaffirmed on many fronts: by the bio-essentialism that drives revelation, search and reunion, and open *or* closed adoptions; by the bio-narcissistic insistence on family sameness over difference; and by the language of *the same* that family and adoption experts not only speak but also teach and expect us to speak. Its main effect as it produces and separates the subjectivities of biological and adopted children, despite the possibility that this separation might not reflect the intention of many experts, is that it levels and diminishes the possibilities of family experience for all of us.

To be sure, the bio-genealogical imperative is not in decline. Its operations are and remain in evidence everywhere; divorce rates, blended families, and interracial and/or LGBTQ marriages and families have not significantly altered the cultural value that continues to be placed on biological ties. Instead, the real change lies only in its new or additional formations. It is simply more varied because, for instance, divorce rates, changes in marriage or common law unions, and new fertility practices have essentially heightened the individual's existential panic over the realization of a bio-normative sense of self, identity, and belonging. In fact, the contemporary fascination with, and emerging markets for, ancestry and fertility are colossal because the imperative is omnipresent. You need only consider the proliferation, popularization, and marketing of DNA testing to see that the imperative has continued to adapt and that its reach and consequences for family subjectivities are hardly diminished. Obvious examples are online slogans like AncestryDNA's "Discover the family story your DNA can tell" and 23andMe's "Get to know you," which parrot the bio-genealogical imperative in the form of the promise that each product makes in relation to issues of family, belonging, and identity.[1] AncestryDNA's "Testimonials" television campaign is a further manifestation of the imperative, although it is as paradoxical as it is exemplary. In the testimonial spots, we are presented with individuals who discover, via DNA testing, that the ancestry with which they have identified all their lives is either false or much less true than they originally believed. As a result, each individual rejects or adapts a previous identity to identify with a new bio-genealogical "truth" that is told by the DNA test. The paradox of this outcome, however, is that each individual's rejection of a past identity and embrace of a new or recalibrated one demonstrates how little biology or DNA has to do with identity formation, as opposed to what is the individual's *will to identify* with biology or DNA as the "truth" of identity. For instance, Kyle "trade[s] in [his] lederhosen for a kilt," and Kim, who "want[s] to know who I am," discovers the "shocking result ... that [she is] 26 per cent Native American," a statistic that makes up the greatest part of her DNA chart.[2] In these advertisements, Kyle and Kim flog DNA *as* identity, yet their eagerness to locate the truth of their identities in the bio-materiality of their DNA betrays the fact that the shift in their identities is not causally related to their DNA at all but is due precisely to the *knowledge* of their DNA, which is to say that their DNA discoveries really illustrate the bio-genealogical imperative's onto-epistemological role in the formation of identity and, by extension, the "family" subject.

MyHeritage's "Humanity" commercial featuring rapper, poet, and spoken word artist Prince Ea is another case in point.[3] It demonstrates the imperative's endurance through the popular and tacit embrace of what is essentially the postmodern logic of *both/and*, a logic that this book has challenged too. In it, Prince Ea utilizes his DNA results to resist normative meanings of race as "a collective figment of our imaginations." His DNA discovery is that his bio-heritage is 14 per cent British, 7 per cent western European, 3 per cent eastern European, and 3 per cent Finnish, whereas 72 per cent is West African, which prompts his rhetorical question, "Is race as real as I thought?" His point is that DNA complicates his racial identity, which he further illustrates with questions such as "Which race box do I pick?" and "Should the others get dismissed?" when he is faced, for instance, with "applications" that survey and limit people's racial identities because they entail that a choice *must* be made between categories. His conclusions, fostered by his DNA discovery, are that "who we are is more complex than the labels society gave us," that "there are amazing stories within," and ultimately that you will "discover who you are with MyHeritage.com." The *both/and* in Prince Ea's spot is the idea that multiracial and/or multiethnic DNA material can actually be used to depose race as something that is or should be bounded by meanings of blackness or whiteness. In effect, Prince Ea's message seems to be that race *is* a social construction. But in the ad, this message is accurate only as it relates to race in the singular or taken-for-granted sense that he is "black." Prince Ea's spot does not precisely diminish race *as* biology because he does not also suggest that the now multiple, instead of singular, truths of his race or ethnicity *as* DNA are equally social constructions. He suggests only that what the truth of DNA shows us is that "who we are is more complex." His complexification of racialization with reference to DNA does not, therefore, debunk race *as* biological or genetic. It simply multiplies the bio-material access points through which a body or subject can be racialized, or pathologized, or diminished within from without. Thus Prince Ea's DNA results may diffuse and disrupt the bounds of what is an essentialized (i.e., "obvious") "black" identity but still fail to dispel what is now a multiple set of truths about race that remain linked to him via his DNA; his turn to DNA contours him as a (multiply) racialized subject within an ongoing social context that remains ordered by white bio-supremacy. In other words, DNA testing does not render race or the bio-genealogical imperative inoperative. It merely enhances the complexity and the potential, as well as the reach, of the imperative's operations.

If the bio-genealogical imperative has changed, it is merely with respect to questions of the context and/or formation in which it now operates, but it can hardly be said to have been hampered by our neoliberal and neocolonial present. Indeed, its (future) adaptive function *is* our uninterrupted social-political-historical investment in the biological tie *as* the family's *material* and, therefore, *real* foundation. The fertility market is an obvious case in point: it is a viable market because it enables people to realize the imperative. First and foremost, people generally continue to desire biological over adopted children, and fertility treatments provide them with the (second and third) chance to do so. With the advent of these treatments, the devaluation of adoption has simply remained intact and perhaps worsened because, if and when it is turned to, it is not the first choice but the last option, if it is considered at all, once fertility treatments have failed. The state also wants its citizens to have the biological children they desire. For example, although coverage varies by province across Canada, in Ontario a range of fertility treatments are bankrolled, to greater and lesser degrees, under the Ontario Health Insurance Plan, whereas adoption is not, and thus children who would be better served by government-funded adoptions that, for instance, allowed them to stay in good foster homes remain subject to the precarity of the foster care system. Additionally, the bio-genealogical imperative is realized by fertility science in other familiar ways. It has spawned a similarly motivated search movement and, in popular vernacular, "dibling" or "donor-sibling registries," wherein "donor children" (i.e., born of sperm or egg donation or both) seek their bio-genealogical origins, rights, and open records for much the same reason as adoptees. In Canada, where sperm donors are not compensated, par-

ents and donor children who search are discovering via means such
as social media sites that they may have "half-siblings" in multiples of
ten or even hundreds because there are relatively few unpaid
donors.[4] This situation is not a surprise under the circumstances, but
to *think* that you have forty or more *known* "half-siblings," often in
proximity, is nevertheless a bio-genealogical onto-epistemic exercise
that affirms the imperative and proliferates it (i.e., the conflation of
family, belonging, and identity with genetics) virally through social
media. And even if the search leads to the discovery of numerous,
proximal half-siblings, poses a threat of unwitting incest (or genetic
sexual attraction), creates anxiety over "how I create a connection
with 18 families," or elicits "'freaky and creepy'" experiences, the
impetus (i.e., the imperative) behind the search, the anxiety, and
these unsettling experiences remains the same.[5] Moreover, these bio-
genealogical threats and anxieties are already being reined in with
calls to limit same-donor pregnancies, the effects of which are the
(re)normalization of the bio-family and the protection of its exclusive
pleasures. Within the confines of the imperative, the fact that you cannot easily create a connection, let alone one that is meaningful, with
eighteen, forty, or a hundred families to whom your donor child is
related is going to be a very good reason to limit same-donor pregnancies; if people are permitted so many biological ties that it makes
it impossible for them to make a connection with their "families," it
exposes the fact that the biological tie in and of itself is not really a
connection at all. As a result, the call for a limit on same-donor pregnancies is a rarifying strategy that renews the illusion of the biological tie as a de facto connection. Coupled with calls for limits, therefore, fertility science is widening, not lessening, the imperative's grip
on families. Indeed, it is annexing *other* families *as* bio-families
because, for instance, it is enabling LGBTQ families to depart from
what were once "chosen families" in order to pursue biological ties, or
bio-homonormativity, in that as they accrue the rights of heterosexuals and can access fertility treatments, they will choose biological ties
first. This is not to say that LGBTQ families will completely cease to
adopt but that LGBTQ access to fertility treatments will diminish
adoption as a purported "first choice."[6] Indeed, if Suzanne Pelka is
right about the direction of queer parenting, as I think she is, "[i]t is
little wonder then, when we are financially able, that we often appropriate reproductive technologies to create families such that our children are biologically representative of both parents or in some way

biologically related to their siblings."[7] The "little wonder" that any of us may typically experience concerning things like reproductive technologies *as* an effect of the bio-genealogical imperative, and thus as a choice that has implications for the systemic devaluation of the adoptive tie, is precisely the kind of problem that this book has sought to address.

Of course, there are the exceptions. There are atypical individuals who choose adoption first and do so in spite of their ability to biologically reproduce. But exceptions in and of themselves do not undo the imperative; the meanings of social abnormality (i.e., why would you choose someone else's children over your own?) and exceptionalism (i.e., they must be very special people to adopt!) that surround adoption, or the people who choose it, are still too easily enlisted as grounds that justify a normative rejection of adoption as a first choice at all. Where the meaning of family is concerned, exceptions, *as such*, do not disprove the rule. They normalize it because they are always and already *outside* of the ordinary. Changing the landscape of family in ways that ensure families are equally valued, regardless and because of their differences, is an onto-epistemological project that has yet to gain any significant social-political-historical ground. And as I have argued, it begins with our readiness to critically observe the role of the bio-genealogical imperative in the structure and maintenance of our identities, our familial experiences and relations, and our social-political institutions insofar as they rely on and, thereby, overdetermine normative family formations. It entails a willingness to acknowledge not only the pleasures but also the pain, shame, suffering, and neglect that are facilitated within families if and when we deny the bio-genealogical imperative *as* a powerful and ongoing social-political-historical imperative, a denial that simply leaves its bio-heteronormative, bio-homonormative, and monoracializing effects unchecked.

To that end, this book's critical analysis of the institution of adoption as a *scientia familialis* – one that engenders, as it diminishes, adoptive subjects at the discursive crossroads of sociobiology (or genetics) and epigenetics, psychiatry, psychology, sociology, the social sciences, adoption social work, and the adoption rights movement – is a direct challenge to bio-genealogical thought, as well as to the family experience that it produces, limits, and determines. The intent of this analysis has been to disturb and disrupt bio-normativity by demonstrating how the *will to think, reproduce, experience, and identify with bio-family* devalues adoptive ties. Hopefully, it has also encouraged a re-examination of how the knowledge, not the phenomenon, of adoption engages all family subjects in devaluing the adoptive tie's ontological status. Although the institution of adoption may claim to support adopted children and their families, this book has suggested that its effects are otherwise: adoption theory and practice onto-epistemologically devalue adoptive ties in relation to biological ties. What the book has shown is that adoption discourse, whether in the form of adoption science and psychology, law, social work, or rights, supports a biological family order at the expense of adoptee and adoptive family experience because the institution of adoption is a discursive apparatus that, either explicitly or implicitly, is bio-essentialist at its core. It has argued that the effects of adoption discourse are not confined formally to the institution of adoption or to those plugged into it but are ubiquitous in our culture and mainstream attitudes about *nature* as both a necessary and sufficient condition for the foundation of what counts first and foremost as a *real* family tie. If this book has accomplished anything, therefore, it is hopefully the initiation of a shift in thought and thus in the discussions about adoption that are possible. It has diverted thought away from dominant understandings of adoption and adoptee identity as *problems* that need to be solved, and it has offered different understandings of our identities and family experiences as effects of bio-normativity. It has exposed how the uncritical *normalization* of the need to know bio-genealogy works in ways that drive us always to query adoptive ties, to treat them as suspect, and to do so in order to chart, manage, and maintain the heightened value of our own and others' biological family ties (i.e., as the core of being, identity, and connection), just as the people at my brother's funeral did.

The idealized experience of "family" that we are encouraged to seek in the Western context, as in many others, corresponds onto-epistemologically to the biological tie. Undoing this experience entails a critical rethinking of what amounts to a blind faith in biology as an exclusive and material conduit for *being* family – a mode of being that promises seemingly unmatched pleasures and experiences, along with a complete sense of self. Nevertheless, serious critique of this faith remains, and is perhaps becoming even more so, a taboo both inside and outside the institution of adoption, a truism that is evidenced by the bio-genealogical imperative's ongoing operations within modern and postmodern Western "family" experience.

Thwarting the ideal demands that we identify the various modes and strategies of knowledge that propel the imperative. It requires repeated demonstrations of how biases that favour the biological family operate onto-epistemologically in and through us, as well as within and through our institutions of family. It means we must reveal *how* the varied and capricious forces of family knowledge effectively differentiate family subjects and family experience in such a way that biological ties are always assumed to be superior to adoptive ties. It requires a rejection of the domination of "family" experience in and through the bio-genealogical episteme, wherein the self, to be recognized as normal and whole, is expected to demonstrate its knowledge and the experience of its genetic similarity relative to its family, an idea or expectation that permeates not only the institution of adoption, but also any institution that currently addresses the family.

Whether or not Western families are reshaped by globalization and (bio-)technology, divorce, common law unions, interracial marriage, LGBTQ rights, and so on, the practical implications of this philosophical project are pertinent to all family subjects. It does not matter whether an individual's identity or family is biracial, transracial, and/or transnational, adoptive or biological, queer or straight, or all of the above. As of yet, there is still no outside of the bio-genealogical imperative. People with the most complicated and nonconforming ties continue to be vulnerable to the imperative's onto-epistemic effects. Shelley M. Park theorizes the family that is postmodern and "polymaternal" (i.e., "two or more mothers") as a "(queer) assemblage" in that it is "created through adoption, lesbian parenting, divorce-extended and marriage-extended kinship networks, or some combination of these," yet she reiterates the imperative because her "model of kinship that embraces *both* the connections *and* the differences between and among kin" is a *both/and* approach.[8] Although she asserts that "the difference between biological mothers and adoptive mothers is an epistemological one," she also lists the *"obvious bodily connections"* that adoptive mothers "lack": they "do not experience conception, pregnancy, or giving birth to their children, nor do they (typically) nourish them with milk from their breasts, nor do their children carry forward their DNA or resemble them in socially salient ways."[9] Park's list is obvious with respect to the question of differentiated *experience* but not as it concerns *connection*. In short, biological bodily *experiences* are not necessarily bases for *connection* between a woman and child, but because she conflates these *experiences* with *connection*, she reiterates the imperative. Indeed, there are many women for whom these bodily experiences turn out to be bases for abjection: many biological mothers do not connect to all of their children (e.g., many pick favourites due, perhaps, to their racism, their sexism, or one child being needier than another); they reject a child due to (what is constructed currently as) postpartum depression; and/or they neglect, abuse, and/or even murder the children they have experienced bodily.[10] Thus Park capitulates to the imperative not because she differentiates the bodily experience of biological and adoptive mothers but because she uncritically assumes that biological bodily experience is identical to connection. The point is that even among the queerest of families, the bio-genealogical imperative is very, very hard to overcome. Resisting it, therefore, entails that *you* begin to question, repeatedly and deeply, (your) identity and family bonds *as* bio-genealogy and, by extension, *as* race, nation, genetics, and/or sexuality. Ask yourself what the cost of the bio-genealogical episteme is, including the cost of the desire and commitment to be intelligible within its terms of pleasure and pain, intimacy and vulnerability, abuse and neglect, belonging and exclusion, racism and ethnocentrism, and ultimately subjection. To engage this question is to challenge the bio-centricity of "family" and/or "identity," or what amounts to our bio-subjection as an effect of the critical questions that new and old family experts have either failed or dared not to ask.

This book does *not* suggest that biological ties are never a basis for family ties. It is not invested in adoption over and above biological ties but in undoing the idealization of biological ties over and above, or at the expense of, adoptive ties. Its main project has been to problematize the taken-for-granted idea that biological ties, as such, are *inherently* the best basis for family ties. Its main conclusion is that the presence of a biological tie between two people, in and of itself, is not a sufficient basis for the nevertheless normative assumption that "family" ties really do, or indeed should, exist between them. Indeed, it is the false promise of this assumption that explains how and why so many people feel compelled, even against their will, to maintain associations and alliances with people they would have little or nothing to do with if they were not biologically tied. The idea that the biological tie coerces the self to exclaim a love for people it does not like, and sometimes for people who threaten its very existence (as in cases of neglect and abuse), is a testament to the ways that the bio-genealogical imperative imposes shameful, terrible, and even dangerous limits on the possibilities of identity and "family" experience.

Ultimately, this book is a resistance against the social, political, and historical forces within dominant modes of modern and postmodern Western knowledge that continue to impact the family sciences and the institution of adoption. It is a defence against the totalizing impact of these forces on family subjectivities and a critique of the idea that genetic similarity or sameness is *the*, as opposed to *a*, basis for a "family" bond, which is to say that it is a direct challenge to the bio-genealogical imperative. It is an epistemological prompt that calls on you, the reader, to consider and recognize difference, specifically its ontological role and possibility, as an*other* foundation for family bonds. Although this book has focused on adoption to address questions of identity, belonging, and subjectivity, the processes of bio-normalization that it examines also impact racialization, sex, gender, sexuality, and ability. The ways that adoption and adoptee identity are set up as problems to be solved by the human sciences are relevant to historical and contemporary questions about race, sex, gender, sexuality, and ability as problems of knowledge; these issues, like adoption, emerge and converge as problems within the human sciences (albeit in different ways) because these sciences beget not only family and adoption psychologies but also scientific racism, sexology, and eugenics. For similar reasons, therefore, the critical approach to adoption and adoptee identity presented here speaks also to contemporary theorists, practitioners, and activists in philosophy, the psychologies, the social sciences, and social work who examine identity and subjectivity from feminist, critical race, postcolonial, disability, and queer perspectives; regardless of whether adoption is a focus of such studies, the bio-family, including its lack, is first and foremost the location from which individuals are expected to experience their identities and belonging.

The work of this book is completed, therefore, if it leaves you questioning the hierarchies of family, family subjectivity, and identity that are ordered by the knowledge, rather than the presence or absence, of biology or bio-genealogy. Its chief aspiration is to challenge you to interrogate your unconditional beliefs in the biological tie as a talisman that, in and of itself, secures authentic family experience or, conversely, your unconditional beliefs in the adoptive tie as a presentiment that forecloses the possibility of this experience. Its final suggestion is that we fail our families and ourselves when we ignore the idea that *difference* as much as *sameness*, or in conjunction with it, is a basis for real and meaningful family bonds, even if family experts let it go unrecognized as such. Indeed, adoption is a phenomenon wherein family bonds are founded upon difference every day; however, the sameness that adoption experts encourage adoptive families to simulate displaces this realization and, therefore, the successful or unmitigated function of difference as a bond. For instance, this effect is reflected in the frequency with which adoption experts attribute pathology and dysfunction in adoptive families to biological difference. It is also evident in the fundamental commitment of experts to the idea that overt or covert matching practices help to prevent adoption breakdown. The greatest threat to adoptive families and their ties is the bio-genealogical imperative's demand for sameness, its location of the *problem* of adoption in the adoptee or the lack of biological ties, and our neglect of the imperative as the source of adoptee subjectivity.

The possibilities of family experience are greatest when we reject the devaluation of biological family difference as the negative side of a binary that sustains the positioning of biological sameness above such difference. In the end, the treatment of sameness or difference, or both, as bases for meaningful family bonds is in our hands, not our blood, because family bonds are onto-epistemic choices.

Notes

INTRODUCTION

1 Insofar as the "individual" subject is discussed in context as an outcome of particular historical discourses (i.e., individualism, naturalism, and psychonalysis), I utilize male pronouns precisely to indicate the gender these discourses took for granted or imposed upon the concept of the individual. I enlist female pronouns in discussion related to contemporary contexts and with respect to the "adoptee" because she so often is the subject of adoption and reunion discourse.

2 Hill Collins, "Defining Black Feminist Thought," 351.

3 Haslanger and Witt, "Introduction," 9.

4 Ibid., 9–10.

5 Miller, *Passion of Michel Foucault*, 255–6.

6 Ibid., 53.

7 Foucault, *Foucault Reader*, 101–20.

8 Foucault, *Discipline and Punish*, 182–3, original emphasis.

9 Although Jacques Derrida and Foucault were at odds because, as Foucault later argued, Derrida reduced "discursive practices to textual traces," their ideas about differentiation, not *différance*, were alike in that both understood it to be something that elicited and/or sustained hierarchies. Foucault, *History of Madness*, xxiv.

10 Bartky, "Sympathy and Solidarity," 178.

11 Fuss, *Identification Papers*, 142.

12 Ashcroft, Griffiths, and Tiffin, "Introduction Eleven," 289.

13 I initially explored the idea that a biological tie is neither a necessary nor a sufficient condition for *being* either a "biological child" or a "biological fam-

ily," not to mention for a normal identity, in my 2003 doctoral dissertation. See Latchford, "Family Intravenous," v, 3, 6, 50, 59–60, 263, 266.

14 I am taking somewhat of a liberty here with respect to Foucault's notion of "bio-power," wherein power/knowledge penetrates the body.

15 There is a distinction to be made between *essential* as opposed to *natural*. A natural criterion can be wholly irrelevant to the essence of a thing or category. The essence of "chair" entails a four-legged object with a seat and back that is designed and crafted for sitting upon; putting Platonic arguments aside, nothing about the essence of "chair" in and of itself is natural or predetermined by nature. However, in the context of adoption, the essence of being "adopted" currently turns on a definition that pertains to a criterion that is also a natural fact (i.e., the biological tie is absent), and this fact is largely assumed to imply that the essence of adoptees' needs is rooted in nature. In effect, adoption experts treat the essence of being adopted, or the adoptee's *difference* from the biological child, as though it were an issue of nature; and, as I will show, this treatment is implicit in the work of adoption experts who claim to take what are traditionally regarded as nurture perspectives on the issue of the essence of adoptee identity. So although there is a distinction to be made between the treatment of adoption as an essential difference as opposed to being a natural difference, I argue that no such distinction is successfully made by adoption experts.

16 My use of the word "ontological" is not a traditional usage. It does not refer to a transcendental notion of being that defines being in conjunction with a set of necessary characteristics. My usage is in the spirit of mapping out and analyzing the effects of ontological characteristics or claims being made about being (as though they were necessary), which then form and limit a being, as a subject, in the sense described by Foucault. For instance, as Alan Schrift explains, "Foucault's works can be regarded as a 'critical ontology of the present': insofar as the subject position delivered to us by modernity is not an ontological necessity, other subject positions will be historically possible in terms of the contingencies of the present moment." See Schrift, "Foucault's Reconfiguration of the Subject," 157. Today, the "ontological status" of the biological tie is superior to that of the adoptive tie because the characteristics associated with it, such as by adoption experts, are treated as though they really are necessary and inherent to the presence or nature of that tie, and it is this treatment that informs what it means *to be* a "biological" child. Furthermore, necessary and inherent characteristics are attached to the adoptive tie *as* a lack of the presence of the biological tie, which confers an inferior ontological status on the being of those who are known *to be* "adopted." The subject positions "biological" child and "adoptee" (and the ties to which

these positions refer) incur different ontological statuses through social relations and modes of knowledge that, nonetheless, treat each status as though it were real, essential, and necessary *to being* one or the other.

17 Carp, *Family Matters*, 88–9, 94–5.

18 Foucault's ideas regarding the "human sciences" would include any science that takes human being as its object; it would thus include behavioural genetics and epigenetics (and their precursors eugenics and sociobiology), as well as psychology, psychoanalysis, and the social sciences.

19 Foucault, *History of Sexuality*, vol. 1, 109.

CHAPTER ONE

1 Etezachy, Akhatar, and Kramer, "Multifaceted Psychosocial Impact of Adoption," 4.

2 Triseliotis, *In Search of Origins*, 109–23.

3 Anderson, "Nature of the Adoptee Search," 623.

4 Although I generally refer to the "adoptee" or "adoptive family," many of the issues and concerns pertaining to identity problems that I raise are relevant to "stepfamilies," "foster families," and, indeed, any family, depending on the degree to which children are or are not prevented from knowing their bio-genealogy.

5 Baden and O'Leary Wiley, "Counseling Adopted Persons in Adulthood," 868.

6 Wegar, *Adoption, Identity, and Kinship*, 45.

7 Carp, *Family Matters*, 139.

8 Notably, a series of extremely influential articles written jointly by the psychiatrist Arthur D. Sorosky and social workers Annette Baran and Reuben Pannor strongly supports the idea that sealed birth records should be made available to adoptees in order to resolve identity conflicts. See Sorosky, Baran, and Pannor, "Identity Conflicts in Adoptees"; and Sorosky, Baran, and Pannor, "Reunion of Adoptees and Birth Relatives."

9 Carp discusses the historical impact of Sorosky, Baran, and Pannor's ideas at length. Carp, *Family Matters*, 147–66.

10 Sorosky, Baran, and Pannor, "Identity Conflicts in Adoptees," 18; Sorosky, Baran, and Pannor, "Reunion of Adoptees and Birth Relatives," 195.

11 Sorosky, Baran, and Pannor, *Adoption Triangle: The Effects*, 207–14.

12 Melosh, *Strangers and Kin*, 276.

13 The idea that adoptee identity conflicts are due to bio-genealogical alienation, a state that is remedied by adoptees being granted such knowledge, informs the ARM's central belief that adoptees have a right to unlimited

access to their legally sealed birth records. This assumption underpins the work of the prominent search activist Betty Jean Lifton. See Lifton, *Journey of the Adopted Self*.

14 Clothier, "Psychology of the Adopted Child"; Schechter, "Observations on Adopted Children"; Sorosky, Baran, and Pannor, "Identity Conflicts in Adoptees"; Brodzinsky, Schechter, and Henig, *Being Adopted*.

15 Melosh, *Strangers and Kin*, 246.

16 Wegar, "Adoption and Mental Health," 540.

17 Carp, *Family Matters*, 151.

18 On "adoption syndrome," see Carp, *Family Matters*, 151–2. On "adopted child syndrome," see Melosh, *Strangers and Kin*, 263; and Carp, *Family Matters*, 188, 227.

19 Carp notes that Kirshener, who testified for DeGelleke, "later admitted that he had not used a representative sample or a control group of normal children and in fact he had not conducted any research at all." But he also observes that this fact in and of itself has not stopped the use of this concept in certain court cases, such as Rifkin's, since his work on the subject was exposed as "bogus." Carp, *Family Matters*, 188, 227.

20 Loxterkamp, "Contact and Truth," 423.

21 Bartholet, *Family Bonds*, 181–2; Wegar, *Adoption, Identity, and Kinship*, 136.

22 By "adoption handbook," I mean a popular, practical guide written for people contemplating or engaging in adoptive ties.

23 Brodzinsky, "Foreword," xiii.

24 Strauss, *Birthright*, 8.

25 Melina, *Raising Adopted Children*, 157–73.

26 Ibid., 158.

27 Ibid., xi–xii, xix, 7, 110, 154–6.

28 Ibid., 6.

29 Clothier, "Psychology of the Adopted Child," 222.

30 Ibid.

31 Ibid.

32 Ibid.

33 Ibid., 223.

34 Sants, "Genealogical Bewilderment," 136.

35 Ibid., 133.

36 Ibid., 136.

37 Sants did not consider adopted children to be the only children who were susceptible to bewilderment. Any child who had "at least one unknown parent" could suffer some degree of bewilderment. Ibid., 133.

38 Frisk, "Identity Problems and Confused Conceptions," 7.

39 Ibid., 9.

40 Ibid.

41 Freud, *Collected Papers*, vol. 5, 74.

42 Ibid., 74–8.

43 Hoopes, "Adoption and Identity Formation," 152. With regard to the issue of children knowing their adoptive status, Carp observes that telling a child that he or she is adopted (adoption revelation) has long been considered an acceptable practice, although some adoptive parents do not tell and some experts have made cases against telling. Nevertheless, as early as 1927, some American adoption agencies already prescribed telling as a condition of legal adoption. See Carp, *Family Matters*, 88.

44 The adoption experts who consider these ideas to be accurate accounts of the possible causes of identity problems in adoptees are too numerous to list, but the following works have been influential in this regard: Triseliotis, *In Search of Origins*; Triseliotis, "Identity and Genealogy in Adopted People"; Sorosky, Baran, and Pannor, "Identity Conflicts in Adoptees"; McRoy, Grotevant, and Zurcher Jr, *Emotional Disturbance*; and Brodzinsky, Schechter, and Henig, *Being Adopted*.

45 McRoy, Grotevant, and Zurcher Jr, *Emotional Disturbance*, 3.

46 Ibid., 3–11.

47 As discussed in chapter 6, various sociobiologists and behavioural geneticists have also enlisted psychoanalysis and its implications for evolutionary biology, genetics, and epigenetics, arguing that Freud's theories are not at all in conflict with their own nature-based theories.

48 Ibid., 4.

49 Ibid., 4–5.

50 Hoksbergen and Laak, "Psychic Homelessness," 477.

51 McRoy, Grotevant, and Zurcher Jr, *Emotional Disturbance*, 5–7.

52 Ibid., 5.

53 Balcom, *Traffic in Babies*, 32, 31.

54 For instance, debate over transracial adoption does not target matching as a sound adoption practice in and of itself but the question of race as an (in)appropriate criteria for a match when all other criteria have been met.

55 For obvious reasons, some semblance of this theory is cited often as a justification for opposing transracial and transnational adoption.

56 McRoy, Grotevant, and Zurcher Jr, *Emotional Disturbance*, 7–9.

57 Balcom, *Traffic in Babies*, 33.

58 Ibid., 197.

59 Patton, *BirthMarks*, 139.

60 Balcom, *Traffic in Babies*, 222–31.

61 Roberts, *Shattered Bonds*, 166.

62 Patton, *BirthMarks*, 139, 142; Balcom, *Traffic in Babies*, 231; Roberts, *Shattered Bonds*, 166.

63 Balcom, *Traffic in Babies*, 231.

64 Roberts, *Shattered Bonds*, 167.

65 Patton, *BirthMarks*, 155; National Association of Black Social Workers, "Kinship Care"; Canadian Pediatric Society, "Position Statement."

66 Ontario Ministry of Children and Youth Services, "Forever Families."

67 Wegar, "Adoption, Family Ideology," 367.

68 Dorow and Swiffen, "Blood and Desire," 564.

69 Brodzinsky, Schechter, and Henig, *Being Adopted*, 156.

70 McRoy, Grotevant, and Zurcher Jr, *Emotional Disturbance*, 9.

71 Ibid.

72 Kirk, *Shared Fate*, 1–15.

73 Ibid.

74 McRoy, Grotevant, and Zurcher Jr, *Emotional Disturbance*, 9–10.

75 Jones and Davis, "From Acts to Perceptions."

76 McRoy, Grotevant, and Zurcher Jr, *Emotional Disturbance*, 10–11, original emphasis.

77 Ibid.

78 Carp notes that since at least 1910 relinquishing a child for adoption has led to birth mothers being unfairly stigmatized. In part, this stigma is due to the main precursor of genetic theory. Specifically, the eugenics movement linked being an unwed mother with being "feebleminded," which led to adoptees being stigmatized as prone to "inherited mental defects" due to their genetic origins. Carp, *Family Matters*, 18.

79 Kirk makes this nature assumption in a discussion of matching. Kirk, *Shared Fate*, 23–4.

80 In his later work, *Adoptive Kinship: A Modern Institution in Need of Reform*, Kirk argues that, because the definition of the adoptive tie is not equivalent to that of the biological tie, "a first priority ought to be the attempt to redefine the nature of adoptive kinship so as to conform to realities." Kirk, *Adoptive Kinship*, 159.

81 Kirk acknowledges "primitive societies" where adoption is a central, normalized cultural practice and thus is not stigmatized, but he merely notes this fact without pursuing it as a foundation upon which to challenge the structure of adoption as difference in the West. His proposal that adoptive families acknowledge their difference by pursuing role competence, therefore, seems to result from a resignation to the Western structure of adoption as difference. Kirk, *Shared Fate*, 1; Kirk, *Adoptive Kinship*, 19.

82 Kirk, *Shared Fate*, 70, 156–74.

83 McRoy, Grotevant, and Zurcher Jr, *Emotional Disturbance*, 11.

84 Brodzinsky, Schechter, and Henig, *Being Adopted*, 40–2, 107–8, 33, 76–9, 156.

85 Lifton, *Journey of the Adopted Self*, 55, 68, 33, 60–1, 226.

86 Triseliotis, "Identity and Genealogy in Adopted People," 36.

87 Ibid., 39–40, 39, my emphasis.

88 Ibid., 40.

89 Ibid., 38.

90 "reductive fallacy," *Dictionary of Philosophy*, ed. Angeles, 242. My thanks to Samantha Mills for suggesting that I discuss this bias in light of the reductive fallacy too.

91 Charlene E. Miall and Karen March also investigate the role of the social in relation to adoption, but for the sake of this discussion I have chosen to limit myself to Bartholet and Wegar because Miall and March tend to focus more generally on the social stigma of adoption as a family form. Their work, however, is certainly relevant and complementary to that of Bartholet and Wegar. See March and Miall, "Adoption as a Family Form"; Miall, "Social Construction of Adoption"; Miall, "Stigma of Adoptive Parent Status"; and March, "Perception of Adoption as Social Stigma."

92 Bartholet, *Family Bonds*, 24.

93 Bartholet, "Adoption and the Parental Screening System," 122.

94 Ibid., 121. See also Bartholet, *Family Bonds*, 114–17.

95 Race and biology intersect in the context of adoptee identity theories wherever sameness is deemed the necessary foundation of identification processes in both nature and nurture theories. Bartholet, *Family Bonds*, 158–9, 174–82.

96 Ibid., 158.

97 Ibid., 174–86.

98 Ibid., 158.

99 Ibid.

100 Ibid., 181, 175.

101 Ibid., 86–117.

102 Ibid., 183.

103 Ibid., 182.

104 See the Introduction for a discussion of difference and hierarchy.

105 Ibid., 181, 225.

106 Ibid., 181.

107 Ibid.

108 Ibid.

109 Ibid., 182.

110 Wegar, *Adoption, Identity, and Kinship*, 18.
111 Ibid., 131.
112 Ibid., 122.
113 Ibid., 121–3, 136–7.
114 Ibid., 123, original emphasis.
115 In the context of this discussion, Wegar cites Kenneth J. Gergen and Mary
     M. Gergen and states that "the need for self-narratives is as much social as it
     is innate." Although she does not elaborate on what could be read as a con-
     tradiction in her argument, it seems that she would not conflate what is
     referred to as an innate need for self-narrative with the need for genealogi-
     cal knowledge. I suspect that is because the latter need could be character-
     ized as a socially produced narrative, among any number, that could be
     used to satiate the need that she refers to as innate. Wegar, *Adoption, Identity,
     and Kinship*, 136; Gergen and Gergen, "Narratives of the Self," 254–73.
116 Wegar, *Adoption, Identity, and Kinship*, 137.
117 Haslanger, "Family, Ancestry and Self."
118 Velleman, quoted in ibid.
119 Ibid.
120 Ibid.
121 The visibility of race that situates a self's identity within a racial hierarchy is
     not onto-epistemologically identical with the magical thinking that is nec-
     essary to sustain the biological tie as either a bond between selves or a con-
     duit for identity that is materially real; the visibility of race, at least as
     colour, displaces some of the self's or a family's choices with respect to situ-
     ated identity, which the invisibility of the biological tie, insofar as biological
     sameness is a narcissistic projection, does not.
122 My emphasis.
123 Similarly, analytic arguments that rely on comparative differentiations, such
     as that of Tina Rulli, that *explicitly* emphasize the "unique" or "special value
     of adoption in its own right" reproduce the same kind of epistemic doubt
     about *the valuation* of the value of adoption that is being affirmed in a con-
     text that is already informed by a bio-bias. See Rulli, "Unique Value of
     Adoption," 109.
124 Patton, *BirthMarks*, 112–13, original emphasis.
125 Ibid., 110, 111, my emphasis.
126 Ibid., 16.
127 Ibid., 171.
128 Ibid., 113.
129 Ibid., 173, original emphasis.
130 Derrida, *Specters of Marx*, 63.

131 Dorow, *Transnational Adoption*, 281.

132 Ibid., 25, 281.

133 Ibid., 22.

134 Ibid.

135 Ibid.

136 Ibid., 279, original emphasis.

137 Ibid., 22.

138 Ibid., 281.

139 Ibid., 271–2.

140 Ibid., 270.

141 Javier et al., eds, *Handbook of Adoption*, 449.

142 Dorow, *Transnational Adoption*, 270.

143 Javier et al., eds, *Handbook of Adoption*, 449.

144 Dorow, *Transnational Adoption*, 270.

145 Wade, *Troublesome Inheritance*; Shulman, "Book Review."

CHAPTER TWO

1 This account of an adoption revelation experience is one that was shared with me some time ago by a former student.

2 Carp, *Family Matters*, 88–9, 94–5.

3 Triseliotis, *In Search of Origins*, 20–1.

4 Carp, *Family Matters*, 88.

5 Herman, *Kinship by Design*, 276.

6 Ibid., 273, my emphasis.

7 Ibid., 273, 282.

8 Ansfield, quoted in ibid., 276.

9 Melina, *Raising Adopted Children*, 91.

10 Ibid.

11 Ibid.

12 Ibid.

13 Ibid., 91–2.

14 Ibid., 91.

15 Herman, *Kinship by Design*, 276.

16 Wieder, quoted in Carp, *Family Matters*, 129, original emphasis.

17 Melosh, *Strangers and Kin*, 237.

18 Melina, *Raising Adopted Children*, 91.

19 Borders, Penny, and Portnoy, "Adult Adoptees and Their Friends," 407.

20 Brodzinsky, Schechter, and Henig, *Being Adopted*, 103.

21 Watson, "Late Revelation," 1–2.

22 Ibid., 1.

23 In December 2017, I learned that Karen Barad has used the term *"onto-epistem-ology"* since 2003, whereas I have used the term "onto-epistemology" in the course of writing this book since 2011. The ideas I use "onto-epistemology" to convey are distinct from Barad's ideas. In the broadest sense, I employ "onto-epistemology" to refer to any *idea* or episteme of self that is disguised as the *being* or ontology of self. In this book, it refers to *a materiality of self that is said to be real or there (i.e., the bio-tie) but is not there or real, even as it is experienced as such.* Although it could refer to any episteme that poses as a/the material core of being, it is used herein to characterize and critique the ways that bio-ties are set up as the *matter of truth* about the self, being, and identity; I enlist it to create suspicion about bio-genealogy as the material truth of self, being, and identity. It allows me to capture the biological tie's *taken-for-grantedness as a material*, rather than discursive, conduit for self-knowledge and identity, and it allows me to highlight the tie's uncritical treatment as a material(-ethereal) weld between self and other. Foucault's ideas about ontology, or "critical ontology," have been the most important influence on my thought on this front; see note 16 of the Introduction.

Conversely, Barad, a feminist, posthumanist, and new materialist working within the field of science studies, uses *"onto-epistem-ology"* as a response to treatments of matter as discursive (e.g., Butler's notion of materialization). Barad rejects the idea that matter is passive in relation to knowledge, as well as the idea that there "is an inherent difference between the human and nonhuman, subject and object, mind and body, matter and discourse"; she enlists the term *"onto-epistem-ology"* to name "practices of knowing in being" and the idea that matter is enlivened, actively intertwined with, and impacts knowledge or discourse. See Barad, "Posthuman Performativity," 829; and Barad, *Meeting the Universe Halfway*, 185.

24 Woo, "Judy Lewis Dies at 76"; Vitello, "Judy Lewis, Secret Daughter."

25 Woo, "Judy Lewis Dies at 76."

26 Ibid.

27 Ibid.

28 Ibid.

29 Ibid.; Vitello, "Judy Lewis, Secret Daughter."

30 Seligmann, *Broken Links*, 280, 1.

31 I am using "reiteration" in line with Butler's ideas on the subject. Butler, *Bodies That Matter*, 2.

32 Ibid., 3.

33 "fact, brute," *Dictionary of Philosophy*, ed. Angeles, 93.

34 The idea that biology determines racial difference is now suspect in the context of genetic science because no single gene or group of genes occurs solely in blacks, whites, Asians, and so on, yet both the natural and human sciences have a history of taking assumptions like this one for granted. An obvious example is eugenics.

35 Of course, in the context of this book, this idea has implications for whether it is possible to be a "biological" child in the absence of a biological tie, but I return to this later.

36 Butler, *Bodies That Matter*, 30.

37 Ibid., 28.

38 Ibid.

39 Ibid., 30, original emphasis.

40 Ibid.

41 Ibid., 28.

42 Ibid., 12.

43 Butler, "Gender as Performance," 33.

44 Butler, *Bodies That Matter*, 12–13.

45 Ibid., 10.

46 Ibid.

47 Ibid., 1–2.

48 Butler, "Gender as Performance," 33.

49 Ibid.

50 Ibid.

51 Ibid.

52 Butler, *Bodies That Matter*, 29, 28.

53 These observations are inspired by Butler's questions about reproduction in "Gender as Performance." She suggests that "[w]hen people ask the question 'Aren't *these* biological differences?' they're not really asking a question about the materiality of the body. They're actually asking whether or not the social institution of reproduction is the most salient one for thinking about gender. In that sense, there is a discursive enforcement of a norm." Butler, "Gender as Performance," 34, original emphasis.

54 I examine the idea of genetic history as a basis for identity in chapter 5. Nevertheless, behavioural geneticists do suggest that the presence of biological ties creates an environment that reinforces normal identity formation insofar as the child's environmental access to people who are genetically similar reinforces their shared genetic personality traits. In the case of the adoptee, therefore, the lack of genetic similarity, relative to her parents, is understood to cause environmental conflict, which is what essentially undermines her identity formation.

55 This right, as we will see in the next chapter, is central in a Western social context that deeply values the individualistic principle of private property.

56 In the following chapter, I explore how this *need* is located in the modern Western subject partly through the emergence of the discourse of individualism.

57 This also speaks to the experiences of mixed-race children who grow up in the midst of two cultures when their parents are from two different places of origin and they are born and/or raised in one or the other, or even in the midst of three cultures when they are born and/or raised in a third context. CBC Radio's *The Current*, "Mixed Blessings," which aired on 10–13 September 2007, documents the experiences of adult mixed-race children and the complexity, as well as the lack, of identification with one, both, or neither of their parents.

58 Walcott, *Black Like Who?* xii, 20, 23, 29.

59 Ibid., 28, 29.

60 Leighton, "Being Adopted and Being a Philosopher," 160, original emphasis.

61 Ibid., 161.

62 In 1989 Jessica Lange played the character of Ann Talbot in *Music Box*, directed by Costa-Gavras. Ann Talbot discovers as an adult that her father, a Hungarian immigrant to the United States, has committed heinous war crimes. The film explores the impact of this revelation on the character and its impact on her relationship with her (biological) father.

63 Hurdis, quoted in Walton, "Supporting the Interests of Intercountry Adoptees," 449–50.

64 Kathleen Caswell, quoted in Fleisher, "Decline of Domestic Adoption," 182.

65 Manning, "Baby Needs," 681.

66 "Mixed Blessings."

67 Brzović, "Natural Kinds."

68 Moore, "Mourning Loss," 7.

69 Ibid., 5.

70 Phillips, *On Kissing, Tickling, and Being Bored*, 99.

71 Ibid., 100.

72 Ibid., 99.

73 Various genealogical events that historically facilitate this association are examined in the next chapter.

74 White, "Revolutionary Theory," 102, my emphasis.

75 Ibid.

76 Palmer, "On Refusing Who We Are," 405.

77 Foucault, *Foucault Reader*, 93, 78.

78 Foucault, *History of Sexuality*, vol. 1, 155–6.

79 In *The History of Sexuality*, Foucault largely focuses on the effects of the external relationship between forces of knowledge and the production of the subject. He develops his ideas concerning how power and knowledge begin to work within the subject, even at the level of the body, in later interviews and works such as *Power/Knowledge* and "Technologies of the Self." Still, even though he does not fully develop it here, he does begin to discuss the notion of "bio-power" in *The History of Sexuality*. Foucault, *Power/Knowledge*, 55–62; Foucault, "Technologies of the Self"; Foucault, *History of Sexuality*, vol. 1, 140–4.

80 Dreyfus and Rabinow, *Michel Foucault*, 168.

81 Foucault, *History of Sexuality*, vol. 1, 39.

82 Dreyfus, "Foreword," xviii, xxx, xxxv, xxxviii.

83 Ibid., viii–xiii.

84 Ibid., xii, xxiii.

85 Foucault, *Foucault Reader*, 87–8.

86 Palmer, "On Refusing Who We Are," 405.

87 Ibid.

88 Foucault, *Order of Things*, 327.

89 Ibid.

90 Although Foucault would reject his theistic philosophy, Søren Kierkegaard's observation that "[i]f a person does not become what he understands, he does not really understand it" offers us a useful way to think about how Foucault views the relationship between being and thought. Kierkegaard, *Diary of Søren Kierkegaard*, 126.

91 Foucault, *History of Sexuality*, vol. 2, 4.

92 Foucault, *Archaeology of Knowledge*, 49.

93 Foucault, *Foucault Reader*, 94.

94 Wilson, "Foucault, Genealogy, History," 158.

95 Schrift, "Foucault's Reconfiguration of the Subject," 153.

96 Foucault, *Foucault Reader*, 79.

97 Ibid., 78, 95.

98 I say "eventually" because the onset of a new subjectivity as an "adoptee," such as in the case of Celina, is garnered through the self's induction into the institution of adoption, a process that she was in the midst of at the time we met because she had begun to seek information and emotional support from professionals who specialized in adoption issues.

99 Foucault, *History of Sexuality*, vol. 2, 6–7.

100 Foucault, *Foucault Live*, 296.
101 Foucault, *History of Sexuality*, vol. 2, 11.
102 Foucault explores this idea in *The History of Sexuality*, where he suggests that, like the classical and the Christian experiences of sex, the modern emergence of "sexuality" is intelligible only in light of "the theoretical and practical context with which it has been associated." Thus, even though sex is an object of concern in each context, the problematization of the object changes with the contemporary modes and applications of knowledge that *are* morality and science and medicine in each period. In antiquity, Foucault suggests that the distinctiveness of the problematization, and thus the experience, of sex is due to its location in the matrices of concern with the role of pleasure and the ethic of "self-mastery" in the "'arts of existence.'" In Christianity, the problem of sex becomes different because it is reticulated through ascetic knowledges and the problem of sin. So although there is a certain but limited historical continuity to sex as an object and practice of knowledge, it is vastly transformed as it is permeated by other historical modes of knowledge. As a result, the experience of sex, known and practised as it is in one age, becomes largely unintelligible in another if it, as an object, is problematized in a sufficiently new way. Foucault, *History of Sexuality*, vol. 2, 3, 82, 10, 3–13.

Of course, Foucault does not suggest that the physical experience of sex is mediated in singular and predictable ways that are indubitably confined to a dominant discourse in a particular social-political-historical moment. Experience, indeed pleasure, can mutate within dominant modes of knowledge and in ways that are completely unanticipated. A given mode of knowledge can present the self with inadvertent and variform opportunities for experience. To exemplify this idea, Foucault discusses "reverse discourses." Generally, these discourses do not so much oppose or "run counter to" a dominant discourse but appear and multiply within and throughout the interstices of that discourse. For instance, at the same time that modern science and medicine produced a discourse of "normal" sexuality – one that attempts to sequester "perverse" sexualities, such as homosexuality – they also created conditions under which "homosexuality began to speak in its own behalf, to demand that its legitimacy or 'naturality' be acknowledged, often in the same vocabulary, using the same categories by which it was medically disqualified." Reverse discourses, therefore, also mediate experience (again, in limited and determined ways), but they do so not as ideologies or moralities that oppose or "run counter to" a dominant discourse. Instead, they occur in and through the very relations and strategies of power that, for example, would suppress them. Thus a repressive discourse of homosexuality is also an impetus for new sexual pleasures that are "homosexuality" because power and knowledge are essentially reciprocal and (re)productive.

Finally, the problem related to reverse discourses as modes of resistance is worth mentioning; reverse discourses are not necessarily as productive as the dominant discourses out of which they emerge, and so they may not sufficiently minimize or resist the effects of the latter; and where a reverse discourse is as, or more, productive than the discourse out of which it aris-es, it will nonetheless produce new forms of subjugation that also restrict, limit, and determine human experience. Thus resistance lies not in the self becoming and maintaining itself as a new subject but in its attempt to remain infinitely open to trying on and casting off old subjectivities for new. Foucault, *History of Sexuality*, vol. 1, 101, 101–2.

103 Wilson, "Foucault, Genealogy, History," 167.

104 Sorosky, Baran, and Pannor, *Adoption Triangle: The Effects*, 26–7, 32; Gager, *Blood Ties and Fictive Ties*, 37–40.

105 Jacques Donzelot suggests the problem of child preservation arose when concerns with increasing infant mortality rates, child education, and state interests in production intersected in the eighteenth century. Elisabeth Bad-inter reiterates these trends and explores how earlier Enlightenment con-cerns with population, equality, and happiness, prompted by Jean-Jacques Rousseau, among others, also instigated a new interest in the child. Donzelot, *Policing of Families*, 9–47; Badinter, "Defense of the Child"; Sorosky, Baran, and Pannor, *Adoption Triangle: The Effects*, 28, 32.

106 Carp, *Family Matters*, 11.

107 Ibid.

108 Ibid., 11–12.

109 Although no longer recommended by adoption experts, this is a reference to the "chosen baby" narrative that adoptive parents were often counselled throughout the 1970s to tell their children in order to put their adoptions in a positive light. Lifton, *Journey of the Adopted Self*, 39.

110 For Foucault's discussion of origins and self-recognition, see Foucault, "Niet-zsche, Genealogy, History"; and Foucault, *Foucault Reader*, 77–88.

111 Ibid., 94.

112 This idea underpins Foucault's suspicion toward using identity categories at all, as well as his preference, instead, for the language of the "subject." The idea of the subject better reflects the contingency of experience and its dependency on systems of knowledge and power – systems that are not only externally imposed upon the individual but that also further begin to function in him *as* the "forms of understanding which the subject creates

about himself." Foucault, *Essential Works of Michel Foucault*, vol. 1, 177. It is also worth noting that Foucault always personally resisted identity categories to avoid being "equated with" and thus limited by any particular category. He has often presented his ideas about this type of resistance, but a very good discussion occurs in his essay "What Is an Author?" See Foucault, *Foucault Reader*, 101–20.

CHAPTER THREE

1 Foucault, *Politics of Truth*, 177.
2 Dumont, *Essays on Individualism*, 10.
3 Mannheim and Weber, each quoted in Lukes, "Meanings of 'Individualism,'" 45.
4 These themes are the subject of Lukes's classic text *Individualism*.
5 Foucault, "Nietzsche, Genealogy, History," 154.
6 Canguilhem, "Death of Man?" 78.
7 Foucault, "Nietzsche, Genealogy, History," 145.
8 Foucault, "Political Technology of Individuals," 162; Dreyfus, "'Being and Power' Revisited," 43.
9 Foucault, "Nietzsche, Genealogy, History," 144.
10 Bouchard, "Introduction," 23.
11 Deleuze, quoted in Huffer, *Mad for Foucault*, 93.
12 Foucault, *Foucault Reader*, 46.
13 Plummer, *Intimate Citizenship*, 24. Ken Plummer makes this claim in a discussion of the idea that although "personal choices seem to proliferate" with respect to modern intimacies that are familial or sexual, these "'free' choices" are merely "socially patterned" as such by individualist ideology. Ibid., 24–5.
14 Lukes, *Individualism*, 19.
15 Levin, *Theories of the Self*, 7.
16 Lukes, *Individualism*, 107.
17 Ibid.
18 Ibid.
19 Foucault, quoted in Han, "Analytic of Finitude," 188.
20 Huffer, *Mad for Foucault*, 265.
21 Hicks, "Nietzsche, Heidegger and Foucault," 89.
22 Han, "Analytic of Finitude," 197.
23 Shanahan, *Toward a Genealogy of Individualism*, 18.
24 Levin, *Theories of the Self*, 13.
25 Ibid.

26 Glover, *I: The Philosophy and Psychology*, 90.

27 Lukes, *Individualism*, 57.

28 Levin, *Theories of the Self*, 33.

29 Glover, *I: The Philosophy and Psychology*, 125.

30 Kant, quoted in Lukes, *Individualism*, 55, original emphasis.

31 Foucault, *Politics of Truth*, 34, 35.

32 Shanahan, *Toward a Genealogy of Individualism*, 82–5.

33 Canguilhem, "Death of Man?" 89, original emphasis.

34 Shanahan, *Toward a Genealogy of Individualism*, 84, original emphasis.

35 Canguilhem notes that at the turn of the nineteenth century, "biology, economy, and linguistics" addressed the question "What is man?" Notably, biology and economy also converged within naturalism, as the proceeding discussion suggests. Canguilhem, "Death of Man?" 89.

36 Furst and Skrine, *Naturalism*, 4–5.

37 Smith, "Art, Science, and Visual Culture," 94.

38 Ibid.

39 Clark, "'Ants Were Duly Visited,'" 151.

40 Ibid., 157.

41 Ibid.

42 Furst and Skrine, *Naturalism*, 2, 2–3.

43 Clark, "'Ants Were Duly Visited,'" 151.

44 Müller-Wille and Rheinberger, *Cultural History of Heredity*, 10.

45 Durant, "Scientific Naturalism and Social Reform," 34, 49, 34.

46 Darwin, *On the Origin of Species*.

47 Müller-Wille and Rheinberger, *Cultural History of Heredity*, 2.

48 Phillips, *Darwin's Worms*, 6.

49 Hawkins, *Social Darwinism*, 216, 216–18.

50 Young, *Darwin's Metaphor*, 40–3, 86–7.

51 Darwin, *On the Origin of Species*, 31.

52 Ibid., 108.

53 Ibid.

54 Lewontin, *Biology as Ideology*, 9–10, original emphasis.

55 Ibid., 9, 13.

56 Staffan Müller-Wille and Hans Jörg Rheinberger argue that the historical socio-economic conditions necessary for the early modern "knowledge regime of heredity ... started to unfold as people, goods, and the relationships they mediated began to move and change on a global scale," a thesis that sheds another light on how and why Darwin's ideas could come to enjoy such easy currency. Müller-Wille and Rheinberger, *Cultural History of Heredity*, 3.

57 Riesman, *Individualism Reconsidered*, 28, 29.

58 Lewontin, *Biology as Ideology*, 10–11.

59 Bernardes, "'Family Ideology,'" 281.

60 Ibid., 281–2.

61 Ibid., 283.

62 Ibid., 284.

63 Donzelot, *Policing of Families*, 20, 48–50, 77.

64 Ibid., 81.

65 Throughout her book *Mother Love*, Elisabeth Badinter shows how up until the eighteenth century both upper- and lower-class western European women commonly sent their infants great distances, and in good conscience, to live in the care of wet nurses, often until between the ages of three and six. Her book concludes that it was only as the state began to take an interest in lowering infant mortality rates that this practice began to meet with social disapproval.

66 Donzelot, *Policing of Families*, 46–9.

67 Ibid., 13, 448–9.

68 The biological tie, *as* race, also has a history of being socially, politically, and historically manipulated in order to control or rule out who is responsible for a given child. For instance, Dorothy Roberts explains that during the history of American slavery, the responsibility for the children of slaves was determined in law "by making slave status inheritable from the mother." This law ensured that the mixed-race children of white, male masters and black, female slaves could make no claim to "free" status on the basis of their biological/racial lineage to a "free" white father. What this fact and Donzelot's observations illustrate is that the biological tie is a fluid strategy that is utilized to exert power and control over individuals for the purpose of social-political-historical aims. Roberts, "Genetic Tie," 226–7.

69 Shaffer, "Familial Love," 74.

70 Shelley, *Frankenstein*, 121.

71 Ibid., 139.

72 Wegar, *Adoption, Identity, and Kinship*, 97.

73 Ibid., 97–8.

74 Carp, *Family Matters*, 144.

75 Lifton, *Journey of the Adopted Self*, 136.

76 Ibid., 135.

77 Cumette and Testa, "Consuming Genomes," 159, 178.

78 Zwart, "Genomics and Self-Knowledge," 192.

79 Ibid., 182.

80 Clinton and Blair, each quoted in ibid., 188, original emphasis.

81 Collins et al., "Vision for the Future."

82 Ibid.

83 Hauskeller, "Genes, Genomes and Identity," 286.

CHAPTER FOUR

1 Wright, *Twins: Genes, Environment*, 5.

2 "In our own culture," Wright notes, "we tend to dote on twins and mythologize their specialness through daytime talk shows, which turn them into freaks but which also, to be fair, provide a forum to marvel at the wonder and the mystery of the twin event." Wright, *Twins: Genes, Environment*, 6. The ability of twins to capture the popular imagination arguably points to a collective concern with the meaning and value of biological sameness that is similar to the concern that Katarina Wegar, as we have seen, claims is reflected in the popularity of adoptee searches as a talk show topic. Wegar, *Adoption, Identity, and Kinship*, 97.

3 Bryan, *Nature and Nurture of Twins*, 9.

4 Scheinfeld, *Twins and Supertwins*, 273. Thomas J. Bouchard Jr indicates that "Galton introduced the use of both twins and adoptees," citing Galton's published works "The History of Twins" (1876) and *Inquiries into Human Faculty and Its Development* (1883) respectively. Bouchard Jr, "Genetic and Environmental Influences," 257.

5 Galton, "History of Twins"; Galton, *Inquiries into Human Faculty*.

6 Galton, "History of Twins," 392, 395.

7 Ibid., 391–2; Wright, *Twins: And What*, 12.

8 Lichtenstein et al., "Socioeconomic Status and Physical Health"; Eckert et al., "Homosexuality in Monozygotic Twins."

9 Ehrlich and Feldman, "Genes and Cultures," 89.

10 Stewart, *Exploring Twins*, 40.

11 Bouchard Jr, "Genetic and Environmental Influences," 257.

12 Galton is not reputed to have proposed studies on *reared-apart* twins, according to Thomas J. Bouchard Jr's discussion of Galton's personal letters (which reside in the University of London Archives). Notably, however, Bouchard did discover that Galton had begun to seek out samples of twins with the help of an insurance company that for some reason could and did provide him with confidential information concerning the whereabouts of a number of twin pairs. Bouchard Jr, "Behavioral Studies of Twins and Adoptees," 12.8–12.9.

13 Harris, *The Nurture Assumption*, 23.

14 Bouchard Jr, "Behavioral Studies of Twins and Adoptees," 12.8.

15 Wright, *Twins: And What*, 135.

16 Harris, *Nurture Assumption*, 21–2.

17 Segal, quoted in Miele, "Entwinned Lives," 29.

18 Harris, *Nurture Assumption*, 22–3.

19 Watson, *Twins*, 69.

20 Ibid., 69–73.

21 Bryan, *Nature and Nurture of Twins*, 1.

22 Ibid., 1–3.

23 Ibid., 5.

24 Stewart, *Exploring Twins*, 10.

25 Watson, *Twins*, 70.

26 With the advancement and increasing use of fertility treatments by childless couples, more multiple births are occurring, and the day may come when twins no longer command the awe and curiosity that they do today. This outcome, in turn, could alter the impact of twin discourse on subjectivity.

27 This discourse occurs with, in, and through a bio-genealogical imperative that is already operative.

28 Wright, *Twins: And What*, 146–8, 152. Wright also discusses how twin studies began to be used to measure the heritability of personality and notes that Thomas J. Bouchard Jr, who conducted the influential Minnesota Study of Twins Reared Apart, suggests that "about fifty percent" of personality is heritable. Ibid., 147.

29 The idea that genes determine the kinds and quality of ties is not limited to the family. For instance, in a recent study, Karen Thorpe and Karen Gardner examined "friendship patterns" and the likelihood of friend sharing between MZ, DZ same-sex, and DZ opposite-sex twins, concluding that MZ twins will share friends 50 per cent of the time compared to DZ same-sex twins at 25 per cent and DZ opposite-sex twins at 5 per cent. What is fascinating about this study is its overemphasis or narrow focus on genes, as opposed to sex and gender, as the main correlate in friend-sharing patterns. Indeed, sex and gender, as particular kinds of sameness and difference that can be distinguished from genetic similarity and difference as correlate bases for friendship, are not considered seriously at all. Thorpe and Gardner, "Twins and Their Friendships."

30 For a general introduction to the structure and goals of the Minnesota Study of Twins Reared Apart and to the use of reared-apart twins in their ongoing study, see Lykken et al., "Minnesota Twin Family Registry"; and Bouchard Jr et al., "Sources of Human Psychological Differences."

31 Bouchard Jr, "Behaviorial Studies of Twins and Adoptees," 12.8.

32 Ibid., 12.7.

33 Ibid.

34 Segal, quoted in Miele, "Entwinned Lives," 31.

35 Ibid.

36 Secrecy and controversy continue to surround Neubauer's study because he somehow obtained permission to observe Amy and Beth prior to and following their adoptions. He did so without the adoptive parents or the twins themselves being made aware of their twins or the purpose of the study. How he managed this arrangement has yet to come fully to light, although all twins were placed by the same adoption agency, so it appears the agency played a role in misleading the adoptive parents in order to support Neubauer's study, especially since it was ongoing throughout much of the children's lives. Wright, *Twins: And What*, 1–3. A CNN documentary film, Tim Wardle's *Three Identical Strangers* (2018), also examines the Neubauer study. The film tells the story of reunited reared-apart triplets who were subjects in the study, and it discusses their efforts to have the complete study made public because it is currently sealed within the Yale University Archives until 2065.

37 The "first *report* on identical twins separated in infancy and reared apart" was made by Paul Popenoe in 1922. Scheinfeld, *Twins and Supertwins*, 274 my emphasis. For Shienfeld's chronology of the earliest twin studies, see ibid., 273–5.

38 Wright, *Twins: Genes, Environment*, 1.

39 Harris, *Nurture Assumption*, 293.

40 Ibid., 294.

41 Wright, *Twins: Genes, Environment*, 5.

42 Ibid., 7–8.

43 Harris, *Nurture Assumption*, 294.

44 Given that Neubauer's long-term study began in 1960, it is plausible to assume Amy and Beth would have been aware of being "adopted," as adoption psychologists and social workers, at this time, advocated parents telling children of their adoptions as early as possible.

45 Elsewhere, I critically examine how discourses of naturalized motherhood, which operate in line with the bio-genealogical imperative, subject (some) birth mothers to being portrayed and to portraying themselves not as agents but as traumatized and coerced, partly to secure their rights *as* mothers in the context of search and reunion. Latchford, "Reckless Abandon."

46 The following studies show that children not originally prone to enuresis can experience this symptom following various traumatic events, such as natural disasters, car accidents, or sexual abuse. Durkhin et al., "Effects of a Natural Disaster"; Eidlitz-Markus, Shuper, and Amir, "Secondary Enuresis"; Klevan and DeJong, "Urinary Tract Symptoms."

47 Hill, Hutton, and Easton, "Adoptive Parenting," 20.

48 Bunyan, "Modifying Behaviour," 52.

49 Foucault, *Power/Knowledge*, 186.

50 Mara B. Adelman and Marie Siemon note that sometimes singleton children can experience "pseudo-twinning ... reminiscent of the behaviour found between twins," but these relationships are not thought to occur with the same persistence or to the degree that they do in identical twins. Adelman and Siemon, "Communicating the Relational Shift," 97.

51 Schave and Ciriello, *Identity and Intimacy in Twins*, 11.

52 For instance, the twin bond – even though its constituents are hotly debated – is thought to be so powerful that it has led to a proliferation of psychological investigations and guides on how best to raise twins in light of this bond. As recent examples, see Sandbank, ed., *Twin and Triplet Psychology*; and Woodward, *Lone Twin*.

53 Bouchard Jr et al., "Sources of Human Psychological Differences." Watson discusses Bouchard Jr's work and the questions it raises about whether reared-apart twins can be said to lead "parallel lives" as an effect of their genetic similarity. Watson, *Twins*, 25–65. Notably, Bouchard Jr does not consider adoption literature in relation to the fact that reunited adoptees often claim to experience strong affinities with newfound biological family members. Still, he would not see any contradiction in this finding because reunited bio-family members share genes, which on his view explains the "magnetic" pull that singleton reunitees experience.

54 Athanassiou, "Study of the Vicissitudes," 330.

55 Lassers and Nordan, "Separation-Individuation," 469.

56 Athanassiou, "Study of the Vicissitudes," 329.

57 Lassers and Nordan, "Separation-Individuation," 469; Adelman and Siemon, "Communicating the Relational Shift," 98–9.

58 Adelman and Siemon, "Communicating the Relational Shift," 98.

59 Bryan, "Death of a Twin," 198.

60 Harris, *Nurture Assumption*, 34.

61 Wright, *Twins: And What*, 122; Harris, *Nurture Assumption*, 33–4.

62 Harris, *Nurture Assumption*, 37.

63 Klein, *Alone in the Mirror*, 1.

64 Ibid., 2.

65 Klein, *Not All Twins Are Alike*, xvii.

66 Ibid., 106.

67 For instance, as Watson discusses extensively, Bouchard Jr's ongoing Minnesota Study of Twins Reared Apart has recorded many "uncanny" similari-

ties between reunited reared-apart twins, including attire, body language, and interests. Watson, *Twins*, 23–68.

68 Schave and Ciriello, *Identity and Intimacy in Twins*, 4–6, 12.

69 Hayashi et al., "Relationship between Parents' Report Rate," 165.

70 Bryan, *Nature and Nurture of Twins*, 164.

71 Schave and Ciriello, *Identity and Intimacy in Twins*, 5.

72 Ibid., 11.

73 A concern in the environmental psychology of twins is the psychic impact on twins' ability to develop an individual identity when they are treated as though they are *identical*, such as when their parents dress them in the same clothes, mix up their names, or consistently refer to them as "the twins." Pat Preedy notes that in a study of twins, "one-fifth [of parents] made no effort to distinguish between the children." Like Neubauer, Preedy concludes that every effort should be made to identify twins individually, or else they "may not be able to function as individuals." Preedy, "Meeting the Educational Needs," 78, 79.

74 Harris, *Nurture Assumption*, 29.

75 For instance, some monozygotic twins are so underindividuated that they may develop what is referred to as a "unit identity," wherein each twin, to varying degrees, is unable to distinguish her self from the self of her twin. Hagedorn and Kizziar, *Gemini*, 33.

76 In philosophical terms, a "necessary condition for something is one without which the thing does not exist or occur." "Necessary and Sufficient Conditions," *Dictionary of Philosophy*, ed. Lacey, 228.

77 Harris, *Nurture Assumption*, 23.

78 Boyle, "Everybody DOES Have a Twin."

79 Spector, *Identically Different*, 27, 8.

80 Ibid., 10, 27.

81 Ibid., 29, 293. Darwin's concept of pangenesis proposed the idea that what he called "gemmules" were "'capable of transmission in a dormant state to future generations and may then be developed." Quoted in Müller-Wille and Rheinberger, *Cultural History of Heredity*, 77.

82 Spector, *Identically Different*, 7.

83 Ibid.

84 Ibid., 18.

85 Ibid., 20.

86 Gopnik, "Innateness," 195.

87 It is noteworthy that this *thought* about family bonds encompasses marriage: the reprosexual act that consummates marriage (symbolically) materi-

alizes a biological tie that is "materially" realized if and when offspring result. As Claude Lévi-Strauss suggests, marriage "is never superimposed upon blood ties but replaces them." Lévi-Strauss, *Elementary Structures of Kinship*, 480.

88 Foucault, *Power/Knowledge*, 56–7.

89 This point is much the same as that made by Foucault with regard to the distinction between the human as opposed to natural sciences. See also note 15 of the Introduction for a discussion of the distinction between what is essential versus natural, a distinction that adoption experts fail to observe or maintain.

CHAPTER FIVE

1 Lamb, *I Know This Much Is True*, 234.

2 According to Jean Laplanche and Jean-Bertrand Pontalis, Freud initially dated the term "narcissism" to 1899 and attributed it to Paul Nacke in his paper "On Narcissism" (1914). In 1920 he added a note to the *Three Essays on the Theory of Sexuality* (1905) with the correction "that it was to Havelock Ellis that the introduction of the term should be rightfully attributed" because "it was Ellis who first ... invoked the myth of Narcissus to help describe a case of perverted behaviour" in 1898. Laplanche and Pontalis, *Language of Psycho-Analysis*, 257.

3 The bio-logic of Freud's concept of narcissism is critically examined in the following chapter.

4 This idea is evidenced in psychoanalytic interpretations of normal and abnormal identity formation discussed in chapters 1 and 4.

5 Freud, *Totem and Taboo*, 130.

6 Freud, "On Narcissism," 85.

7 Schwartz, *Cassandra's Daughter*, 1.

8 Ibid.

9 Ibid.

10 Foucault, *Power/Knowledge*, 213.

11 Ibid.; Freud, *Interpretation of Dreams (First Part)*, 1.

12 Freud discusses how dreams are understood historically in scientific literature prior to psychoanalysis at some length. See Freud, *Interpretation of Dreams (First Part)*, 1–95.

13 Toews, "Foucault and the Freudian Subject," 117.

14 Foucault, *Power/Knowledge*, 218.

15 Badcock, *Essential Freud*, 161.

16 The intersection of naturalism and individualism is discussed in detail in chapter 3.

17 Freudian psychoanalysis interpreted from a sociobiological perspective would read the id's failure in this regard as genetically determined and, therefore, due to the structure of the id itself. Psychoanalysts who emphasize the import of nurture would reject the sociobiological claim that Freud understands biology to be the determining factor in the function of the id, ego, and super-ego. Instead, they would locate the cause of the id's failure in the unreasonable demands that civilization can and does make upon the self. Either way, Freud's idea that the self's participation in or alienation from civilization turns on the ego's *ability* to negotiate the demands of the id and the super-ego still has implications for and lends itself to individualist and naturalist concerns with the self's *ability* to adapt and survive, regardless of the role that genetics and/or the unreasonable demands of civilization play in that ability.

18 Freud, *Civilization and Its Discontents*, 45–7.

19 Freud, *Historical and Expository Works*, 272–3, original emphasis.

20 Ferris, *Dr. Freud*, 31, 26.

21 Gildiner, "Evolutionary Foundations of Freud's Theory."

22 Freud, *Historical and Expository Works*, 252.

23 Freud, *Totem and Taboo*, 141–3.

24 Freud, *Historical and Expository Works*, 252–3.

25 Phillips, *Darwin's Worms*, 13.

26 Foucault, *Archaeology of Knowledge*, 46; Foucault, *Foucault Reader*, 7. Even if Darwin and Freud are understood to posit radically different views of the self – that is, the self as a process of natural selection as opposed to the self as an (un)conscious legacy of historical psychic events – Foucault would still consider naturalism and psychoanalysis to be allied to the extent that they intersect within "human sciences." Both Darwinian naturalism – which is manifested in eugenics, sociobiology, and behavioural genetics – and psychoanalysis assume that the self is something that can be objectively analyzed, an assumption that Foucault finds particularly problematic, as I discuss in chapter 2.

27 As somewhat of an aside, it is worth mentioning, as Linda Alcoff does, that even "[c]ritical theoretical discourses and practices themselves are allied and aligned with power, as Michel Foucault would warn us"; Alcoff, "Expert Discourses of Critique: Foucault as Power/Knowledge," 307.

28 Foucault, *Madness and Civilization*, 254.

29 Bursten, "Some Narcissistic Personality Types," 400.

30 This is one of the main reasons why psychoanalysis plays a pivotal role in enacting the modern Western bio-genealogical imperative.

31 Foucault, *History of Sexuality*, vol. 1, 159.

32 Ibid., 159, 56.

33 For Foucault, the import of there being "no absolute outside" of power, and thus psychoanalysis as a discursive mode of power, is that as long as psychoanalysis is a dominant discourse, there is no position from which psychoanalysis can be *objectively* and wholly critiqued. However, this idea does not rule out the possibility of any and all critique from within or by those who are subject to a social-political-historical moment that is psychoanalysis. For instance, my goal in this work is to examine some of the naturalistic assumptions embedded in the discourse of psychoanalysis. Although I do not have the critical distance in an objective sense to identify all of the naturalistic assumptions of psychoanalysis, particularly those to which I am unaware that I am subject, I do have an ability to critically assess some of its assumptions. Simply being subject to psychoanalysis does not generally preclude the possibility of making critical observations about aspects of it. I can critique psychoanalysis at the same time that I am subject to it, albeit partially, in that my subjection renders me nonobjective in a transcendental sense but not absolutely incapable of critique. Ibid., 95.

34 Ibid., 130.

35 Although psychoanalysts might view a life as an ongoing narrative, a narrative is linear, or at the very least constrained, so Foucault would treat it as a continuity. Foucault would hold this position even if it is granted that a narrative can be rewritten in light of formerly repressed material that continuously surfaces throughout a life because even a rewritten *narrative* functions as a continuity; moreover, new material can be analyzed to fit a pre-existing narrative, particularly the Oedipal narrative, which psychoanalysis relies upon as a source of meaning through which it reads formerly repressed material. In many respects, rewriting a narrative falls prey to the same problems that Foucault locates in trading one identity for another. A new self-narrative is like a new identity in that both produce a sense of self-continuity that locates the self in a subject position that, albeit new, is a constraint on the self's possibility.

36 Freud assumes that this desire is both universally historical and repressed. He traces it back to a primary and originally unrepressed Oedipal event. Freud, *Totem and Taboo*, 141–3.

37 Rose, *Governing the Soul*, 133–4.

38 Ibid., 163–5.

39 Ibid., 169.

40 Freud often introduced his papers and theories with qualifying statements of this kind. In this instance, he is introducing a discussion on the "riddle of femininity," which identifies the main differences between gender identity formation and sexual object-choice in the male and female as a result of the normal resolution of the Oedipal complex. Freud, "Femininity," 140.

41 Foucault, *Power/Knowledge*, 218.

42 Dreyfus, "Foreword," viii–ix.

43 Bird, "Thomas Kuhn."

44 Kuhn, *Structure of Scientific Revolutions*, 5.

45 Ibid.

46 Hoeller, "Editor's Foreword," 8, original emphasis.

47 Ibid., 66.

48 For Foucault's discussion of the relationship between images and the possibility of worlds for being, see ibid., 66–75.

49 Ibid., 73.

50 Ibid., 51.

51 Ibid., 71.

52 Fully free being would entail that the imagination infinitely shed old images (i.e., old worlds) for new.

53 Ibid., 72.

54 Ibid., 73.

55 Foucault, *Foucault Live*, 330.

56 Foucault argues that psychoanalysis is both like and unlike other human sciences with respect to the "knowledge of man," which refers to the historical moment in which "man constituted himself in Western culture as both that which must be conceived of and that which is to be known." Essentially, man offers himself up *as* an object of knowledge to be observed in ways that the natural sciences observe the natural world by conceiving of himself as a positivity. As a result, this historical moment is also concurrent with the event of the human sciences as the institutionalized forms of knowledge that take man as their object. The knowledge of man manifests within the human sciences as an epistemological shift toward a new "analytic of finitude" wherein man now knows and experiences his being essentially as finite. According to Foucault, this analytic is deployed through the norms, rules, and systems that the human sciences impose upon man's understanding of himself. In other words, the human sciences' image of man imposes limits on his being, which undermines his ability to know and experience the possibilities of his being as infinite. Foucault, *Order of Things*, 344–87, 345, 351, 312–18.

57 Foucault, *Religion and Culture*, 118.

58 The implications of incest discourse for the bio-genealogical imperative are discussed at length in the final three chapters of this book.

59 As new modes of knowledge efface Freud's and Darwin's knowledge, they will no doubt one day displace the experiences and modes of being that Freud and Darwin continue to make possible at present.

CHAPTER SIX

1 Ovid, *Metamorphoses of Ovid*, trans. Slavitt, 53.

2 Javanbakht, "Was the Myth of Narcissus?" 63–4. As Arash Javanbakht observes, in psychoanalysis "mythical and religious stories are believed to be representatives of intrapsychic life." Ibid., 63.

3 Freud first introduces the term "narcissism" in *Leonardo da Vinci and a Memory of His Childhood* to explain the phenomenon of homosexuality, wherein the homosexual, by choosing a male love object, is understood to choose a version of himself as opposed to making a normal (heterosexual) object-choice. Freud, *Leonardo da Vinci*, 140–2.

4 Freud, "'Uncanny,'" 235.

5 Wright, *Twins: And What*, 157–8.

6 Schwartz, *Culture of the Copy*, 19.

7 Frosh, *Identity Crisis*, 68, 9.

8 Foucault, *History of Sexuality*, vol. 1, 58, 57.

9 Foucault, *Power/Knowledge*, 214, 212–17.

10 Freud, "Aetiology of Hysteria," 267, original emphasis.

11 Ibid., 271, 276–7.

12 The question of why is answered in different ways. The traditional explanation is that Freud rejected the theory because of the contradiction it posed in light of his further belief that neurotic symptoms are universally experienced by adults, including himself, and vary only by degree. Christopher Badcock explains that this belief is what ultimately led Freud to reject the hypothesis that child sexual abuse is the cause of *all* neurotic symptoms. If neurotic symptoms are experienced universally, *all* individuals have experienced child sexual abuse, which Freud decidedly felt was impossible. Conversely, Jeffrey M. Masson argues that because Freud's theory met great resistance from his contemporaries, who had the power to alienate him and did, he simply rejected the theory out of a lack of moral courage. Masson interprets the main argument against the seduction theory, which Freud first articulated in a letter to Wilhelm Fliess, as little more than "the beginning of an internal reconciliation with his colleagues and with the whole of nineteenth-century psychiatry." Badcock, *Essential Freud*, 35–6; Masson, *Assault on Truth*, 107–10.

13 Freud did not actually use the term "Oedipus complex" until 1910. Laplanche and Pontalis, *Language of Psycho-Analysis*, 283.

14 Freud, *Interpretation of Dreams (First Part)*, 262.

15 Freud, "Infantile Sexuality."

16 Masson, *Assault on Truth*, 122–3.

17 For Freud, the abnormal can be used to explain and map out the normal because they are on the same continuum. For instance, in a discussion of sexual perversions, Freud writes that "[t]he importance of these abnormalities lies in the unexpected fact that they facilitate our understanding of normal development." Assuming somatic causes are ruled out, abnormal psychic processes are understood as magnifications of normal processes. The difference between them is really only the manifestation of a normally occurring psychodynamic being magnified to such an extent that it brings the individual into conflict with the norms of his social environment, be it the family or society. Freud, *Three Essays on the Theory of Sexuality*, 7; Freud, "On Narcissism," 75.

18 This is not to say that adoptees never seek grief counselling but that, sought out and apprehended, bio-genealogy first and foremost is the cure.

19 Herman, *Kinship by Design*, 258.

20 Ibid.

21 Ibid., original emphasis.

22 Ibid., 259.

23 Freud, *Interpretation of Dreams (Second Part)*, 553–4, 568–70.

24 In other words, it is possible that if Freud's discovery of the unconscious and the significance that he gives to childhood history occurred in a social-political-historical context where there was no invention of a primal father, and/or where children were not raised by the biological family but communally, and/or where there was no practice of delineating social groups on the basis of biological ties, the conditions that currently produce adoptee experience would be absent to such an extent that the "adoptee" as we know her would not exist.

25 Freud, "On Narcissism," 65.

26 Ibid., 66.

27 Ibid., 67. Freud introduced the concept of narcissism prior to the second phase of psychoanalysis, wherein he eventually developed his ideas concerning the id and super-ego. Nonetheless, narcissism remained a central component of psychoanalytic theory throughout and continues to widely influence many current notions of psychological development.

28 Ibid.

29 Ibid., 68.

30 Hamilton, *Narcissus and Oedipus*, 34.

31 Freud, "Lecture XXVI," 416.

32 Freud, "On Narcissism," 78–81.

33 Ibid., 82.

34 Ibid., 84.

35 Ibid., 80.

36 Ibid., 76.

37 Ibid., 84.

38 Ibid., 82.

39 The developmental importance of the ego-ideal is ultimately the social purpose it serves as a standard against which the self will begin to measure
itself or as an ideal that the self will actually try to attain, thereby ensuring
that its libido seeks acceptable forms of gratification and is directed toward
appropriate objects.

40 Freud, "On Narcissism," 87–8.

41 Ibid., 84–5.

42 Ibid., 85.

43 Ibid., 82–3.

44 Ibid., 83, my emphasis.

45 Given scientific advances with regard to surrogacy, it is interesting to consider whether Freud must necessarily be read to imply that a child need
only emerge from a woman's body, as opposed to being composed of her
genetic material, in order to revive narcissism.

46 Ibid., 82–5.

47 Ibid., 84, 85.

48 Freud's precursory discussion of women as mothers also serves as an illustration of the narcissistic as opposed to anaclitic object-choices he generally
associates with women as opposed to men. However, given that Freud notes
that either sex can potentially make either choice, it seems "parental love" is
an instance where men, whose repressed primary narcissism is also subject
to revival, are inclined toward a narcissistic object-choice. This conclusion is
clearly plausible given that Freud so obviously addresses fathers in the cited
passage on parental love.

49 Initially, perhaps, this idea seems obvious in the case of the mother simply
because of the bio-physical facts of pregnancy and birth. Given that Freud
does not explicitly say the same about fathers, it is somewhat less obvious,
at least until the social-political-historical import of paternity tests in the
modern Western context is considered. Where paternity is contested,
shared biology is the basis used to determine those for whom one is
responsible. And if a father extends love to a child *only* when paternity
has confirmed his tie, which is not uncommon, a "father" does currently

love to the extent that he experiences the child as a bio-physical part of his body.

50　Schneider and Rimmer, "Adoptive Parents' Hostility," 347.

51　Ibid.

52　Ibid.

53　Witt, "Family Resemblances," 144.

54　Ibid., 141–2.

55　Ibid., 135–6.

56　Ibid., 143.

57　Ibid.

58　Ibid., 139, 145.

59　Ibid.

60　Ibid., 144.

61　Keller, "Rethinking Ruddick's Birthgiver," 175, 175–9.

62　Ibid., 182, 181, my emphasis.

63　Ibid., 181.

64　Ibid., 182.

65　Ibid., my emphasis.

66　Fisher, *Search for Anna Fisher*; Holtz, *Of Unknown Origin*; Lifton, *Journey of the Adopted Self*; Lifton, *Twice Born*.

67　Hipchen, "Images of the Family Body," 169.

68　Ibid.

69　Ibid.

70　Ibid., original emphasis.

71　McRoy, Grotevant, and Zucher Jr, *Emotional Disturbance*, 132.

72　In the event that a *known* "adoptive parent" or "adoptee" imagined herself to be a *biological* parent or child and identified with her adopted child or adoptive parent as such, adoption psychology, given the import it attaches to adoption revelation, would treat the identification as a manifestation of adoption-related pathology, which would nonetheless differentiate the relation between this parent and child and the status of their "family" tie. Conversely, if a parent and child who share no biological tie believed they did, along with the rest of the world – for instance, because babies were mistakenly swapped in a maternity ward – there is no reason, from a Foucauldian perspective, to suggest that they could not have a *real* experience of biological narcissism because this experience is discursively produced by the bio-genealogical imperative.

73　Imagine, however, if psychoanalysis depicted parental love as determined by the child's function as a narcissistic object-choice but in a way and/or in a social-political-historical context that did not conflate genetic similarity with selfsameness. Under these circumstances, or others, adoptees and biological children could arguably function equally as objects that instigate *parental* love. That such circumstances could be made to exist seems, at least, plausible given that the association between genetic similarity and sameness, as opposed to difference, is a relatively new one.

74 Freud, *Group Psychology*, 37.

75 Ibid.

76 Ibid.

77 Ibid. Arguably, identification need not always assume a biological bias, such as when the individual identifies with civilization. Freud, *Civilization and Its Discontents*, 76, 79. But then again, identification does assume this bias if and when the individual's ability to identify with civilization is affected by considerations of race because race historically and frequently is still treated *as* biology. For an interesting discussion of identification in regard to race and civilization, see Fuss, *Identification Papers*, 141–65.

78 In a lengthy footnote, Freud finds that the family romance is one among a number of fantasies characteristic of the Oedipal complex. Freud, *Three Essays on the Theory of Sexuality*, 92.

79 Freud, *Totem and Taboo*, 130.

80 Freud, *Group Psychology*, 37.

81 Freud, "Ego and the Id," 371.

82 In "The Ego and the Id" (1923) Freud proposed that the Oedipal complex is analogous in boys and girls. He would later reject this idea in "Some Psychical Consequences of the Anatomical Distinction between the Sexes" (1925). This distinction is noted here given the controversy it created within psychoanalysis, particularly between Freud and Carl Jung, who later posited the "Electra complex" as the analogous phase in women, which Freud also rejected. Generally, however, this distinction does not tend to be pursued within the context of adoption psychology. The idea that the Oedipal complex is analogous in male and female adoptees typically operates as a general assumption among adoption experts insofar as they simply do not explore the implications of Freud's later distinction between the sexes as it relates to male and female adopted children. For this reason, I have decided to focus solely on the implications of the Oedipal complex for adoptees in general, regardless of sex. Freud, "Ego and the Id," 371, 371n4; Freud, "Some Psychical Consequences," 332–5.

83 Freud, "Ego and the Id," 371–2.

84 Freud, *Group Psychology*, 38, original emphasis.

85 The relationship between adoptee subjectivity and Oedipal or incest discourse, which is disseminated in large part by psychoanalysis, is examined in the following chapters.

86 Aversa, Baldieri, and Marozza, "Mythic Function of Narcissism," 565.

87 Ibid., 553.

88 Freud, *Interpretation of Dreams (First Part)*, 261.

89 Laplanche and Pontalis, *Language of Psycho-Analysis*, 255.

90 Ovid, *Metamorphoses of Ovid*, trans. Slavitt, 53.

91 André Green's description of therapeutic analysis nicely demonstrates the elusive quality psychoanalysis attributes to its object: "Doing analysis involves subjecting a dense and often confused body of facts – particularly as the analyst will have given up any attempt to understand them in terms of the outward unity of the discourse – to the test of differentiation; and, according to principles that should reveal a different composition of the object, which this time is not apparent, thereby allowing its real nature to emerge." Green, *Life Narcissism, Death Narcissism*, ix.

92 Although the Ovidian version of the myth is more often read as though Narcissus initially mistakes his image for another youth, realizing only after his love has taken root and it is too late that it is a mere reflection of himself that he desires, there is some disagreement. For example, in Rolfe Humphries's translation of the myth, Narcissus is characterized as "[n]ot knowing what he sees." Ovid, *Metamorphoses*, trans. Humphries, 70. The same is true in the myth as told by Mark P.O. Morford and Robert J. Lenardon: Narcissus "did not understand what he was looking at." Morford and Lenardon, *Classical Mythology*, 225. Conversely, David R. Slavitt's translation of Ovid's tale implies that Narcissus initially "knows it is hopeless, knows it is only his own reflection." Ovid, *Metamorphoses of Ovid*, trans. Slavitt, 55.

93 Christopher Lasch argues that in the context of American life, and due to the rise of a "therapeutic sensibility," narcissism has become a cultural ideal, one that has created a population of individuals who, by consciously seeking an authentic sense of self or identity, have become isolated, lonely, and self-absorbed, all of which is to the detriment of society, politics, history, culture, and religion. Lasch, *Culture of Narcissism*, 7–13. Jean M. Twenge more recently has made a similar argument about today's American youth, whom she refers to as "Generation Me." Twenge suggests that, having been raised on family psychologies that focus on the child, or "me," which has nourished a conscious narcissism in today's youth, this generation is the most ill-equipped yet with respect to maintaining either personal or social relationships that are psychologically healthy and reciprocal. Twenge, *Generation Me*.

94 Ovid, *Metamorphoses of Ovid*, trans. Slavitt, 53.

95 Steinhart examines the myth of Narcissus in order to critique the narcissism

that is entailed by and drives dominant theories about artificial intelligence. Steinhart, "Self-Recognition and Countermemory," 303.

96 For an introductory discussion of this phenomenon, see Trinder, Feast, and Howe, "Rejection and Reunions."

97 Steinhart, "Self-Recognition and Countermemory," 304.

98 Ibid.

99 Ibid., 305.

100 Ibid.

101 Ovid, *Metamorphoses of Ovid*, trans. Slavitt, 56; Morford and Lenardon, *Classical Mythology*, 225.

102 Ovid, *Metamorphoses of Ovid*, trans. Slavitt, 56.

103 Pausanias, *Description of Greece*, xxxi, 6–9, 311.

104 Unfortunately, Pausanius does not appear to have known the twin's name, at least insofar as he does not provide it.

105 Ibid., 311.

106 Ibid.

107 Holmes, *Gender*, 18.

108 Ibid., 69.

109 Simons, *Beauvoir and the Second Sex*, 222.

110 Beauvoir, *Second Sex*, 139.

111 Changfoot, "Second Sex's Continued Relevance," 20.

112 Beauvoir, *Second Sex*, 141.

113 Kirby, *Judith Butler*, 24, 25.

114 Irigaray, *Ethics of Sexual Difference*, 134, 140.

115 Ibid., 135.

116 Ibid., 139.

117 For an excellent overview of these debates, see Stone, "From Political to Realist Essentialism."

118 Irigaray, *Conversations*, 2, original emphasis.

119 Irigaray, *Ethics of Sexual Difference*, 13.

120 Butler, *Senses of the Subject*, 154, 159.

121 Ibid.

122 Ibid., 154.

123 Ibid.

124 Beardsworth, "Freud's Oedipus and Kristeva's Narcissus," 63.

125 The idea that sexual difference is already an extant foundation for mutual recognition between self and other is logically consistent with a notion of such difference as either essential or socially/culturally constructed, although I propose the latter.

CHAPTER SEVEN

1 Lifton, *Journey of the Adopted Self*, 226.
2 McColm, *Adoption Reunions*, 20; Carp, *Family Matters*, 12. Michelle McColm notes that adoption legislation throughout North America has historically used the phrase "'as if born to'" in order to emphasize the idea that the biological tie is legally severed.
3 Adoptive parents are also asked these sorts of questions, which maintain the status of the biological tie as a family tie throughout the adoptive family.
4 As discussed in chapter 1, even poststructuralist approaches to adoption leave the biological tie's superior status unchecked because they take both/and positions that, in failing to take on such questions, effectively maintain the differentiation and devaluation of adoptive family subjects and their ties.
5 Pelka, "Sharing Motherhood," 201.
6 Nordqvist, "Out of Sight," 1130, 1138.
7 Wegar, "Adoption, Family Ideology," 367.
8 Rubin, "My Co-World," 122.
9 For instance, section 155.1 of the *Criminal Code of Canada* states, "Every one commits incest who, knowing that another person is by blood relationship his or her parent, child, brother, sister, grandparent or grandchild, as the case may be, has sexual intercourse with that person." Section 155.4 also states that "'brother' and 'sister', respectively, include half-brother and half-sister," but there is no reference to adopted grandparents, parents, or siblings. In contrast, Canada's *Marriage (Prohibited Degrees) Act*, which pertains to "laws prohibiting marriage between related persons," does address individuals related by means of adoption. Paragraph 2(2)(a) of this act states that marriage is prohibited between persons who are related "by consanguinity, affinity or adoption." Taken together, what these two pieces of legislation suggest is that although adopted relatives are legally barred from marriage, they are incapable of committing incest, at least in the criminal sense of the word. *Martin's Annual Criminal Code*, 296; Payne and Payne, *Canadian Family Law*, 40–1.
10 *Bohall v. State*, 546 N.E.2d 1214 (1989).
11 *R. v. Schmidt*, 5 CR 165 at 171.
12 Popple, ed., *Criminal Reports*, vol. 5, 171.
13 Ibid., 173, 177, 180.
14 Two recent Canadian cases that further illustrate the idea that charges of sexual abuse, not incest, apply categorically to nonbiological ties, which

involve an adoptive father and a stepfather repectively, are *R. v. G.D.B.*, [2000] 1 SCR 520; and *R. v. R.W.B.*, (2000) 185 Nfld. & P.E.I.R. 212 (NFCA).

15 "Incest: The Last Taboo?"; Aziza, "Forbidden Love"; Tsoulis-Reay, "What's It Like?"; Miller, "Can You Really Justify?"

16 Adoptees who decide to search can also access basic literature, obtain pamphlets, and go to workshops on the topic through either public or private search and social service adoption agencies, as well as on the Internet. For instance, the Toronto Children's Aid Society readily provides adoptees with these resources.

17 Kirsta, "Genetic Sexual Attraction."

18 Feast, "Working in the Adoption Circle," 50.

19 In the earlier mentioned article "What's It Like to Date Your Dad?" Alexa Tsoulis-Reay claims that "[a]ccording to [the] article in *The Guardian*, experts estimate that these taboo feelings occur in about 50 percent of cases where estranged relatives are reunited as adults." This is an incautious reformulation of the *Guardian*'s already seemingly broad claim, one that further pathologizes adoptees, as it leaves readers with the distinct impression that GSA occurs very, very frequently in adoption reunion. This misrepresentation of the *Guardian* article also speaks to the problem of the medium as it concerns many depictions of GSA within mainstream media.

20 Speirs et al., "Mediated Reunions in Adoption," 860.

21 Greenberg, "Post-Adoption Reunion," 8; Greenberg and Littlewood, "Post-Adoption Incest." Littlewood republished the latter 1995 text as a chapter in his 2002 monograph *Pathologies in the West*, although with a new title and brief introduction. See Littlewood, "Genetic Sexual Attraction," 130–45.

22 Greenberg, "Post-Adoption Reunion," 14, 9.

23 Ibid., 11.

24 Ibid.

25 Ibid.

26 Greenberg and Littlewood, "Post-Adoption Incest," 35, my emphasis.

27 Paul, "Incest Avoidance," 1096.

28 Smith, "Beyond Westermarck," 206.

29 It is not uncommon for the direct influence of these disciplines to remain unidentified in search literature that does not address an academic audience.

30 I have come across only one paper, by Marcie A. Griffin, that has entertained the idea that adoptees need not necessarily be discouraged from acting on GSA. The gist of Griffin's argument is that as long as reunitees are truly aware of the potential consequences of their actions, "Who am I to tell

them they shouldn't?" This argument, however, in no way denies that the consequences are, or should be, severe; it suggests only that reunitees should be able to subject themselves to such consequences if they so choose. See Griffin, "Genetic Sexual Attraction and Adoptees."

31 Gonyo, "Genetic Sexual Attraction," in *The Decree*. In transcribed notes of a 1988 conference, Gonyo also explains, "I don't know if I coined the phrase or it's been here all along and I never knew it." Gonyo, "Genetic Sexual Attraction," in *Adoption into the 90's*, 25.1.

32 Gonyo explains that when she was reunited with her son and experienced GSA toward him, she had no idea that other reunitees were experiencing the same sorts of feelings "because nobody talked about it." Gonyo, "Genetic Sexual Attraction," in *Adoption into the 90's*, 25.18.

33 *Search Manual for Adoptees*, 106; Gonyo, "Genetic Sexual Attraction," in *The Decree*.

34 Lifton, *Journey of the Adopted Self*, 225.

35 Lifton gives a general discussion of the sexual encounters that have and may occur between reunited adoptees and birth parents or siblings; Lifton, *Journey of the Adopted Self*, 225–40.

36 Adoption Community Outreach Project, *Search Manual for Adoptees*, 106. This attraction is also characterized as "natural" by Lifton, *Journey of the Adopted Self*, 237.

37 Lifton, *Journey of the Adopted Self*, 239. Lifton also uses the metaphor of a "storm" and "battening down the hatches" to illustrate how adoptees and birth relatives should approach the possibility of GSA. Ibid., 238–40. The Adoption Community Outreach Project's search manual states that consummating GSA "will cause untold emotional upheaval and damage." Adoption Community Outreach Project, *Search Manual for Adoptees*, 106.

38 Lifton, *Journey of the Adopted Self*, 233.

39 Lifton, "Ghosts in the Adopted Family," 77.

40 Gonyo, "Genetic Sexual Attraction," in *The Decree*.

41 Brodzinsky, Schechter, and Henig, *Being Adopted*, 144. Although Barbara Gonyo likely coined the term "genetic sexual attraction" as early as 1987, Brodzinsky, Schechter, and Henig appear to have no knowledge of the term or Gonyo's work.

42 Childs, "Genetic Sexual Attraction"; Cusak, *Twins and Deviance*, 126.

43 Carp, *Family Matters*, 138.

44 Adoption Community Outreach Project, *Search Manual for Adoptees*, 105; McColm, *Adoption Reunions*, 165. On the same page, Michelle McColm also reiterates the utility of adoptees being "forewarned of the possibility."

45 For instance, an adoptee's experience of GSA might occur for reasons that are distinct from those of a biological parent even though both share a feeling of desire.

46 In the context of adoption discourse, Gonyo is the first to propose some semblance of this idea, and although she does not go into great detail, it retains a general currency among adoption experts. Gonyo, "Genetic Sexual Attraction," in *Adoption into the 90's*, 25.3, 25.5.

47 Ibid., 25.3.

48 McColm, *Adoption Reunions*, 165.

49 Brodzinsky, Schechter, and Henig, *Being Adopted*, 144.

50 Adoption Community Outreach Project, *Search Manual for Adoptees*, 106.

51 This idea echoes behavioural genetic theories with regard to the uncanny likenesses of twins reared apart; in fact, twin theorists will apply GSA theories to explain sexual desire when it occurs between reunited reared-apart twins, and the application in the context of twin theories implies an even greater intensity between twins insofar as twins similarities are greater. See Cusak, *Twins and Deviance*, 126.

52 Twins reared together who have sexual feelings and engage in sexual relations do not precisely experience GSA. Rather, whereas GSA theories treat reunion as a condition that makes it possible with respect to the absence of the incest taboo, when reared-together twins are sexual, they are presumed to commit incest, or "twincest" as it is sometimes called, such as in twin-themed pornography. Ibid., 10, 21–4.

53 Lifton, "Ghosts in the Adopted Family," 77.

54 Lifton, *Journey of the Adopted Self*, 229, 230; Adoption Community Outreach Project, *Search Manual for Adoptees*, 106.

55 Lifton, *Journey of the Adopted Self*, 236.

56 Ibid., 236–40.

57 Ibid., 226.

58 Notably, Lifton does not seem to differentiate between the sexes with regard to the Oedipal drama, as Freud eventually did. Instead, she discusses its general implications for all adoptees.

59 Lifton, *Journey of the Adopted Self*, 238, 239.

60 Ibid., 226.

61 Lifton, "Ghosts in the Adopted Family," 77.

62 Lifton, *Journey of the Adopted Self*, 228.

63 Adoption Community Outreach Project, *Search Manual for Adoptees*, 106.

64 Lifton, *Journey of the Adopted Self*, 229.

65 See chapters 4 and 5, which demonstrate the implicit bio-narcissistic logic of psychoanalysis.

66 Lifton, *Journey of the Adopted Self*, 236.

67 Ibid., 235.

68 Ibid., 237.

69 Ibid., 239.

70 "Bob Childs."

71 Ibid.

72 Childs, "Genetic Sexual Attraction," 30.

73 Ibid., 25.

74 Ibid., 29–30.

75 Ibid., 262, 267, 270.

76 Ibid., 257, 264.

77 Ibid., 292, 27, 133–4.

78 Ibid., 274.

79 Ibid., 29.

80 Ibid.

81 Brodzinsky, Schechter, and Henig, *Being Adopted*, 156.

82 Ibid., 32.

83 Childs, "Genetric Sexual Attraction," 280.

84 Ibid.

85 Matson, "Genetic Attraction (GA)," 16.

86 Ibid., 3, 6, 11; Laplanche and Pontalis, *Language of Psycho-Analysis*, 278.

87 Matson, "Genetic Attraction (GA)," 4.

88 Ibid., 15.

89 Ibid., 16.

90 Ibid., 6, 7.

91 Ibid., 7.

92 Ibid., 15, original emphasis.

93 Ibid., 13.

94 Ibid., 15.

95 Ibid., 14, 15, original emphasis.

96 This argument assumes that fully genital desire occurs in the absence of possible narcissistic projections or identifications that might again imply that desire is oral in some way. It also assumes that the self's sense of separation from the other is developed and remains intact during the experience of sexual desire.

97 Lifton, *Journey of the Adopted Self*, 228.

98 Add to this an inoperative incest taboo, and her experience of her "son/brother" *as* a "spouse/stranger" is even more complicated.

 99 Corliss, "Scenes from a Breakup," 37.
100 Although unknown, "[t]he birth year of Soon-Yi Previn is believed to be
     1970 or 1972." Farrow, *What Falls Away*, 345.
101 Isaacson, "Heart Wants What It Wants," 43.
102 Farrow includes the legal judgment that concluded their custody battle in
     an appendix to her memoir. Farrow, *What Falls Away*, 343–70.
103 Ibid., 290.
104 Isaacson, "Heart Wants What It Wants," 42.
105 Ibid. 41, original emphasis. In 2013 Farrow implied that her "biological
     child" with Allen, originally named Satchel, now Ronan, might be Frank
     Sinatra's progeny, an idea Allen entertains in the *New York Times*, or so it
     appears, to undermine Farrow's "integrity and honesty" during their earlier
     custody battle; Allen was investigated for "child molestation" of his and Far-
     row's adopted daughter, Dylan, when she was seven. Dylan recently reiterat-
     ed these allegations. See Nye, "'Is He My Son?'"; Allen, "Woody Allen Speaks
     Out"; Farrow, "Open Letter from Dylan Farrow"; and Kristof, "Dylan Far-
     row's Story."
106 Isaacson, "Heart Wants What It Wants," 41, my emphasis. See also "Soon-Yi
     Speaks"; the title "Soon-Yi Speaks" is curiously at odds with the text, which
     includes no verbatim quotes from Previn. Additionally, the author of the
     text is listed as "Newsweek Staff," although its key points and arguments are
     pretty much identical to Allen's interview in *Time*, indeed hauntingly so.
107 Isaacson, "Heart Wants What It Wants," 41.
108 Ibid., 41, 42.
109 Ibid., 41, original emphasis.
110 Ibid.
111 See "Inbred Obscurity," 2475.
112 Toufexis, "What Is Incest?" 39; Cornacchia, "Woody Allen's Revelations," A2.
     Many of the letters in *Time*, 21 September 1992, 4, comment on Allen's
     complete lack of "conscience" surrounding his choice to sleep with Farrow's
     daughter.
113 Toufexis, "What Is Incest?" 39; Cornacchia, "Woody Allen's Revelations," A2.
114 The Allen example is important in relation not only to questions about the
     devaluation of legal adoptive ties but also to questions about the devalua-
     tion of any nonbiological tie that purports to be (informally) "familial."
     Allen's relationship with Previn, although peripheral to adoption in the
     important respect that he is not her legally adoptive father, is significant
     insofar as the interrogation of his nonbiological ties by the media clarifies
     current social and legal meanings of incest that nonetheless have implica-
     tions for adoptive ties.

115 Fragoso, "At 79, Woody Allen."
116 An unmarried man who acted on sexual desire for his partner's biological
     mother or sibling would be subject to less social stigma than if he and his
     partner were married, but he would be understood to cross a sexual line,
     which may raise the spectre of incest for some and not others. Sex with
     one's in-laws, however, is on a continuum with incest in Western, as well as
     other, cultures. For example, in the Bible, Leviticus 18:6–18, which delin-
     eates prohibited sexual-familial relations, prohibits sex between father and
     daughter-in-law and mother and son-in-law. Moreover, today, in the United
     States, "[a] number of states categorize incest prohibitions as applicable to
     step-relatives and in-laws." There are even American "statutes under which
     terminated marriages continue to be relevant for purposes of incest"
     because "[h]istorically, the very notion that one is related to one's in-laws
     drew on the idea that 'the sexual union makes man and woman one flesh,'
     and thus one's relatives by affinity are transformed into relatives by blood."
     "Inbred Obscurity," 2474, 2475.

CHAPTER EIGHT

 1 Morford and Lenardon, *Classical Mythology*, 152.
 2 Ibid., 304.
 3 James B. Twitchell suggests that the basic trends in arguments concerning
    incest are biological, psychological, and sociological. Whereas Twitchell con-
    flates feminist perspectives on incest with those that are sociological, Vikki
    Bell argues that feminists reject sociological (and anthropological) perspec-
    tives on incest. The meaning of incest and its prohibition is discussed from
    these four vantage points, but these categories are neither exhaustive nor
    hard and fast. The lines between them often blur, or are sometimes nonexis-
    tent. Thus incest can be examined under different rubrics. For instance,
    Bell's Foucauldian analysis of the *problem* of incest examines many of the
    same arguments under the headings of "health," "abuse," and "family."
    Twitchell, *Forbidden Partners*, 33–4; Bell, *Interrogating Incest*, 57, 130, 135, 141.
 4 Atwood, "When Love Hurts," 309.
 5 See chapters 2 and 5; and Foucault, *History of Sexuality*, vol. 1, 109.
 6 Masters, *Patterns of Incest*, 52, original emphasis.
 7 Ibid., 52.
 8 Ibid., 53.
 9 Ibid.
10 "Incest," *Oxford English Dictionary*.
11 Shepher, *Incest*, 27.

12 "Incest," *Oxford English Dictionary*.

13 "Incest," *Encyclopedia of Anthropology*.

14 "Incest," *Dictionary of Psychology*.

15 Turner, "Incest, Inbreeding," 39; Twitchell, *Forbidden Partners*, 7.

16 Jones, *In the Blood*, 74.

17 Childs, "Genetic Sexual Attraction," 217.

18 Jones, *In the Blood*, 70.

19 Ibid., 72.

20 Foucault, *History of Sexuality*, vol. 1, 38–41, 41.

21 Aldridge, "Meaning of Incest from Hutcheson to Gibbon," 309.

22 Ibid., 309–13.

23 Darwin, *On the Origin of Species*, 128, 389, original emphasis.

24 Foucault would consider eugenics, sociobiology, behavioural or behaviour genetics, and epigenetics to be human sciences because they locate the origins of human personality and psychology in human biology or genetics and thus "attempt to combine organic pathology and mental pathology" in order to arrive at a "science of the self." Dreyfus, "Foreword," x, xxiii.

25 Foucault, *History of Sexuality*, vol. 1, 129; see also 109–10.

26 Foucault, *Politics, Philosophy, Culture*, 302.

27 Bell, *Interrogating Incest*, 98, original emphasis.

28 For more obvious reasons, *psychoanalytic* and liberal (i.e., individualistic) feminisms can be shown to reiterate the logic of incest as a universal too.

29 Lambert, "Review of *Everybody's Family Romance*," 185.

30 Workman and Reader, *Evolutionary Psychology*, 20.

31 Wilson, *Sociobiology*, 4.

32 Morehead, "Oedipus, Darwin, and Freud," 348.

33 Shepher, *Incest*, 7.

34 Ibid., 69.

35 Gopnik, "Innateness," 195.

36 Sociobiologists generally attribute this line of reasoning, or these bases for "the familiarity argument," to Edward Westermarck, whom Robin Fox quotes at the same time that he queries, "who can say who originated it?" Fox, *Red Lamp of Incest*, 20.

37 Shepher, *Incest*, 43

38 Peakman, *Pleasure's All Mine*, 287.

39 Twitchell, *Forbidden Partners*, 33.

40 Fox, *Red Lamp of Incest*, 20.

41 Westermarck, *Short History of Marriage*, 80.

42 Bittles, *Consanguinity in Context*, 179. See also Wolf, "Introduction," 9.

43 Joseph Shepher notes that Westermarck referred to this effect as the "law of

similarity," but subsequently it is known as the "law of homogamy." Shepher, *Incest*, 46.

44 Ibid., 45.

45 Morehead, "Oedipus, Darwin, and Freud," 352.

46 Bittles, *Consanguinity in Context*, 179.

47 Shepher discusses both the kibbutzim and *sim-pua* studies at some length. Shepher, *Incest*, 51–67.

48 Shepher, cited in Morehead, "Oedipus, Darwin, and Freud," 352.

49 Shepher, *Incest*, 63–7; Morehead, "Oedipus, Darwin, and Freud," 352.

50 Wolf, "Introduction," 10.

51 Shepher, *Incest*, 47.

52 Morehead, "Oedipus, Darwin, and Freud," 353; Shepher, *Incest*, 48, original emphasis.

53 Mansfield et al., "Responses to Fukuyama," 36.

54 Harkins, *Everybody's Family Romance*, 93.

55 Wolf, "Introduction," 9.

56 Arnhart, "Incest Taboo," 202.

57 Freud, *Totem and Taboo*, 123; Freud, *Interpretation of Dreams (First Part)*, 262.

58 The word "instinct," also characterized as a "drive," within the Freudian corpus is the "term generally accepted by English-speaking psycho-analytic authors as a rendering of the German '*Trieb*': dynamic process consisting in a *pressure* (charge of energy, motricity factor) which directs the organism towards an aim. According to Freud, an instinct has its *source* in a bodily stimulus; its *aim* is to eliminate the state of tension obtaining at the instinctual source; and it is in the *object*, or thanks to it, that the instinct may achieve its aim." Laplanche and Pontalis, *Language of Psycho-Analysis*, 214, original emphasis. It is often argued, therefore, that Freud's notion of instinct should not be confused with "traditional" and "modern" theories of instinct that pertain solely to heredity, although, as we shall see, bio-determinists can interpret his views to suit their own ends. It is not entirely clear where Freud actually locates the origins of instinct, in the sense of drive. As Jean Laplanche and Jean-Bertrand Pontalis point out, Freud writes in *Three Essays on the Theory of Sexuality*, "instinct is defined as 'lying on the frontier between the mental and the physical,'" which may explain why his theory of sexuality has been interpreted to support both nature and nurture perspectives. Laplanche and Pontalis, *Language of Psycho-Analysis*, 214–15. To confuse matters, Freud also suggests, in a footnote added in 1915 to *Three Essays on the Theory of Sexuality* (1905), that incest is in some way instinctual in the biological sense when he writes that "[t]he barrier against incest is probably among the historical acquisitions of mankind, and, like other moral taboos,

has no doubt already become established in many persons by organic inheritance." Freud, *Three Essays on the Theory of Sexuality*, 91n3.

59 Freud, *Totem and Taboo*, 123.

60 Twitchell, *Forbidden Partners*, 33.

61 Freud, *Totem and Taboo*, 123.

62 Freud's notion of incest, as Oedipal desire, can be interpreted to refer broadly to ties of kinship as opposed to ties that are biological. Depending on
social-cultural rules of kinship, it encompasses nonconsanguine child-parent relations, or it does not treat "incest" as categorically limited to the idea
that the child must direct his first sexual desire toward a *biological* parent in
order for such desire to be Oedipal. This idea implies that any kind of
child-parent relation is "incestuous" for Freud if and when a child directs
his first sexual desire toward a main *nonbiological* caregiver. Indeed, in discussions that pertain to the role of the incest barrier in redirecting "the
child's sexual inclination towards his parents and others in charge of him,"
Freud sometimes makes overt qualifications that reinforce this interpretation. Freud, *Three Essays on the Theory of Sexuality*, 101. However, this argument neglects that Freud makes other qualifications that suggest he understands the child's reaction to the incest barrier, which redirects desire away
from *others* in charge of him, to be dependent on the child (mis)identifying
those factual nonbiological others *as*, or as identical to, a blood relation. He
illustrates this idea when he writes that "the child can erect, amongst other
restraints on sexuality, the barrier against incest, and can thus take up into
himself the moral precepts which expressly exclude his object-choice, as
being blood-relations, the persons whom he has loved in his childhood."
Ibid., 91. Freud's use of J.G. Frazer's argument against Westermarck, discussed in the preceding paragraph, additionally implies that his view of
incest turns, at least, on the necessity of the child's (mis)identification of an
other as a blood relation. Freud also categorically blurs what is or is not at
issue, biologically speaking, in what motivates and directs psychic rites of
initiation, such as the child's erection of the incest barrier, which begins the
painful process of the individual's separation from the family, when he
states "that these are difficulties which are inherent in all psychical – and,
indeed, at bottom, in all organic – development." Freud, *Civilization and Its
Discontents*, 59. This blurring is compounded by the fact that Freud chooses
the Oedipus myth as *the* metaphor for child-parent relations because in it
the crime of incest is defined solely with reference to biological ties as
opposed to nurturing; the incest occurs between Oedipus and his biological
mother, Jocasta, in spite of the fact that Oedipus, possessing no knowledge
of his adoption, has lived to adulthood thinking that Merope is his biologi-

cal mother, which, given Freud's nod to primary caregivers, should make Merope the logical object of Oedipus's desire. Freud's choice to place the Oedipal narrative at the centre of human psychology therefore implies that, for him, the presence of blood ties really is the defining feature of incest. For instance, Freud might have chosen a myth where the threat of *incest* with a *nonbiological* child occurs. He might have used Phaedra and Hippolytus as either a possible or additional model for incest in child-parent relations to reinforce his passing reference to primary cargivers. Given the liberties Freud takes with myth and interpretation, Hippolytus's horror at Phaedra's desire might be read to lie in an unwillingness to transgress an incest taboo if incest can refer to family bonds in general, as opposed to blood ties in particular. Morford and Lenardon, *Classical Mythology*, 152. At the very least, Freud's reliance on Oedipus implies that the idea that blood relations are the basis for *family* and *incest* is largely unproblematic and taken for granted by him. The bio-logic of the Oedipal metaphor with which Freud works, together with the meaning of incest in the modern Western context, in which he lived and worked, logically excludes nonbiological parents from being parents for whom a child feels *incestuous* or Oedipal desire. Indeed, that is why Freudian psychoanalysis, when applied to issues of adoption, so readily lends itself to reading the "adoptee," due to her prolonged separation from her *biological* parents, as unable to normally resolve Oedipal desire.

63 Freud, *Civilization and Its Discontents*, 59.

64 Ibid., 59–60.

65 Ibid., 29, original emphasis.

66 Ibid.

67 Ibid., 84.

68 For instance, incest can be due to the individual not passing fully through an earlier psychic stage of primary narcissism.

69 Morehead, "Odeipus, Darwin, and Freud"; Badcock, *Essential Freud*; Fox, *Red Lamp of Incest*.

70 Twitchell, *Forbidden Partners*, 33.

71 Morehead, "Odeipus, Darwin, and Freud," 360.

72 Dawkins, *Selfish Gene*, 293.

73 Arnhart, "Incest Taboo," 205.

74 Fox, *Red Lamp of Incest*, 80, original emphasis.

75 Twitchell, *Forbidden Partners*, 35.

76 Erickson, "Evolutionary Thought," 170.

77 Arnhart, "Incest Taboo," 205.

78 Ibid.

79 Arnhart, "Incest Taboo," 206, 205–6.

80 Durham, "Assessing the Gaps," 121, quoting Wilson.

81 Stein, *Incest and Human Love*, x–xi.

82 Harkins, *Everybody's Family Romance*, 31.

83 Freud, quoted in Godelier, *Metamorphoses of Kinship*, 393.

84 Laplanche and Pontalis, *Language of Psychoanalysis*, 283; Stein, *Incest and Human Love*, x–xi.

85 Twitchell, *Forbidden Partners*, 34.

86 Bell, *Interrogating Incest*, 7, 57.

87 Twitchell, *Forbidden Partners*, 34.

88 Durkheim, *Incest*, 13.

89 Ibid., 60, 68–9.

90 Ibid., 60–2.

91 Ibid., 27–8.

92 Ibid., 25.

93 Ibid., 15.

94 Ibid., 53.

95 Ibid., 68, 98.

96 Ibid., 70.

97 Ibid., 70, 101.

98 Ibid., 100.

99 Ellis, "Origins and the Development of the Incest Taboo," 124.

100 Malinowski, *Sex and Repression in Savage Society*, 244–5, 142–3.

101 Ibid., 247.

102 Ibid., 256–61.

103 Lévi-Strauss, *Elementary Structures of Kinship*, 24.

104 Ibid.

105 Ibid., 51, 54.

106 Ibid., 478–81.

107 Ibid., 490.

108 Ibid., 493.

109 Other feminists who take a psychoanalytic perspective do not reject the idea that children experience incestuous desire as much as they reject the idea that this desire is a biological instinct. Indeed, poststructuralist feminists like Judith Butler, who also incorporate psychoanalysis into their approach, do not deny that the experience of such desire is real, although they explore the social, political, and historical forces that underpin such an experience.

110 Atwood, "When Love Hurts," 310.

111 Ibid., 288.

112 Bell, *Interrogating Incest*, 57.

113 Harkins, *Everybody's Family Romance*, 57.

114 Waldby et al., "Theoretical Perspectives," 97.

115 Faller, "Mother-Blaming in the Shadow of Incest," 130.

116 Devlin, "'Acting Out the Oedipal Wish,'" 609.

117 Bell, *Interrogating Incest*, 85–6.

118 Ward, *Father-Daughter Rape*, 102.

119 Armstrong, *Rocking the Cradle of Sexual Politics*, 16–17.

120 Gallup, *Daughter's Seduction*, xii, 56, 71.

121 Ibid., 71.

122 Harkins, *Everybody's Family Romance*, 60.

123 Ibid., 66, 67, original emphasis.

124 Whittier, "Where Are the Children?" 103, 97.

125 Ibid., 97.

126 Ibid.

127 Butler, "Quandries of the Incest Taboo," 40, original emphasis.

128 Harkins, *Everybody's Family Romance*, 80.

129 Whittier's 2016 survey of major feminist journals in sociology over a twenty-year period located only fourteen articles on "child sexual abuse or incest." Whittier, "Where Are the Children?" 96, 97.

130 Mardorossian, "Toward a New Feminist Theory," 747.

131 Butler, "Quandries of the Incest Taboo," 45, 46.

132 Ibid., 45.

133 Ibid., 44.

134 Foucault, *History of Sexuality*, vol. 1, 106.

135 The use of marriage is not distinguished from bloodlines by Foucault because marriage primarily operates as a bloodline in the modern Western context. The normative function of marriage as a biological tie is also illustrated on page 33, note 87, and on page 244.

136 Foucault, *History of Sexuality*, vol. 1, 106–7.

137 Ibid., 105–6.

138 Ibid., 108.

139 Ibid., 106.

140 Ibid., 107.

141 Foucault argues that medical science, as opposed to morality, sets up the interdiction against "casual pleasures" in a modern economy that does not support "unproductive activities." Ibid., 36–7.

142 Bell, *Interrogating Incest*, 93.

143 Freud's Oedipal theory can therefore be understood to support increasing controls placed on modern bodies and families in this regard.

144 Ibid.
145 Foucault, *History of Sexuality*, vol. 1, 108–9.
146 Ibid., 109.
147 Ibid.

CHAPTER NINE

1 Bernard Knox observes that Sophocles's *Oedipus the King* has "been almost universally regarded as the classic example of the 'tragedy of fate.'" Knox, "Introduction to Oedipus the King," 131.
2 Freud, *Totem and Taboo*, 156.
3 Ibid., 68.
4 Turner and Maryanski, *Incest*, 4–5.
5 Johnson and Price-Williams argue that Oedipal tales are a cross-cultural phenomenon, occurring on every continent and found in an overwhelming number of social contexts ranging from "smaller societies" to "complex societies." Johnson and Price-Williams, *Oedipus Ubiquitous*, 3–7, 98–103.
6 Paul, "Incest Avoidance," 1091.
7 Fox, *Red Lamp of Incest*, 80.
8 Shepher, *Incest*, 137, original emphasis.
9 As an example, although Mark T. Erickson does not reject Freud outright, he does make the ultimate case that "Freud's perception of familial relationships could have been significantly distorted" if, as he suspects, Freud "was sexually abused by someone whose relationship was held dear," particularly his nanny. The point here is less the abuse and more that Erickson, like many in his field, is still so engaged in debate with Freud. Erickson, "Evolution of Incest Avoidance," 212, 225.
10 Josephs, "Evolved Function of the Oedipal Conflict," 948.
11 Stevens, "Jungian Analysis and Evolutionary Psychology," 94.
12 Smith, "Freud and Evolutionary Anthropology's First," 51. American biologist Michael Ghiselin is said to have coined the term "evolutionary psychology" in 1973, and Jerome H. Barkow, Leda Cosmides, and John Tooby "popularized" it in 1992 in their edited volume *The Adapted Mind*. See Boundless Psychology, "Evolutionary Psychology."
13 Josephs, "Evolved Function of the Oedipal Conflict," 938, 941.
14 Littlewood, "Genetic Sexual Attraction," 143.
15 Paul, "Incest Avoidance," 1095.
16 Arnhart, "Incest Taboo," 205.
17 Paul, "Incest Avoidance," 1092.
18 Erickson, "Evolution of Incest Avoidance," 211–12.

19 Ibid., 217, 226, 221–2.

20 Evolutionary psychologists Randolph M. Nesse and Alan T. Lloyd, quoted in Buller, "DeFreuding Evolutionary Psychology," 102.

21 Ibid., 102, 101, original emphasis. For Buller's discussion of *subpersonal psychology*," see ibid., 100–2, original emphasis.

22 Here, Erickson goes so far as to say that "[c]linical and anthropological findings now illuminate this myth in a way not anticipated by Freud. Oedipus portrays the literal truth that early separation undermines a natural adaptation for incest avoidance." Erickson, "Evolutionary Thought," 170.

23 Malinowski, *Sex and Repression in Savage Society*, 2, 169–72, 2, original emphasis.

24 Turner and Maryanski, *Incest*, 41–2.

25 Godelier, *Metamorphoses of Kinship*, 305.

26 Paul, "Incest Avoidance," 1096.

27 Lévi-Strauss, *Elementary Structures of Kinship*, 491.

28 Huffer, *Mad for Foucault*, 128, 129, 128.

29 Park, *Mothering Queerly*, 10.

30 Ibid., 1, 10–11.

31 Hipchen, "Genetic Sexual Attraction," 7.

32 Ibid., 6.

33 In what is a transcribed interview, the text reads, "Oediphile Complex," which appears to be a mispelling of "Oedipal." Gonyo, "Genetic Sexual Attraction," in *Adoption into the 90's*, 25.5.

34 With respect to the logic of the Oedipal psyche, this regression can also be further complicated by a reactivation of primary narcissism.

35 Notably, one of the strategies Gonyo recommends to ward off GSA is that the reunited adoptee make a point of calling a birth mother "Mom" and, we can assume, a birth father "Dad" instead of using their first names. Doing so, she suggests, helps the reunitee to internalize the real meaning of the relationship between adoptee and birth parents. Gonyo, "Genetic Sexual Attraction," in *Adoption into the 90's*, 25.33.

36 Lifton, *Journey of the Adopted Self*, 226.

37 Greenberg, "Post-Adoption Reunion," 6, original emphasis.

38 Twitchell, *Forbidden Partners*, 3.

39 Quoted in Gonyo, "Genetic Sexual Attraction," in *Adoption into the 90's*, 25.7.

40 Quoted in Lifton, *Journey of the Adopted Self*, 231.

41 Gill, "Disgusted by Incest?"; Marshall, "Of Course Twitter Calls It 'Incest'"; Doe, "This Mother/Son GSA Couple."

42 Butler, *Antigone's Claim*, 70, original emphasis.

43 Ibid., 24, 79.

44 To further confound what Antigone represents, Butler suggests that she also acts symbolically "'in the place of the mother.'" Ibid., 22, quoting Robert Graves.

45 Ibid.

46 Ibid., 29.

47 Ibid., 17.

48 Edmunds, *Oedipus*, 5.

49 Ibid., 7.

50 Johnson and Price-Williams, *Oedipus Ubiquitous*, 113.

51 Bettelheim, *Freud and Man's Soul*, 20.

52 Edmunds, *Oedipus*, 7.

53 The import of this possibility is that it highlights the superiority deemed intrinsic to the biological tie in that it functions extra-legally as a right or entitlement to be a "parent," even in the absence of parent-*like* behaviour. Rights derived from adoptive ties are utterly dependent on the law and are granted only after potential adoptive parents are rigorously scrutinized and interrogated regarding their ability to be parents prior to adoption. Conversely, the biological tie, as the ability to conceive, wholly circumvents any prior scrutiny of a would-be biological parent's ability to be a "parent." The biological parent is scrutinized only if and when evidence of abuse is established. Adoptive parents are treated unequally in that the lack of a biological tie requires that they be subjected to an investigation without any evidence of abuse before they may obtain the right to be "parents": they are suspect from the start. To establish equality between ties, therefore, both adoptive and biological parents could be subjected to parental licensure, for certainly to conflate a right to parent with the mere ability to give birth is not in the best interests of children. Carolyn McLeod and Andrew Botterell have recently made the contrary argument about adoptive versus biological parents because it is "unfair that one class of prospective parents [i.e., adoptive] is subject to potentially intrusive licensing and screening requirements while other groups of prospective parents are not." McLeod and Botterell, "Not for the Faint of Heart," 166. Although I agree that it is unfair for adoptive parents to be subject to requirements that differ from those of other prospective parents, I tend toward the reverse conclusion that all parents should be subject to licensure because neither the biological tie *nor* the desire to be a parent in and of itself should be a sufficient ground for the legal right to parent and it is unlikely that adoptive parents will cease to be subjected to such intrusions.

54 Sophocles, *Three Theban Plays*, 219.

55 Ibid., 205.
56 Bettelheim, *Freud and Man's Soul*, 23.
57 Ibid.
58 Ibid.
59 Bettelheim's observation that the story of Oedipus is about self-knowledge, or "his discovery of the truth" as it is manifested through Oedipus's realization that he has committed patricide and incest, is quite common. Knox, "Introduction to Oedipus the King," 131.
60 As important as adoption revelation might be in a social-political-historical context that subjects the self to a bio-genealogical imperative, this new tragedy in the myth suggests that an injustice is nonetheless perpetrated against the self through adoption revelation. Adoption experts impose revelation upon adoptees to prevent trauma or identity crisis, yet this trauma imaginably ceases to exist outside a biological family order. In this way, adoption revelation reinscribes the bio-genealogical imperative, which devalues, or makes traumatic, the experience and revelation of adoptive ties in the first place. This is not to say that withholding bio-genealogy from adoptees is preferable to revelation in this social-political-historical moment but to say that revelation, for all the trauma it prevents, still serves the aims of a biological family order.

CONCLUSION

1 "Discover the Family Story"; "Get To Know You."
2 AncestryDNA, "Testimonial: Kyle"; AncestryDNA, "Kim."
3 MyHeritage DNA, "'Humanity' Featuring Prince Ea."
4 Blackwell, "Limit Pregnancies."
5 Ibid.
6 Based on a 2004 study, Nancy J. Mezey suggests that "[w]hereas most heterosexuals see adoption as a second choice that they use after facing infertility, lesbians and gay men often look to adoption as a first choice means of becoming parents," a claim that arguably obscures the realities of choice in LGBTQ contexts anyway because the points of departure for first and second choices among would-be heterosexual versus LGBTQ parents, particularly as regards (in)fertility, are simply not the same. Mezey, *LGBT Families*, 88.
7 Pelka, "Making and Unmaking of Biological Ties," 85.
8 Park, *Mothering Queerly*, 1, 163, original emphasis. Park draws on Gilles Deleuze and Felix Guattari's concept of "assemblage" to explore queer and polymaternal recombinations of kinship or novel layouts of biological, adoptive, blended, and/or (same-)sexual relations that challenge hetero- and homonormativity, "reprosexuality," and biocentrism. Ibid., 1, 163, 18, 27, 257.

9 Ibid., 69, 61, my emphasis.

10 Anne Kingston has examined the fact that "more and more women are no longer afraid to admit that they hate being a mom" and its implications for ideals about maternal love and the primary bond. Kingston, "I Wish I Never Had Kids"; the quotation is from the cover of the issue of *Maclean's* magazine in which this article appears.

Bibliography

Adelman, Mara B., and Marie Siemon. "Communicating the Relational Shift: Separation among Adult Twins." *American Journal of Psychotherapy* 40, no. 1 (1986): 96–109.

Adoption Community Outreach Project. *Search Manual for Adoptees and Birth Relatives*. Toronto: Parent Finders Incorporated and Adoption Council of Ontario, 1997.

Alcoff, Linda. "Expert Discourses of Critique: Foucault as Power/Knowledge." In Lenore Langsdorf, Stephen H. Watson, and Karen Anne Smith, eds, *Reinterpreting the Political: Continental Philosophy and Political Theory*, 307–16. Albany, NY: SUNY Press, 1998.

Aldridge, Alfred Owen. "The Meaning of Incest from Hutcheson to Gibbon." *Ethics: An International Journal of Social, Political, and Legal Philosophy* 61, no. 4 (1951): 309–13.

Allen, Woody. "Woody Allen Speaks Out." *New York* Times, 7 February 2014. https://www.nytimes.com/2014/02/09/opinion/sunday/woody-allen-speaks-out.html.

Altman, Robert, dir. *Gosford Park*. Film. USA Films, 2001.

AncestryDNA. "Kim." TV commercial. *iSpot.tv*. https://www.ispot.tv/ad/wKqV/ancestrydna-kim?autoplay=1.

– "Testimonial: Kyle." TV commercial. *iSpot.tv*. https://www.ispot.tv/ad/7c4Y/ancestrydna-testimonial-kyle?autoplay=1.

Anderson, Robert S. "The Nature of the Adoptee Search: Adventure, Cure or Growth?" *Child Welfare* 68, no. 6 (1989): 624–32.

Armstrong, Louise. *Rocking the Cradle of Sexual Politics: What Happened When Women Said Incest*. Reading, MA: Addison-Wesley, 1994.

Arnhart, Larry. "The Incest Taboo as Darwinian Natural Right." In Arthur P. Wolf and William H. Durham, eds, *Inbreeding, Incest, and the Incest Taboo:*

The State of Knowledge at the Turn of the Century, 190–218. Stanford, CA: Stanford University Press, 2004.

Ashcroft, Bill, Gareth Griffiths, and Helen Tiffin. "Introduction Eleven." In Bill Ashcroft, Gareth Griffiths, and Helen Tiffin, eds, *The Post-Colonial Studies Reader*, 2nd ed., 289–90. London: Routledge, 2009.

Athanassiou, C. "A Study of the Vicissitudes of Identification in Twins." *International Journal of Psycho-Analysis* 67, no. 3 (1986): 329–35.

Atwood, Joan D. "When Love Hurts: Preadolescent Girls' Reports of Incest." *American Journal of Family Therapy* 35, no. 4 (2007): 287–313.

Aversa, G. Luigi, Vittorio Baldieri, and Maria Ilena Marozza. "The Mythic Function of Narcissism." *Journal of Analytical Psychology* 49, no. 4 (2004): 553–68.

Aziza, Sindhu. "Forbidden Love: Genetic Sexual Attraction." CBC Radio, *The Current*, 23 November 2010. https://www.cbc.ca/andthewinneris/2010/11/23/forbidden-love-genetic-sexual-attraction.

Badcock, Christopher. *Essential Freud*. 2nd ed. Oxford: Blackwell, 1992.

Baden, Amanda L., and Mary O'Leary Wiley. "Counseling Adopted Persons in Adulthood: Integrating Practice and Research." *Counseling Psychologist* 35, no. 6 (2007): 868–901.

Badinter, Elisabeth. "The Defense of the Child." In *Mother Love: Myth and Reality*, 120–67. New York: Macmillan, 1981.

Balcom, Karen A. *The Traffic in Babies: Cross-Border Adoption and Baby-Selling between the United States and Canada, 1930–1972*. Toronto: University of Toronto Press, 2011.

Barad, Karen. *Meeting the Universe Halfway: Quantum Physics and the Entanglement of Matter and Meaning*. Durham, NC: Duke University Press, 2007.

– "Posthuman Performativity: Toward an Understanding of How Matter Comes to Matter." *Signs* 28, no. 3 (2003): 801–31.

Barkow, Jerome H., Leda Cosmides, and John Tooby, eds. *The Adapted Mind: Evolutionary Psychology and the Generation of Culture*. New York: Oxford University Press, 1992.

Bartholet, Elizabeth. "Adoption and the Parental Screening System." In Peg Tittle, ed., *Should Parents Be Licensed? Debating the Issues*, 119–29. New York: Prometheus Books, 2004.

– *Family Bonds: Adoption, Infertility, and the New World of Child Production*. Boston: Beacon, 1999.

Bartky, Sandra Lee. "Sympathy and Solidarity: On a Tightrope with Scheler." In Diana Tietjens Meyers, ed., *Feminists Rethink the Self*, 177–96. Boulder, CO: Westview, 1997.

Beardsworth, Sara. "Freud's Oedipus and Kristeva's Narcissus: Three Hetero-geneities." *Hypatia* 20, no. 1 (2005): 54–77.

Beauvoir, Simone de. *The Second Sex*. Trans. H.M. Parshley. New York: Vintage, 1989.

Bell, Vikki. *Interrogating Incest: Feminism, Foucault and the Law*. New York: Routledge, 1993.

Bernardes, Jon. "'Family Ideology': Identification and Exploration." *Sociological Review* 33, no. 2 (1985): 275–97.

Bettelheim, Bruno. *Freud and Man's Soul: An Important Re-Interpretation of Freudian Theory*. New York: Alfred A. Knopf, 1983.

Bird, Alexander. "Thomas Kuhn: Criticism and Influence." In Edward N. Zalta, ed., *The Stanford Encyclopedia of Philosophy*. Fall 2013. https://plato.stanford.edu/archives/fall2013/entries/thomas-kuhn/#6.

Bittles, Alan H. *Consanguinity in Context*. Cambridge, UK: Cambridge University Press, 2012.

Blackwell, Tom. "Limit Pregnancies by Same Sperm Donor: Fertility Experts." *National Post*, 8 September 2011. http://nationalpost.com/news/canada/limit-pregnancies-by-same-sperm-donor-fertility-experts.

"Bob Childs." *Psychology Today*. https://therapists.psychologytoday.com/rms/name/Bob_Childs_PsyD_Cambridge_Massachusetts_132845.

Bohall v. State, 546 N.E.2d 1214 (1989).

Borders, L. DiAnne, Judith M. Penny, and Francie Portnoy. "Adult Adoptees and Their Friends: Current Functioning and Psychosocial Well-Being." *Family Relations* 49, no. 4 (2000): 407–18.

Bouchard, Donald F. "Introduction." In Donald F. Bouchard, ed., *Language, Counter-Memory, Practice: Selected Essays and Interviews by Michel Foucault*, 15–25. Ithaca, NY: Cornell University Press, 1977.

Bouchard, Thomas J., Jr. "Behavioral Studies of Twins and Adoptees." In American Adoption Congress and TRIAD Society for Truth in Adoption, eds, *Adoption into the 90's: Trends and Issues*, proceedings of the 10th Annual Conference of the American Adoption Congress and TRIAD Society for Truth in Adoption, Calgary, 28 April to 1 May 1988, 12.1–12.28. Washington, DC: American Adoption Congress, 1988.

– "Genetic and Environmental Influences on Adult Intelligence and Special Mental Abilities." *Human Biology* 70, no. 2 (1998): 257–79.

Bouchard, Thomas J., Jr, David T. Lykken, Matthew McGue, Nancy L. Segal, and Auke Tellegen. "Sources of Human Psychological Differences: The Minnesota Study of Twins Reared Apart." *Science* 250, no. 4978 (1990): 223–8.

Boundless Psychology. "Evolutionary Psychology." In "Theoretical Perspectives in Modern Psychology." https://courses.lumenlearning.com/boundless-psychology/chapter/theoretical-perspectives-in-modern-psychology/.

Boyle, Louise. "Everybody DOES Have a Twin: Photographer Creates Amazing Portraits of STRANGERS Who Look the Double of Each Other." *Daily Mail* (London), 13 December 2012. http://www.dailymail.co.uk/news/article-2247797/Twin-portraits-Quebec-photographer-Francois-Brunelle-takes-pictures-look-alikes.html.

Brodzinsky, David. "Foreword." In Rafael A. Javier, Amanda L. Baden, Frank A. Biafora, and Alina Camacho-Gingerich, eds, *Handbook of Adoption: Implications for Researchers, Practitioners, and Families*, xiii–xvi. London: Sage, 2007.

Brodzinsky, David, Marshall D. Schechter, and Robin Marantz Henig. *Being Adopted: The Lifelong Search for Self*. New York: Doubleday, 1992.

Bryan, Elizabeth A. "The Death of a Twin." In A.C. Sandbank, ed., *Twin and Triplet Psychology: A Multi-Professional Guide to Working with Multiples*, 186–200. London: Routledge, 1999.

– *The Nature and Nurture of Twins*. London: Baillière Tindall, 1983.

Brzović, Zdenka. "Natural Kinds." In *Internet Encyclopedia of Philosophy: A Peer-Reviewed Academic Resource.* https://www.iep.utm.edu/nat-kind.

Buller, David J. "DeFreuding Evolutionary Psychology: Adaptation and Human Motivation." In Valerie Gray Hardcastle, ed., *Where Biology Meets Psychology: Philosophical Essays*, 99–114. Cambridge, MA: MIT Press, 1999.

Bunyan, Andrew. "Modifying Behaviour: Enuresis." *Adoption and Fostering* 10, no. 4 (1986): 51–3.

Bursten, Ben. "Some Narcissistic Personality Types." In Andrew P. Morrison, ed., *Essential Papers on Narcissism*, 377–402. New York: New York University Press, 1986.

Butler, Judith. *Antigone's Claim: Kinship between Life and Death*. New York: Columbia University Press, 2000.

– *Bodies That Matter*. New York: Routledge, 1993.

– "Gender as Performance: An Interview with Judith Butler." *Radical Philosophy* 67 (1994): 32–9.

– "Quandaries of the Incest Taboo." In Peter Brooks and Alex Woloch, eds, *Whose Freud? The Place of Psychoanalysis in Contemporary Culture*, 39–46. New Haven, CT: Yale University Press, 2000.

– *Senses of the Subject*. New York: Fordham University Press, 2015.

Canadian Pediatric Society. "Position Statement: Transracial Adoption." http://www.cps.ca/documents/position/adoption-transracial.

Canguilhem, Georges. "The Death of Man, or Exhaustion of the Cogito?" Trans. Catherine Porter. In Gary Gutting, ed., *The Cambridge Companion to Foucault*, 2nd ed., 74–94. Cambridge, UK: Cambridge University Press, 2005.

Carp, E. Wayne. *Family Matters: Secrecy and Disclosure in the History of Adoption*. Cambridge, MA: Harvard University Press, 1998.

Changfoot, Nadine. "The Second Sex's Continued Relevance for Equality and Difference Feminisms." *European Journal of Women's Studies* 16, no. 1 (2009): 11–31.

Childs, Robert M. "Genetic Sexual Attraction: Healing and Danger in the Reunions of Adoptees and Their Birth Families." PhD diss., Massachusetts School of Professional Psychology, 1998.

Clark, J.F.M. "'The Ants Were Duly Visited': Making Sense of John Lubbock, Scientific Naturalism and the Senses of Social Insects." *British Journal for the History of Science* 30, no. 2 (1997): 151–76.

Clothier, Florence. "The Psychology of the Adopted Child." *Mental Hygiene* 27 (1943): 222–30.

Collins, Francis S., Eric D. Green, Alan E. Guttmacher, and Mark S. Guyer. "A Vision for the Future of Genomics Research: A Blueprint for the Genomic Era." *Nature*, 24 April 2003, 835–47. https://www.genome.gov/11007524/nhgris-vision-for-the-future-of-genomic-research/.

Columbus, Chris, dir. *Harry Potter and the Sorcerer's Stone*. Film. Warner Bros. Pictures, 2001.

Corliss, Richard. "Scenes from a Breakup." *Time*, 31 August 1992, 36–40.

Cornacchia, Cheryl. "Woody Allen's Revelations Show Need for Clearer Definition of Incest: Therapists." *Montreal Gazette*, 21 August 1992, A2.

Cumette, Margaret, and Giuseppe Testa. "Consuming Genomes: Scientific and Social Innovation in Direct-to-Consumer Genetic Testing." *New Genetics and Society* 31, no. 2 (2012): 159–81.

Cusak, Carmen M. *Twins and Deviance: Law, Crime, Sex, Society, and Family*. Newcastle, UK: Cambridge Scholars, 2016.

Darwin, Charles. *On the Origin of Species by Means of Natural Selection, or The Preservation of Favoured Races in the Struggle for Life*. New York: Modern Library, 1998.

Dawkins, Richard. *The Selfish Gene*. Oxford: Oxford University Press, 1989.

Derrida, Jacques. *Specters of Marx: The State of Debt, the Work of Mourning and the New Intellectual*. New York: Routledge Classics, 2006.

Devlin, Rachel. "'Acting Out the Oedipal Wish': Father-Daughter Incest and the Sexuality of Adolescent Girls in the United States, 1941–1965." *Journal of Social History* 38, no. 3 (2005): 609–33.

Dictionary of Philosophy. Ed. Peter A. Angeles. New York: Barnes and Noble, 1981.

Dictionary of Philosophy. 3rd ed. Ed. A.R. Lacey. New York: Routledge, 1996.

A Dictionary of Psychology. Ed. James Drever. 1952. Reprint, Middlesex, UK: Penguin, 1975.

"Discover the Family Story Your DNA Can Tell." *Ancestry*. https://www.ancestry.ca/dna/?cj=1&geo_a=r&geo_s=us&geo_t=ca&geo_v =2.0.0&o_iid=64405&o_lid=64405&o_sch=Web+Property.

Doe, Jane. "This Mother/Son GSA Couple Do NOT Need 'Help.'" *Consanguinamory: A Blog for the Intelligent Discussion of Relationships between Family Members*, 8 April 2016. https://consanguinamory.wordpress .com/2016/04/08/this-motherson-gsa-couple-do-not-need-help/.

Donzelot, Jacques. *The Policing of Families*. Trans. Robert Hurley. Baltimore, MD: Johns Hopkins University Press, 1997.

Dorow, Sara K. *Transnational Adoption: A Cultural Economy of Race, Gender and Kinship*. New York: New York University Press, 2006.

Dorow, Sara K., and Amy Swiffen. "Blood and Desire: The Secret of Heteronormativity in Adoption Narratives of Culture." *American Ethnologist* 36, no. 3 (2009): 563–73.

Dreyfus, Hubert L. "'Being and Power' Revisited." In Alan Michman and Alan Rosenburg, eds, *Foucault and Heidegger: Critical Encounters*, 30–54. Minneapolis: University of Minnesota Press, 2003.

– "Foreword to the California Edition." In Michel Foucault, *Mental Illness and Psychology*, trans. Alan Sheridan, vii–xliii. Berkeley: University of California Press, 1987.

– "Foucault's Critique of Psychiatric Medicine." *Journal of Medicine and Philosophy* 12, no. 4 (1987): 311–33.

Dreyfus, Hubert L., and Paul Rabinow. *Michel Foucault: Beyond Structuralism and Hermeneutics*. Chicago: University of Chicago Press, 1983.

Dumont, Louis. *Essays on Individualism: Modern Ideology in Anthropological Perspective*. Chicago: University of Chicago Press, 1986.

Durant, John R. "Scientific Naturalism and Social Reform in the Thought of Alfred Russel Wallace." *British Society for the History of Science* 12, no. 1 (1979): 31–58.

Durham, William H. "Assessing the Gaps in Westermarck's Theory." In Arthur P. Wolf and William H. Durham, eds, *Inbreeding, Incest, and the Incest Taboo: The State of Knowledge at the Turn of the Century*, 121–38. Stanford, CA: Stanford University Press, 2004.

Durkheim, Émile. *Incest: The Nature and Origin of the Taboo*. Trans. Edward Sagarin. New York: Lyle Stuart, 1963.

Durkhin, M.S., N. Khan, L.L. Davidson, S.S. Zaman, and Z.A. Stein. "The Effects of a Natural Disaster on Child Behavior: Evidence for Posttraumatic Stress." *American Journal of Public Health* 83, no. 11 (1993): 1549–53.

Eckert, Elke D., T.J. Bouchard Jr, J. Bohlen, and L.L. Heston. "Homosexuality in Monozygotic Twins Reared Apart." *British Journal of Psychiatry* 148, no. 4 (1986): 421–5.

Edmunds, Lowell. *Oedipus: The Ancient Legend and Its Later Analogues*. Baltimore, MD: Johns Hopkins University Press, 1985.

Ehrlich, Paul, and Marcus Feldman. "Genes and Cultures: What Creates Our Behavioral Phenome?" *Current Anthropology* 44, no. 1 (2003): 87–107.

Eidlitz-Markus, T.A. Shuper, and J. Amir. "Secondary Enuresis: Post-Traumatic Stress Disorder in Children after Car Accidents." *Israel Medical Association Journal* 2, no. 2 (2000): 135–7.

Ellis, Albert. "The Origins and the Development of the Incest Taboo." In Émile Durkheim, *Incest: The Nature and Origin of the Taboo*, trans. Edward Sagarin, 121–74. New York: Lyle Stuart, 1963.

Encyclopedia of Anthropology. Ed. David E. Hunter and Phillip Whitten. New York: Harper and Row, 1976.

Encyclopedia of World Problems and Human Potential. Vol. 1. 4th ed. Ed. Union of International Associations. Munich: K.G. Saur, 1994.

Erickson, Mark T. "Evolutionary Thought and the Current Clinical Understanding of Incest." In Arthur P. Wolf and William H. Durham, eds, *Inbreeding, Incest, and the Incest Taboo: The State of Knowledge at the Turn of the Century*, 161–89. Stanford, CA: Stanford University Press, 2004.

– "The Evolution of Incest Avoidance: Oedipus and the Psychopathologies of Incest." In Paul Gilbert and Kent G. Bailey, eds, *Genes on the Couch: Explorations in Evolutionary Psychotherapy*, 211–31. London: Routledge, 2000.

Etezachy, M. Hossein, Salman Akhatar, and Selma Kramer. "The Multifaceted Psychosocial Impact of Adoption." In Salman Akhatar and Selma Kramer, eds, *Thicker Than Blood: Bonds of Fantasy and Reality in Adoption*, 3–17. Northvale, NJ: Jason Aronson, 2000.

Faller, Kathleen Coulborn. "Mother-Blaming in the Shadow of Incest: Commentary on 'Motherhood in the Shadow of Incest' by Rachel Lev-Wiesel." *Journal of Child Sexual Abuse* 16, no. 1 (2007): 129–36.

Farrow, Dylan. "An Open Letter from Dylan Farrow." *New York Times*, 1 February 2014. https://kristof.blogs.nytimes.com/2014/02/01/an-open-letter-from-dylan-farrow/.

Farrow, Mia. *What Falls Away: A Memoir*. New York: Doubleday, 1997.

Feast, Julia. "Working in the Adoption Circle – Outcomes of Section 51 Counselling." *Adoption and Fostering* 16, no. 4 (1992): 46–52.

Ferris, Paul. *Dr. Freud: A Life*. Washington, DC: Counterpoint, 1998.

Fisher, Florence. *The Search for Anna Fisher*. New York: Arthur Fields, 1973.

Fleisher, Alison. "The Decline of Domestic Adoption: Intercountry Adoption as a Response to Local Adoption Laws and Proposals to Foster Domestic Adoption." *Southern California Review of Law and Women's Studies* 13, no. 1 (2003): 171–97.

Foucault, Michel. *The Archaeology of Knowledge and the Discourse on Language*. Trans. A.M. Sheridan Smith. New York: Pantheon, 1972.

– *Discipline and Punish: The Birth of the Prison*. Trans. Alan Sheridan. New York: Vintage, 1979.

– *Essential Works of Michel Foucault, 1954–1984*. Vol. 1, *Ethics: Subjectivity and Truth*. Ed. Paul Rabinow. New York: New Press, 1997.

– *Foucault Live: Interviews, 1966–84*. New York: Semiotext(e), 1989.

– *The Foucault Reader*. Ed. Paul Rabinow. New York: Pantheon, 1984.

– *History of Madness*. Trans. Jonathan Murphy and Jean Khalfa. Ed. Jean Khalfa. London: Routledge, 2006.

– *The History of Sexuality*. Vol. 1, *An Introduction*. Trans. Robert Hurley. New York: Vintage, 1990.

– *The History of Sexuality*. Vol. 2, *The Use of Pleasure*. Trans. Robert Hurley. New York: Vintage, 1990.

– *Madness and Civilization: A History of Insanity in the Age of Reason*. Trans. Richard Howard. New York: Vintage, 1965.

– *Mental Illness and Psychology*. Trans. Alan Sheridan. Berkeley: University of California Press, 1987.

– "Nietzsche, Genealogy, History." In Donald F. Bouchard, ed., *Language Counter-Memory, Practice: Selected Essays and Interviews by Michel Foucault*, 137–64. Ithaca, NY: Cornell University Press, 1977.

– *The Order of Things: An Archaeology of the Human Sciences*. 1970. Reprint, New York: Vintage, 1994.

– "The Political Technology of Individuals." In Luther H. Martin, Huck Gutman, and Patrick H. Hutton, eds, *Technologies of the Self: A Seminar with Michel Foucault*, 145–62. Amherst: University of Massachusetts Press, 1988.

– *The Politics of Truth*. Ed. Sylvère Lotringer and Lysa Hochroth. New York: Semiotext(e), 1997.

– *Politics, Philosophy, Culture: Interviews and Other Writings, 1977–1984*. Trans. Alan Sheridan. Ed. Lawrence D. Kritzman. New York: Routledge, 1990.

– *Power/Knowledge: Selected Interviews and Other Writings, 1972–1977*. Ed. Colin Gordon. New York: Pantheon, 1980.

– *Religion and Culture*. Ed. Jeremy R. Carrette. New York: Routledge, 1999.
– "Technologies of the Self." In Luther H. Martin, Huck Gutman, and Patrick H. Hutton, eds, *Technologies of the Self: A Seminar with Michel Foucault*, 16–49. Amherst: University of Massachusetts Press, 1988.

Foucault, Michel, and Ludwig Binswanger. "Dream, Imagination, and Existence." In Michel Foucault and Ludwig Binswanger, *Dream and Existence*, ed. Keith Hoeller, 31–78. New Jersey: Humanities Press, 1993.

Fox, Robin. *The Red Lamp of Incest: An Enquiry into the Origins of Mind and Society*. New York: E.P. Dutton, 1980.

Fragoso, Sam. "At 79, Woody Allen Says There's Still Time to Do His Best Work." *NPR*, 29 July 2015. http://www.npr.org/2015/07/29/426827865/at-79-woody-allen-says-theres-still-time-to-do-his-best-work.

Freud, Sigmund. "The Aetiology of Hysteria." In Jeffrey M. Masson, *The Assault on Truth: Freud's Suppression of the Seduction Theory*, 259–90. New York: Pocket Books, 1998.

– *Civilization and Its Discontents*. Trans. James Strachey. New York: W.W. Norton, 1961.

– *Collected Papers*. Vol. 5. Ed. M.M. Khan. Trans. Joan Riviere. London: Hogarth, 1971.

– "The Ego and the Id." In *On Metapsychology: The Theory of Psychoanalysis: Beyond the Pleasure Principle, The Ego and the Id, and Other Works*, trans. James Strachey, ed. Angela Richards, 339–407. Penguin Freud Library, vol. 11. London: Penguin, 1991.

– "Femininity." In *New Introductory Lectures on Psycho-Analysis: The Standard Edition*, trans. James Strachey, 139–67. New York: W.W. Norton, 1965.

– *Group Psychology and the Analysis of the Ego*. Trans. James Strachey. New York: W.W. Norton, 1959.

– *Historical and Expository Works on Psychoanalysis: History of the Psychoanalytic Movement, An Autobiographical Study, Outline of Psychoanalysis and Other Works*. Trans. James Strachey. Ed. Albert Dickson. Penguin Freud Library, vol. 15. London: Penguin, 1993.

– "Infantile Sexuality." In *Three Essays on the Theory of Sexuality*, trans. James Strachey, 39–109. New York: Basic Books, 1975.

– *The Interpretation of Dreams (First Part)*. Trans. James Strachey. Standard Edition of the Complete Psychological Works of Sigmund Freud, vol. 4. London: Vintage, 2001.

– *The Interpretation of Dreams (Second Part)*. Trans. James Strachey. Standard Edition of the Complete Psychological Works of Sigmund Freud, vol. 5. London: Vintage, 2001.

– "Lecture XXVI: Libido Theory and Narcissism." In *Introductory Lectures on*

Psychoanalysis (Part III), trans. James Strachey, 412–30. Standard Edition of the Complete Psychological Works of Sigmund Freud, vol. 16. London: Vintage, 2001.

– *Leonardo da Vinci and a Memory of His Childhood*. Trans. Alan Tyson. Harmondsworth: Pelican, 1966.

– "On Narcissism: An Introduction." In *On Metapsychology: The Theory of Psychoanalysis: Beyond the Pleasure Principle, The Ego and the Id, and Other Works*, trans. James Strachey, ed. Angela Richards, 59–97. Penguin Freud Library, vol. 11. London: Penguin, 1991.

– "Some Psychical Consequences of the Anatomical Distinction between the Sexes." In *On Sexuality: Three Essays on the Theory of Sexuality and Other Works*, trans. James Strachey, ed. Angela Richards, 323–43. Penguin Freud Library, vol. 7. London: Penguin, 1977.

– *Three Essays on the Theory of Sexuality*. Trans. James Strachey. New York: Basic Books, 1975.

– *Totem and Taboo and Other Works*. Trans. James Strachey. Standard Edition of the Complete Psychological Works of Sigmund Freud, vol. 13. London: Vintage, 2001.

– "The 'Uncanny.'" In *An Infantile Neurosis and Other Works*, trans. James Strachey, 219–52. Standard Edition of the Complete Psychological Works of Sigmund Freud, vol. 17. London: Hogarth, 1986.

Frisk, Max. "Identity Problems and Confused Conceptions of the Genetic Ego in Adopted Children during Adolescence." *Acta Paedopsychiatria* 31 (1964): 6–12.

Frosh, Stephen. *Identity Crisis: Modernity, Psychoanalysis and the Self*. London: Macmillan, 1991.

Furst, Lillian R., and Peter N. Skrine. *Naturalism*. London: Methuen, 1971.

Fuss, Diana. *Identification Papers*. New York: Routledge, 1995.

Gager, Kristin E. *Blood Ties and Fictive Ties: Adoption and Family Life in Early Modern France*. Princeton, NJ: Princeton University Press, 1996.

Gallup, Jane. *The Daughter's Seduction: Feminism and Psychoanalysis*. Ithaca, NY: Cornell University Press, 1982.

Galton, Francis. "The History of Twins, as a Criterion of the Relative Powers of Nature and Nurture." *Journal of the Anthropological Institute of Great Britain and Ireland* 5 (1876): 391–406.

– *Inquiries into Human Faculty and Its Development*. New York: Macmillan, 1883.

Gavras, Konstantinos (Costa-Gavras), dir. *Music Box*. Film. Carolco Pictures, 1989.

Gergen, K.J., and M.M. Gergen. "Narratives of the Self." In T.R. Sarbin and

K.E. Scheibe, eds, *Studies in Social Identity*, 254–72. New York: Praeger, 1983.

"Get To Know You." *23andMe*. https://www.23andme.com.

Gildiner, Catherine Ann. "The Evolutionary Foundations of Freud's Theory of Female Psychology." PhD diss., York University, 1983.

Gill, Charlotte. "Disgusted by Incest? Genetic Sexual Attraction Is Real and on the Rise." *Telegraph* (London), 9 September 2016. https://www.telegraph.co.uk/family/relationships/disgusted-by-incest-genetic-sexual-attraction-is-real-and-on-the/.

Glover, Jonathon. *I: The Philosophy and Psychology of Personal Identity*. London: Penguin, 1991.

Godelier, Maurice. *The Metamorphoses of Kinship*. Trans. Nora Scott. London: Verso, 2011.

Gonyo, Barbara. "Genetic Sexual Attraction." In American Adoption Congress and TRIAD Society for Truth in Adoption, eds, *Adoption into the 90's: Trends and Issues*, proceedings of the 10th Annual Conference of the American Adoption Congress and TRIAD Society for Truth in Adoption, Calgary, 28 April to 1 May 1988, 25.1–25.33. Washington, DC: American Adoption Congress, 1988.

– "Genetic Sexual Attraction." *The Decree: A Quarterly of the American Adoption Congress* 4, no. 2 (1987): 12–18. http://poundpuplegacy.org/node/18705.

Gopnik, Alison. "Innateness." In John Brockman, ed., *This Idea Must Die: Scientific Theories That Are Blocking Progress*, 192–5. New York: Harper-Perennial, 2015.

Green, André. *Life Narcissism, Death Narcissism*. Trans. Andrew Weller. London: Free Association Books, 2001.

Greenberg, Maurice. "Post-Adoption Reunion – Are We Entering Uncharted Territory?" *Adoption and Fostering* 17, no. 4 (1993): 5–15.

Greenberg, Maurice, and Roland Littlewood. "Post-Adoption Incest and Phenotypic Matching: Experience, Personal Meanings and Biosocial Implications." *British Journal of Medical Psychology* 68, no. 1 (1995): 29–44.

Griffin, Marcie A. "Genetic Sexual Attraction and Adoptees: Can we Legislate Morality?" *Adoption Triad Forum*, January-February 1998. http://poundpuplegacy.org/node/18702.

Griffith, Keith C. *The Right to Know Who You Are: Reform of Adoption Law with Honesty, Openness and Integrity*. Ottawa: Katherine W. Kimbell, 1991.

Gutman, Huck. "Rousseau's *Confessions*: A Technology of the Self." In Luther H. Martin, Huck Gutman, and Patrick H. Hutton, eds, *Technologies of the Self: A Seminar with Michel Foucault*, 99–120. Amherst: University of Massachusetts Press, 1988.

Hagedorn, Judy W., and Janet W. Kizziar. *Gemini: The Psychology and Phenomena of Twins*. Chicago: Center for the Study of Multiple Birth, 1983.

Hamilton, Victoria. *Narcissus and Oedipus: The Children of Psychoanalysis*. London: Routledge and Kegan Paul, 1982.

Han, Béatrice. "The Analytic of Finitude and the History of Subjectivity." Trans. Edward Phile. In Gary Gutting, ed., *The Cambridge Companion to Foucault*, 2nd ed., 176–209. Cambridge, UK: Cambridge University Press, 2005.

Harkins, Gillian. *Everybody's Family Romance: Reading Incest in Neo-Liberal America*. Minneapolis: University of Minnesota Press, 2009.

Harris, Judith Rich. *The Nurture Assumption: Why Children Turn Out the Way They Do*. New York: Touchstone, 1998.

Haslanger, Sally. "Family, Ancestry and Self: What Is the Moral Significance of Biological Ties?" *Adoption and Culture* 2, no. 1 (2009). https://dspace.mit.edu/handle/1721.1/64650.

Haslanger, Sally, and Charlotte Witt. "Introduction: Kith, Kin and Family." In Sally Haslanger and Charlotte Witt, eds, *Adoption Matters: Philosophical and Feminist Essays*, 1–15. Ithaca, NY: Cornell University Press, 2005.

Hauskeller, Christine. "Genes, Genomes and Identity: Projections on Matter." *New Genetics and Society* 23, no. 3 (2004): 285–99.

Hawkins, Mike. *Social Darwinism in European and American Thought, 1860–1945: Nature as Model and Nature as Threat*. New York: Cambridge University Press, 1997.

Hayashi, Chisato, Kazuo Hayakawa, Chika Tsuboi, Keiko Oda, Yukiko Amau, Yoko Kobayashi, and Kenji Kato. "Relationship between Parents' Report Rate of Twin Language and Factors Related to Linguistic Development: Older Sibling, Nonverbal Play and Preschool Attendance." *Twin Research and Human Genetics* 9, no. 1 (2006): 165–74.

Herman, Ellen. *Kinship by Design: A History of Adoption in the Modern United States*. Chicago: University of Chicago Press, 2008.

Hicks, Steven V. "Nietzsche, Heidegger and Foucault: Nihilism and Beyond." In Alan Michman and Alan Rosenburg, eds, *Foucault and Heidegger: Critical Encounters*, 74–109. Minneapolis: University of Minnesota Press, 2003.

Hill Collins, Patricia. "Defining Black Feminist Thought." In Carole R. McCann and Seung-kyung Kim, eds, *Feminist Theory Reader: Local and Global Perspectives*, 2nd ed., 341–56. New York: Routledge, 2010.

Hill, Malcom, Sandra Hutton, and Shona Easton. "Adoptive Parenting – Plus and Minus." *Adoption and Fostering* 12, no. 2 (1988): 17–23.

Hipchen, Emily. "Genetic Sexual Attraction and the Creation of Fatherhood: Making Daddy (Infamous) in *The Kiss*." *Journal of the Midwest Modern Language Association* 42, no. 2 (2009): 5–22.

– "Images of the Family Body in the Adoptee Search Narrative." In Christopeher Stuart and Stephanie Todd, eds, *New Essays on Life Writing and the Body*, 168–89. Newcastle, UK: Cambridge Scholars, 2009.

Hoeller, Keith. "Editor's Foreword." In Michel Foucault and Ludwig Binswanger, *Dream and Existence*, ed. Keith Hoeller, 7–18. New Jersey: Humanities Press, 1993.

Hoksbergen, Rene, and Jan Ter Laak. "Psychic Homelessness Related to Reactive Attachment Disorder." In Rafael A. Javier, Amanda L. Baden, Frank A. Biafora, and Alina Camacho-Gingerich, eds, *Handbook of Adoption: Implications for Researchers, Practitioners, and Families*, 474–90. London: Sage, 2007.

Holmes, Brooke. *Gender: Antiquity and Its Legacy*. Oxford: Oxford University Press, 2012.

Holtz, Debra Levy. *Of Unknown Origin: A Memoir*. San Francisco, CA: Council Oak, 2001.

Hoopes, J.L. "Adoption and Identity Formation." In David M. Brodzinsky and Marshall D. Schechter, eds, *The Psychology of Adoption*, 144–66. New York: Oxford University Press, 1990.

Huffer, Lynne. *Mad for Foucault: Rethinking the Foundations of Queer Theory*. New York: Columbia University Press, 2010.

"Inbred Obscurity: Improving Incest Laws in the Shadow of the 'Sexual Family.'" *Harvard Law Review* 119, no. 8 (2006): 2464–85.

"Incest: The Last Taboo?" *Current TV*, 23 April 2010. https://www.youtube.com/watch?v=fo7tk2I2UgQ.

Irigaray, Luce. *Conversations*. Trans. C. Collins. Ed. S. Lotringer. London: Continuum, 2008.

– *An Ethics of Sexual Difference*. Trans. Carolyn Burke and Gillian C. Gill. Ithaca, NY: Cornell University Press, 1993.

Isaacson, Walter. "The Heart Wants What It Wants: From His Fifth Avenue Penthouse, Woody Defends His Love for Soon-Yi and Heatedly Denies Allegations of Child Abuse." *Time*, 31 August 1992, 41–3.

Javanbakht, Arash. "Was the Myth of Narcissus Misinterpreted by Freud? Narcissus, a Model for Schizoid–Histrionic, Not Narcissistic, Personality Disorder." *American Journal of Psychoanalysis* 66, no. 1 (2006): 63–71.

Javier, Rafael A., Amanda L. Baden, Frank A. Biafora, and Alina Camacho-Gingerich, eds. *Handbook of Adoption: Implications for Researchers, Practitioners, and Families*. London: Sage, 2007.

Johnson, Allen W., and Douglass Price-Williams. *Oedipus Ubiquitous: The Family Complex in World Folk Literature*. Stanford, CA: Stanford University Press, 1996.

Jones, E.E., and K.E. Davis. "From Acts to Perceptions: The Attribution Process in Person Perception." In Leonard Berkowitz, ed., *Cognitive Theories in Social Psychology*, 283–330. New York: Academic Press, 1978.

Jones, Steve. *In the Blood: God, Genes and Destiny*. London: Harper Collins, 1996.

Josephs, Lawrence. "The Evolved Function of the Oedipal Conflict." *International Journal of Psychoanalysis* 91, no. 4 (2010): 937–58.

Keller, Jean. "Rethinking Ruddick's Birthgiver/Adoptive Mother Distinction." In Andrea O'Reilly, ed., *Maternal Thinking: Philosophy, Politics, Practice*, 173–87. Toronto: Demeter, 2009.

Kierkegaard, Søren. *The Diary of Søren Kierkegaard*. Ed. Peter Rohde. New York: Citadel, 1960.

Kingston, Anne. "I Wish I Never Had Kids. There. I Said It." *Maclean's*, February 2013, 50–5.

Kirby, Vicki. *Judith Butler: Live Theory*. London: Continuum, 2006.

Kirk, H. David. *Adoptive Kinship: A Modern Institution in Need of Reform*. Toronto: Butterworths, 1981.

– *Shared Fate: A Theory of Adoption and Mental Health*. New York: Free Press of Glencoe, 1964.

Kirsta, Alex. "Genetic Sexual Attraction." *Guardian* (London), 17 May 2003. https://www.theguardian.com/theguardian/2003/may/17/weekend7 .weekend2.

Klein, Barbara Schave. *Alone in the Mirror: Twins in Therapy*. New York: Routledge, 2012.

– *Not All Twins Are Alike: Psychological Profiles of Twinship*. Westport, CT: Praeger, 2003.

Klevan, J.L., and A.R. DeJong. "Urinary Tract Symptoms and Urinary Tract Infections Following Sexual Abuse." *American Journal of Diseases of Children* 144, no. 2 (1990): 242–4.

Knox, Bernard. "Introduction to Oedipus the King." In Sophocles, *The Three Theban Plays: Antigone, Oedipus the King, Oedipus at Colonus*, trans. Robert Fagles, 131–53. Toronto: Penguin, 1984.

Kristof, Nicholas. "Dylan Farrow's Story." *New York Times*, 1 February 2014. https://www.nytimes.com/2014/02/02/opinion/sunday/kristof-dylan-farrows-story.html.

Kuhn, Thomas S. *The Structure of Scientific Revolutions*. 3rd ed. Chicago: University of Chicago Press, 1996.

Lamb, Wally. *I Know This Much Is True*. New York: Regan Books, 1998.

Lambert, Kristen. "Review of *Everybody's Family Romance: Reading Incest in*

Neoliberal America, by Gillian Hawkins." *Journal of International Women's Studies* 11, no. 4 (2010): 185–8.

. Laplanche, Jean, and Jean-Bertrand Pontalis. *The Language of Psycho-Analysis*. Trans. Donald Nicholson-Smith. New York: W.W. Norton, 1973.

Lasch, Christopher. *The Culture of Narcissism: American Life in an Age of Diminishing Expectations*. New York: W.W. Norton, 1979.

Lassers, Elisabeth, and Robert Nordan. "Separation-Individuation of an Identical Twin." *Adolescent Psychiatry* 6 (1978): 469–79.

Latchford, Frances J. "Family Intravenous: The Modern Western Bio-Genealogical Imperative and the Production of 'Family' Experience." PhD diss., York University, 2003.

– "Reckless Abandon: The Politics of Victimization and Agency in Birth-mother Narratives." In Frances J. Latchford, ed., *Adoption and Mothering*, 73–87. Bradford: Demeter, 2012.

Leigh, Mike, dir. *Secrets & Lies*. Film. Third Man Films, 1996.

Leighton, Kimberly. "Being Adopted and Being a Philosopher: Exploring Identity and the 'Desire to Know' Differently." In Sally Haslanger and Charlotte Witt, eds, *Adoption Matters: Philosophical and Feminist Essays*, 146–70. Ithaca, NY: Cornell University Press, 2005.

"Letters." *Time*, 21 September 1992, 4.

Levin, Jerome D. *Theories of the Self*. Washington, DC: Hemisphere, 1992.

Lévi-Strauss, Claude. *The Elementary Structures of Kinship*. Boston: Beacon, 1969.

Lewontin, Richard C. *Biology as Ideology: The Doctrine of DNA*. Concord, ON: House of Anansi, 1991.

Lichtenstein, Paul, Jennifer R. Harris, Nancy L. Pederson, and G.E. McClear. "Socioeconomic Status and Physical Health, How Are They Related? An Empirical Study Based on Twins Reared Apart and Twins Reared Together." *Social Science and Medicine* 36, no. 4 (1993): 441–50.

Lifton, Betty Jean. "Ghosts in the Adopted Family." *Psychoanalytic Inquiry: A Topical Journal for Mental Health Professionals* 30, no. 1 (2009): 71–90.

– *The Journey of the Adopted Self: A Quest for Wholeness*. New York: Basic Books, 1994.

– *Twice Born: Memoirs of an Adopted Daughter*. New York: McGraw Hill, 1975.

Littlewood, Roland. "Genetic Sexual Attraction and the Theory of Incest." In *Pathologies in the West: An Anthropology of Mental Illness in Europe and America*, 130–45. Ithaca, NY: Cornell University Press, 2002.

Loxterkamp, Lorne. "Contact and Truth: The Unfolding Predicament in

Adoption and Fostering." *Clinical Child Psychology and Psychiatry* 14, no. 3 (2009): 423–35.

Lukes, Steven. *Individualism*. Oxford: Blackwell, 1990.

– "The Meanings of 'Individualism.'" *Journal of the History of Ideas* 32, no. 1 (1971): 45–66.

Lykken, D.T., T.J. Bouchard Jr, M. McGue, and A. Tellegen. "The Minnesota Twin Family Registry: Some Initial Findings." *Acta Geneticae Medicae et Gemellologiae: Twin Research* 39, no. 1 (1990): 35–70.

Malinowski, Bronislaw. *Sex and Repression in Savage Society*. London: Routledge and Kegan Paul, 1937.

Manning, Paula J. "Baby Needs a New Set of Rules: Using Adoption Doctrine to Regulate Embryo Donation." *Georgetown Journal of Gender and the Law* 5, no. 2 (2004): 677–721.

Mansfield, Harvey C., Edward O. Wilson, Gertrude Himmelfarb, Robin Fox, Robert J. Samuelson, and Joseph S. Nye. "Responses to Fukuyama." *National Interest* 56 (1999): 34–44.

March, Karen. "Perception of Adoption as Social Stigma: Motivation for Search and Reunion." *Journal of Marriage and the Family* 57, no. 3 (1995): 653–60.

March, Karen, and Charlene E. Miall. "Adoption as a Family Form." *Family Relations* 49, no. 4 (2000): 359–62.

Mardorossian, Carine M. "Toward a New Feminist Theory of Rape." *Signs* 27, no. 3 (2002): 743–75.

Marshall, Carrie. "Of Course Twitter Calls It 'Incest' but Mother and Son in Relationship Together Need Help, Not Hate." *Metro* (London), 8 April 2016. http://metro.co.uk/2016/04/08/of-course-its-incest-but-mother-and-son-in-relationship-together-need-help-not-hate-5803252/.

Martin's Annual Criminal Code 2008. Aurora, ON: Canada Law Book, 2008.

Masson, Jeffrey M. *The Assault on Truth: Freud's Suppression of the Seduction Theory*. New York: Pocket Books, 1998.

Masters, R.E.L. *Patterns of Incest: A Psycho-Social Study of Incest, Based on Clinical and Historical Data*. New York: Julian, 1963.

Matson, Suzanne G. "Genetic Attraction (GA) and Genetic Sexual Attraction (GSA): Challenging the Status Quo Thinking on GSA, a Multi-Theoretical Discussion." *Adoption Dynamics: A Psychoeducational Website for Issues in Relinquishment and Adoption*. http://msnhomepages.talkcity.com/Support St/adoptiondynamics/page23.html. Accessed 1 December 2000 to 24 March 2002. URL now defunct.

McColm, Michelle. *Adoption Reunions: A Book for Adoptees, Birth Parents and Adoptive Families*. Toronto: Second Story, 1993.

Mcleod, Carolyn, and Andrew Botterell. "'Not for the Faint of Heart': Assessing the Status Quo on Adoption and Parental Licensing." In Françoise Baylis and Carolyn McLeod, eds, *Family-Making: Contemporary Ethical Challenges*, 151–67. Oxford: Oxford University Press, 2014.

McRoy, Ruth G., Harold Grotevant, and Louis A. Zurcher Jr. *Emotional Disturbance in Adopted Adolescents: Origins and Development*. New York: Praeger, 1988.

Melina, Lois Ruskai. *Raising Adopted Children: Practical, Reassuring Advice for Every Adoptive Parent*. New York: Harper Perennial, 1998.

Melosh, Barbara. *Strangers and Kin: The American Way of Adoption*. Cambridge, MA: Harvard University Press, 2002.

Mezey, Nancy J. *LGBT Families*. London: Sage, 2015.

Miall, Charlene E. "The Social Construction of Adoption: Clinical and Community Perspectives." *Family Relations* 45, no. 3 (1996): 309–17.

– "The Stigma of Adoptive Parent Status: Perceptions of Community Attitudes toward Adoption and the Experience of Informal Social Sanctioning." *Family Relations* 36, no. 1 (1987): 34–9.

Miele, Frank. "Entwinned Lives." *Skeptic* 14, no. 3 (2008): 27–37.

Miller, James. *The Passion of Michel Foucault*. New York: Anchor Books, Doubleday, 1993.

Miller, Korin. "Can You Really Justify Wanting to Have Sex with Your Mom?" *New York Post*, 12 April 2016. http://nypost.com/2016/04/12/can-you-really-justify-wanting-to-have-sex-with-your-mom/.

"Mixed Blessings." CBC Radio, *The Current*, 10–13 September 2007.

Moore, Kerry Lynn. "Mourning Loss: The Place of the Object in Narrative Fantasy." PhD diss., University of Pennsylvania, 2000.

Morehead, Daniel. "Oedipus, Darwin, and Freud: One Big, Happy Family?" *Psychoanalytic Quarterly* 68, no. 3 (1999): 347–75.

Morford, Mark P.O., and Robert J. Lenardon. *Classical Mythology*. 3rd ed. New York: Longman, 1985.

Müller-Wille, Staffan, and Hans Jörg Rheinberger. *A Cultural History of Heredity*. Chicago: University of Chicago Press, 2012.

MyHeritage DNA. "'Humanity' Featuring Prince Ea." TV commercial. *iSpot.tv*. https://www.ispot.tv/ad/wYFV/myheritage-dna-humanity-featuring-prince-ea.

National Association of Black Social Workers. "Kinship Care." https://cdn.ymaws.com/www.nabsw.org/resource/resmgr/position_statements_papers/kinship_care_position_paper.pdf.

Nordqvist, Petra. "Out of Sight, Out of Mind: Family Resemblances in Lesbian Donor Conception." *Sociology* 44, no. 6 (2010): 1128–44.

Nye, James. "'Is He My Son? He Looks a Lot Like Frank with the Blue Eyes':

Woody Allen Claims That If Ronan Farrow Is Sinatra's Child Then Mia
    Farrow Lied under Oath to Get Child Support." *Daily Mail* (London), 8
    February 2014. http://www.dailymail.co.uk/news/article-2554717/Woody-
    Allen-says-Ronan-Farrow-Frank-Sinatras-child-Mai-Farrow-lied-oath-hits-
    child-support-paid.html.

Ontario Ministry of Children and Youth Services. "Forever Families:
    Ontario's Adoption System." In *Raising Expectations: Recommendations of
    the Expert Panel on Infertility and Adoption*, 31–84. 2009. https://www
    .scribd.com/document/19113829/Recommendations-of-the-Expert-Panel-
    on-Infertility-and-Adoption.

Ovid. *Metamorphoses*. Trans. Rolfe Humphries. Bloomington: Indiana Uni-
    versity Press,1983.

– *The Metamorphoses of Ovid.* Trans. David R. Slavitt. Baltimore, MD: Johns
    Hopkins University Press, 1994.

Oxford English Dictionary. 2nd ed. Oxford University Press, 1961.

Palmer, Daniel E. "On Refusing Who We Are: Foucault's Critique of the
    Epistemic Subject." *Philosophy Today* 42, no. 4 (1998): 402–10.

Park, Shelley M. *Mothering Queerly, Queering Motherhood: Resisting Monoma-
    ternalism in Adoptive, Lesbian, Blended, and Polygamous Families*. Albany,
    NY: SUNY Press, 2013.

Patton, Sandra. *BirthMarks: Transracial Adoption in Contemporary America*.
    New York: New York University Press, 2000.

Paul, Robert A. "Incest Avoidance: Oedipal and Preoedipal, Natural and
    Cultural." *Journal of the American Psychoanalytic Association* 58, no. 6
    (2010): 1087–112.

Pausanias. *Description of Greece*. Vol. 4. Trans. W.H.S. Jones. Cambridge, MA:
    Harvard University Press, 1935.

Payne, Julien D., and Marilyn A. Payne. *Canadian Family Law*. Toronto:
    Irwin Law, 2001.

Peakman, Julie. *The Pleasure's All Mine: A History of Perverse Sex*. London:
    Reaktion Books, 2013.

Pelka, Suzanne. "The Making and Unmaking of Biological Ties in Lesbian-
    Led Families." In Rachel Epstein, ed., *Who's Your Daddy? And Other Writ-
    ings on Queer Parenting*, 83–92. Toronto: Sumach, 2009.

– "Sharing Motherhood: Maternal Jealousy among Lesbian Co-Mothers."
    Journal of Homosexuality 56, no. 2 (2009): 195–217.

Phillips, Adam. *Darwin's Worms: On Life Stories and Death Stories*. New York:
    Basic Books, 2000.

– *On Kissing, Tickling, and Being Bored: Psychoanalytic Essays on the Unexam-
    ined Life*. 1993. Reprint, Cambridge, MA: Harvard University Press, 1997.

Plummer, Ken. *Intimate Citizenship: Private Decisions and Public Dialogues.*
Montreal and Kingston: McGill-Queen's University Press, 2003.

Popple, A.E., ed. *Criminal Reports (Canada): A Series of Reports with Annotations and Practice Notes on Criminal Cases Arising in the Courts of the Various Provinces in Canada.* Vol. 5. Toronto: Carswell, 1948.

Preedy, Pat. "Meeting the Educational Needs of Pre-School and Primary Aged Twins and Higher Multiples." In A.C. Sandbank, ed., *Twin and Triplet Psychology: A Professional Guide to Working with Multiples*, 70–99. London: Routledge, 1999.

Return to Sender. Documentary. CBC Television, *The Passionate Eye*, February 2005.

Riesman, David. *Individualism Reconsidered and Other Essays.* London: Collier-Macmillan, 1964.

Roberts, Dorothy. "The Genetic Tie." *Chicago Law Review* 62, no. 1 (1995): 209–73.

– *Shattered Bonds: The Color of Child Welfare.* New York: Basic Civitas Books, 2002.

Rose, Nikolas. *Governing the Soul: The Shaping of the Private Self.* New York: Routledge, 1990.

Rubin, Aviva. "My Co-World and Welcome to It: Adventures in Non-Conjugal Parenting." In Rachel Epstein, ed., *Who's Your Daddy? And Other Writings on Queer Parenting*, 117–23. Toronto: Sumach, 2009.

Rulli, Tina. "The Unique Value of Adoption." In Françoise Baylis and Carolyn McLeod, eds, *Family-Making: Contemporary Ethical Challenges*, 109–28. Oxford: Oxford University Press, 2014.

R. v. G.D.B., [2000] 1 SCR 520.

R. v. R.W.B., (2000) 185 Nfld. & P.E.I.R. 212 (NFCA).

R. v. Schmidt, 5 CR 165 at 171.

Sandbank, A.C., ed. *Twin and Triplet Psychology: A Professional Guide to Working with Multiples.* London: Routledge, 1999.

Sants, H.J. "Genealogical Bewilderment in Children with Substitute Parents." *British Journal of Medical Psychology* 37 (1964): 133–41.

Schave, Barbara, and Janet Ciriello. *Identity and Intimacy in Twins.* New York: Praeger, 1983.

Schechter, Marshall D. "Observations on Adopted Children." *Archives of General Psychiatry* 3, no. 1 (1960): 21–32.

Scheinfeld, Amram. *Twins and Supertwins.* Philadelphia: Lippincott, 1967.

Schneider, Stanley, and Esti Rimmer. "Adoptive Parents' Hostility toward Their Adopted Children." *Children and Youth Services Review* 6, no. 4 (1984): 345–52.

Schrift, Alan D. "Foucault's Reconfiguration of the Subject: From Nietzsche to Butler, Laclau/Mouffe, and Beyond." *Philosophy Today* 41, no. 1 (1997): 153–9.

Schwartz, Hillel. *The Culture of the Copy: Striking Likenesses, Unreasonable Facsimiles*. New York: Zone Books, 1996.

Schwartz, Joseph. *Cassandra's Daughter: A History of Psychoanalysis*. New York: Viking, 1999.

Seligmann, Linda J. *Broken Links, Enduring Ties: American Adoption across, Race, Class, and Nation*. Stanford, CA: Stanford University Press, 2013.

Shaffer, Julie. "Familial Love, Incest, and Female Desire in Late Eighteenth- and Early Nineteenth-Century British Women's Novels." *Criticism* 41, no. 1 (1999): 67–99.

Shanahan, Daniel. *Toward a Genealogy of Individualism*. Amherst: University of Massachusetts Press, 1992.

Shelley, Mary. *Frankenstein, or The Modern Prometheus: The 1818 Text*. Oxford: Oxford University Press, 1998.

Shepher, Joseph. *Incest: A Biosocial View*. New York: Academic Press, 1983.

Shulman, Seth. "Book Review: 'A Troublesome Inheritance: Genes, Race and Human History,' by Nicholas Wade." *Washington Post*, 23 May 2014. http://www.washingtonpost.com/opinions/book-review-a-troublesome-inheritance-genes-race-and-human-history-by-nicholas-wade/2014/05/23/d0dbbde4-bf34-11e3-b574-f8748871856a_story.html.

Simons, Margaret A. *Beauvoir and the Second Sex: Feminism, Race, and the Origins of Existentialism*. New York: Rowman and Littlefield, 2001.

Smith, David Livingstone. "Beyond Westermarck: Can Shared Mothering or Maternal Phenotype Matching Account for Incest Avoidance?" *Evolutionary Psychology* 5, no. 1 (2007): 202–22. https://journals.sagepub.com/doi/pdf/10.1177/147470490700500112.

Smith, Pamela H. "Art, Science, and Visual Culture in Early Modern Europe." *Isis: A Journal of the History of Science Society* 97, no. 1 (2006): 83–100.

Smith, Richard J. "Freud and Evolutionary Anthropology's First Just-So Story." *Evolutionary Anthropology* 25, no. 2 (2016): 50–3.

"Soon-Yi Speaks: 'Let's Not Get Hysterical.'" *Newsweek*, 30 August 1992. http://www.newsweek.com/soon-yi-speaks-lets-not-get-hysterical-197958.

Sophocles. *The Three Theban Plays: Antigone, Oedipus the King, Oedipus at Colonus*. Trans. Robert Fagles. New York: Penguin, 1984.

Sorosky, Arthur D., Annette Baran, and Reuben Pannor. *The Adoption Triangle: The Effects of the Sealed Record on Adoptees, Birth Parents, and Adoptive Parents*. New York: Doubleday, 1978.

– "Identity Conflicts in Adoptees." *American Journal of Orthopsychiatry* 45, no. 1 (1975): 18–27.

– "The Reunion of Adoptees and Birth Relatives." *Journal of Youth and Adolescence* 3, no. 3 (1974): 195–206.

Spector, Tim. *Identically Different: Why You Can Change Your Genes*. London: Weidenfeld and Nicolson, 2012.

Speirs, Carol Cumming, Sydney Duder, Richard Sullivan, Silvia Kirstein, Mona Propst, and Dolores Meade. "Mediated Reunions in Adoption: Findings from and Evaluation Study." *Child Welfare* 84, no. 6 (2005): 843–66.

Stein, Robert. *Incest and Human Love: The Betrayal of the Soul in Psychotherapy*. 2nd ed. Texas: Spring, 1984.

Steinhart, Eric. "Self-Recognition and Countermemory." *Philosophy Today* 33, no. 4 (1989): 302–18.

Stevens, Anthony. "Jungian Analysis and Evolutionary Psychotherapy: An Integrative Approach." In Paul Gilbert and Kent G. Bailey, eds, *Genes on the Couch: Explorations in Evolutionary Psychotherapy*, 93–117. Hove, East Sussex: Brunner-Routledge, 2000.

Stewart, Elizabeth A. *Exploring Twins: Towards a Social Analysis of Twinship*. Hampshire, UK: Macmillan, 2000.

Stone, Alison. "From Political to Realist Essentialism: Rereading Luce Irigaray." *Feminist Theory* 5, no. 1 (2004): 5–23.

Strauss, Jean A.S. *Birthright: The Guide to Search and Reunion for Adoptees, Birthparents, and Adoptive Parents*. New York: Penguin, 1994.

Thorpe, Karen, and Karen Gardner. "Twins and Their Friendships: Differences between Monozygotic, Dizygotic Same-Sex and Dizygotic Mixed-Sex Pairs." *Twin Research and Human Genetics* 9, no. 1 (2006): 155–64.

Toews, John E. "Foucault and the Freudian Subject: Archaeology, Genealogy, and the Historicization of Psychoanalysis." In Jan Goldstein, ed., *Foucault and the Writing of History*, 116–34. Oxford: Blackwell, 1994.

Toufexis, Anastasia. "What Is Incest?" *Time*, 31 August 1992, 39.

Trinder, Liz, Julia Feast, and David Howe. "Rejection and Reunions That Break Down." In *The Adoption Reunion Handbook*, 97–110. Chichester, UK: John Wiley and Sons, 2004.

Triseliotis, John. "Identity and Genealogy in Adopted People." In D. Hibbs, ed., *Adoption: International Perspectives*, 35–44. Madison, CT: International Universities Press, 1991.

– *In Search of Origins: The Experiences of Adopted People*. Boston: Routledge and Kegan Paul, 1973.

Tsoulis-Reay, Alexa. "What's It Like to Date Your Dad?" *New York Magazine*,

15 January 2015. https://www.thecut.com/2015/01/what-its-like-to-date-your-dad.html.

Turner, Ashley P. "Incest, Inbreeding, and Intrafamilial Conflict: Analyzing the Boundaries of Sexual Permissiveness in Modern North America." *Sexuality and Culture* 12, no. 1 (2008): 38–44.

Turner, Jonathon, and Alexandra Maryanski. *Incest: Origins of the Taboo.* Boulder, CO: Paradigm, 2005.

Twenge, Jean M. *Generation Me: Why Today's Young Americans Are More Confident, Assertive, Entitled – and More Miserable Than Ever Before.* New York: Free Press, 2006.

Twitchell, James B. *Forbidden Partners: The Incest Taboo in Modern Culture.* New York: Columbia University Press, 1987.

Vitello, Paul. "Judy Lewis, Secret Daughter of Hollywood, Dies at 76." *New York Times*, 30 November 2011. http://www.nytimes.com/2011/12/01/arts/television/judy-lewis-secret-daughter-of-hollywood-dies-at-76.html?_r=0.

Wade, Nicholas. *A Troublesome Inheritance: Genes, Race and Human History.* New York: Penguin, 2014.

Walcott, Rinaldo. *Black Like Who? Writing Black Canada.* Toronto: Insomniac, 1997.

Waldby, Cathy, Atosha Clancy, Jan Emetchi, and Caroline Summerfield. "Theoretical Perspectives on Father-Daughter Incest." In Emily Driver and Audrey Droisen, eds, *Child Sexual Abuse: Feminist Perspectives*, 88–106. 1989. Reprint, London: Macmillan, 1990.

Walton, Jessica. "Supporting the Interests of Intercountry Adoptees beyond Childhood: Access to Adoption Information and Identity." *Social Policy and Society* 11, no. 3 (2012): 443–54.

Ward, Elizabeth. *Father-Daughter Rape.* London: Women's Press, 1984.

Wardle, Tim, dir. *Three Identical Strangers.* Film. CNN Films, 2018.

Watson, Kenneth W. "Family-Centered Adoption Practice." *Families in Society: The Journal of Contemporary Human Services* 77, no. 9 (1996): 523–34.

Watson, Margaret. "Late Revelation – The Impact of Adoption in Midlife." *Australian Journal of Adoption* 6, no. 1 (2012): 1–9. http://pandora.nla.gov.au/pan/98265/20130416-0013/www.nla.gov.au/openpublish/index.php/aja/article/view/2543/2993.html.

Watson, Peter. *Twins: An Uncanny Relationship?* 1981. Reprint, New York: Viking, 1982.

Wegar, Katarina. "Adoption and Mental Health: A Theoretical Critique of the Psychopathological Model." *American Journal of Orthopsychiatry* 65, no. 4 (1995): 540–8.

– "Adoption, Family Ideology, and Social Stigma: Bias in Community Attitudes, Adoption Research, and Practice." *Family Relations* 49, no. 4 (2000): 363–9.

– *Adoption, Identity, and Kinship: The Debate over Sealed Birth Records.* New Haven, CT: Yale University Press, 1997.

Westermarck, Edward. *A Short History of Marriage.* New York: Macmillan, 1926.

White, Renée T. "Revolutionary Theory: Sociological Dimensions of Fanon's *Sociologie d'une révolution*." In Lewis R. Gordon, T. Denean Sharpley-Whiting, and Renée T. White, eds, *Fanon: A Critical Reader,* 100–12. Oxford: Blackwell, 1996.

Whittier, Nancy. "Where Are the Children? Theorizing the Missing Piece in Gendered Sexual Violence." *Gender and Society* 30, no. 1 (2016): 95–108.

Wilson, Edward O. *Sociobiology: The New Synthesis.* Cambridge, MA: Belknap Press of Harvard University Press, 1975.

Wilson, Timothy H. "Foucault, Genealogy, History." *Philosophy Today* 39, no. 2 (1995): 157–70.

Witt, Charlotte. "Family Resemblances: Adoption, Personal Identity, and Genetic Essentialism." In Sally Haslanger and Charlotte Witt, eds, *Adoption Matters: Philosophical and Feminist Essays,* 135–45. Ithaca, NY: Cornell University Press, 2005.

Wolf, Arthur P. "Introduction." In Arthur P. Wolf and William H. Durham, eds, *Inbreeding, Incest, and the Incest Taboo: The State of Knowledge at the Turn of the Century,* 1–23. Stanford, CA: Stanford University Press, 2004.

Woo, Elaine. "Judy Lewis Dies at 76; Daughter of Stars Loretta Young and Clark Gable." *Los Angeles Times,* 1 December 2011. http://articles.latimes .com/2011/dec/01/local/la-me-judy-lewis-20111201.

Woodward, Joan. *The Lone Twin: Understanding Twin Bereavement and Loss.* London: Free Association Books, 1998.

Workman, Lance, and Will Reader. *Evolutionary Psychology: An Introduction.* 3rd ed. Cambridge, UK: Cambridge University Press, 2014.

Wright, Lawrence. *Twins: And What They Tell Us about Who We Are.* New York: John Wiley and Sons, 1997.

– *Twins: Genes, Environment and the Mystery of Identity.* London: Weidenfeld and Nicolson, 1997.

Young, Robert M. *Darwin's Metaphor: Nature's Place in Victorian Culture*.
    Cambridge, UK: Cambridge University Press, 1985.
Zwart, Nijmegen Hub. "Genomics and Self-Knowledge: Implications for
    Societal Research and Debate." *New Genetics and Society* 26, no. 2 (2007):
    181–202.

Index

Adapted Mind, The (Barkow, Cosmides, and Tooby), 358n12

Adelman, Mara B., 332n50

adopted child syndrome, 31

adoptees: bio-family not perceived as family, 278, 285–6, 296–7; as chosen child, 107, 325n109; experience of, 78–9, 103–4; questions asked of, 7, 224, 299–300; unable to function as a (biological) narcissistic object-choice (psychoanalysis), 196. *See also* adoption identity problems; Amy, reared-apart twin; Beth, reared-apart twin; genetic sexual attraction (GSA); search and reunion / search activism

Adoptee's Liberty Movement Association, 129

adoption, 27–70; legal act/ requirements, 112, 360n53; open, 30–2, 93, 189, 224, 301; Roman laws on, 107; special value of, 318n123. *See also* adoption identity problems; adoptive tie, equality of; adoptive tie, inferiority of; genetic sexual attraction (GSA); incest; search and reunion / search activism

Adoption and Fostering (Feast), 229

adoption/birth records, 29–30, 50, 55, 129–30, 223, 313–14n13, 313n8

adoption discourses. *See* genetic sexual attraction (GSA); incest; individualism; naturalism; psychoanalysis; twins

Adoption, Identity, and Kinship (Wegar), 32, 128

adoption identity problems: from absence of biological tie, 5, 69, 86–7, 91; assumption of, 29, 31, 32–3, 66–7; from bio-genealogical alienation, 31, 313–14n13; compared to national identity problems, 100; early psychoanalytic theories on, 34–6; from exposure to abusive biological family, 31–2; from knowledge, 76–81, 139; pathologization of, 111; from severing of mother-child relationship, 34. *See also* adoption revelation